Free Trade and Cultural Diversity in International Law

This book attempts to reconcile the concept of free trade with a key non-trade social value – cultural diversity – in an era of economic globalisation. It first shows how we can look at culture in many different ways, and explains why we should care about cultural diversity. The book then examines the challenges that policymakers are faced with in formulating cultural measures in the new media environment, and analyses UNESCO's theories and approaches to cultural diversity.

This is followed by a comprehensive examination of the treatment of 'culture' in global and regional trade agreements, including the framework of the GATT/WTO system, the WTO's judicial practice involving cultural products, and the treatment of culture under the EC/EU and NAFTA. This identifies the challenges trade norms encounter in dealing with cultural products.

The author seeks to formulate a balanced view of the challenge of protecting and promoting cultural diversity while also recognising the important goal of trade liberalisation. To this end Professor Shi proposes a dual method through which the norms found in WTO agreements and in UNESCO cultural instruments may be brought into alignment: the first highlighting the compatibility of cultural policy measures with trade obligations on a domestic level, the second suggesting potential linkages between the WTO rules and the UNESCO Convention from the perspectives of treaty interpretation.

Studies in International Trade Law: Volume 14

Studies in International Trade Law
Titles in this series

Volume 1 *Basic Legal Instruments for the Liberalisation of Trade*
Federico Ortino

Volume 2 *The Power to Protect: Trade Health, and Uncertainty in the WTO*
Catherine Button

Volume 3 *The WTO, the Internet and Trade in Digital Products*
Sascha Wunsch-Vincent

Volume 4 *Good Faith in the Jurisprudence of the WTO: The Protection of Legitimate Expectations, Good Faith Interpretation and Fair Dispute Settlement*
Marion Panizzon

Volume 5 *Globalisation and Labour Rights: The Conflict between Core Labour Rights and International Economic Law*
Christine Kaufmann

Volume 6 *The World Trade Organization and Human Rights*
Fiona Macmillan

Volume 7 *Redefining Sovereignty in International Economic Law*
Edited by Wenhua Shan, Penelope Simons and Dalvinder Singh

Volume 8 *Law and Ethics in International Trade and Environment Debates*
Ilona Cheyne

Volume 9 *Constitutionalism, Multilevel Trade Governance and Social Regulation*
Edited by Christian Joerges and Ernst-Ulrich Petersmann

Volume 10 *The Human Rights Impact of the World Trade Organisation*
James Harrison

Volume 11 *Developing Countries and the Multilateral Trade Regime: The Failure and Promise of the WTOs' Development Mission*
Donatella Alessandrini

Volume 12 *Constitutionalism, Multilevel Trade Governance and International Economic Law*
Edited by Christian Joerges and Ernst-Ulrich Petersmann

Volume 13 *The Right to Development and International Economic Law: Legal and Moral Dimensions*
Isabella Bunn

For the complete list of titles in this series, see the 'Studies in International Law' link at www.hartpub.co.uk/books/series.asp

Free Trade and Cultural Diversity in International Law

Jingxia Shi

• HART •
PUBLISHING
OXFORD AND PORTLAND, OREGON
2013

Published in the United Kingdom by Hart Publishing Ltd
16C Worcester Place, Oxford, OX1 2JW
Telephone: +44 (0)1865 517530
Fax: +44 (0)1865 510710
E-mail: mail@hartpub.co.uk
Website: http://www.hartpub.co.uk

Published in North America (US and Canada) by
Hart Publishing
c/o International Specialized Book Services
920 NE 58th Avenue, Suite 300
Portland, OR 97213-3786
USA
Tel: +1 503 287 3093 or toll-free: (1) 800 944 6190
Fax: +1 503 280 8832
E-mail: orders@isbs.com
Website: http://www.isbs.com

British Library Cataloguing in Publication Data
Data Available

ISBN: 978-1-84946-425-3

Typeset by Forewords Ltd, Oxford
Printed and bound in Great Britain by
MPG Printgroup Ltd

This book is in memory of my parents,
Tijian SHI and Ruzhen QI,

AND

Dedicated to my husband, Wenhui Yang,

and my daughter, Yishi Yang

Foreword

'When we scrutinize the social processes of the globe,' Harold D Lasswell and Myres S McDougal wrote, 'we cannot fail to observe that some areas are occupied by peoples whose values and institutions are of such distinctiveness that they can readily be contrasted to their neighbors . . . we employ the term "culture" to designate any distinctive and stable pattern of community values and institutions.'[1] Viewed from the perspective of the individual members of those communities, their respective cultures—those distinctive and stable patterns of community values and institutions—constitute the essential ecologies of their 'inner worlds'.[2] No wonder, then, that the incorporation of the international protection of human rights in the modern *corpus juris gentium*, which has focused on individual rights, has also included a concern for the protection of culture.[3]

Paradoxically, these same human rights instruments, by their very act of establishing transcultural standards of achievement, commit those to whom they are directed to changing their cultures to bring them into conformity with those prescribed standards. In other instruments, the international community undertakes to foster 'development', a process which involves imposed social change. Still other planks in contemporary international law's platform commit the world community to foster trade and direct foreign investment as a means of securing development.

At the political level, change can radically transform community values and institutions and the power relations that sustain them. At the personal level, such changes can be traumatic. McLuhan and Fiore may have exaggerated the consequence, but they were surely right when they associated innovation with profound personal distress: 'every major technical innovation will so disturb our inner lives that wars necessarily result as misbegotten efforts to recover the old images'.[4]

Of all of the modes of social change which contemporary international law endorses, none is more constant and potentially yet subtly intrusive than international trade. Every imported item carries the seeds of social

[1] HD Lasswell and MS McDougal, *Jurisprudence for a Free Society, Studies in Law, Science and Policy*, vol 1 (Martinus Nijhoff Publishers, 1992) 348.

[2] WM Reisman, 'International Law and the Inner Worlds of Others' (1996) 9 *St Thomas Law Review* 25.

[3] See, generally, Art 15, Covenant on Economic, Social and Cultural Rights, and especially the UNESCO Convention on the Protection and Promotion of the Diversity of Cultural Expressions (2005); see also, UNESCO, *Declaration of the Principles of International Cultural Cooperation* (1966).

[4] M McLuhan and Q Fiore, *War and Peace in the Global Village* (Ginko Press, 1968) 4.

change. A McDonald's in Changsha,[5] in changing traditional dining habits, can disrupt the dynamics and superordinations of the nuclear and extended family. Levi jeans in Kuala Lumpur can contribute to changing gender relations and even sexual mores. And so on. But the potential for precipitating cultural changes through the transnational sale of goods pales in comparison with the changes that can be wrought by trade in services via the Internet, which Professor Chander has felicitously labeled the modern 'Electronic Silk Road'.[6]

Cultures and sub-cultures have always been subject to the difficult and sometimes traumatic challenge of adjustment when the ecological and political contexts in which they were anchored changed. But usually these were comparatively rare occurrences. The vast processes of cultural interchange that we call globalisation now mean that every culture is continuously exposed to other cultures and, in varying degree, is subject to changes, sometimes wrenching, from without. Subject to continuous exposure to outside influences, a sense of beleaguerment will often excite a need for defense. Nowhere has this been more acute than in the interface of international trade law and international human rights law.

Hence the timeliness of Professor Shi's brilliant study of the tension between the international goals of free trade, on the one hand, and the maintenance of cultural diversity, on the other. The book's great value lies not only in its meticulous presentation and analysis of the policies expressed in the major legal instruments as well as the decision trends applying them, but even more importantly in the author's creative proposals for resolving the antinomies by bringing the conflicting policies of these sectors of international law into a reciprocally beneficial relationship, avoiding both the Scylla of protectionism and the Charybdis of cultural extinction.

This is an important contribution to legal scholarship and policy analysis and invention.

W Michael Reisman
Yale Law School
15 January 2013

[5] Changsha is the capital city of Hunan Province, a central southern province in China (author note).

[6] A Chander, *The Electronic Silk Road: How the Web Binds the World Together in Commerce* (Yale University Press, 2013).

Acknowledgements

It is the time to place the final touch on this work and give thanks to the many individuals and institutions without whom the completion of this book would not have been imaginable.

This book is primarily based on my JSD dissertation 'From Quandary to Synergy: Revisiting Free Trade and Cultural Diversity', written during my study at Yale Law School between 2006 and 2011. Therefore, most of all, I must thank the three professors who made up my JSD dissertation committee: they have helped to fulfill my dream of pursuing an academic odyssey at Yale. Professor Michael Reisman, my most vital source of intellectual stimulation, inspired this research topic and provided profound academic guidance from inception to end. He carefully read drafts and made significant comments and critiques. His thoughtful insights and instruction helped shape the structure and refine the substance of the dissertation, for which I am deeply and infinitely grateful to him. Likewise, I am very much indebted to my two readers, Professor Lea Brilmayer and Professor Amy Chua, for their enduring support throughout my entire stay at Yale.

The faculty and staff at Yale Law School were extraordinarily stimulating and supportive during my academic stay. My sincere gratitude goes to Associate Dean Toni E Davis and Director of Graduate Programs Maria Dino, whose joint efforts helped create a perfect environment for a long-term academic project. Jamie Horsley at the China Law Center helped me with various academic and personal matters in her most kind manner. Thanks to the entire staff of the Yale Law Library for their incomparable research support. The drafts of this book were presented at the JSD colloquium at Yale Law School; my fellow JSD candidates and other participants in the workshop offered valuable comments and critiques. I am very grateful to the Yale Law School, in particular to the Lillian Goldman Fellowship and the Howard M Holtzmann Fellowship in International Arbitration & Dispute Resolution, for their generosity in supporting my studies, which enabled me to concentrate my time and energy on this project.

I owe a debt to the following people for the ways in which they have influenced and enriched my academic pursuits. Professor Jerome Cohen at the New York University School of Law, a pre-eminent and widely respected pioneer in the study of Chinese law, began supporting the development of my academic career even before we met. Professor Guiguo Wang, the dean of the Law School at Hong Kong City University, has been my academic mentor for almost two decades. One of the lucky beneficiaries of his kindness and friendship, I have long been influenced by his invigorating intellectual spirit and motivated by his unsurpassed professional achievement. I am also greatly indebted to all my former professors for their enduring support and valuable advice, including Eric Brunstad at Yale Law School, Jinsong Yu at Renmin University and E'xiang Wan at the Supreme Court of China. The following dear friends, to name just a few, have greatly enriched my life in New Haven: Steven Kargman, Jeffery Prescott, Neysun Mahboubi, Ying Du, Jinhua Cheng, Zhiqiang Wang, Ya-wen Lei, Shitong Qiao, Carol Pang and Taisu Zhang.

Many colleagues at UIBE, my home institution in China, also contributed to this work. Madam Ling Wang, Professor Jianjun Shi, Professor Guijun Lin, Professor Wei Shi and other friends at UIBE supported my stay at Yale by granting me academic leave in the most flexible manner, not to mention their warm encouragement of my research. Madam Ling Wang in particular understands the significance of my research in the face of China's ever-evolving cultural industries, and has kept me abreast of the latest developments in the field. I also owe much to my colleagues at the UIBE Law School, who were there whenever I needed them, and contributed to my academic pursuits in ways that they may not even realise.

Finally, I wish to thank my family for their priceless love and support well beyond this project. I am most grateful to my late parents, who, through their plain words and deeds, taught me the most essential human morals and virtues: achieving success through hard work and kindness to people. They deserve my infinite respect and gratitude. A heartfelt thank to my husband, Wenhui Yang, who has always been my safe harbour and supported me unflinchingly throughout my long academic expedition. My daughter Yishi is the greatest source of my joy and happiness; over the years she has transformed the otherwise lonely experience of JSD research into a pleasant journey, constantly reminding me of the need to balance career and family. For these reasons, and many others, this work is dedicated to these individuals and institutions that offered me varied and essential support.

Some ideas developed in this book were previously published in 'The Specificity of Cultural Products versus the Generality of Trade Obligations: Reflecting on China-Publication and Audiovisual Service' (2011) 45(1) Journal of World Trade 159 and 'Factoring Cultural Element into Deciding the "Likeness" of Cultural Products: A Perspective from the New Haven School' (2012) 20(2) Asia Pacific Law Review 167. I am grateful to the publishers for agreeing to authorise the reproduction of the relevant parts in this book.

I express appreciation to Mr William Lin at Wellslaw Beijing for suggesting that I submit the manuscript to Hart Publishing, a pre-eminent law publisher. Thanks also go to the anonymous peer reviewers for Hart, and Mr Richard Hart, Rachel Turner, Tom Adams, Melanie Hamill, Jane

Parker and Jo Ledger, for their expert help in seeing the enterprise through to completion. They did an excellent job shepherding the project along and finally produced an admirably thorough book before us.

All in all, I am profoundly indebted to all those who have helped me, those few whom I mention and the many I do not; it is hard to fully describe or even sketch my appreciation in such a short note. Deepest thanks remain in my heart forever. Lastly, I am entirely responsible for the final product and any remaining mistakes.

Jingxia Shi
6 January 2013

Contents

Table of GATT/WTO Reports and Rulings

List of full case names and reference for short title citations used in the book.

GATT 1947 REPORTS AND RULINGS

WTO PANEL AND APPELLATE BODY REPORTS

1

Introduction: Globalisation as the Context

> Globalization lies at the heart of modern culture; cultural practices lie at the heart of globalisation . . . The huge transformative processes of our time that globalisation describes cannot be properly understood until they are grasped through the conceptual vocabulary of culture; likewise that these transformations change the very fabric of cultural experience and, indeed, affect our sense of what culture actually is in the modern world. John Tomlinson[1]

GLOBALISATION SETS THE main stage for this book; the balancing of trade norms and cultural values in the context of economic globalisation constitutes the central inquiry throughout the project. This chapter aims to sketch a framework for understanding the research background of this book, exploring the phenomena of globalisation, culture and trade, and the interaction among them.

1.1 GLOBALISATION AND CULTURE

Recent decades have witnessed a marked worldwide move in the direction of globalisation.[2] More than an intensified internationalisation,[3] globalisation can mean many things.[4] At the political and economic level,

[1] J Tomlinson, *Globalization and Culture* (1999) 1. Tomlinson goes far beyond traditional discussions on globalisation and economic issues to analyse the wide-ranging cultural, social and moral aspects of globalisation in this engaging and lucid book. He discusses the uneven nature of the experience of global modernity in different countries, and concludes that a genuinely cosmopolitan culture is unlikely to emerge unless we respect cultural difference and share a common sense of commitment about the world.

[2] See D Held and A McGrew (eds), *Global Transformations: Politics, Economics and Culture* (1999) 1.

[3] See NG Canclini, 'Cultural Policy Options in the Context of Globalization' in UNESCO, *World Culture Report* (1998) 157, 159 (discussing the qualitative differences between globalisation and internationalization); M Keane, 'Exporting Chinese Culture: Industry Financing Models in Film and Television' (2006) 3(1) *Westminster Papers in Communication and Culture* 11, 13–14 (addressing the difference between internationalization and globalisation).

[4] For different definitions or meanings of 'globalisation', see, eg J Liss, 'The Impact of Globalization and Technological Change on Culture and National Identity: A Call for Visionary Pragmatism', in D Browne (ed), *The Culture/Trade Quandary: Canada's Policy Options* (1998) 166 ('globalisation' in the policy literature); ME Footer and Christoph

globalisation is a process of denationalisation of politics, markets and legal systems, characterised by the growing interdependence and interpenetration of human relations alongside with the increasing integration of the world's socio-economic life.[5] In a broader sense, globalisation is a complex, multilayered process that affects the social structures of nations[6] and is erasing 'the traditional boundaries between politics, culture, technology, finance, national security and ecology'.[7] Globalisation has not only radically changed the world's political[8] and economic orders, but also people's ways of conceiving the world.

A universal element of human life, culture manifests itself in a multiplicity of forms. Everyone has culture, and it makes us what we are.[9] Cultural identity is essential to understanding human behaviours.[10] From the perspective of basic human rights, culture represents the opportunities of self-expression and self-development for everyone.[11] From a collective perspective, culture defines the national character and identity.

Globalisation is widely viewed as a 'multidimensional' phenomenon, and culture is one dimension of globalisation.[12] Globalisation has a twofold impact on culture. On the one hand, it generates positive effects on culture through cultural exchange and innovation.[13] Progressive and healthy cultural exchange leads to mutual enrichment that opens up new perspectives and encourages the proliferation of new cultures.[14] Further, a greater degree of cultural exchange arouses awareness of cultural

B Graber, 'Trade Liberalization and Cultural Policy' (2000) 3 *Journal of International Economic Law* 115, 134 ('globalisation' in a psychological point of view).

[5] See F Webster, *Theories of the Information Society* (1995) 141.

[6] See AJ Lodge, 'Globalization: Panacea for the World or Conquistador of International Law and Statehood?' (2005) 7 *Oregon Review of International Law* 224, 224.

[7] See TL Friedman, *The Lexus and the O Tree: Understanding Globalization* (1999) 15.

[8] See Held and McGrew, above n 2, 1 (pointing out that globalisation suggests the limits to national politics).

[9] See HJ Morgenthau, *Politics among Nations: The Struggle for Power and Peace*, 3rd edn (1962) 262; see also C Brown, *Sovereignty, Rights and Justice: International Political Theory Today* (2002) 189–90.

[10] United Nations, 'Cultural Diversity and Globalization: A Document for Reflection on the Subtheme of 'Culture' from the Millennium Forum of the United Nations', available at http://www.forumsocialmundial.org.br/download/tconferencias_identidadecultural_prop_eng.pdf (last accessed on 1 June 2012) (hereinafter UN, Cultural Diversity and Globalization) 7.

[11] This is perhaps the most widely accepted understanding of culture adopted by UNESCO. According to this conception of culture, in addition to art and literature, culture encompasses lifestyles, basic human rights, value systems, traditions and beliefs. See UNESCO, 'Mexico City Declaration on Cultural Policies, World Conference on Cultural Policies, Mexico City, 26 July—6 August 1982', available at portal.unesco.org/culture/en/files/../11919410061mexico../mexico_en.pdf (last accessed on 1 June 2012).

[12] See Tomlinson, above n 1, 13.

[13] See UNESCO, 'Our Creative Diversity: Report of the World Commission on Culture and Development' (finalised by J Pérez de Cuéllar, 1995), Executive Summary, 66 (discussing the celebratory picture of globalisation given by Mexican theorist Néstor G Canclini in his conception of culture as hybridization).

[14] See UNESCO, above n 11, 3.

difference, which, together with cultural specialisation, can expand the menu of choices for everyone.[15]

On the other hand, numerous texts have described globalisation's negative effects on culture.[16] The literature is replete with bleak forecasts for the fate of a national cultural identity faced with the hegemonic ideology of neo-liberalism; this pessimistic outlook prevails for several reasons.[17] First, cultural exchange is rarely a steady advance on all fronts at once. Globalisation is an unequal and asymmetric process that does not always involve a greater degree of exchange among different cultures. While certain cultures expand rapidly, others may shrink or even wither away.[18] Accompanied by the process of market deregulation and economic concentration, globalisation tends to impose one culture upon the others, which may result in a homogeneous global culture.[19] Rather than fostering mutual understanding among people, this reality may give rise to certain social and economic exclusions.[20] In particular, globalisation poses a serious challenge to ethnic minorities whose languages, customs, and ideas are easily drowned out by the din of mass media catering to the interests of majority communities.[21]

Meanwhile, the idea of 'culture' implicitly connects meaning construction with a particularity and fixed locality, while one of the effects of

[15] See JN Pieterse, *Globalization and Culture—Global Mélange* (2004) 57–58.

[16] See, eg N Obuljen, 'From our Creative Diversity to the Convention on Cultural Diversity: Introduction to the Debate' in N Obuljen and J Smiers (eds), *UNESCO's Convention on the Protection and Promotion of the Diversity of Cultural Expressions: Making It Work* (2006) 19–20; UNESCO, 'Meeting of the Experts Committee on the Strengthening of UNESCO's Role in Promoting Cultural Diversity in the Context of Globalization', Working Document, CLT/CIC/BCI/DC/DOC 5E (Paris, 21–22 September 2000)1–2.

[17] Neo-liberalism is a political–economic school of thought built upon neo-classical price theory and encourages deregulation, privatisation and free trade. For an unflattering account of neo-liberalism, see, eg S George, 'A Short History of Neoliberalism: Twenty Years of Elite Economics and Emerging Opportunities for Structural Change', available at http://www.globalexchange.org/campaigns/econ101/neoliberalism.html (last accessed on 1 June 2012).

[18] See T Cowen, *Creative Destruction: How Globalization is Changing the World's Cultures* (2002) 11.

[19] See UN, Cultural Diversity and Globalization, above n 10, 2; see also J Mandle, 'Globalization and Justice' (2000) 570 *Annals* 126, 134; DS Petito, 'Sovereignty and Globalization: Fallacies, Truth, and Perception' (2001) 17 *New York Law School Journal of Human Rights* 1139, 1139. The most classic example is that a standard form of American culture is being systematically transmitted to other cultures. A possible danger of spreading popular American mass culture is that the size and scale of the media of communication dominate what is promulgated, and that tastes and interests of minorities get lost. See, eg UNESCO, above n 13, 27. Prominent critics like TL Friedman have argued that globalisation has its own dominant culture, which is why it tends to be homogenising: 'Culturally speaking, globalisation is largely, though not entirely, the spread of Americanization—from big Macs to iMacs to Mickey Mouse—on a global scale.' See Friedman, above n 7, 1.

[20] See J Reeves, *Culture and International Relations: Narratives, Natives and Tourists* (2004) 185; see also UN, Cultural Diversity and Globalization, above n 10, 2–3.

[21] See E Brooks, 'Cultural Imperialism vs Cultural Protectionism: Hollywood's Response to UNESCO Efforts to Promote Cultural Diversity' (2006) 5 *Journal of International Business & Law* 112, 128–29.

globalisation is proximity. Promoting more physical mobility that ever before,[22] globalisation has rendered the world a smaller place. The interaction between people from different cultures has increased accordingly.[23] This may weaken or destroy ethos, a given group's unique perspective on the world.[24] Globalisation tends to damage ethos particularly in economically disadvantaged societies, and has caused local culture to lose its uniqueness; as a result, these societies have in their artistic creativity.[25] This gives rise to the concern that development may lead to the loss of identity, sense of community and personal meaning.

Thus far, no investigation, no matter how comprehensive, has been able to provide an authoritative evaluation of the exact impact of globalisation on culture. But it seems fair to state that globalisation may lead to both the best and the worst for culture. If the phenomenon manifests in a process in which different cultures and societies can participate with equality, globalisation can benefit all. If the process is directed and decided exclusively by economic powers, however, it may result in cultural homogenisation and social exclusion.[26] This raises the question of how different cultures can efficiently adapt to globalisation.

Culture's importance to individuals and nations means that cultural diversity is a fundamental aspect of modern society. As well as the assertions of national identity, cultural sovereignty and human rights,[27] other arguments, such as cultural pluralism and the natural occurrence of culture, also illustrate how imperative it is to defend culture from extinction, to protect culture against homogenisation and to celebrate culture in its diversity.

1.2 GLOBALISATION AND TRADE

This book touches upon economic globalisation, a much criticised process that integrates national economies into the international economy through trade, investment, and flows of capital and technology.[28] Among these elements, trade is the most commonly identified driving force behind

[22] See Tomlinson, above n 1, 27–29.

[23] See Diana Ayton-Shenker, United Nations Background Note: The Challenge of Human Rights and Cultural Diversity, available at http://www.un.org/rights/dpi1627e.htm (last accessed on 1 June 2012).

[24] See Cowen, above n 18, 50–51 (2002).

[25] Ibid, 47–72 (discussing ethos and the tragedy of cultural loss).

[26] See UN, Cultural Diversity and Globalization, above n 10, 3.

[27] See R Jennings and A Watts (eds), *Oppenheim's International Law*, 9th edn (1992) 87–88; see also AS Akermark, *Justifications of Minority Protection in International Law* (1997) 78–83.

[28] See CJ Bhagwati, *In Defense of Globalization* (2004) 3.

economic globalisation.[29] Free trade augments global welfare and helps achieve goals such as preventing war, elevating living standards, creating jobs, the equitable distribution of wealth, etc. It would be unthinkable to revert to the era of escalating trade protectionism. Economic globalisation follows the lead of trade agreements, which enables the process to occur fast and efficiently.[30] The most powerful trading system currently in place is the World Trade Organization (WTO), often cited as an icon of trade globalisation.[31]

The political sustainability of global economic development requires the adoption of common social safeguards.[32] This is particularly true when the effects of trade expansion and consequent economic integration are not uniformly positive. Furthermore, as trade liberalisation has advanced, it constrains the free exercise of regulatory power in non-trade matters by sovereign states, which were hitherto thought of as purely domestic regulatory decisions.[33] In fact, the WTO has been faced with increasing tensions between free markets and state regulation in recent years, termed 'trade-related' or 'trade linkage' problems.[34] Arguably, no such problem arises where the competing objectives are merely about trade protectionism, since liberalisation generally trumps protectionism in the absence of other considerations. However, the fact remains that numerous social considerations do exist and should not be ignored.

As pointed out, the relationship between free trade and state regulations tends to be a zero sum game: if one is pushed too far, any benefit for one is likely to come at a cost to the other.[35] In this sense, one essential mission of a global trading system is to reconcile the clashes between free trade and other social values; otherwise it may lead to a dual crisis—trade failure and regulatory failure. Although the concerns that motivate non-trade issues are diverse, one common aspiration is the harmonisation of regulatory standards, laws and business practices at both the national

[29] See Renato Ruggiero (the former WTO Director-General), 'A Borderless World', address to the OECD Ministerial Conference, Ottawa, 7 October 1998), available at http://www.wto.org/english/news_e/sprr_e/ott_e.htm (last accessed on 2 June 2012).

[30] See Lodge, above n 6, 271–86.

[31] Ibid, 300–01.

[32] See P Sutherland et al, 'Challenges Facing the WTO and Policies to Address Global Governance' in GP Sampson (ed), *The Role of the World Trade Organization in Global Governance* (2001) 92.

[33] See M Wolf, 'What the World Needs From the Multilateral Trading System' in Sampson, ibid, 183–86.

[34] These problems include culture, environment, development, human rights and labour standards. The growth of relevant debates derives from two converging forces. First, more issues are now regarded as being trade related in the narrow sense that the norms governing those issues affect trade. Secondly, an increasing number of substantive areas become the subjects of internationally coordinated action or multilateral agreements. See, eg D Leebron, 'Linkages' (2002) 96 *American Journal of International Law* 5.

[35] See S Cho, *Free Markets and Social Regulation: A Reform Agenda of the Global Trading System* (2003) 2.

and international levels. This sets the stage for the discussion of the trade and culture issue in this book.

1.3 RAISING THE ISSUE: GLOBALISATION, CULTURE AND TRADE

One of the debates over global governance boils down to a conflict between free trade and cultural protection[36] in which globalisation—the simultaneous liberalisation and acceleration of trade—is deemed incompatible with the coexistence and development of local cultures.[37] The trade of cultural products in particular brings to light different conceptions of economic development, collective identity and cultural diversity, and illuminates the clash between the homogenising forces of economic globalisation and unhindered free trade on the one hand and the protection of local cultures for the sake of diversity on the other.[38]

1.3.1 The Conflicting Conceptions about Trade and Culture

Starkly conflicting conclusions can be drawn about the trade of cultural products. On the positive side, the evidence strongly suggests that free trade represents a significant increase in human freedom by promoting the international exchange of cultural products and expanding consumer choice.[39] Tyler Cowen, an established cultural economist, offered a 'gains from trade' model to understand cultural exchange, which demonstrates how cross-cultural exchange drives cultural blossoming.[40]

Notwithstanding the tendency of trade to increase diversity over time

[36] See generally D Kennedy, 'New Approaches to Comparative Law: Comparativism and International Governance' [1997] *Utah Law Review* 545, 551, 563–75 (discussing how public international law manages the conflict between national culture and global governance). The debate between trade and cultural values goes back to the 1920s, when a number of countries introduced quotas in order to protect their fledgling film industries from a sudden influx of American films. See P Sauvé and K Steinfatt, 'Towards Multilateral Rules on Trade and Culture: Protective Regulation or Efficient Protection?' in *Achieving Better Regulation of Services,* Conference Proceedings, AusInfo, Canberra (Productivity Commission and Australian National University, November 2000) 323.

[37] See R Prodi, 'Globalization and Cultural Diversity: The Contribution of European Institutions', in Ricciardelli, M, et al (eds), *Globalization and Multicultural Societies—Some Views from Europe* (2003) 137.

[38] T Franck has framed this opposition in international legal discourse as one between 'legal-culture' on the one hand—the staple of which is equal application to all regardless of difference, and 'culture-culture' on the other—the main concern of which is the protection of diversity in the face of the homogenising forces of an egalitarian application of international law. See T Franck, 'The Legal-Culture and the Culture-Culture' [1999] *American Society of International Law Proceedings* 271.

[39] See Cowen, above n 18, 5–6, 18.

[40] Ibid, 12–13.

by accelerating the pace of exchange between new cultures,[41] trade liberalisation and economic growth do not always guarantee positive effects on the progress of culture. According to Cowen, trade commercialises and homogenises culture, and gives individuals, regardless of nationality, a similarly rich set of consumption opportunities. It makes countries or societies 'commonly diverse', as opposed to making them different from each other.[42] During this process, while the world as a whole has a broader menu of choices, some regions have lost their distinctiveness.[43] In particular, it has frequently been alleged that the worldwide diffusion and dissemination of mass culture products under the free trade regime has led to the suffocation of domestic cultural expressions.[44]

Cowen also outlines several exceptions or problems with the 'gains from trade' approach to cultural exchange. (i) Societal ethos: trade may harm or foster societal ethos when some small societies may require isolation to maintain their ethos; (ii) cost disease: traditional skills like hand weaving may fall out of use because of the adoption of less costly technologies; (iii) excess clustering: this likely happens where one country's industry dominates the world market; and (iv) quality of consumer tastes: foreign buyers may corrupt the standards of local taste.[45]

Further, Cowen points out that there are different types of cultural diversity. He distinguishes four types: cultural diversity within societies, diversity across societies, diversity across time, and operative or practical diversity. Cowen maintains that globalisation impacts these diversities differently; it is good for some, but not all, types of diversity. Trade increases cultural diversity within societies, even while it may reduce diversity across them: formerly culturally distinct societies will become more alike, offering the same rich menu of consumption.[46]

A common thread in Cowen's analysis is the belief that trade tends to foster both homogenisation and greater niche diversity at the same time. He further argues that trade provides societies with vastly more effective access to objective diversity. Cowen's own nuanced analysis leads him to

[41] Ibid, 15–16.

[42] Ibid, 129.

[43] Ibid, 17.

[44] See, eg Footer and Graber, above n 4, 134; Petito, above n 19, 1139–72; J Gray, *False Dawn: The Delusions of Global Capitalism* (1998) (arguing that global free trade is ruining the world's polities, economies, and cultures). J Tunstall, *Media are American* (1977) 57 (defining the 'cultural imperialism thesis' as the view that 'authentic, traditional and local culture in many parts of the world is being battered out of existence by the indiscriminate dumping of large quantities of slick commercial and media products, mainly from the US'); F Jameson, 'Globalization and Strategy', *New Left Review*, July/August 2000, 49–68 (holding that the standardization of world culture, with local popular or traditional forms driven out or dumbed down to make way for American television, American music, food, clothes and films, has been seen by many as the very heart of globalisation).

[45] See Cowen, above n 18, 49–65.

[46] Ibid, 125–29.

observe that cultural criticisms of globalisation often amount to a narrow or one-sided view of a multifaceted process.

In addition to these concerns, it should be noted that cultural issues could not be adequately addressed solely through a trade prism, as trade rules are not the only threat to a cultural regulatory framework. Rapid progress in technological developments has shrunk the world and driven economic globalisation to an unprecedented degree. The digital revolution renders it easier and less expensive to produce and distribute cultural products. While the practical benefits of these advances have been accompanied by an increase in the choice of modes and quality of cultural products, and explosions of cultural creativity, new technologies have further fuelled the debate around culture shock, national identity and the threats to cultural sovereignty.[47] There has been growing concern that the technology-driven developments in the production and distribution of cultural products might well be beyond the reach of effective regulation. This adds an extra layer of complexity to the problem of trade and culture.

1.3.2 Three 'Duals'—Dual Nature, Dual Legislators and Dual Systems

Cultural products present themselves dually, as both tradable objects and vectors of identity.[48] This creates a drastic confrontation between two divergent logics—'culture-as-commerce' and 'culture-as-identity'—with little likelihood of a plausible synthesis.[49] Typically, one group of countries (with France and Canada at the forefront) is concerned that economically predominant forces homogenise or dilute national cultures or identities.[50] Positing the importation of cultural products as a threat to national identity, they frequently invoke cultural protection as a strategy to restrict trade in culture. On the other side of the debate is the contention that, with the advent of a knowledge-based economy, the prosperity of the media industry and the rapid innovation of technology, cultural industries have become more strategically critical to national economies.

47 EG McAnany and KT Williams, *Mass Media and Free Trade: NAFTA and Cultural Industries* (1996) vii.

48 For a detailed account of this dual nature, see T Knight, 'The Dual Nature of Cultural Products: An Analysis of the World Trade Organization's Decisions Regarding Canadian Periodicals' (1999) 57 *University of Toronto Faculty of Law Review* 165; see also RJ Neuwirth, 'The "Cultural Industries": A Clash of Basic Values?—A Comparative Study of the EU and the NAFTA in Light of the WTO' in F Palermo and GN Toggenburg (eds), *European Constitutional Values and Cultural Diversity* (2003) 95.

49 See Kennedy, above n 36, 563–75 (discussing how international law manages the conflict between national culture and global governance).

50 See D Goulet, 'The Evolving Nature of Development in the Light of Globalization' (2004) 6 *Journal of Law & Social Challenges* 1, 11–13; see also CE Baker, 'An Economic Critique of Free Trade in Media Products' (2000) 78 *North Carolina Law Review* 1357, 1357–435.

Given the huge economic interests represented by cultural industries, it comes as no surprise that the US, as the largest exporter of cultural products, criticises trade restriction as a pretext for economic protectionism. Alongside these traditional players, more and more developing countries with time-honoured cultural heritages and emerging cultural industries paint different pictures of the culture–trade nexus.[51]

The coexistence of dual lawmakers and legal instruments adds further discord to the issue. Historically, while the idea of cultural protection can arguably be traced as far back as the origins of state sovereignty,[52] the modern doctrine of cultural diversity did not begin to take shape until the emergence of multilateral trading systems,[53] represented by the General Agreement on Tariffs and Trade (GATT)/WTO framework. With free trade as its leitmotif, the WTO regime does not legalise 'cultural exception', nor does it grant cultural products any special treatment. The United Nations Educational, Scientific and Cultural Organization (UNESCO), one of whose central mandates is to promote cultural diversity, adopted the Convention on the Protection and Promotion of the Diversity of Cultural Expressions (hereinafter 'the UNESCO Convention on Cultural Diversity' or 'the UNESCO Convention'), which came into force on 18 March 2007. An indication that the UNESCO strengthens its role in cultural protection, the Convention further intensifies the collision between culture and trade.[54]

The conflict between culture and trade has existed over a long period of time. It persists, particularly on the present international law agenda, and has procured prime attention with the implementation of the UNESCO Convention. The coexistence of the two international organisations WTO and UNESCO, and the corresponding legal instruments charged

[51] Traditionally, the debate over trade–culture is defined as a choice between American hegemony and cultural diversity, or a choice between Hollywood films and domestic films. Accordingly, the issue of culture and trade has been mostly argued among the US, French and Canada, with few voices heard from other countries. The situation has recently changed, however, with more participation of other countries, including Australia, China, Korea, Japan and India. In addition, while Europe has a keen interest in the protection of cultural expression, particularly relating to its audiovisual sector, most developing countries pay more attention to the protection of their traditional cultures. See Lee Seunghwan, Heritage Conventions Intertwine with the Concept of Cultural Diversity: Asian and European Perspectives, in Obuljen and Smiers, above n 16, 219–20.

[52] See Petito, above n 44, 1139.

[53] The discourse over trade and culture has its antecedents in the work of the Frankfurt School in the 1930s and 1940s, which coined the term 'cultural industry' in its criticism of the emerging radio, film and recorded music sectors. After the Frankfurt School approach lost ground to the political economy approach in the 1970s and 1980s, the discourse over trade and culture began to be formulated as a debate, which has continued up to the present. See, eg J Sinclair, 'Culture and Trade: Theoretical and Practical Considerations', in McAnany and Williams, above n 47, 30.

[54] The UNESCO Convention on Cultural Diversity was adopted at UNESCO's 33rd general conference on 25 October 2005. Some 148 Members of UNESCO supported the final draft, with Israel and the US voting against and Australia, Honduras, Liberia and Nicaragua abstaining. For more discussions on the UNESCO and UNESCO Convention, see Chapter 4 below.

with different missions, exemplifies the continuously asserted decentralisation or fragmentation of international law,[55] a topic ripe for attention at a higher level.[56] How the WTO and UNESCO can tackle the issue in a cooperative way presents an important subject for international law scholars.

In short, economic globalisation has caused a widespread panic regarding the loss of cultural identity, leading to the resistance to trade in cultural products. The increasing interface and dissonance between trade and culture has resulted in an escalating number of irritants and disputes, which call for an appropriate response from international law. The strife has gradually morphed into a topic of global concern with the heightened collision, the decentralised international legal enforcement and the more diverse participation of various countries.

Against this backdrop, this book seeks to address the juxtaposition between neoliberal trading system and cultural policy options. It intends to provide a balanced view of the challenges inherent in protecting and promoting cultural diversity while at the same time pursuing trade liberalisation. Touching upon an intractable issue in international law, the interrogation of this topic is of an indisputable theoretical and practical necessity.

1.4 THE STRUCTURE OF THE BOOK

Centring on the reconciliation of free trade with cultural diversity in the context of economic globalisation, the book is divided into nine chapters and follows the path described below.

Subsequent to this introduction, Chapter 2 is rooted in a variety of theoretical orientations with a view to exploring how we should understand 'culture' as a complicated social phenomenon and extremely dynamic concept. The objective of the chapter is to draw together diverse publications from social science and offer a synthesis that helps us to

[55] See, eg J Pauwelyn, *Conflict of Norms in Public International Law—How WTO Law Relates to Other Rules of International Law* (2003) head page ('with no single "international legislator" and a multitude of states, international organizations and tribunals making and enforcing the law, the international legal system is decentralized').

[56] On 5 May 2002, the International Law Commission (ILC) set up a Study Group on the topic of the 'fragmentation of international law' to address this urgent issue. See G Hafner, 'Risk Ensuring from Fragmentation of International Law', ILC Report on the Work of its 52nd session, General Assembly Official Records, 56th session, supplement No 10 (A/55/10), 321–29. The Study Group concluded four years of work and stated that the emergence of new and special types of law, self-contained regimes, and geographically or functionally limited treaty systems create problems of coherence in international law. See International Law Commission, 'Fragmentation of International Law: Difficulties Arising from the Diversification and Expansion of International Law—Report of the Study Group (Finalized by Martti Koskenniemi)', UN Doc A/CN.4/L.682, 3 October 2006, available at http://untreaty.un.org/ilc/guide/1_9.htm (last accessed on 1 June 2012).

understand 'culture' from comparative perspectives and, more importantly, our imperative to protect culture and cultural diversity. To this end, Chapter 2 presents an array of approaches for interrogating culture: humanist, anthropological, culture-as-commerce, culture-as-identity, culture as human rights and culture as resource. It concludes with some further thoughts on the interrelationship among these different viewpoints.

In an era of globalisation, domestic cultural regulation holds the key to resolving the culture and trade issue, because each state is obliged to bring its regulatory framework into compatibility with its trade obligations. Chapter 3 begins with a discussion of the justifications for necessary and appropriate cultural policy measures, and the challenges that policymakers are faced with in formulating these measures in the new media environment. The chapter continues with an examination of several of the most frequently used measures, including foreign ownership restriction, content regulation featuring quota system, subsidies, intellectual property rights mechanisms and censorship. It also seeks to identify the dialectic relationships among culture, economy, technology and politics in framing tenable cultural policy measures. The discussion in this chapter is of particular relevance to the proposed design for a WTO-compatible domestic cultural policy measures outlined in Chapter 8.

Chapter 4 begins with a study of the evolution of UNESCO's cultural missions. Next, it discusses the developments of UNESCO's theories and approaches to culture and cultural diversity, with a focus on culture and development, and culture and globalisation. This section continues with an examination of the newly adopted UNESCO Convention on Cultural Diversity, focusing on its negotiation disputes, main contents, advantages and disadvantages, successes and failures. The chapter then lays the foundation for the examination of potential channels of connection between WTO rules and the UNESCO Convention later in Chapter 8.

Chapter 5 presents a study of the theoretical and legislative framework regarding the treatment of culture under the existing GATT/WTO system. First, it reviews an institutional transformation from the Havana Charter to the WTO Agreement on Establishing the WTO. The second section of Chapter 5 analyses the 'screen quota' contained in GATT Article IV, the Uruguay Round negotiation and conflict around audiovisual services, the 'agreement to disagree' compromise finally reached, the exception clauses applying to cultural products, anti-dumping, subsidies, safeguard measures and their applicability to cultural products. In an attempt to offer a full picture of the treatment of culture in the GATT/WTO, this chapter also touches upon several emerging issues, including investment and intellectual property, and explores to what extent they may be related to cultural protection.

Chapter 6 focuses on the judicial practice involving cultural products under the GATT/WTO regime. The detailed case studies provide a critical analysis of the WTO's approach to trade disputes that concern cultural issues. Following an introduction of the GATT/WTO dispute settlement mechanism, Chapter 6 analyses two WTO cases, *Canada—Periodicals*[57] and *China—Publications and Audiovisual Products*.[58] The examination centres on several key issues, including the possibility of invoking the UNESCO cultural instruments as a general defence, the applicability of a public morals exception to cultural products, the incoherence among WTO agreements arising from the overlap of cultural goods and services, and the degree to which cultural content may be used to distinguish 'like products'. This chapter relies heavily on case studies, but offers some analysis as well, identifying problems that take precedence over mere fact statements. This chapter also reiterates the challenges faced by the WTO in settling disputes around the culture and trade issue.

Chapter 7 analyses the treatment of culture under regional frameworks, featuring the EC/EU and the North American Free Trade Agreement (NAFTA). Beginning with the observation that cultural diversity in the EC/EU is a constitutional value, this chapter traces the status of culture at the EC/EU treaty level, then discusses the EC directives on audiovisual service and judicial practice on cultural diversity by the European court. Next, the chapter turns to NAFTA and explores its cultural exception clause, and the weakness and strength of the clause in practice. The chapter concludes with a brief look at the interface of global (WTO) and regional regimes regarding cultural issues.

Chapters 5–7 furnish a comprehensive examination of the status quo treatment of culture in global and regional trade agreements. This trend analysis seeks to identify the challenges trade regimes encounter in dealing with cultural products and tries to diagnose the problems in resolving culture-related trade disputes. These chapters serve as the groundwork for mapping out international and domestic reform proposals in Chapter 8.

Based on the research set out in in previous chapters, Chapter 8 proposes a jurisprudence through which the two separate international legal norms—ie the UNESCO Convention and the WTO agreements—might change from a state of coexistence to one of cooperation, and, by extension, the conflict between trade liberalisation and cultural diversity might move towards synergy. Following the review of the necessity and urgency of addressing the trade and culture stalemate, Chapter 8 makes a two-level proposal: the compatibility of cultural policy measures with

[57] WTO, *Canada—Certain Measures Affecting Periodicals*, complained by the US, WT/DS/31, request for consultations received on 11 March 1996, Panel Report circulated on 14 March 1997 and Appellate Body Report circulated on 30 June 1997.

[58] WTO, *China—Measures Affecting Trading Rights and Distribution Services for Certain Publications and Audiovisual Entertainment Products*, complained by the US, WT/DS/363, request for consultations received on April 10, 2007, Panel Report circulated on 12 August 2009 and the Appellate Body Report circulated on 21 December 2009. DSB adopted the reports on 19 January 2010.

trade obligations on a domestic level and the potential linkage of WTO rules with the UNESCO Convention at the international level. In the latter, this chapter suggests possible procedural links and, more importantly, methods of treaty interpretation that might help bridge the gap between these two sets of instruments.

Chapter 9 concludes with a summary of the broader lessons learned throughout this work and looks beyond, to the challenges faced ahead. It emphasises again that international trade and cultural diversity should not be enemies, that, instead, WTO and UNESCO should work together to bring cultural concerns into trade framework against the backdrop of economic globalisation.

2

Culture and Cultures in Comparative Perspectives: Towards a Synthesis

There are cultures in which sheer experience is so precarious that human beings find it hard to transcend the immediate task of obtaining food and shelter to survive. There are cultures whose members are primarily concerned with the integration of their individual existences into the pattern of nature and tradition. They are preoccupied with spirits, deities, or ancestors. There are cultures that value time, indolence, the warmth of personal relationships, the cultivation, for mere pleasure, of skills that cannot be sold. Leo Bogart[1]

2.1 INTRODUCTION

ONE OF THE most complicated words in the English language,[2] 'culture' defies an easy definition because of its complexity and ever-widening applications.[3] Culture is more than technical infrastructure and information content, although these are certainly its most visible elements.[4] Historically, culture has referred to 'high culture'—the intellectual, musical, artistic and literary products of a society[5]—while in a contemporary sense, culture may take many more forms. Depending on the context, the term may refer to the arts, to the media, to the rituals and other practice by which nations or social groups symbolically reproduce themselves, or to the differences by which some groups distinguish

[1] L Bogart, *Commercial Culture: The Media System and the Public Interest* (1995) 67.

[2] See R Williams, *Keywords: A Vocabulary of Culture and Society* (1985) 87 (claiming that 'Culture is the two or three most complicated words in the English language'.)

[3] See R Borofsky, 'Cultural Possibilities' in UNESCO, *World Culture Report* (1998) 64 (suggesting that the attempts to define culture are 'akin to trying to encage the wind', which captures the protean nature of culture and emphasises how hard to be precise about what the term means).

[4] See V Rabinovitch, 'The Social and Economic Rationales for Domestic Cultural Policies' in D Browne (ed), *The Culture/Trade Quandary: Canada's Policy Options* (1998) 25.

[5] See SP Huntington, Foreword: Cultures Count, in LE Harrison and SP Huntington (eds), *Culture Matters: How Values Shape Human Progress* (2000) XV.

themselves from others.[6] All of these cultural forms must be considered equal under the ethic of cultural relativism.[7]

The word 'culture' also indicates different concerns in different disciplines.[8] Such claims as 'culture is our identity', 'cultural expressions reflect the traditions and convictions of an existing community' or 'cultural diversity is a constitutional value in the EU'[9] mirror many of the distinctions and dynamics associated with the concept of culture, as well as an evolution from cultural pluralism as a public policy[10] to cultural diversity as a notion in international law. International law conforms to the human tendency to objectify by first extending cultural protection to specific items, such as folklore, crafts and skills,[11] despite the fact that a major portion of culture is now present in the realm of popular culture. This book focuses on cultural products, including cultural goods such as publications, films, videos, music recordings and cultural services in the audiovisual sectors.[12] These products are more tradeable and thus pose a more salient threat to local culture.[13]

[6] See G Yúdice, *The Expediency of Culture: Uses of Culture in the Global Era* 214–15 (2003).

[7] Cultural relativism propounds the view that the beliefs, customs, practices and rituals of an individual culture must be observed and evaluated from the perspective of the culture in which they originate and are manifested. See T Barfield (ed), *The Dictionary Anthropology* 98 (1997).

[8] See D Throsby, *Economics and Culture* 3 (2001); see also CE Baker, 'An Economic Critique of Free Trade in Media Products' (2000) 78 *North Carolina Law Review* 1357, 1363.

[9] See, eg C Carmody, 'When "Cultural Identity Was Not At Issue": Thinking about Canada—Certain Measures Concerning Periodicals' (1999) 30 *Law & Policy International Business* 231, 242–43.

[10] See generally W Kymlicka, *Multicultural Citizenship: A Liberal Theory of Minority Rights* (1996); see also W Kymlicka, *The Rights of Minority Cultures* (1995).

[11] See T Knight, The Dual Nature of Cultural Products: An Analysis of the World Trade Organization's Decisions Regarding Canadian Periodicals, 57 *University of Toronto Faculty of Law Review* 165, 169 (1999).

[12] It should be emphasised that cultural products may include folk culture and high culture as well, such as publications on folklore and videos of ballet performance. The distinction between high culture and the concept of entertainment is indeed less valid today because, in the era of information society, high culture is becoming accessible to everyone and much of the culture acquired by individuals now comes from mass cultural products. On another front, also note that culture is embodied in something other than cultural products. For example, McDonald's in Beijing or Paris or Jakarta displaces the distinctive local cuisines that are a major vehicle for culture. Levi jeans replace traditional costumes with their indigenous values (eg female modesty and subordination). One must realise that almost every commercial thing moving from one community to another has inevitable cultural effects. There are willed and unwilled intercultural exchanges. In an age of globalisation, intercultural exchanges will take place on a wider scale and the politics of recognition will escalate. During this process, trade is only one factor forcing intercultural change and the ensuing obliteration of cultures. In other words, culture is very much contingent on many social and economic factors—such as urbanisation and technological advancement—in addition to international trade. Note that this book limits the scope of its discussion to cultural products in a contemporary sense; that is, cultural goods and services that are subject to trade agreements.

[13] Advocates of protectionism generally assert that there is a strong link between exposure to cultural works and the shaping of societal attitudes. This debate is rarely about high

Although there is too much dispute to posit a consensus concept of culture, it is helpful at the outset of this book to foster an understanding of culture from comparative perspectives. Without pretending to exhaust the subject, this chapter draws on the literature of different disciplines to observe 'culture' from comparative perspectives.

2.2 HUMANIST: CULTURE AS 'THE BEST OF EVERYTHING'

An etymological analysis reveals that the word 'culture' began from a primitive idea rooted in cultivation, originally referring to the tillage of soil and the cultivation of good matters.[14] Gradually the meaning was extended to embrace a whole range of intellectual and social activity and improvement.[15] During this etymologic transformation, the influence of early German counter-enlightenment intellectuals helped broaden the meaning of 'culture' from the cultivation of better habits to a more spiritual concept. Later, the concept of 'culture' took shape independently of the concept of 'civilisation' in Britain and Germany, albeit in different ways.[16]

The humanist attitude essentially considers culture to be the high art enjoyed by a happy few, or the highest intellectual achievements, such as philosophy and literature.[17] Accordingly, culture was put into the province of art and literature, of intellectual endeavour and personal achievement, especially their higher manifestations. The humanist views 'culture' as an artifact to be visited at a gallery or watched at a theatre. In the humanist conception, 'culture' is attained through education and knowledge; it is closely connected to aspiration and denotes a measure of success.

The humanist concept of culture rests on the elitist assumption that culture is 'the best of everything', a sense of self-awareness, spiritual

culture—painting, sculpture, literature, opera, and the like. It is, rather, focused on mass-produced popular culture—film, television, mass-market books and periodicals. This is where money is truly at stake on both sides. See, eg OR Goodenough, 'Defending the Imaginary to the Death? Free Trade, National Identity, and Canada's Cultural Preoccupation' (1998) 15 *Arizona Journal of International and Comparative Law* 203, 209–10 (asserting that what is truly at stake is control over the flow of, and capacity of profit from, popular culture, instead of high culture).

[14] See Throsby, above n 8, 3.

[15] See J Reeves, *Culture and International Relations: Narratives, Natives and Tourists* (2004) 15.

[16] In the nineteenth century, 'culture' was thought to be the means for improving civilisation in Britain, while in Germany, the concept of 'Kulture' was more nationalistic and exclusive. The concept of 'civilisation' later evolved and became allied with race theory and biological determinism. It should be noted, however, that early international relations theorists rejected the connection between biological determinism and the concept of 'civilisation'. Ibid, 36.

[17] See LV Prott, 'Cultural Rights as Peoples' Rights' in J Crawford (ed), *The Rights of People* (1992) 94.

growth and improvement.[18] Writing in this tradition, the nineteenth-century cultural critic Matthew Arnold described the word 'culture' as 'sweetness and light'. Far from making us what we are, 'culture' was the thing that would, in Arnold's view, save us from the intellectual and spiritual anarchy that industrialisation had unleashed.[19]

Alongside the emergence of new international machinery in the form of the League of Nations, the humanist concept of 'culture' helped give international relations a new lease on life. Before the First World War broke out, culture was thought to be able to fulfil a significant mission in international politics, ie improving civilisation with 'the best of everything' or 'the pursuit of perfection'.[20] If this held true on an international scale, culture would spread the benefits of 'sweetness and light' by exchanging 'the best of everything' among nations. The rationale behind this assumption was straightforward—if people become more cultured, they will change their imperfect habits and behaviours. As a result, they would become more civilised, which would, in turn, affect the nature of international relations. In the short term, the spread of culture could prevent war, while in the long term, it might even lead to a new world order.[21] The outbreak of the First World War, however, indicated that civilisation was indeed a more fragile structure than previously imagined. Culture failed to perform the role that had been envisioned for it, a failure demonstrated once more when the Second World War broke out.

2.3 AN ANTHROPOLOGICAL VIEW: WE ARE OUR CULTURE[22]

The idea of 'culture' has travelled a long way since Arnold claimed culture to be 'the best of everything'. While the humanist cultural project got underway in international relations, the 'anthropological' notion of culture was being established. Compared to the humanist concept, the anthropological conception of culture is much broader and involves many aspects of one's ways of life, including food, clothing, housing, family values

[18] See Reeves, above n 15, 2–3.

[19] M Arnold, *Culture and Anarchy* (1869/1994) 5. In Arnold's view, 'Culture . . . is a study of perfection'. He further wrote that: '[Culture] seeks to do away with classes; to make the best that has been thought and known in the world current everywhere; to make all men live in an atmosphere of sweetness and light' (idem).

[20] See Reeves, above n 15, 61.

[21] Ibid, 40–41.

[22] Margaret Mead, an American cultural anthropologist, made this renowned claim in 1942. M Mead, *Keep Your Powder Dry: An Anthropologist Looks at America* (1943) 21. She put the word 'are' in italics to emphasise that culture defines us in certain way. This claim emphasised culture's demonstration of the uniqueness of individuals and their communities. See Reeves, above n 15, 1.

and the like.[23] Anthropologists—notable among them Clifford Geertz—use 'culture' to refer to the entire way of life of a society, including its values, practices, symbols, institutions and human relationships.[24] Within this understanding, culture is everywhere, and everyone is implicated in culture.[25] Culture defines us and our ways of life, and is accepted and known as the thing that distinguishes each of us.[26] There is a considerable difference between the claim that culture represents 'the best of everything' and the premise that 'we are our culture'—a claim that admits everything, even the worst.

The twentieth century witnessed the fall of the humanist view, and the anthropological understanding of culture became commonplace. The anthropological notion of culture first emerged in the US during the 1910s and 1920s. After the Second World War, work in cultural field continued to raise the profile of an anthropological concept of culture in the American context, and interest in the humanist concept of culture gradually declined. From the time Mead made her famous statement, 'we *are* our culture', in the 1940s, the anthropological idea of culture has advanced across the world at a considerable pace. In the late 1940s, the anthropological concept of culture was even hailed as 'the foundation stone of social sciences'.[27]

During the cold war, culture came to represent American values and way of life instead of 'the best of everything'.[28] After the cold war, the 1990s witnessed a widespread revival of interest in the idea of culture. Samuel Huntington argued, in his controversial work, *The Clash of Civilizations and the Remaking of World Order*, that the major differences in political and economic development among civilisations are clearly rooted in their distinct cultures. He contends that conflict often erupts along cultural fault lines.[29] He further held that post-cold-war world politics was entering a new phase in which international relations would be determined by cultural differences. Huntington posits, in other words, that the difference between cultures is the dominant source of international conflicts.[30] Even if one does not agree with Huntington's view of international politics, the idea that culture has a broad effect on people's lives seems hard to reject. Huntington's vision, another manifestation of the anthropological

[23] See Reeves, ibid, 179–80.

[24] See Huntington, above n 5, XV.

[25] See A Kuper, *Culture—The Anthrologists' Account* (1999) 2.

[26] See Reeves, above n 15, 2.

[27] See GW Stocking, *Race, Culture, and Evolution: Essays in the History of Anthropology* (1968/82) 302.

[28] See Reeves, above n 15, 87–111.

[29] See SP Huntington et al, 'Samuel P Huntington's "The Clash of Civilizations?" The Debate' [1993/1996] *Foreign Affairs* 29; see also JN Pieterse, *Globalization and Culture—Global Mélange* (2004) 42–44.

[30] Ibid, 3.

notion of culture in international relations, was, and still is, influential in the field of cultural politics.

Despite its prevalence, however, the anthropological concept of culture carries substantive and theoretical difficulties. It has been argued that this all-inclusive definition of culture is analytically empty and operationally meaningless.[31] The concept was also criticised as merely existing in a state of 'taken-for-grantedness'.[32] Indeed, anthropologists themselves expressed concerns over the politics of culture and the theoretical implications such a broad concept might generate.[33] Nevertheless, it is undeniable that culture, however we define it, is central to everything we do and think.[34] The conceptual difficulties do not prevent our understanding the anthropological idea of culture as synonymous with 'way of life'.

2.4 CULTURE AS IDENTITY: CENTERING ON IDENTITY CRISIS

There has long been a noticeable tendency to equate cultural studies with the politics and theory of identity.[35] This close relationship can be seen in the omnipresence of culture in works on the subject of identity, especially in the wake of the influence of postcolonial and critical race theory.[36]

2.4.1 On Identity and Cultural Identity

The concept of 'identity' is itself manifold, and its various facets fail to converge on a central theme. Huntington defined 'identity' as 'an individual's or a group's sense of self', a product of self-consciousness or distinct qualities possessed by people to differentiate themselves from others.[37] This definition indicates that identity is a crucial factor in shaping human attitude and behaviour.[38]

[31] See Throsby, above n 8, 3.

[32] See J Kahn, 'Culture: Demise or Resurrection?' (1987) 9(2) *Critique of Anthropology* 17.

[33] See Reeves, above n 15, 161.

[34] See B Ostry, 'Culture and Trade: One Policy/No Options' in Browne, above n 4, 18–19.

[35] See, eg L Grossberg, 'Identity and Cultural Studies: Is That All There Is?' in ST Huall and P Du Gay (eds), *Questions of Cultural Identity* (1996) 87.

[36] Critical Race Theory (CRT) is based on the American encounter, and it embodies and embraces race consciousness. CRT places race at the centre of American experience. For more details, see, eg R Gordon, 'Symposium: Critical Race Theory and International Law: Convergence and Divergence Foreword' (2000) 45 *Williamette Law Review* 827.

[37] See SP Huntington, *Who Are We? The Challenges to America's National Identity* (2004) 21.

[38] Huntington further set out several key points concerning identities. First, both individuals and groups have identities. Secondly, identities are overwhelmingly constructed. Thirdly, individuals and to a lesser extent groups have multiple identities. Fourthly, identities

Though the term 'identity' is often inflated to cover almost everything that characterises an individual or a group, it is more closely related to those chosen or inherited characteristics that define a certain group and form an integral part of an individual's self-understanding.[39] In *Patterns of Culture*, Ruth Benedict viewed human culture as 'personality writ large'. She believed that each culture has been selected from the great arc of human potentialities and certain characteristics.[40] She explains that people are culturally embedded in the sense that they grow up and live within a culturally structured world, organise their lives and social relations in terms of its system of meaning and significance, and place considerable value on their cultural identity.[41] Furthermore, people are born into, and shaped by, a cultural matrix: no one can exist outside a particular culture.[42] In reality, people often turn to culture as a means of self-definition and mobilisation, and assert their cultural values.

Taken together, these suggest a strong connection between culture and identity. Accordingly, we associate given cultures with certain ethnic groups or nationalities, and these markers become a natural way to speak about culture.[43] 'Cultural identity' is understood as the sum of all cultural references through which a person, alone or in community with others, defines or constitutes himself and his community, and by which he wishes to be recognised. Political scientist Adda Bozeman reinforces this opinion, writing that 'the destiny of each linguistically and morally unified community depends ultimately upon the survival of certain primary structuring ideas around which successive generations have coalesced and which thus symbolise the society's continuity'.[44] This view, termed the 'essentialist model of culture', ie there is an unchanging essence in a particular culture, has been popularised by Huntington.[45] It is important to note that even though this view claims that culture deeply shapes human beings, it does not posit that human beings are

are defined by the self, but they are the product of the interaction between the self and others. Fifthly, the relative salience of alternative identities for any individual or group is situational. See Huntington, ibid, 22–24.

[39] See B Parekh, *Rethinking Multiculturalism: Cultural Diversity and Political Theory* (2006) 1.

[40] See M Mead, 'Preface' in R Benedict, *Patterns of Culture* (1989) xi–xii.

[41] See Parekh, above n 39, 336.

[42] See UNESCO, 'Our Creative Diversity: Report of the World Commission on Culture and Development' (finalised by J Pérez de Cuéllar, 1995), Executive Summary, 28.

[43] See LC Wai, 'The Ownership of Cultural Hybrids', available at inter-disciplinary.net/ati/diversity/interculturalism/ic1/lau%20paper.pdf (last accessed on 8 June 2012) 1. Note that the author mainly discusses in this article how problematic the ownership of cultures can be, through the exploration of the nature of cultural hybrid.

[44] A Bozeman, *Strategic Intelligence and Statecraft* (1998) 26.

[45] See S Huntington, *The Clash of Civilizations and the Remaking of World Order* (1996) 48–55.

not merely determined by their culture.[46] Consequently, the idea that an individual is only a cultural being may leave little room to question the world. People should be able to take a critical view of culture and rise above it to varying degrees.[47]

2.4.2 The Collectivity of Identity: Linking Culture with Nation Building

National identity determines who belongs to a community and is entitled to make claims on it. The concept, as Townshend comments, holds that nations are primal, natural communities that may embrace a purported historic destiny.[48] This view is premised on the argument that nations, like individuals, have identities that comprise perceptions of themselves and beliefs about how others view them. One of the distinct matters intricately tied to the complexities of identity,[49] culture acts as the reason for existing as people, as a political entity and as a nation, and therefore reflects the traditions and convictions of an existing community.[50] This understanding of national identity is at the heart of asserting the centrality of culture. Culture plays an unparalleled role in nation building by engraving national history, long-term development trends, changing external relationships and other distinctiveness associated with a nation.

This poses a series of questions: how can nations have cultural identities like individuals? Is this identity different from an individual's identity? In what sense is a culture inseparable from a group? Culture's collective nature lies at the core of this line of inquiry. Individuals have played an active role in creating culture and shaping societies; further, they are tied up in a variety of group affiliations deriving from biological and historical bases—a shared national, cultural, linguistic, gender, religion or alliance.[51] Culture embraces prevailing values and norms found in a community or society, and is viewed as the sum total of attitudes, values

[46] See Parekh, above n 39, 158; see also Wai, above n 43, 2 (arguing that it is inaccurate to view a culture as an accumulation of cultural achievements by a particular ethnic group. With each intercultural exchange, cultures are deeply transformed.)

[47] In fact, people often have multiple cultural identities; even there is a primary one. See Kuper, above n 25, 247. An individual's mix of cultures typically embraces many specialised allegiances with different geographical boundaries. See K Acheson and C Maule, *Much Ado about Culture: North American Trade Disputes* (1999) 7–8.

[48] *Financial Times Magazine*, 17 January 2004. *Cf* EL Jones, *Cultures Merging: A Historical and Economic Critique of Culture* (2006) 242.

[49] See N Horst, 'Creating an Ever Closer Union: The European Court of Justice and the Threat to Cultural Diversity' (2008) 47 *Columbian Journal of Transnational Law* 165, 207.

[50] See Ostry, above n 34, 20.

[51] See JD van der Vyver, 'Book Review: Culture and Equality: An Egalitarian Critique of Multiculturalism by Brian Barry' (2002) 17 *Connecticut Journal of International Law* 323, 323.

and opinions of the individuals.[52] It is the phenomenon whereby a society or group affirms its presence in the world and assures its reproduction and persistence over time.[53] In this sense, culture is necessarily collective in nature and a kind of group phenomenon.[54] Culture is recognised as an outgrowth of collectivity; therefore, affirmation of a given cultural practice is an affirmation of the particular cultural group. Here the transition of ideas from one involving self-definition to a concept denoting community development and group identity merits attention. In the meantime, the anthropological view of culture informs us that culture is meaningful to a specific community.[55] A group of persons who share cultural referents and formulate a common cultural identity constitute a cultural community.

As a collective property of society, culture is conducive to building a healthy community environment, which in turn gives its members a sense of rootedness to an ongoing community of ancient origins. In this sense, culture nourishes the members' sense of belonging and develops and satisfies their need for identity. The members work together to preserve what they consider essential to their community. A case in point is that the African Union, in *Charter for the Cultural Renaissance of Africa*, recognises cultural diversity as a factor for mutual enrichment of peoples and nations, as well as its contribution to the expression of national and regional identities.[56]

Cultural identity goes hand-in-hand with cultural politics. Cultural survival being the bottom line, cultural politics makes the claim that a human being can only be free in a cultural arena where his or her values are honoured. Left without a secure sense of identity amidst the transition to globalisation, people may resort to isolationism, ethnocentrism or intolerance.[57] In a multicultural society, cultural difference and diversity should be fostered and respected.

[52] The view of culture as the sum total of subjective attitudes and opinions of individuals became dominant among social scientists in the 1950s and 1960s. Later on, however, this view was seen as inadequate to account for the complexity of cultural phenomenon. See JD Hunter, 'The Enduring Culture War' in JD Hunter and A Wolfe (eds), *Is There a Culture War?—A Dialogue on Values and American Public Life* (2006) 18–19.

[53] This view also comports with the proposal that culture should be viewed as a style of life, which takes in the whole existential reality of the persons and communities in a society. See P Jones, 'Human Rights and Diverse Cultures: Continuity or Discontinuity?' in ST Caney and P Jones (eds), *Human Rights and Global Diversity* (2001) 43.

[54] See United Nations, 'Cultural Diversity and Globalization: A Document for Reflection on the Subtheme of "Culture" from the Millennium Forum of the United Nations, available at http://www.forumsocialmundial.org.br/download/tconferencias_identidadecultural_prop_eng.pdf (last accessed on 8 June 2012) 5.

[55] See Kuper, above n 25, 3.

[56] See African Union Charter for the Cultural Renaissance of Africa, adopted in Khartoum, Soudan, 22–24 January 2006, available at http://www.acA.org/eng/textesreferenciels/charte.php (last accessed on 8 June 2012) Arts 3 and 4.

[57] See D Ayton-Shenker, 'The Challenge of Human Rights and Cultural Diversity', United Nations Background Note, available at http://www.un.org/rights/dpi1627e.htm (last accessed on 8 June 2012).

2.4.3 Culture and Identity Crisis

The confluence of culture and identity precipitated by globalisation results in an increasingly global, multicultural world brimming with tension, confusion and conflict. The impact of economic globalisation on the traditional ways of human life forces people to reconsider and redefine their identities, and the so-called 'identity crisis' emerges.[58] Despite the variations in its form, substance and intensity, identity crisis in general has distinct causes and common characteristics.

First, culture is a key factor in any search for the root cause of identity crisis. As illustrated above, culture informs people about who they are and what they have in common.[59] On a larger scale, a nation's culture expresses its essential values, beliefs and perspectives, and is key to nation building. Nevertheless, in recent years, the cultural penetration by other nations—through artifacts, modes of production and consumption, and the one-way flow of information—has generated much concern over the loss of local culture and identity.[60] When a threat to culture gradually becomes a threat to the core of identity, people across the globe are compelled to decide what in their cultures can be maintained and what will be lost.

Secondly, national identity that defines nationhood is spontaneous and defined by immutable features. It is not practised, but inherent; it is not achieved, but ascribed.[61] Once national identity is lost, it is hard to reclaim. This means that if individuals or groups lose the freedom to maintain their cultural identities, their dignity may be seriously curtailed.[62]

Thirdly, identity crisis alerts nations of the cultural homogenisation that arises from accelerated globalisation and the surge of foreign cultural products, particularly with respect to the maintenance and survival of indigenous culture.[63] Faced with unequal competition from powerful external political and economic forces, indigenous cultures have often been marginalised.[64] To compound this loss, the newer cultural symbols

[58] See Huntington, above n 37, 12–13.

[59] See Jones, above n 53, 28.

[60] See MC Bateson, 'Foreword' in R Benedict, *Patterns of Culture* (1989) vii–viii.

[61] See J Friedman, *Cultural Identity and Global Process* (1994) 29.

[62] See T McGonagle, 'The Promotion of Cultural Diversity via New Media Technologies: An Introduction to the Challenges of Operationalization' (2008) 2008(6) *IRIS-Plus* 1, 3.

[63] According to the UN's statistics, there are 350 million indigenous people in the world, living in over 70 countries. Of the 6,000 estimated cultures in the world, 4,500 are indigenous. Over the course of their history, indigenous peoples have developed lifestyles and cultures, which are intricately tied to nature. Their value and belief systems have evolved to enable them to respect and live in harmony with nature, conserving the diversity of life upon which they depend. See Cultural Diversity and Biodiversity for Sustainable Development, a jointly convened UNESCO and UNEP high-level roundtable held on 3 September 2002 in Johannesburg during the World Summit on Sustainable Development, Background Documents, 14.

[64] See UNESCO, above n 42, 69.

to which they are exposed, mainly media products, further undermine their social and cultural security.

Fourthly, people are often inclined to esteem their own culture more highly than that of others.[65] Just as membership of any community entails obligations, the members of a cultural community devote loyalty to their culture. This devotion derives from the fact that culture gives human beings the coherence to make sense of the world and stabilises their personalities. At the same time, loyalty to culture entails duties, such as cherishing culture, defending it against perverse misrepresentations and protecting it from being destroyed.[66]

The current crisis of cultural identity presents the question of how to maintain local culture in a globalised world. Canada and France provide a vivid illustration of the urgency a nation may feel about identity crisis. Despite some subtle differences, both countries hold that culture serves as one of the primary sources of identity and the wellspring for their citizens' self-definition, expression and sense of group belonging. Cultural products are important vehicles of social communication and have a major influence on what citizens learn, believe and feel.[67] Concerned that the deluge of American cultural products may push their national identity—and even cultural sovereignty—to the verge of extinction,[68] both Canada and France traditionally tie support for culture and cultural industries to the survival of an independent nation and the construction of a healthy democratic community.[69]

2.5 CULTURE AS COMMERCE: THE PERSPECTIVE OF CULTURAL ECONOMIC INTERESTS

What is framed as a conflict between trade and culture is in fact a clash between two arguments, culture-as-identity and culture-as-commerce. Due

[65] See R Kothari, 'Peace in an Age of Transformation' in Walker, RBJ (ed), *Culture, Ideology and World Order* (1984) 356.

[66] See Parekh, above n 39, 159–60.

[67] See P Sauvé and K Steinfatt, 'Towards Multilateral Rules on Trade and Culture: Protective Regulation or Efficient Protection?' in *Achieving Better Regulation of Services*, Conference Proceedings, AusInfo, Canberra (Productivity Commission and Australian National University, November 2000) 327.

[68] While the term 'cultural sovereignty' was never defined, it was broadly understood as an enabling clause, guaranteeing states the 'sovereign rights to maintain, adopt, and implement policies and measures to protect and promote their culture'. See C Balassa, 'America's Image Abroad: The UNESCO Cultural Diversity Convention and US Motion Picture Exports France', available at sitemason.vanderbilt.edu/files/../Americas%20Image%20Abroad%20 final.pdf (last accessed on 3 June 2011) 9. For more elaboration of the argument on 'cultural sovereignty', see, eg F Griffiths, *Strong and Free: Canada and the New Sovereignty* (1996) (arguing that a strong culture is essential to Canadian national security).

[69] See Knight, above n 11, 167–68.

in large part to its increasing significance to national economies,[70] the rise of market values has become an important factor in understanding the role of modern culture. The culture-as-commerce argument is premised on the view that culture is a commodity capable of generating profit by means of cultural industries.[71]

2.5.1 The US as the Advocate of the Commerce Argument

The US is a powerful advocate of the culture-as-commerce argument. The prevalent American view, held by almost no other nation, is that culture is the 'economic output produced by cultural industries' or the 'product of industries to which an economic quantum can be attached', and that the products of cultural expressions are nothing more than entertainment.[72] When culture and entertainment become hugely profitable export-oriented businesses, they are wrapped up in a trade liberalisation agenda. The US particularly argues that, because culture is quantifiable in monetary terms, there is nothing economically unique about cultural products that can rationalise the repudiation of settled trade premises.[73] Preoccupied with this notion, the US has been pressing hard to subject cultural products to free trade disciplines.[74] Europeans, on the other hand, firmly hold that free trade arrangements would legitimise the colonisation of the European imagination by Hollywood products, not to mention the huge economic interests enjoyed by those transnational entertainment conglomerates.[75]

In short, the logic of the US view rests on the premise that the making of culture is an industry. This makes certain sense since today the most potent expressions of culture are those of mass-market books, popular music, commercial films and television programmes. These forms of culture are products of commercial enterprises. However, this narrative might be too easily taken as positioning the US against other countries. In addition to economic interests, the shift of the US from 'melting pot' to 'cultural

[70] See Yúdice, above n 6, 221–22 (noting that the consumption of immaterial culture has become a potent engine of economic development).

[71] See JW Warnock, *Free Trade and the New Right Agenda* (1988) 217.

[72] See, eg BI Moran, 'Curb Center Special Feature: United States' Trade Policy and the Exportation of United States' Culture' (2004) 7 *Vanderbilt Journal of Entertainment Law & Practice* 41, 53–54; see also A De Fazeskas, 'Free Trade and Culture: An Alternative Approach' (1993) 2 *Dalhousie Journal of Legal Studies* 141, 147.

[73] See S Globerman, *Culture, Governments, and Markets: Public Policy and the Cultural Industries* (1987) 1–52.

[74] See, eg RL Van Harpen, 'Mamas, Don't Let Your Babies Grow Up to Be Cowboys: Reconciling Trade and Cultural Independence' (1995) 4 *Minnesota Journal of Global Trade* 165, 187–89.

[75] See Yúdice, above n 6, 218.

pluralism'[76] readily lends necessary support to a thorough understanding of the culture-as-commerce argument.

First, America is a nation built on immigration. With immigrants as a sizeable fraction of annual additions to its workforce, the US is and has been a multi-ethnic society with a wide range of cultural practices.[77] Multiple ethnicities are taken for granted; and multiculturalism has a natural constituency that has grown in the US. This reality translates into an openness to different cultures. A host of cultural influences from outside the US freely works themselves into America's cultural kaleidoscope. These cultural imports wind up fitting into an ever-expanding mosaic.[78]

Secondly, the US is a net exporter of culture thanks to its enormous cultural vitality and technological creativity, combined with its hegemonic status in world politics.[79] Americans feel no sense of threat to their culture from trade because it is America's culture that spreads to the world.[80] Secure in its unique position of cultural hegemony, the US does not see a need to adopt defensive cultural policies. It is naturally hard for American people to appreciate the connection asserted by others between protecting culture and national identity. Hence, Americans generally treat Canadians' identity claim with less appreciation and view it as a nationalistic concept or an attempt at protectionism.[81] A reciprocal failure manifests itself in the fact that Canadians do not understand the important roles that free markets play in the lives of most American people.[82] One commentator summarised: 'for Canadians, culture is a nation-building exercise. In the US, it is an enormous industry.'[83] The recurring squabbles between the two countries grow out of the collision of these two sets of defining national myths.

[76] This important shift has been documented by American sociologists and legal scholars. See generally, AM Schlesinger, *Disuniting of America: Reflections on a Multicultural Society* (1991); see also P Hansen, 'The Cultural Short Cut: A Road to Exclusion? Notes on Identity Politics in the European Union' in J Gundara and Sidney Jacobs (eds), *Intellectual Europe—Diversity and Social Policy* (2000) 101.

[77] See J Bhagwati, *The Wind of the Hundred Days: How Washington Mismanaged Globalization* (2000) 209.

[78] Ibid, 210.

[79] For a comprehensive account of the US' hegemony, see L Brilmayor, *American Hegemony—Political Morality in a One-Superpower World* (1994).

[80] See Bhagwati, above n 77, 211.

[81] See M Braun and L Parker, 'Trade in Culture: Consumable Product or Cherished Articulation of a Nation's Soul?' (1993) 22 *Denver Journal of International Law and Policy* 155, 157; H Loeb, The Management and Resolution of Cross Border Disputes As Canada/US Enter the 21st Century: Telecommunication and Culture: Transborder Freedom of Information or Cultural Identity?' (2000) 26 *Canada—US Law Journal* 303, 304.

[82] For more details of these cultural battles, see, eg JL Granastein, *Yankees Go Home: Canadians and Anti-Americanism* (1996); JH Thompson, 'Canada's Quest for Cultural Sovereignty: Protection, Promotion, and Popular Culture' in SJ Randall and HW Konrad (eds), *NAFTA in Transition* (1995).

[83] See R Eberschlag, 'Culture Clash: Canadian Periodical Policies and the World Trade Organization' (1998) 26 *Manchester Law Journal* 65, 66.

Thirdly, Americans' perspective is largely shaped by a history of liberal markets and an ingrained suspicion of government measures limiting market freedom. Historian Frank A Ninkovich notes that, in the US, the analogy of culture and commerce was typical of a liberal mentality that looked at politics, culture and trade as a seamless web of mutually reinforcing filaments meant to bring about a 'liberal ecumene'.[84] This view holds that it is the market, instead of the government, that should dictate whether and how products are disseminated,[85] and the most direct means of achieving cultural diversity is to dismantle border impediments to the free flow of ideas, goods and services.[86] Consequently, the defence of domestic cultures by restricting trade in cultural products is criticised as a smokescreen for protectionism.[87]

Fourthly, the US cares about its identity as well. According to Ambassador Louise Oliver, the US, the most culturally diverse country in the world, is a vigorous proponent of cultural diversity.[88] As a nation of immigrants, the US has long insisted on the swift assimilation of aliens into the 'language and culture that has come down to us from the builders of this republic', as Theodore Roosevelt put it.

For all these reasons, Americans find it hard to apprehend why trade is viewed as a menace to culture; when they do understand this fear, they see a protectionist impulse behind the policy response.[89] This, in turn, reinforces the cynical way in which lobbyists for industries exploit the case for free trade to advance their agendas.

2.5.2 An Appraisal of the Root of the Issue

Jagdish Bhagwati convincingly explains how the dynamic, open and multicultural nature of US society could turn into a threat for cultural plurality

[84] See FA Ninkovich, *The Diplomacy of Ideas: US Foreign Policy and Cultural Relations* (1981) 15, 61.

[85] See I Slotin, 'Free Speech and the Visage Culture: Canadian and American Perspectives on Pop Culture Discrimination' (2002) 111 *Yale Law Journal* 2289, 2290.

[86] Ambassador Louise V Oliver, 'Explanation of Vote of the United States on the Convention on the Protection and Promotion of the Diversity of Cultural Expressions', statement to 33rd UNESCO General Conference, 20 October 2005, available at http://www.usunesco.org/texts/GenConf33_Amb_Intervention_CD_Vote.pdf (last accessed on 8 June 2012) 1.

[87] HM Endelman, 'Regulating Culture: Controversy in the GATT Accord' (1995) 18 *Boston College International & Competition Law Review* 443, 452; see Braun and Parker, above n 81, 175.

[88] 'Ambassador to UNESCO speaks to Executive Board in Paris, US Seeks Improved Draft Convention on Cultural Diversity, available at http://www.america.gov/st/washfile-english/2005/September/20050923173845xlrenneFo.6679302.html, September 23, 2005 (last accessed on 8 June 2012).

[89] See Bhagwati, above n 77, 211.

in other countries.[90] Even if the American position might be correct in the opinion of trade advocates, many other countries, like Canada and France, resolutely reject the application of free trade rules to cultural products.[91] In the confrontation between these two profoundly different logics, there seems little likelihood of a plausible synthesis due to the fundamental discontinuity of appreciation.[92] An objective appraisal calls for a holistic perspective.

On the one hand, culture is no longer limited to ballet or museums, but encompasses popular media culture as well. The cultural sector's contribution to a country's GDP is considerably larger than previously thought in many nations. American cultural industry is certainly one of its most profitable sectors. Even in Canada, some European countries, China and India, cultural industries are earmarked as growth areas of strategic economic relevance.[93] As many countries have been suffering the effects of cultural erosion from the pervasive international distribution of American cultural products, they have sought to provide support to maintain domestic cultural industries.

It thus comes as no surprise that, aside from the identity claim, these countries, like the US, are concerned that cultural imports will harm domestic economic interests. This exhibits an ambivalent feeling toward culture and commerce. Since the late 1970s, the economic discourse of cultural industry, instead of the establishment of national culture, has dominated cultural policy discussions in Canada.[94] Alison Beale also demonstrates that, under the cloak of protecting national culture, capital interests in both Canada and France are actually promoting their own cultural industries instead of nonprofit arts or heritage, which would presumably be a bulwark of national identity.[95] Furthermore, the value of modern culture is more closely linked to technology, and in particular, to powerful media technologies. Media products exert an important influence on the shaping of citizenship and of identity, though this influence is

[90] Ibid, 209–13.

[91] See Baker, above n 8, 1358–59.

[92] See LGC Kaplan, 'The European Community's "Television Without Frontiers" Directive: Stimulating Europe to Regulate Culture' (1994) 8 *Emory International Law Review* 255, 345.

[93] The economic impacts of film and television production in Canada are being felt across the country. For example, Vancouver ranks third behind Hollywood and New York City as a North American film production centre. See K Boryskavich and A Bowler, 'Trade and Culture: Hollywood North: Tax Incentives and the Film Industry in Canada' (2002) 2 *Asper Review of International Business & Trade Law* 25, 30, 39–40.

[94] See K Dowler, 'The Cultural Industries Policy Apparatus' in M Dorland (ed), *The Cultural Industries in Canada: Problems, Policies and Prospects* (1996) 328–46.

[95] See A Beale, 'Communication Policy, Media Industries, and Globalization: Identifying a Policy Hierarchy' in D Crane et al (eds), *Global Culture: Media, Arts Policy, and Globalization* (2002) 14.

difficult to specify precisely.[96] As a result, in a time when culture has become big business, elite approaches to culture that ignore market-driven cultural forms neglect an essential ingredient of the current cultural mix.

On the other hand, a nation's culture is the expression of its values, beliefs and perspectives necessary for preserving a healthy community. Cultural production and consumption have a strong impact on the quality of life.[97] Unique amalgams of content, distribution method and exhibition, cultural products are not just products requiring financial investment, but also intellectual, creative works as well.[98] Though the economic impact of cultural industries suggests what is truly at stake in the context of economic globalisation, completely equating culture with income-generating industry eliminates the spirituality, history and value of cultural practices, which serve as the central ingredients that maintain values and celebrate the traditions of communities.[99] Thus, while we do need to take the economic side into account, all forms of cultural expression should certainly not be reduced to mere commercial value. As advocated by Jacques Delor, cultural goods are not like other merchandise and deserve special protection because culture is there to reassure; it is part of our roots.[100]

The combined cultural and economic character of cultural products forms the basis for a critical analysis in social theory, which later becomes exemplified in the concept of 'cultural industry',[101] a key notion in the trade and culture conundrum. Due to the dual nature of cultural products, cultural industries pose an interesting intellectual as much as a practical challenge to the existing normative frameworks and their organisational

[96] See J Liss 'The Impact of Globalization and Technological Change on Culture and National Identity: A Call for Visionary Pragmatism' in D Browne (ed), *The Culture/Trade Quandary: Canada's Policy Options* (1998) 164.

[97] See Rabinovitch, above n 4, 29.

[98] See A Herold, 'Between Art and Commerce: Constitutional Contradictions within the Framework of the EU Film Policy' in F Palermo and GN Toggenburg (eds), *European Constitutional Values and Cultural Diversity* (2003) 74.

[99] See UNESCO, above n 42, 235.

[100] Delor is the Former President of the EC. Quoting from R Collins, 'The Screening of Jacques Tati: Broadcasting and Cultural Identity in The European Community' (1993) 11 *Cardozo Arts & Entertainments Law Journal* 361.

[101] The term 'cultural industry' was first coined by the scholars of the Frankfurt School in the 1930s and 1940s when they criticised the emerging radio, film, and recorded music sectors. See, eg TW Adorno, *The Culture Industry* (2001) 98; TW Adorno and M Horkheimer, 'The Culture Industry: Enlightenment as Mass Deception' in TW Adorno and M Horkheimer (eds), *Dialectic of Enlightenment* (1997) 120–67; J Sinclair, 'Culture and Trade: Theoretical and Practical Considerations' in EG McAnany and KT Williams (eds), *Mass Media and Free Trade: NAFTA and Cultural Industries* (1996) 30. More important for the emergence of cultural industries as a category of analysis as well as criticism has been the work of Garnham, who describes 'cultural industries' as those institutions which employ the characteristic modes of production and organisation of industrial corporations to produce and disseminate symbols in the form of cultural goods and services, generally as commodities. See N Garnham, *Capitalism and Communication* (1990) 155–56.

structures.[102] With the advent of economic globalisation, culture industries have been increasingly export-oriented. Trade in cultural products disseminates all kinds of values, from notions of citizenship to consumer ethos.[103]

Maintaining a society that is rich in quality of life requires a culture replete with civil values, democracy, education, rule of law, community mindedness and tolerance of diversity, and shows a commitment to communication among citizens. These cultural values underpin and ground a distinctive society, yet escape market analysis because they do not show up in any obvious way on the bottom line.[104] The paradigm of competition and comparative advantage that underlies the liberalisation of the world market may not readily apply to the different structure and incentives of the cultural market. For example, fixed production costs are much higher in the US than in other countries, but are easily absorbed by the revenues accrued from a larger domestic market. This economies-of-scale advantage lowers the marginal costs borne by US producers entering foreign markets, and their price discrimination strategies have sometimes been seen as a form of 'cultural dumping'.[105] Considering this, purely market-oriented approaches to cultural policy that advocate a narrowing of the focus of culture to the high arts and to market failures prove inadequate.

In short, culture is commerce, but it is more than that. Despite the difficulty in drawing a clear line between economy and culture in the 'post-cultural-industry' era, the commodification of culture decontextualises and destroys the meaning of cultural practice.[106] Economy and trade are vital aspects of culture,[107] yet market logic has trouble appreciating the intangible values of culture, including its linkage to identity, because quantification in this respect is extremely hard. The values underlying the economic and cultural positions thus collide, intersecting in the idea of the market. Therefore, to overstate the claims of the culture-as-commerce argument, cultural goals are in danger of being overwhelmed by purely commercial objectives.

[102] See RJ Neuwirth, 'The "Cultural Industries": A Clash of Basic Values?—A Comparative Study of the EU and the NAFTA in Light of the WTO' in F Palermo and GN Toggenburg (eds), *European Constitutional Values and Cultural Diversity* (2003) 94–95.

[103] See Yúdice, above n 6, 237.

[104] See Liss, above n 96, 163.

[105] See J Devlin, 'Canada and International Trade in Culture: Beyond National Interests' (2004) 14 *Minnesota Journal of Global Trade* 177, 178–79.

[106] See UNESCO, above n 42, 235.

[107] In rejecting a purely market-oriented view of culture, anthropologist Marshall Sahlins observes that it is meaningless to talk of the relation between culture and the economy, since the economy is part of a people's culture. See Jeffrey, above n 96, 162.

2.6 CULTURE AS HUMAN RIGHTS: REVISITING CULTURAL RIGHTS

One justification for protecting culture in international law is to recognise culture as an essential component of human rights.[108] The transition from the recognition of enjoying culture at large (culture of the dominant society) to the recognition of a specific group of people enjoying culture unique both to them and to their own identity is a leap in human rights law.[109] The basic notion is that every human being has the right to culture, which includes the right to participate, enjoy and develop cultural life and identity.[110] The right to culture in international law is coupled with a long-standing debate between universal human rights (universalism) and cultural relativism.[111] This section tries to explore whether universal human rights exist in a culturally diverse world, the elements necessary to understand cultural rights in a globalised world, and how human rights can be reconciled with the clash of culture and trade characteristic of the era of globalisation.

2.6.1 The Hallmarks of Universalism and Cultural Relativism

Universalism and cultural relativism are two key concepts in understanding the application of human rights to cultural policies and practices.[112] The claim that human rights derive from universally valid and absolute moral principles sets the stage for the battle between these two concepts. The debate proceeds to question whether the legitimacy of human rights

[108] See AS Akermark, *Justifications of Minority Protection in International Law* (1997) 78–83.

[109] See M Hadjioannou, 'The International Human Right to Culture: Reclamation of the Cultural Identities of Indigenous Peoples under International Law' (2005) 8 *Chapman Law Review* 201, 208.

[110] Human rights that relate to cultural diversity encompass a wide range of protections. See United Nations, Universal Declaration of Human Rights, Arts 19 and 27; United Nations, International Covenant on Civil and Political Rights (ICCPR); United Nations, International Covenant on Economic, Social, and Cultural Rights (ICESCR), Art 1; see also Ayton-Shenker, above n 57.

[111] See, eg M Skinner, 'Locating Indigenous Power: Cultural Relativism, Universalism and State Sovereignty Preface' (2001) 7 *New England International & Comparative Law Annual* 69; G Binder, 'Cultural Relativism and Cultural Imperialism in Human Rights Law' (1999) 5 *Buffalo Human Rights Law Review* 211; MA Civic, 'A Comparative Analysis of International and Chinese Human Rights Law—Universality Versus Cultural Relativism' (1995–96) 2 *Buffalo Journal of International Law* 285; J Morgan-Foster, 'A New Perspective on the Universality Debate: Reverse Moderate Relativism in the Islamic Context' (2003) 10 *ILSA Journal of International & Comparative Law* 35.

[112] See E Reichert, 'Human Rights: An Examination of Universalism and Cultural Relativism' (2006) 22(1) *Journal of Comparative Social Welfare* 23.

depends upon the existence of fundamental principles of justice that transcend culture, society and politics.[113]

2.6.1.1 *Universalism*

Universalism proclaims that all human beings are born equal, with human rights as their birthrights. Human rights are universal, intended for everyone in every culture, and belong to everyone wherever he or she resides.[114] In essence, universalism entitles all individuals, regardless of their cultural antecedents, to certain minimal rights without discrimination.[115] This implies that the basic necessities for a decent life must be the first concern of humanity. Strict universalism rejects the idea of cultural diversity, and contends that those primitive cultures will eventually evolve to have the same system of law and rights as Western cultures.[116]

The notion of universalism came into prominence after World War II,[117] when the UN declared the universality of human rights. The 1948 Universal Declaration of Human Rights (UDHR) conceives of human rights as a seamless ideal and affirms consensus around a universal standard of human rights.[118] This is further strengthened by the International Covenant on Economic, Social and Cultural Rights (ICESCR),[119] the International Covenant on Civil and Political Rights (ICCPR)[120] and other related international instruments. Member States of the UN have a

[113] See Binder, above n 111, 211.

[114] Universalism is based largely on Western philosophy and the value it places on the individual. Jack Donnelly best summarises the contemporary doctrine of the Universalist approach. First, all humans have rights by virtue of their humanity; secondly, a person's rights cannot be conditioned by gender or national or ethnic origin; thirdly, human rights exists universally as the highest moral rights. See J Donnelly, *Universal Human Rights in Theory and Practice* (2002); see also UNESCO, above n 42, 16.

[115] A fundamental rule of international law, the non-discrimination principle protects individuals and groups against the denial and violation of their human rights. Hence, to deny human rights on the grounds of cultural distinction is discriminatory. See, eg Ayton-Shenker, above n 57.

[116] See KY Schooley, 'Cultural Sovereignty, Islam, and Human Rights—Toward A Communitarian Revision' (1995) 25 *Cumberland Law Review* 651, 713.

[117] See F Newman and D Weissbrodt, *International Human Rights: Law, Policy, and Process* (1996) 6 (mentioning that, historically, the development of modern human rights law followed the end of the Second World War, the convening of the Nuremberg Tribunals and the creation of the United Nations).

[118] United Nations, The Universal Declaration of Human Rights, Preamble; see also EM Zechenter, 'In the Name of Culture: Cultural Relativism and the Abuse of the Individual' (1997) 53 *Journal of Anthropological Research* 319. With the adoption of the Universal Declaration of Human Rights, countries all over the world discussed and negotiated values that would become the basis for human rights. See Reichert, above n 112, 26.

[119] United Nations, International Covenant on Economic, Social and Cultural Rights, adopted and opened for signature, ratification and accession by General Assembly resolution 2200A (XXI) of 16 December 1966, entry into force 3 January 1976, in accordance with Art 27, Preamble, Arts 5, 13 and 18.

[120] United Nations, International Covenant on Civil and Political Rights, adopted and opened for signature, ratification and accession by General Assembly resolution 2200A

legal obligation to promote and protect human rights.[121] The background to the founding of the UN indicates that only by working together and agreeing upon a universal set of principles can all nations succeed in creating a better world.[122] In this sense, universal human rights reflect the dynamic, coordinated efforts of the international community to achieve and advance a common standard in international law to protect human dignity.

2.6.1.2 *Cultural Relativism*

Cultural relativism first originated with anthropologists, who demonstrated empirically that there are many different cultures in the world, each equally worthy. They expressed concern over placing all peoples across the world within the single aegis of Western culture.[123] Cultural relativism asserts that human values are culturally relative and vary a great deal from different perspectives. The ethic of cultural relativism teaches us that high culture, folk culture and popular culture are all equal. Its fundamental theme is that culture defines individual values, and people's rights are dependent on their nationality, religion and culture.[124]

Holding that traditional local cultures are unchangeable, cultural relativism received its greatest prominence as a means to counter colonialism. Cultural relativists subscribe to the view that all ethical, religious and political beliefs are truths related to the cultural identity of an individual or a society. No outside value is superior to local cultures.[125] They reject the application of universal human rights standards, which they frequently characterise as a reflection of the conflict between Western imperialism and local cultural beliefs.[126]

(XXI) of 16 December 1966, entry into force 23 March 1976, in accordance with Art 49, Preamble, Art 5.

[121] Human rights are emphasised among the purposes of the UN as proclaimed in its Charter, which states that human rights are 'for all without distinction'. The Charter further commits the UN and all Member States to action promoting 'universal respect for, and observance of, human rights and fundamental freedoms'. United States, Charter of the United Nations, Preamble, Arts 1(3), 13(1)(b), 55(c), 62(2), 68, 76(c).

[122] See Reichert, above n 112, 27–28.

[123] See generally TE Higgins, 'Anti-Essentialism, Relativism, and Human Rights' (1996) 19 *Harvard Women's Law Journal* 89.

[124] See Reichert, above n 112, 28–29.

[125] Ibid, 28–29.

[126] See A Eckert, 'The Global and Local: Reconciling Universal Human Rights and Cultural Diversity' (2002) 2(2) *Human Rights & Human Welfare* 2. For example, at the 1993 UN Conference on Human Rights, a delegation led by China, Syria and Iran officially challenged the universality of human rights. They held that human rights as currently defined are not universal but based on Western morality. Human rights should not be imposed as norms on non-Western societies with disregard for those societies' historical and economic development, cultural differences, and perceptions of what is right and wrong. Furthermore, they contend that the imposition of one's standard on another culture is unjust and imperialist in nature. See Reichert, above n 112, 33.

There are variances of cultural relativism. Strict relativism encompasses group identity, explains culture as the sole source of the validity for a moral value[127] and maintains that any contemplation of international human rights is a priori offensive to local cultures.[128] Moderate relativism treats international norms as a neutral benchmark that ought to be achieved. It posits that attention to local cultures precludes the universality of human rights while recognising that certain sets of core rights do transcend cultural boundaries.[129] A relatively new theory, reverse moderate relativism, accepts the virtues of moderate relativism but attempts to avoid the Western-centric focus on international norms as a neutral standard to be achieved.[130] A proposed weak relativist approach views human rights as prima facie universal, but recognises culture as a source of exceptions.[131]

2.6.2 A Critique of Universalism and Cultural Relativism

With the advent of globalisation, the world has become a smaller place and people are no longer governed by national borders. Having fundamental rights instead of rights tied to certain cultures may provide a better solution to the problems with defining human rights. It is a unified solution, but one with a major flaw: it neglects the complexity of human values. The discussions of universalism versus cultural relativism often contemplate a Western tendency towards universalism and a non-Western tendency to highlight cultural identity. Some countries criticise the imperialist nature of universalism and charge that it perpetuates colonialist practices. Nonetheless, cultural relativism also occurs in Western countries, including the US.[132] The fact remains that no country or culture readily accepts the imposition of universal human rights, particularly when the human rights involved would potentially weaken a nation's culture.[133] Moreover, the claim of sovereignty may constitute another barrier to the pursuit of universal human rights,[134] since there has been no consensus answer to the debate about the superiority of human rights and sovereignty across the world. In short, universalism may not be tenable to the extent that it ignores the tensions of different countries and negates the validity of indigenous culture.

[127] See J Donnelly, 'Cultural Relativism and Universal Human Rights' (1984) 6(4) *Human Rights Quarterly* 400.

[128] See Schooley, above n 116, 679–82.

[129] Ibid, 682–90.

[130] See Morgan-Foster, above n 111, 66–67.

[131] See Donnelly, above n 127, 402.

[132] See Reichert, above n 112, 24–27.

[133] See J Donnelly, *International Human Rights* (1993) 36.

[134] Ibid, 28–29.

Cultural relativism calls for considering cultural difference in looking at how human rights are applied and presents a challenge to universalism, claiming it is appropriate to prevent the traditional values of one society from being absorbed into the universal heritage of a more powerful society.[135] However, cultural relativism has deficits and has the potential to be abused. Strict relativism discredits the whole field of human rights and lacks warranty.[136] Moderate relativism is appealing in some senses, but lacks a definite meaning. A general concern is that if cultural traditions alone govern a state's compliance with international standards, then human rights perceived as culturally relative would only be subject to state discretion. This would lead to widespread disregard, abuse and violation of human rights, and threaten the effectiveness of international human rights law that has been painstakingly constructed over the decades.[137] Furthermore, given the elasticity of the concept of culture, cultural relativism may even threaten to erode the foundations of the multilateral trading order.

2.6.3 Reconciling Human Rights with Cultural Diversity

In order to promote and protect both the universality of human dignity and a fair diversity of local culture, a balance should be struck between universalism and cultural relativism. It is not an easy task to pursue, though, particularly because human rights principles sometimes contradict local cultural norms.

2.6.3.1 The Necessity to Reconcile Human Rights with Cultural Diversity

The impact of culture in shaping individuals is systematic and unchangeable. This cultural variability of human nature not only permits, but also requires, cross-cultural variations in human rights.[138] A universal application of human rights without deference to cultural traits diminishes cultural identity and may indeed constitute a human rights violation. By the same token, if all rights rested solely on culturally determined social rules, then there would be no human rights. Historically, a long process of civilisation has imposed norms to restrain human behaviour,

[135] See B Smith, 'Art Objects and Historical Usage' in I McBryde (ed), *Who Owns the Past?* (1985).

[136] See BH Weston, 'Human Rights and Nation-Building in Cross-Cultural Settings' (2008) 60 *Maine Law Review* 317, 325–26.

[137] See Ayton-Shenker, above n 57; P Macklem, 'Distributing Sovereignty: Indian Nations and Equality of Peoples' (1993) 45 *Stanford Law Review* 1311, 1335–1336; Skinner, above n 111, 81.

[138] See Donnelly, above n 127, 403.

and these norms have evolved in parallel across different cultures. There are legitimate and substantive limitations on cultural practices, even on well-entrenched traditions.[139] For instance, no culture today can claim a right to practice slavery. Furthermore, there has been an increasing need to emphasise the common, core values shared by all cultures: the value of life, social order and protection from arbitrary rule. These basic values are embodied in human rights and constitute a valuable instrument for ensuring the dignity of human beings.

Difficulties exist in protecting cultural norms within the framework of universal human rights. It is not proper to resort to human rights to encourage and justify the complete homogenisation of different cultures. Likewise, it is not appropriate to invoke cultural diversity to justify an attack on human dignity.[140] Without giving up either human rights or cultural diversity, it is necessary to come up with a balanced view to address the issue and accomplish the goal through practical strategies.

2.6.3.2 *The Reconcilability of Human Rights with Cultural Norms*

Cultural relativism posits that traditional culture is sufficient to protect human dignity, and therefore universal human rights are not only unnecessary, but also intrusive and disruptive to human life, liberty and security. This is not necessarily the case. Human rights are not representative of or oriented towards one culture to the exclusion of others.[141] Universal human rights represent the hard-won consensus of the international community, rather than the cultural imperialism of any particular region. If the traditional culture can absorb and apply the notion of contemporary human rights, the state is in a better position to implement international standards.

International law establishes a legal standard of minimum protection to maintain human dignity, while universal human rights do not put a uniform cultural standard into place.[142] In fact, while universalism explains that some moral requirements are the same for everyone, it does not require that all human beings have to be the same, nor are there moral requirements to discourage cultural diversity. In this sense, universalism emerges with sufficient flexibility to respect cultural integrity and diversity. This flexibility is further facilitated by the establishment of minimum standards of human rights that incorporate cultural rights.[143] Within this framework, states are granted maximum room for cultural variation without prejudice to the value of human rights.

[139] See Ayton-Shenker, above n 57.
[140] See United Nations, above n 54, 12.
[141] See Ayton-Shenker, above n 57.
[142] See Reichert, above n 112, 27–28.
[143] See Ayton-Shenker, above n 57.

2.6.3.3 *The Strategies to Reconcile Human Rights with Cultural Norms*

In a world of diverse cultural traditions that is simultaneously distinguished by the widespread universalist claim, human rights should in theory extend to every human being without discrimination.[144] In the meantime, international law should approach human rights issues through culturally legitimate means. That said, the task is then to explore channels by which human rights can be reconciled with cultural norms.

The key here is to revive cultural rights and foster respect for cultural diversity. Whether cultural rights should be classed as individual or collective rights is a perennial subject of debate.[145] A balanced view has been proposed which styles cultural rights as individual rights with a powerful collective dimension.[146] Cultural rights are understood as a cluster of rights, including distinct cultural rights, as well as the cultural dimensions of other human rights. The core cultural right is the belief that each person has the right to fully participate in cultural life,[147] including the right to maintain and develop one's cultural identity, lead particular lifestyles, and assemble, associate and organise for certain cultural purposes.

Unfortunately, cultural rights have long been neglected and development in the area has been stunted. The linkage between the goals of maintaining cultural diversity and enforcing cultural rights has yet to be recognised in many countries.[148] In recent years, however, cultural rights have gained more attention alongside the burgeoning protection of minority rights.[149] Considerable progress has been made in promoting cultural democracy and rights. A series of international instruments of human rights contain references to cultural rights, including the UDHR, the ICCPR and the

[144] See Weston, above n 136, 317.

[145] For a representative view of both sides of the debate, see, respectively, A Eide, 'Cultural Rights as Individual Rights', in A Eide et al (eds), *Economic Social and Cultural Rights* (2001) 289–301; LV Prott, 'Cultural Rights as People's Rights in International Law' in J Crawford (ed), *The Rights of Peoples* (1988) 93–106.

[146] See McGonagle, above n 62, 1–2.

[147] See UNESCO, above n 42, 240.

[148] See W Logan, *UNESCO, Cultural Diversity, Cultural Heritage and Human Rights* (2008) 2.

[149] Cultural rights are described as 'the Cinderella of the human rights family'. See H Niec, 'Casting the Foundation for the Implementation of Cultural Rights' in H Niec (ed), *Cultural Rights and Wrongs: A Collection of Essays in Commemoration of the 50th Anniversary of the Universal Declaration of Human Rights* (1998) 176. While cultural rights are indeed of vital importance for minority peoples, dominant societal groups also have valid and vested interests in maintaining their cultures. See W Mannens, 'The International Status of Cultural Rights for National Minorities' in P Cumper and S Wheatley (eds), *Minority Rights in the New Europe* (1999) 185–96.

ICESCR.[150] The Vienna Declaration[151] mentions cultural considerations as well, stating that 'the significance of national and regional particularities and various historical, cultural and religious backgrounds must be borne in mind'.[152] This is a deliberate acknowledgement of the duty of states to protect human rights regardless of their cultural systems.[153]

At the same time, it should be noted that cultural rights are not unlimited. They cannot be invoked or interpreted to justify any act leading to the denial or violation of basic human rights and fundamental freedoms. Moreover, cultural norms are not substitutes for human rights. Rather, they act as the cultural context in which human rights are established, integrated, promoted and protected. Furthermore, recognition and appreciation of particular cultural contexts would serve to facilitate respect for and observance of human rights.[154]

In short, while local cultures protect the well-being of their people, human rights protect and promote human dignity. The intersection of these two values constitutes cultural rights, which are charged to enhance human rights in diverse cultural contexts. Instead of limiting human rights to suit a given culture, it is advisable to draw on compatible cultural values to reinforce human rights. Working in this way inherently recognises cultural integrity and diversity without compromising or diluting the unquestionable universal standard of human rights.

2.6.4 The Margin of Appreciation Doctrine in Reconciling Universalism and Cultural Relativism

The margin of appreciation doctrine, which permeates the jurisprudence of the European Court of Human Rights (ECtHR), is based on the notion that each society is entitled to certain latitude in resolving the inherent conflicts between individual rights and national interests or among different moral

[150] See, eg United Nations, Universal Declaration of Human Rights, Art 27(1) (everyone has the right freely to participate in the cultural life of the community, to enjoy the arts and to share in scientific advancement and its benefits); ICCPR, Art 27 (persons belonging to ethnic, religious or linguistic minorities shall not be denied the right inter alia to enjoy their own culture); ICESCR Art 15 (formulating the right of everyone to participate in cultural life, to benefit from scientific progress and its applications and to enjoy intellectual property rights).

[151] See United Nations, Vienna Declaration and Program of Action, adopted in June 1993 by the UN General Assembly at World Conference on Human Rights held in Austria, Vienna, available at http://www.unhchr.ch/huridocda/huridoca.nsf/(Symbol)/A.CONF.157.23.En (last accessed on 9 June 2012).

[152] Ibid, Part I, ¶5.

[153] See D Otto, 'Rethinking the "Universality" of Human Rights Law'(1997) 29 *Columbia Human Rights Law Review* 1, 11 (this outcome can be read as supporting either the universalist or the relativist position. It reflects the paralysis of the debate and leaves the issue firmly on the international human rights agenda for another day).

[154] See Ayton-Shenker, above n 57.

convictions.[155] The doctrine allows the court to take into account the fact that the European Convention on Human Rights is interpreted differently in different Member States. Judges are obliged to consider the cultural, historical and philosophical differences in a particular state. The doctrine was used for the first time in *Handyside v United Kingdom*,[156] which concerned the publication of a book for school children containing a chapter discussing sexual behaviour in explicit terms. In this case, the ECtHR allowed a limitation of freedom of expression in the interests of the protection of public morals. In later practice, the margin of appreciation doctrine has developed less intrusive, more politically acceptable and cost-effective standards of review for national decisions.

Several policy arguments are cited in favour of the application of the doctrine both in national and international law, such as institutional advantages,[157] democratic accountability,[158] fairness in attributing responsibility[159] and inter-institutional comity.[160] The doctrine embraces two principal elements, ie judicial deference (or judicial restraint)[161]—which relates to norm-application—and normative flexibility[162]—which relates to

[155] For a comprehensive analysis of the margin of appreciation doctrine, see generally, HC Yourow, *The Margin of Appreciation Doctrine in The Dynamics of European Human Rights Jurisprudence* (1996); see also E Brems, 'The Margin of Appreciation Doctrine in the Case-Law of the European Court of Human Rights' (1996) 56 *Heidelberg Journal of International Law* 240.

[156] 5493/72 *Handyside v The United Kingdom* [1976] ECHR 5.

[157] See Y Shany, 'Towards a General Margin of Appreciation Doctrine in International Law?' (2006) 16 *European Journal of International Law* 907, 918–19 (pointing out two prongs of this argument: (i) the judicial decision-making process suffers from chronic deficiencies that support the delegation of decision-making powers to non-judicial decision-makers; and (ii) international courts have more limited decision-making capabilities that their domestic counterparts).

[158] This consideration is premised on the argument that domestic and international courts comprise non-directly elected individuals; their suitability to make important choices regarding social conditions within states is controversial. See SP Croley and JH Jackson, 'WTO Procedures, Standard of Review, and Deference to National Governments' (1996) 90 *American Journal of International Law* 193, 207.

[159] This argument relates to the ex post facto nature of attributing state responsibility for violations of vague legal standards. See Shany, above n 157, 921.

[160] One could maintain that comity represents judicial politics, or even judicious politics. See E Mensch, 'The History of Mainstream Legal Thought' in D Kayris (ed), *The Politics of Law: A Progressive Critique* (1998) 33. Further, the division of labour between national authorities and international courts, instituted by the margin of appreciation doctrine, contributes to the development of a sense of partnership between the two sets of institutions. See PG Carozza, 'Subsidiarity as a Structural Principle of International Human Rights Law' (2003) 97 *American Journal of International Law* 38, 57–58.

[161] International judicial bodies should exercise judicial restraint where necessary. See WTO, 'Argentina—Safeguard Measure on Imports of Footwear, Report of Appellate Body', WT/DS121/AB/R (2000), ¶121; WTO, 'EC—Measures Affecting Asbestos and Asbestos-Containing Products, Report of Appellate Body', WTO Doc WT/DS135/AB/R (2001), ¶168.

[162] See, eg *Sheffield & Horsham v UK*, judgment of 30 July 1998, (1998) 27 EHRR 163, 179 and 192; *Odiévre v France*, judgment of 13 February 2003, ¶40.

norm-interpretation. Margin of appreciation is similar to, but should not be confused with, the principle of subsidiarity in EC law.[163]

An inquiry of particular relevance here is whether the margin of appreciation doctrine is ready to be extrapolated to the human rights field at the world level. The response tends to be affirmative. One way to understand the call for the development of this doctrine is that courts should construe international law norms as introducing minimal side-constraints upon state conduct.[164] Such a construction would leave states with a considerable 'zone of legality' with respect to local cultural norms. The narrowing of the margins of illegality through restrictive interpretation of international norms would minimise international interference with state conduct and promote a vision of subsidiarity in the international setting.

This said, the doctrine has been posited as a means of introducing flexibility in universal human rights standards in response to non-Western human rights discourse, particularly cultural relativism. Moreover, while the doctrine can be seen as a judicial tool for harnessing pernicious trends towards homogeneity, it cannot be ignored that the cultural basis for this technique of flexible applications of human rights standards in specific cases is, by definition, a democratic cultural diversity.[165] However, it should be noted that, although the rationale underlying the margin of appreciation doctrine has been endorsed implicitly in many cases,[166] a systematic recourse to the doctrine is yet to be established. Several caveats with regard to extrapolating the doctrine's application are as follows.

First, the judicial output of the ECtHR carries the promise of setting universal standards for the protection of human rights. These universal aspirations may be compromised by the margin of appreciation doctrine, which, with its principled recognition of moral relativism, is at odds with the concept of universal human rights. The main arguments militating against the application of the doctrine include the risk of stymying the elaboration of international human rights norms, fears of bias, the problem of externalities and *jus cogens* norms.[167] In practice, some cases that rely

[163] Subsidiarity is considered a fundamental principle of EU law. According to this principle, the EU may only act (ie make laws) where action of individual countries is insufficient. The principle was established in the 1992 Treaty of Maastricht. However, at the local level, it was already a key element of the European Charter of Local Self-Government, an instrument of the Council of Europe promulgated in 1985 (which states that the exercise of public responsibilities should be decentralised). The link between the principle of subsidiarity and the margin of appreciation was discussed by the ECHR in *Use of Languages in Belgium* (1968) 1 EHRR 252, 281–82; see also H Petzold, 'The Convention and the Principle of Subsidiarity' in RStJ Macdonald et al (eds), *The European System for the Protection of Human Rights* (1993) 41, 59; Carozza, above n 160, 57–58.

[164] See R Nozick, *Anarchy, State and Utopia* (1974) 29–34.

[165] See I De La Rasilla Del Moral, 'The Increasingly Marginal Appreciation of the Margin of Appreciation Doctrine' (2006) 7(6) *German Law Journal* 612, 623.

[166] See JG Merrilis, *The Development on International Law by the European Court of Human Rights* (1993) 19.

[167] See Shany, above n 157, 922–26.

on this doctrine have been criticised as denials of justice for individuals and abdications by the Court of its duty to adjudicate in sensitive issues, or as a technique of judicial dilution.[168] If applied liberally, the doctrine may seriously undermine the promise of international enforcement of human rights.

Secondly, the doctrine may lead national institutions to resist external review of local cultural practice based on the claim that they are better judges of particular domestic constraints.[169] It is thus feared that the doctrine will increasingly become an opening for abusive limitation in the exercise of human rights in states, which have traditionally inclined towards cultural relativism.[170] In this respect, the doctrine has also been described as an insidious method of enabling powerful states to evade the objective rule of international law,[171] including human rights rules.

Thirdly, the inconsistent application of the doctrine in which seemingly similar cases are granted different margins by the court may raise concerns about judicial double standards.[172] Perpetuating normative ambiguity might even encourage states to evade human rights obligations and render them meaningless.[173]

One way or another, it would be deplorable if the application of the margin of appreciation doctrine were to result in the dilution of the legal certainty that pertains to important human rights norms. To avoid this outcome, it should be stressed that the margin afforded to states is never unlimited—ie it does not constitute total deference to local cultural norms.[174] On the one hand, states must always exercise their discretion with regard to human rights issues in good faith.[175] On the other hand,

[168] See P Mahoney, 'Marvelous Richness of Diversity or Invidious Cultural Relativism?' (1998) 19 *Human Rights Law Journal* 4, 4.

[169] See E Benvenisti, 'Margin of Appreciation, Consensus, and Universal Standards' (1999) 31 *New York University Journal of International Law & Policy* 843, 844.

[170] See JA Sweeney, 'Margins of Appreciation: Cultural Relativity and the European Court of Human Rights in the Post-Cold War Era' (2005) 54 *International & Comparative Law Quarterly* 461.

[171] See, eg CS Feingold, 'The Doctrine of Margin of Appreciation and the European Convention of Human Rights' (1977) 53 *Notre Dame Law Review* 90, 95. See also L Henkin, 'That "S" Word: Sovereignty, and Globalization, and Human Rights, et cetera' (1999) 68 *Fordham Law Review* 1, 7.

[172] See FN Aolain, 'The Emergency of Diversity: Differences in Human Rights Jurisprudence' (1995) 19 *Fordham International Law Journal* 101, 114, 119 (arguing that states more sympathetic to democratic principles are granted a wider margin).

[173] As regards the link between norm determinacy and legitimacy, see TM Franck, *The Power of Legitimacy among Nations* (1990) 50.

[174] WTO, 'EC—Measures Concerning Meat and Meat Products', Report of Appellate Body, WT/DS26/AB/R (1998), ¶117.

[175] See Vienna Convention on the Law of Treaties, 23 May 1969, 1155 UNTS 311, Art 26; see also D Akande and S Williams, 'International Adjudication on National Security Issues: What Role for the WTO?' (2003) 43 *Virginia Journal of International Law* 365, 389–91.

the doctrine does not preclude universalism, but rather works to limit its scope of operation.

2.7 CULTURE AS RESOURCE: A SUSTAINABILITY PERSPECTIVE

2.7.1 Culture as Resource

Globalisation has accelerated the pace of transforming many things into resources. Culture is not an exception in this regard. In the 1940s and 1950s, much attention was paid to culture because of its role in understanding societies, analysing differences between them, and explaining their economic and political development.[176] Then, in the 1980s, a growing number of scholars, politicians and development practitioners began focusing on the role of cultural values and attitudes as facilitators of, or obstacles to, social progress.[177] For instance, when he explains why South Korea and Ghana, whose economic data were similar in the 1960s, are so different now, Samuel Huntington comes to the conclusion that cultures count.[178] David Landes elaborated on the theory that 'culture makes all the difference'.[179]

In the same vein, a large body of literature has explored the links between culture and human progress from different perspectives. The question is not whether culture has a role but rather how to understand this role in the context of broader determinants of prosperity.[180] Related questions include: to what extent cultural factors shape economic and social development; how cultural obstacles to development can be removed or changed; and how cultural factors can be mobilised to facilitate social progress.

Viewing culture as a resource may readily lend support to addressing these inquiries. The concept of 'resource' absorbs and cancels out hitherto prevailing distinctions between high culture, anthropological and mass culture definitions.[181] In modern times, a nation's prosperity, or standard

[176] See Huntington, above n 5, xiii–xiv.

[177] See LE Harrison, 'Introduction: Why Culture Matters' in Harrison and Huntington, above n 5, xxi.

[178] See Huntington, above n 5, xiii.

[179] See D Landers, *The Wealth and Poverty of Nations* (1998) 516; see also D Landers, 'Culture Makes Almost All the Difference', in Harrison and Huntington, above n 5, 2–13 ('If we learn anything from the history of economic development, it is that culture makes almost all the difference. But on the other hand, culture does not stand alone').

[180] See ME Porter, 'Attitudes, Values, Beliefs, and the Microeconomics of Prosperity', in Harrison and Huntington, above n 5, 14.

[181] High culture becomes a resource for urban development in contemporary museums, while mass media industries, particularly the entertainment and copyright industries, which have increasingly integrated music, film, video, television, magazines, satellite and cable

of living, is determined by the productivity with which it uses its human, capital and natural resources. The central issue in social development is how to create the conditions for rapid and sustained productivity growth.[182] Of late, culture has been increasingly wielded as a valuable resource for both sociopolitical amelioration and economic growth.[183] Among others, Inglehart noted a powerful link between cultural values and the political and economic performance of nations.[184] Michael Porter acknowledges that culture influences economic development and competitiveness.[185] In an often-cited quote on the role of culture in human affairs, Daniel P Moynihan writes: 'The central conservative truth is that it is culture, not politics, that determines the success of a society. The central liberal truth is that politics can change a culture and save it from itself.'[186]

Culture, as a resource, is invested and distributed in the most inclusive ways. It is not only employed as an attraction for capital development and tourism, but also, more importantly, as the prime engine of culture industries and an inexhaustible kindling for new industries dependent on intellectual property.[187] Investment in culture may strengthen the fibre of civil society, which in turn serves as an ideal host for political and economic development. In the meantime, globalisation easily sources many things from anywhere and circulates culture globally with ever increasing velocity. In this context, cultural differences that give rise to distinctive products can contribute to improving the prosperity of nations in the global economy.[188] This makes cultural differences more worthy of celebration.

2.7.2 Culture as Resource and Sustainable Development

Culture-as-resource means more than culture-as-commerce, which embraces the management of culture, a view that was not characteristic of either high culture or mass culture in the anthropological sense.[189]

diffusion, constitute a major contributor to the GDP in many countries. See Yúdice, above n 6, 3–4.

[182] See Porter, above n 180, 15–17.

[183] See Yúdice, above n 6, 9–10.

[184] See Harrison, above n 177, xxii.

[185] He also stressed that globalisation includes cultural transmission that will tend to homogenise culture and make it easier for countries to overcome cultural and geographic disadvantages. Ibid.

[186] See Huntington, above n 5, xiv.

[187] A UNESCO official once lamented that culture is invoked to solve problems that previously were the province of economics and politics. It seemed to her that the only way to convince government and business leaders that it is worth supporting cultural activity is to argue that it will reduce social conflicts and lead to economic development. See Yúdice, above n 6, 1–2.

[188] See Porter, above n 180, 28.

[189] See Yúdice, above n 6, 1.

The question arising out of this notion is how to manage such resources, knowledge, technologies and the attendant risks. Inspired by the notion of culture-as-resource, one prevalent solution seems to stem from the interaction between culture and nature, and, accordingly, cultural diversity and biodiversity, from the perspective of sources (both social and natural) and sustainable development.

Contemporary international law has recognised biodiversity as a common concern of humankind. The 1992 Convention on Biological Diversity transcends the traditional approach based on the conservation of individual species and recognises the interconnected nature of the components of the global ecosystem.[190] By the same token, cultural diversity as a value extends beyond a single cultural object. As the world becomes more economically integrated, countries need strong local cultures and cultural expression to maintain their sovereignty and senses of belonging.[191] It is beyond doubt that cultural diversity shall be preserved and nurtured. It is interesting and relevant here to question whether, just as has happened with biodiversity, cultural diversity might gain a new valuation in the international arena.

In framing the answer, one cannot ignore the differences between culture and nature. Biodiversity, which finds expression in the infinite variety of forms of life in the biosphere, is more permanent and resilient; culture, in contrast, is a more adaptable, social phenomenon. Culture is subject to constant exchange, and its evolution may be measured within the span of generations instead of millennia. Notwithstanding these differences, however, there seems no convincing justification for the premise that the more dynamic and adaptable character of culture constitutes a hindrance to a legal recognition of the value of cultural diversity and of the need to safeguard such diversity as a general interest of humanity.[192] Rather, it is the evolutionary character of culture that necessitates the maintenance of robust cultural traditions whose richness and diversity allow fruitful exchange and interaction among different groups of people.

When culture is identified as a fundamental resource—like ecological resources—human beings ought to use it wisely and sustainably, with a view to sustainable development. Sustainable development, in the words of Gro Harlem Brundtland, the Chairman of the World Commission on Environment and Development, is 'development that meets the needs of the present without compromising the ability of future generations to meet

[190] See generally Convention on Biological Diversity, 5 June 1992, available at http://www.cbd.int/(last accessed on 9 June 2012).

[191] See Baker, above n 8, 1435.

[192] See F Francioni, 'Beyond State Sovereignty: The Protection of Cultural Heritage As A Shared Interest of Humanity' (2004), 25 *Michigan Journal of International Law* 1209, 1221–22.

their own needs'.[193] The idea of sustainability brings into question the way nature itself is conceived, and consequently, how the cultural values that condition a society's relationship to nature should be conceived and preserved.[194]

We have inherited a wealth of tangible and intangible cultural resources that embody the collective memory of communities and buttress their senses of identity in times of uncertainty.[195] Held in trust for humankind, these resources are essentially non-renewable and merit careful preservation for the generations to come. In this sense, culture should be seen organically, as akin to the natural resources that should be preserved for the collective future good. As such, there is a crucial cultural aspect to sustainability that has long been underemphasised. Globalisation, however, brings the call for cultural sustainability front and centre. Important variants in attitudes to ecological sustainability demonstrate an urgent need for a culturally diversified approach to issues of social development. Such an approach should genuinely consider and contemplate culture as a non-substitutable resource for the future of humanity, analogous to the considerations of biodiversity treaties.[196] An era of increasing homogeneity and growing convergence also makes it imperative to protect the natural occurrence of culture in the same way that environmentalism has come to protect biodiversity.[197]

In sum, it is not wise to treat sustainability as a development tool limited to the natural environment. Instead, the constitutive role of culture in promoting social development should be stressed, alongside the premise that cultural diversity is parallel to biodiversity.

2.8 CHAPTER RECAP AND FURTHER REFLECTIONS

The objective of this chapter is to synthesise literatures from social science to help us understand culture, a complex social phenomenon. As discussed, culture can be viewed from different perspectives thanks to the concept's great elasticity. Following is a summary of the different views of culture and their interconnectedness.

[193] See United Nations, 'Report of the World Commission on Environment and Development: Our Common Future', transmitted to the General Assembly as an Annex to document A/42/427—'Development and International Co-operation: Environment', available at http://www.un-documents.net/wced-ocf.htm (last accessed on 9 June 2012).

[194] See UNESCO, above n 42, 210.

[195] Ibid, 176.

[196] See Carmody, above n 9, 243–44.

[197] See UNESCO, above n 42, 207.

2.8.1 From Humanist to Anthropological Notions of Culture

The humanist and anthropological notions of culture both derive from the perspective of historic evolution. The humanist view narrates a narrow meaning for 'culture' that focuses largely on the highest intellectual achievements of humans, such as philosophy, literature and art, while the anthropological notion initiates a much broader definition. Culture was first interpreted in terms of artistic products,[198] then was taken in a more anthropological direction. This evolution demonstrates a profound shift in understanding the scope and function of culture.

The anthropological notion of culture holds that culture defines our ways of life and highlights the uniqueness of individuals and their communities. In the modern era, a more robust concept of culture includes technologically enabled new forms of culture, as opposed to emphasising the high arts. The anthropological notion is not only associated with the culture-as-identity argument, but is also of paramount relevance on the idea of cultural diversity. It informs us that the value contained in different cultures is so important that we should defend culture from being homogenised into extinction, find ways of living with a multiplicity of diverse cultures and celebrate culture in its diversity.

2.8.2 Culture-as-Identity versus Culture-as-Commerce

The process of globalisation challenges both the humanist and anthropological concepts of culture and calls for a careful revisiting of the nature of culture. The shift from a humanist to an anthropological notion of culture reflects a historical evolution of the widening scope and functions of culture, while culture-as-identity and culture-as-commerce are two arguments gestated by the essential, contemporary duality of cultural products, ie cultural products are both commercial objects and assets which convey values, ideas and meaning.

It is these two contrasting logics that occasion an intense clash between culture and trade, and the identity claim is a wellspring of this quandary. The recurring confrontations between Canada and the US over cultural

[198] Artistic products conceivably fall into three categories: (i) live performance art—theatre, music and dance; (ii) unique, non-reproducible art—architecture, painting, sculpture and installations; and (iii) reproducible art—literature, sound recordings, film and television productions. Only the last of these is truly tradeable, but the three categories are rather artificial, as the recording, storage and reproduction of a live orchestral concert on compact disc clearly demonstrates. This categorisation is borrowed from Gunther Schulze, who claims that the economic characteristics of each is distinct with respect to durability of the products, the production technology and the degree of uniqueness, which in turn have an impact on their production, consumption and trade. See GG Schulze, 'International Trade in Art' (1999) 23 *Journal of Cultural Economics* 109, 111.

products furnish a vivid illustration of the complexity of cultural products. In this perennial debate, however, the main concern rests less with culture per se than with the means by which culture is carried and delivered, ie cultural industries and products.[199] This complicates the scenario, given the difficulty in distinguishing genuine cultural protection from the protection of the economic interests of cultural industries.

I submit that in modern times, culture is commerce, but more than commerce. With this in mind, cultural identities should be preserved, but an overemphasis on identity might lead to the exclusion of other considerations. It is a meaningful task to explore a dialectical relationship between a closely held value of cultural identity and a philosophical idea of free trade.

2.8.3 Culture as Human Rights and Culture as Resource

The debate on universalism and cultural relativism reflects different attitudes towards human rights issues. It generates implications on the role of culture in achieving human dignity as well.[200] I subscribe to the view that many culturally based beliefs do not come into direct conflict with human rights. Rather, these two values share a degree of compatibility. On this premise, human rights and cultural norms can be reconciled through the notion of cultural rights and corresponding practical strategies. On the one hand, human rights should be approached in a way that is compatible with diverse cultural contexts. On the other hand, cultural norms should be recognised as partners to promote greater respect for and observance of human rights. This not only encourages cultural pluralism, but also fosters more effective international cooperation between cultural norms and human rights. The margin of appreciation doctrine originated from the judicial practice of the ECtHR also provides a promising possibility of adhering to universally recognised human rights while pursuing cultural objectives.

Cultural diversity and biodiversity are intimately related to each other in the sense that cultural diversity mirrors biodiversity, and human diversity and natural diversity are inseparable. They are both assets that produce prosperity for present and future generations and fill essential roles in achieving sustainable development. When cultural diversity is aligned with biodiversity, they will be oriented towards the same goals: minimising homogenising and hegemonising effects, and maximising the role of all cultures in all their dimensions and expressions, and in all the scenarios of human life.

[199] See Knight, above n 11, 168–69.
[200] See Eckert, above n 126, 2.

2.8.4 Towards an Integrated Concept of Culture?

The different notions of culture discussed above often fall into the so-called 'reductionist trap', as they feature one or more aspects of culture while failing to offer a comprehensive notion of what culture truly is. At the same time, every culture represents the equilibrium between certain economic and social forces. Such equilibrium is unlikely to be permanent; it will slowly change their positions in a gradual way.[201] Therefore culture is a dynamic process, which cannot be best illustrated by sets of stills. A great deal remains to be done in defining the key elements that characterise culture in the era of economic globalisation.

While Chapter 4 sets out more specifics of UNESCO's understanding of culture and cultural diversity, it should be noted here that the UN, particularly through the work of UNESCO, has developed definitions of culture from a more sustainable perspective. The most often cited definition was adopted in the 1982 Mexico Declaration on Cultural Policies,[202] which states that 'in its widest sense, culture is now the whole complex of characteristic spiritual, material, intellectual and emotional features that characterise a society or a social grouping'. The recent Fribourg Declaration on Cultural Rights further defines the term 'culture' as covering those values, beliefs, convictions, languages, knowledge and arts, traditions, institutions and ways of life through which a person or a group expresses their humanity, and the meanings that these give to their existence and to their development.[203] These definitions are more integrated and compatible with the context of globalisation.

To conclude, conceptual and methodological strategies have been evolving in social science conducive to understanding 'culture'. This chapter sets up a foundation for discussing the complexity of culture and the difficulty in disentangling the quandary of culture and trade, a foundation that will be elaborated in detail in subsequent chapters.

[201] See Jones, above n 48, 258.

[202] The Declaration was approved in Mexico on 6 August 1982, and is reaffirmed in the Preamble to the Final Declaration of the Intergovernmental Conference on Cultural Policies Favorable to Development, held in Stockholm on 30 March to 2 April 1998.

[203] Art 2(b), Fribourg Declaration on Cultural Rights, adopted in Fribourg on 7 May 2007.

3

Domestic Cultural Policy and Measures: The Case of the Audiovisual Sector

Every lawyer quickly learns that, though the law is beautiful in its complexity, reality is often more complex, while particularly legislative or general law arrangements are insufficiently so. By its very nature, every application of the policies expressed in an open-textured rule to new situations supplements existing law. Particularly in modern industries, like biotechnology or information technology, in which national legislation lags behind technical or scientific developments, the most scrupulous application of the parties' choice of national law may still require the identification of the relevant policies of that state and their extrapolation to new situations.

Michael Reisman[1]

3.1 INTRODUCTION

GLOBALISATION HAS BEEN affecting domestic policymaking and raising a number of controversial issues. One such issue concerns the interaction between economic globalisation and domestic cultural policies and measures. This is an area that has not been fully explored, partly because cultural policymaking is additionally burdened with the complexities associated with the duality of cultural products and cultural industries. First of all, domestic cultural policymaking is affected by the government's interest in presenting a favourable image of national culture. Meanwhile, government is ultimately responsible for ensuring that its cultural regulatory framework is not unnecessarily trade-restrictive while at the same time protecting cultural diversity. In parallel to the duality of cultural products, cultural policies and measures are endowed with the dual mission of promoting cultural industries and protecting cultural identity and diversity. In the meantime, the dynamics of cultural industries and the evolution of cultural policies cannot be

[1] WM Reisman, 'Law, International Public Policy (So-called) and Arbitral Choice in International Commercial Arbitration' in AJ Van Den Burg (ed), *International Arbitration 2006: Back to Basics?* (2006) 849, 851.

fully captured without understanding the technological forces affecting the industry.[2]

Therefore, prior to exploring the treatment of cultural products under the trade frameworks, it is worthwhile examining domestic cultural regulation and assess its effectiveness in pursuing both cultural and economic goals, as well as its compatibility with trade obligations. One of the most challenging aspects of the trade and culture conflict involves audiovisual products, especially in light of the fact that, since the 1980s, the term 'culture' has gradually become synonymous with the word 'audiovisual'.[3] In general, audiovisual products reach people more directly than other media and have a higher potential to shape public opinions.[4] Audiovisual sectors[5] are thus closely linked to the preservation of cultural identity and understood to be the 'hornets' nest' in the dilemma of trade and culture.[6] The audiovisual sector is a domain in which political pressure has been very strong to accommodate different culture-oriented measures;[7] this pressure has even spilled over to other sectors (such as telecommunication services) and to other themes (such as the WTO Work Programme on Electronic Commerce).[8] This justifies allocating a significant portion of this chapter to the discussion of audiovisual policies and measures.

This chapter will first lay out an overview of cultural policies, highlighting two polar views in cultural policymaking—'protectionist' and 'liberalist'—and their basic stances on cultural industries and trade theories. Next it will study several cultural policy tools frequently invoked by governments to sustain national culture, including foreign ownership limitation, content restriction, screen quotas, subsidies, censorship and copyright regulation.

[2] See K Acheson and C Maule, *Much Ado about Culture: North American Trade Disputes* 23 (1999).

[3] See T Voon, 'A New Approach to Audiovisual Products in the WTO: Rebalancing GATT and GATS' (2007) 14 *UCLA Entertainment Law Review* 1, 3. Audiovisual media are perhaps the most fluid field of regulation because of the advent and widespread use of digital technologies and their spillover effect over the regulation. See M Burri-Nenova, 'Cultural Diversity and the EC Audiovisual Media Services Directive: Beyond the Handsome Rhetoric', NCCR Trade Regulation Working Paper No 2009/09 (2 April 2009) 1.

[4] UNESCO, 'Meetings of Experts on Audiovisual Services: Improving the Participation of Developing Countries, organised jointly by the United Nations Conference on Trade and Development (UNCTAD) and the UNESCO', Working Document prepared by the UNESCO Secretariat, CLT/2002/RP/H/1 (Geneva, 13–15 November 2002) (hereinafter UNESCO, 'Meetings of Experts on Audiovisual Services') 4–6.

[5] Motion pictures, videotapes, radio and television, sound recordings, and multimedia services are the main sub-sectors of this industry, whose characteristics and boundaries are rapidly changing as a result of an intense process of technical innovation.

[6] See P Guerrieri et al (eds), *Cultural Diversity and International Economic Integration: The Global Governance of the Audio-Visual Sector* (2005) 2.

[7] See M Burri-Nenova, 'The Law of the World Trade Organization and the Communications Law of the European Community: On a Path of Harmony or Discord?' 41 *Journal of World Trade* 833 (2007).

[8] See WTO, 'Work Program on Electronic Commerce Adopted by the General Council on 25 September 1998', WT/L/274 (30 September 1998); WTO, 'WTO Programme on Electronic Commerce: Background Note by the Secretariat', G/C/W/128 (5 November 1998).

The following section examines the tension between trade liberalisation and the pursuit of cultural policies, and explores the best vehicles to achieve cultural goals in the era of globalisation. From the perspective of the effectiveness of cultural policy measures, this chapter attempts to find out whether protectionism is an ideal way to protect culture. It concludes by suggesting that, although national cultural interest and state sovereignty can provide rationales for cultural protection, protectionism is often not the right choice in the context of trade liberalisation.

This chapter aims to further an understanding of the evolution and effectiveness of cultural policy measures and to advise policy options for dealing with the conundrum of trade and culture. In addition to presenting the views and practice from the major players in this field—the US, Canada and France—the cultural policies or measures implemented by other countries—China, India, Korea, Egypt, Italy, etc[9]—are considered as well.

3.2 AN OVERVIEW OF CULTURAL POLICIES AND MEASURES

The UNESCO Convention defines 'cultural policies and measures' as

> those policies and measures relating to culture as such, or those designed to have a direct effect on cultural expressions of individuals, groups or societies, including the creation, production, dissemination, distribution of and access to cultural activities, goods and services.[10]

This definition is broad enough to encompass financial support and incentive programmes undertaken by governments to protect and promote domestic culture. Given the theme of this book, this chapter focuses its analysis on government measures to protect domestic cultural industries under trade pressure, including, but not limited to, foreign ownership restriction, content regulation, screen quotas, subsidies and tax concessions, and other regulatory support mechanisms.

[9] While a substantial market share of cultural products is still concentrated in the US, countries such as China, India, Korea, Brazil, Mexico and Japan boast thriving culture industries that have global reach. UNESCO lists the US, Japan, Hong Kong (combined with China), Philippines and India as the top five film production centres in the world. See PS Grant and C Wood, *Blockbusters and Trade Wars: Popular Culture in a Globalized World* (2004) 111–20; F Pinto, 'Book Review—Blockbusters and Trade Wars: Popular Culture in a Globalized World' (2004) 7 *Journal of International Economic Law* 922.

[10] UNESCO Convention on Cultural Diversity, Art 4(6).

3.2.1 Two Polar Views on Cultural Policymaking

It is never easy to develop coherent cultural policies and measures. Many states, including the US, maintain various forms of controls on cultural sectors, disregarding the pressure to abolish such intervention. In addition to the heated debates on government intervention in cultural matters,[11] much of the confusion over the objectives of cultural policies derives from the term 'culture' itself, as discussed in Chapter 2. In the past, when culture referred primarily to artistic expression, cultural policy was largely concerned with government funding and promotion of the arts. Now, culture in a contemporary sense is more associated with mass media, and cultural expressions are more bound up with the cultural industries that play a key role not only in disseminating works but also in forming the way in which the culture itself is perceived. Two polar views on cultural policymaking can be identified: the 'protectionist' view—based on the cultural nationalist perspective—and the 'liberalist' view—reflecting a relatively open alternative.

The protectionist view, rooted in cultural nationalism, posits that cultural products made by nationals differ significantly from those made by foreigners, and that, therefore, policies should be adopted to support the displacement of foreign products with domestic cultural products.[12] Cultural policies crafted in this vein emphasise the need to preserve or invigorate cultural identity, or to create an environment in which a distinctive culture can emerge. The aspiration to prevent the cultural decay that results from the domination of foreign products and secure a national cultural space provides an enduring rationale for an affirmative model of cultural policies in which regulation, legislation and other supportive measures are used to encourage domestic cultural production and consumption.[13] Canada and France are among the leading national proponents of this view. In Canada, for instance, cultural industries have succeeded in attracting overt political support for protectionist policies. Protectionist policies—measures directly or indirectly restricting the inflow of content from other countries—control foreign ownership engaged in cultural production and distribution and encourage the production and consumption of Canadian content. Cultural nationalism is often interwoven with other goals that ensure that the material produced and distributed is socially acceptable.[14] In France, for example, where linguistic nationalists believe that the popularity of English-language materials poses

[11] See B Schwartz, 'Canadian Cultural Policy in a World Context' (2002) 2 *Asper Review of International Business & Trade Law* 1, 3.

[12] See Acheson and Maule, above n 2, 15.

[13] See M Hahn, 'A Clash of Cultures? The UNESCO Diversity Convention and International Trade Law' (2006) 9 *Journal of International Economic Law* 515, 517–18.

[14] See K Acheson and C Maule, 'Canada's Audio-visual Policies: Impact on Trade' in Guerrieri et al, above n 6, 156.

a threat to local culture, the government's concern with foreign cultural products embraces both the cultural content and its effect on the national and international roles of the French language.[15]

As far as the trade in cultural products is concerned, nationalists, invoking state sovereignty, maintain that free trade does not alter the coherence of a consistent commitment to domestic cultural expressions.[16] Fearing that greater international integration might result in a higher risk of cultural homogenisation, protectionists have resisted the pressure for trade liberalisation and imposed restrictions to protect the receiving society from foreign cultural influence.[17] Alternatively, they advocate exempting culture from trade norms.

Many countries have adopted protectionist policies as an antidote to the effect of the popularity of American cultural products and as a bulwark against the cultural homogeneity these products may produce. For instance, the EU uses various policies to limit the US entertainment industry's dominance of local marketplace. France has been the most aggressive and vocal in opposing free trade in cultural products. Moreover, France has maintained its protectionist cultural policy so far, without being seriously constrained by France's membership in the EU and the WTO. Canada has maintained the same negotiation position at formal talks concerning trade rules—that is, everything but culture is on the table. Italy is one of the countries most actively in favour of strong audiovisual policies; it shelters its cultural sectors somewhat from the jurisdiction of WTO rules.[18] While these cultural policies and measures form a web of protection for domestic industries, they often cause discrimination against the foreign content, service providers and distributors. As they are susceptible to challenges from WTO trade disciplines, it is very likely that they are not sustainable as long-term policy options.

The US, which defines cultural products in economic terms, typically represents a liberalist position in cultural policymaking. The contrast between the term 'cultural industries'—used by Canada—and 'entertainment industries'—used by the US—indicates the significant differences in their cultural policymaking.[19] Basic to the American sense of itself is a historical aversion to the idea that government shapes or mediates national identity. The US holds that the control of cultural content should

[15] See Acheson and Maule, above n 2, 3–4.

[16] See J Jeffrey, 'The Impact of Technology Change on Canada's Affirmative Policy Model in the Cultural Industry and New Media Sectors' (1999) 25 *Canada—US Law Journal* 379, 387.

[17] See S Andreano and PL Iapadre, 'Audiovisual Policies and International Trade: The Case of Italy' in Guerrieri et al, above n 6, 96; see also Arpita Mukherjee, Audiovisual Policies and International Trade: The Case of India, in Guerrieri et al, above n 6, 218.

[18] See Andreano and Iapadre, ibid, 97.

[19] See Acheson and Maule, above n 2, 2.

rest with individuals and groups, not with the government.[20] These arguments firmly stand on a commercial footing. One exception is that, in order to promote what is considered 'good' in American culture, the US government plays a pivotal role in regulating broadcasting.[21] An examination of the US broadcasting regulations reveals the concerns motivated by a protectionist attitude towards cultural policymaking. The barriers to trade in audiovisuals built by the US include ownership restrictions in the television sector and restrictions on live performance.[22] In practice, the US has increasingly raised the profile of trade barriers imposed on its cultural products by other countries, including Canada and China, which makes the continuation and extension of protectionist policies more costly.

3.2.2 Justifying Government Intervention in Cultural Matters

While the general trend in economic relations has been to liberalise trade, cultural policies have become more restrictive in many countries, even against a global backdrop characterised by the increased commoditisation and homogenisation of mass-consumption cultural products. The world's first national multiculturalism act, the Canadian Multiculturalism Act,[23] gave statutory authority to a range of government policies and programmes to support cultural diversity as a fundamental feature of Canadian society. This was seen as a big step towards supporting the call to 'diversify the mainstream' of cultural policy in Canada.[24] A wide range of policies and measures have also been put into place to promote domestic cultural sectors in other countries.[25] Part of the explanation

[20] Ibid, 18.

[21] The regulation of sex and violence in television is another demonstration of the US' regulation of broadcasting based on cultural protectionism. By attempting to place limits on the amount of sex and violence that can be shown on television, the US defines what is and what is not acceptable in American society and culture through the regulation of broadcasting. For more discussion on this issue, see SJ Kim, 'Comment, Viewer Discretion Is Advised: A Structural Approach to the Issue of Television Violence' (1994) 142 *University of Pennsylvania Law Review* 1383.

[22] See, eg A Addis, 'Who's Afraid of Foreigners? The Restrictions on Alien Ownership of Electronic Media' (2000) 32 *Columbian Human Rights Law Review* 133; see also S Jones, 'Mass Communication, Intellectual Property Rights, International Trade, and the Popular Music Industry' in EG McAnany and KT Williams (eds), *Mass Media and Free Trade: NAFTA and Cultural Industries* (1996) 333–35.

[23] Canadian Multiculturalism Act, 1985, c 24 (4th Supp), available at http://laws.justice.gc.ca/eng/C-18.7/FullText.html (last accessed on 2 June 2012).

[24] See UNESCO, 'Our Creative Diversity: Report of the World Commission on Culture and Development' (finalised by J Pérez de Cuéllar, 1995), Executive Summary, 240.

[25] The main categories of tools contain public ownership regulations (including border measures on goods); market access restrictions on services; content requirements based on nationality, language or type of contents (screen quotas for cinemas, television broadcasting quotas, investment quotas, restrictions on dubbing of foreign films and restrictions based on film ratings); licensing procedures and qualification requirements; technical standards; IP protection; financial support; and international co-production agreements. See Guerrieri

for this phenomenon is a commonly perceived connection between what cultural products deliver and concerns about national identity. Several policy arguments are advanced to justify the government's intervention in cultural matters; a detailed examination of these arguments follows.

3.2.2.1 *The Duality of Cultural Products*

The reluctance to treat cultural products by the same standards as other merchandise lends support to a public choice claim that these products cannot be viewed simply as the output of an economic process.[26] Over and above their commercial and commoditised characteristics, cultural products exhibit unique characteristics.[27] Cultural products play a pivotal role in affecting individual development as well as fostering a strong national culture.[28] Governments feel vulnerable when the local culture is swamped by foreign products. They are concerned that the unfettered free trade may lead to a loss of cultural identity. This fear goes beyond economic concerns and brings into play the notion of cultural value as a desired aspect of human existence. In short, the intrinsically different social nature of cultural products calls for distinct policy regimes.

In an effort to promote national value, cultural sovereignty—a key institution of international law protecting national cultures against uniformisation from the outside—is invoked to justify government intervention to protect domestic culture.[29] The traditional conception of sovereignty assumes, in part, that a nation is identified with a particular culture. It is the fact that the nation acts within such a cultural context that legitimates the exercise of its power. At the same time, the conventional view of state power assumes that culture precedes and constitutes the state, and the state exists to protect national culture from being lost.[30] This justifies the use of state power to protect national values. Governments should factor the cultural mission of cultural industries into their policymaking in

et al, above n 6, 1; for a good overview of this measures, see also UNESCO, 'Meetings of Experts on Audiovisual Services', above n 4, pp. 9–19.

[26] See Hahn, above n 13, 523–25.

[27] One such characteristic the important external effects produced by cultural products, in particular non-use values such as the creation of a national identity. See G Perino and GG Schulze, 'Competition, Cultural Autonomy and Global Governance: The Audio-Visual Sector in Germany', in Guerrieri et al, above n 6, 52.

[28] See Acheson and Maule, above n 2, 10; see also J Liss, 'The Impact of Globalization and Technological Change on Culture and National Identity: A Call for Visionary Pragmatism' in D Browne (ed), *The Culture/Trade Quandary: Canada's Policy Options* (1998) 157.

[29] See D Throsby, *Economics and Culture* 131–33 (2001); A von Bogdandy, 'The European Union as Situation, Executive, and Promoter of the International Law of Cultural Diversity—Elements of a Beautiful Friendship' (2008) 19 *European Journal of International Law* 241, 251.

[30] See JR Paul, 'Cultural Resistance to Global Governance' (2000) 22 *Michigan Journal of International Law* 1, 3.

order to provide a healthy environment for developing domestic culture. Even the forces of globalisation cannot rescind the sovereign right of each state to devise measures for defending cultural identity. The UNESCO Convention on Cultural Diversity reaffirms the sovereign right of governments to formulate and implement cultural policies and to adopt measures to protect and promote cultural diversity.[31]

3.2.2.2 *The Dual Mission of Cultural Policies and Measures*

In parallel to the duality of cultural products, cultural policies are endowed with dual missions, both industrial (or economic) and cultural. On the one hand, the specificity of cultural products justifies the cultural mission of cultural policies and measures. Governments fear cultural impoverishment through the loss of homegrown cultural offerings at the hands of globalisation. A typical example of this is Hollywood's dominance over local film screens and markets.[32] The ubiquity of American cultural products is widely believed to have a negative impact on producing and marketing domestic cultural expressions. The fact that the heaviest consumers of television tend to be either very young or socially disadvantaged adds more concern to the analysis of this situation.[33] This fuels the fear that a populace growing up with the products of American popular culture will lose touch with its own cultural roots, that a possible extinction of domestically produced products would go hand in hand with a replacement by foreign cultural products.

In France, for example, it is claimed that culture policies aim to preserve national cultural independence, unity and prestige, and to increase cultural diversity.[34] In Germany, given the important role that mass media plays in the political process, one of the motivations for the TV regulation is identified as the preservation of cultural identity.[35] In addition to cultural reasons, retaining cultural policies has important symbolic meanings because the market share of domestic products is related to preserving a state's cultural sovereignty.

On the other hand, culture is an industry in modern time and cultural products are commodities.[36] As pointed out, trade in cultural products is often motivated by profit.[37] The overall vitality of national culture is often

[31] UNESCO, UNESCO Convention on Cultural Diversity, Art 5.

[32] According to the statistics from US Census Bureau, the US entertainment industry collects more revenue from foreign sales than any other US industry except commercial aircraft. These international revenues have become increasingly important to the US economy. The entertainment industry also significantly contributes to US employment.

[33] See Hahn, above n 13, 517–18.

[34] See A Jäckel, 'The Inter/Nationalism of French Film Policy' (2007) 15(1) *Modern & Contemporary France* 21, 22.

[35] See Perino and Schulze, above n 27, 54.

[36] See, eg TW Adorno, *The Culture Industry* (2001) 86.

[37] See T Voon, *Cultural Products and the World Trade Organization* (2007) 39–40.

associated with the financial health of domestic cultural industries.[38] Trade negotiations are traditionally about economic interests, and the suggestion that cultural value should be taken into account in determining trade rules is likely to be dismissed.[39]

Taking the above considerations together, it is apparent that one important aspect of cultural policy boils down to the choice between the free trade premise and the value of preserving culture. In one way or another, the economic significance of cultural products cannot be ignored in evaluating justifications for cultural policy and measures. The linkage between culture and industrial instruments is necessary, because without a sustainable economic environment, distinctive local content cannot be produced in any significant volume. This renders the ability to protect cultural industries vital to cultural development, and further, to the survival of local culture.[40]

Cultural policies in many countries indeed reflect a complex compromise between industrial and cultural interests. For example, France's policy has been remarkably consistent in ensuring that both its industrial and cultural goals are realised. Similarly, the regulation of audiovisual industries in the UK covers a wide scope and embraces a range of support measures, which target both economic and cultural objectives.[41] Audiovisual services are one of the fastest growing sectors in the Indian economy.[42] The main objective of Indian audiovisual policy aims to strike a balance between preserving the rich cultural heritage of the nation and increasing the efficiency and global competitiveness of the sector.[43]

3.2.2.3 *Public Goods and Externalities Theory*

Notwithstanding the acknowledgement of culture's economic dimension, the market system is often unable to generate an optimal social outcome. Markets alone do not seem to be in a position to ensure diversity of choice, access for everyone and fair competition. Market failure occurs particularly when marginally successful export-oriented products prevent

[38] See Jeffrey, above n 16, 381–82.

[39] Many economists point to the economic costs and inefficiencies induced by cultural protection. Although they admit that non-economic value might be considered, they tend to disparage reliance on such values. See Throsby, above n 229, 132–33.

[40] See T Magder, 'Franchising the Candy Store: Split-Run Magazines and A New International Regime for Trade in Culture' (1998) *Canadian–American Public Policy*, 1, 8; Jeffrey, above n 16, 379 (1999).

[41] See G Doyle and M Hibberd, 'The Case of the UK Audiovisual System', in Guerrieri et al, above n 6, 135–42.

[42] India has the largest film production in the world, producing an average of 800 feature films and 900 short films annually in 52 different languages and dialects. See Mukherjee, above n 17, 225.

[43] Ibid, 238.

the survival of domestic-oriented products with smaller audiences.[44] A prominent pro-culture response to this observation is that market failures indeed arise in relation to cultural industries, and government intervention is needed to correct these failures.[45] The following explores the reasons for market failure in the case of cultural products and corresponding justifications for government intervention.

In addition to a substantial public goods aspect,[46] the market's failure to provide consumers with appropriate cultural products occurs due to the economies of scale in the production and distribution of cultural products and the impact of externalities on the pricing of cultural products, as well as collective action problems.

First of all, cultural products share an important public goods characteristic because their use is substantially non-rival in economics, which means that the consumption of a product does not reduce the amount available for consumption by others.[47] This readily explains the dominance of American cultural products. At the same time, 'public goods' are those that the private sector cannot produce at prices that the general public can afford, but are nevertheless much valued by the general public.[48] This concept recognises a difference between cultural products and other commodities, and reiterates the fact that trade in cultural products is not an end in itself, but rather should be understood as a means to the end of a higher quality of life.[49] Consequently, there is a general consensus that some degree of government intervention for the purpose of promoting culture is required in the same sense that the government must provide for national defence and public safety.[50] In this respect, Professor Edwin Baker aptly comments:

> The government has . . . always engaged in regulation to advance its conception of a desirable communications order—a conception that includes promotion of viewpoint diversity, quality of discourse, education, and ease of participation.

[44] CE Baker, 'An Economic Critique of Free Trade in Media Products' (2000) 78 *North Carolina Law Review* 1357, 1386–88.

[45] See Voon, above n 37, 43.

[46] See I Kaul, I Grunberg and M Stern, 'Defining Global Public Goods' in I Kaul and M Stern (eds), *Global Public Goods: International Cooperation in the 21st Century* (1999) 2, 5; see also I Bernier, 'Cultural Goods and Services in International Trade Law', in Browne, above n 28, 146.

[47] See P Sauvé and K Steinfatt, 'Towards Multilateral Rules on Trade and Culture: Protective Regulation or Efficient Protection?' in *Achieving Better Regulation of Services*, Conference Proceedings, AusInfo, Canberra (Productivity Commission and Australian National University, November 2000) 329–31.

[48] See I Serageldin, 'Cultural Heritage As Public Good: Economic Analysis Applied to Historic Cities', in Kaul and Stern, above n 46, 240.

[49] See Jeffrey, above n 16, 163–64.

[50] See V Rabinovitch, 'The Social and Economic Rationales for Domestic Cultural Policies', in Browne, above n 28, 26.

> A democracy concerned with promoting collective conceptions of the good arguably requires this form of regulation.[51]

In Canada, the history of federal support of cultural industries reflects a consensus that culture is a 'public goods' requiring concerted government intervention where necessary to promote domestic content production and distribution capacity, to compete effectively with cultural products of other countries. The 'public goods' basis for cultural policymaking centres on the shared experience and information inherent in Canadian cultural content.[52] The stated rationale for these policies is that in the absence of government intervention, the market for domestic authors would be undersupplied and national unity and identity would suffer.[53]

In addition to 'public goods', it is worthwhile mentioning the externalities generated by cultural products in justifying government intervention. The positive externalities arise where people other than the consumer benefit from the consumption of cultural products.[54] There is some evidence that people might be willing to pay something to protect expressions of local cultural identity. In other words, if domestic cultural expressions specifically produce 'public goods', such as feelings of national pride and solidarity, or some beneficial externalities, such as a pool of trained local talent, there may be sound economic reasons for a certain degree of government intervention in the market to support such activities; if so, the efficiency cost imposed may be seen as the price paid to secure the external benefits or the public goods in question.[55] On the other hand, a negative externality analysis would suggest that unrestrained trade in cultural products may well reduce consumer welfare in the importing country in the sense that the improper pricing of cultural products prevents audiences from getting what they want, ie domestic content.

Opening up to international competition adds new dimensions to cultural policymaking. Market integration policies characterising international economic relations have been posing new challenges to national policymakers. The political sensitivity of the trade-off between the benefits of economic globalisation and the social values pursued through cultural policies is high.[56] Even when markets are competitive, free trade does not necessarily ensure variety in content. It is also unlikely to yield efficient or

[51] CE Baker, 'Turner Broadcasting: Content-Based Regulation of Persons and Presses' in DJ Hutchinson et al (eds), *The Supreme Court Review* (1994) 81.

[52] See Rabinovitch, above n 50, 26.

[53] See Acheson and Maule, above n 2, 245.

[54] For example, cultural products that celebrate local culture may encourage social bonding or inspire consumers to contribute more the their community. See Voon, above n 37, 50–54; see also WJ Baumol, 'Applied Welfare Economics' in R Towse, (ed), *A Handbook of Cultural Economics* (2003) 22.

[55] See Throsby, above n 29, 132.

[56] See T O'Regan and B Goldsmith, 'Making Cultural Policy: Meeting Cultural Objectives in a Digital Environment' (2006) 7(1) *Television New Media* 69.

welfare-maximising outcomes due to the imbalance of cultural industries in different countries. Hence the 'global' public goods characteristics of cultural diversity may explain the perceived need for international cooperation in promoting cultural diversity.[57]

In short, economic theory cannot predict that free trade in cultural products will be better at giving audiences what they want than would a set of policies imposing some restrictive effect on imports. If the ultimate goals of different societies extend beyond immediate economic concerns, cultural values can be specifically admitted into the policymaking process in certain cases.[58] This indicates that a fundamental question in framing policy to maintain culture is not whether, but how.

3.2.3 The Changing Landscape of Technology and its Impact on Culture Policymaking

A historically sensitive technocultural perspective should not be omitted from the discussion of culture policymaking. Technology is a source of great cultural changes.[59] Culture and technology are indissolubly linked, and together form a dynamic relationship; changes in one cannot be adequately comprehended without considering the other.[60] The credibility of protectionist and liberalist views on cultural policies is affected by technology as well. As a result, examining how the changing technological landscape alters the persuasiveness of these views is critical to understanding the evolution of cultural policy measures.

The impact of technology on cultural industries is pervasive and ongoing. First, technology is altering the way in which cultural content is produced and delivered from producers to consumers. New technologies facilitate the production and distribution of cultural products and dissolve the traditional boundaries among cultural sectors.[61] In particular, the internet quickens the conveyance of different kinds of content, and digitalisation has greatly enhanced transmission capacity and allowed for the market entry of foreign and domestic competitors onto a level playing field. These changes render trade in cultural products more economically crucial and foreign markets increasingly more important for cultural industries.

Secondly, although technical progress has the potential to weaken market access barriers for new entrants, strong forces are driving greater

[57] See generally L Martin, 'The Political Economy of International Cooperation', in Kaul and Stern, above n 46, 51.

[58] See Throsby, above n 29, 133.

[59] Every major technological change affects both the processes and the relations of production, and hence the economic, political, and cultural organisation of society. See B Parekh, *Rethinking Multiculturalism: Cultural Diversity and Political Theory* (2002) 153.

[60] See Jeffrey, above n 16, 157.

[61] See Sauvé and Steinfatt, above n 47, 324.

concentration in cultural production. Technological changes have brought an intense process of restructuring to audiovisual markets.[62] The huge economies of scale characterising the distribution of cultural products confer a high degree of international openness on this sector.[63] This trend is further accentuated by the dismantling of obstacles to international trade.[64] The overall result is that a few large groups, mainly based in the US, dominate worldwide distribution of audiovisual products. This partly accounts for the fact that in the debates on culture and trade, one of the main risks cited is the standardisation of content stemming from the processes of technological convergence and economic globalisation.[65]

Thirdly, the gradual shift in power from public interventions to the private sector rests partly with technology as well. This shift coincides with a more general transformation of public policy from direct intervention to indirect intervention. The transfer may also have a negative impact on national cultures.[66]

Turning to culture policymaking, we first take note of the fact that technical advancement is beneficial to cultural industries as it enhances competition and the variety of content, but it has contributed to the growing complexity of cultural policy and posed challenges for regulatory setting,[67] particularly in the case of audiovisual services. The convergence led by the economic and technological changes further weakens the effectiveness of cultural policies.[68] Nevertheless, the forces of technological change do not eliminate the need for cultural policy. Instead, transformations in policies must be fashioned to take account of the public interest in emerging media environments.[69]

Government policies for cultural industries are generally developed in a specific set of existing conditions. In the face of advancing technology, the policy framework must change accordingly.[70] In recent decades, technological evolution has reduced the costs of distribution and created an economic imperative to distribute content on a wider basis. Cultural industries have responded to the new commercial opportunities within the constraints imposed by protectionist policy.[71] In this regard, the UK may provide a good illustration. One theme that has emerged clearly in the UK over recent years is a distinct shift in government policy—namely,

[62] See Guerrieri et al, above n 6, 3.

[63] See GG Schulze, 'International Trade in Art' (1999) 23 *Journal of Cultural Economics* 109.

[64] See Guerrieri et al, above n 6, 3.

[65] See UNESCO, above n 24, 232.

[66] See HB Feigenbaum, 'Public Policy and the Private Sector in Audiovisual Industries' (2002), 49 *UCLA Law Review* 1767, 1768.

[67] See Perino and Schulze, above n 27, 70–71.

[68] See Andreano and Iapadre, above n 17, 96–97.

[69] See Jeffrey, above n 16, 157–59.

[70] See Acheson and Maule, above n 2, 37–38.

[71] Ibid, 329.

a gradual moving away from the traditional regulatory model to policies that encourage a more market-driven cultural industry.[72] The UK is not alone in this trend. Indeed, this shift may be seen as a natural response to technological changes that are opening up the cultural industry worldwide. The pattern that appears to emerge can be described as broadly supportive, but is neither radical nor strongly interventionist.

In sum, technology has played, and will continue to play, a crucial role in cultural policymaking. In particular, the pervasive digitally networked environment calls for a re-evaluation or readjustment of the policy tools employed to achieve fundamental cultural objectives.[73] With the increasing interactivity and internationalisation of production and delivery, the challenge before policymakers is to initiate appropriate regulation so that a country can enhance its cultural resilience while also benefiting from the process of globalisation.[74] In order to design compatible and workable cultural policies, prudent policymakers must understand the profound impacts of media and technology, evaluate the relationship between particular measures and cultural goals, and assess the measures' trade-restrictiveness.

Given the great cultural, political and economic significance of cultural sectors, governments carry out complex support policies, providing direct and indirect incentives to foster the growth and competitiveness of their domestic industry. While there is a basic consensus around the need for cultural policies, the forms that particular policy instruments take differ from country to country due to the often sharp differences in the views on public intervention.[75] The following examines several main policy areas where the support for cultural industries impacts economic and cultural aims, including the regulation of content, ownership restrictions, subsidies, screen quotas and censorship.

3.3 FOREIGN OWNERSHIP RESTRICTION

Foreign ownership regulations have been used to achieve cultural objectives, with the assumption that ownership makes a difference as to what is produced and delivered by producers. The premise is that, if an enterprise is owned by nationals, it is more likely to produce and distribute domestic content. In contrast, it holds that foreign ownership would result in inappropriate programming for developing an informed

[72] See Doyle and Hibberd, above n 41, 153.

[73] See M Burri-Nenova, 'Trade versus Culture in the Digital Environment: An Old Conflict in Need of a New Definition' (2009) 12(1) *Journal of International Economic Law* 19, 32–45 (setting out the reality of the digital networked environment and its impact on cultural industry and policy).

[74] See Mukherjee, above n 17, 218.

[75] UNESCO, 'Meetings of Experts on Audiovisual Services', above n 4, 1.

and wise citizenry. The main objectives of ownership regulation are to maintain a balanced diversity of owners of cultural enterprises and to prevent a foreigner from having a dominant control.[76]

3.3.1 Domestic Legislations on Foreign Ownership Restriction

Many countries impose foreign ownership constraints on cultural industries, including divestiture policies. In Canada, the Canadian Radio Television Commission (CRTC) enforces the provisions contained in the Broadcasting Act and Telecommunications Act, which limit foreign ownership in broadcasting and telecommunications enterprises to 20% as a condition of licensure. Foreign investment rules under the Investment Canada Act prohibit foreign acquisitions of Canadian publishing companies, and restrict foreign companies from distributing films unless they hold worldwide distribution rights or have invested at least 50% of production costs.[77] Trade barriers in the Indian audiovisual sectors include a foreign-equity ceiling and ownership restrictions limiting the entry of foreign providers.[78]

Interestingly, the US, in the Communication Act of 1934, also imposes foreign ownership restrictions on radio stations, broadcast television and telephone companies that use wireless communication links.[79] According to the provision, the Federal Communication Commission (FCC) may not grant broadcasting licences to aliens or foreign corporations.[80] No corporation in which more than 20% of the stock is owned by an alien or a foreign corporation may receive a broadcast licence.[81] The FCC has the discretion to deny a licence to any corporation that is directly or indirectly held by another corporation with alien or foreign ties if the FCC finds that the public interest will be served by the refusal or revocation of such licence.[82]

These provisions were originally enacted to restrict foreign ownership for the sake of national security interests. Today, however, parties invoke

[76] See J Smiers, 'Unregulated Markets Don't Exist: What Kinds of Regulations will Promote Cultural Diversity? in Obuljen, N and Smiers, J (eds), *UNESCO's Convention on the Protection and Promotion of the Diversity of Cultural Expressions: Making It Work* (2006) 196.

[77] See respectively, Canada Broadcasting Act (1991, c 11, assented to 1 February 1991); Telecommunications Act (1993, c 38, assented to 23 June 1993); Investment Canada Act (1985, c 20, assented to 20 June 1985).

[78] For more information about the existing trade barriers, see Mukherjee, above n 17, 232–38.

[79] 47 USC s 310(b) (1994), as amended by Telecommunication Act of 1996, Pub L No 104–104, 110 Stat 56, 131–32 (1996).

[80] 47 USC s 310(b)(1)–(2).

[81] 47 USC s 310(b)(3).

[82] 47 USC s 310(b)(4).

the provisions to challenge foreign ownership of or foreign investment in American television broadcasting stations.[83] In a recent case, *In re The Seven Hills Television Co*,[84] the FCC ordered Seven Hills to limit its financial ties with a Mexican family.[85] This decision has led to speculation that the provision now acts as a protectionist device to shield the American telecommunication market from foreign influence and ownership, or that it is used to restrict the influx of foreign speech and programming into the US.[86] These provisions seem to show that a certain degree of cultural protectionism exists even in the US.

In China, the government understands that there is enormous interest in the culture market and has accordingly opened up some aspects of it and invited investment in areas where China needs to develop. China nevertheless denies business opportunities to foreign companies in many cultural fields. In particular, China has long put media ownership within the context of so-called 'socialist culture'. The overriding objectives are 'to direct the enthusiasm of the whole society to participate in cultural construction, gradually form a cultural industry with predominant public ownership, and improve the overall competitiveness of China's cultural industry'.[87]

In recent years, the State Council has issued a series of national plans and regulations on cultural industries, including the Blueprints for Reinvigorating National Cultural Industries[88] and the Directive Governing the Investment of Non-Public Capital into Cultural Industries.[89] These regulations clarify China's media restrictions and regulations. For instance, China encourages foreign investment in printing, distribution and advertising. Similarly, cultural tourism service is open to investment, a signal that China considers it a growing area that needs the injection of foreign capital. The door has also been opened to artwork management, suggesting that foreign capital can be involved in the management of art, and even ownership in this regard is allowed. In a similar manner, China welcomes investment in building its cable infrastructure and developing satellite technology. China also calls for foreign participation in joint ventures to distribute video and sound recordings, as well as in cinema ownership

[83] See IM Rose, 'Note, Barring Foreigners from Our Airways: An Anachronistic Pothole on the Global Information Highway' (1995) 95 *Columbia Law Review* 1188, 1195–97.

[84] *In re The Seven Hills Television Co*, m 2 FCCR 6867 (Rev Bd 1987).

[85] See Rose, above n 83, 1197.

[86] Ibid, 1229.

[87] The State Council of China, 'Several Decisions on the Entry of Non-Public Capital into Cultural Industries' [Guo wu yuan guan yu fei gong you zi ben jin ru wen hua chan ye de ruo gan jue ding,], 8 August 2005, preface.

[88] The State Council of China, 'Blueprints for Reinvigorating National Cultural Industries' [Guo wu yuan wen hua chan ye zhen xing gui hua], 22 July 2009.

[89] The State Council of China, above n 87.

and operation. The Provisional Rules on Foreign Invested Cinemas permits foreign investors to hold stakes of such a joint venture up to 49%.[90]

At the same time, China makes it clear that foreigners cannot invest in, set up or operate content management in newspapers, magazines, radio, television or the internet. Radio and TV signal broadcasting and relay stations, satellites and backbone networks are closed to non-public capital as well. Given China's long-held restrictions on the control of news content, the purpose of these regulations seems to be the control of content in various media. These regulations constitute a setback to those foreign media giants that are trying hard to enter the enormous Chinese market. It thus comes as no surprise that some of these regulations were targeted and challenged before the WTO.[91]

Not every country imposes foreign ownership constraints. In Germany, for example, there is no bias against foreign investors. Almost a quarter of the German TV market has been sold to foreign nationals.[92] Likewise, no provisions in Egypt discriminate against foreign firms registering for activities in the cinema industry; the foreign commercial presence in cultural sectors there faces no discriminatory measures. There is even a tendency to encourage foreign investment in Egypt.[93]

3.3.2 Disputes Arising from Foreign Ownership Restrictions

Foreign ownership restrictions are the outcome of governmental limitations on the influx of foreign cultural products. To some extent, they may be justified as culturally, rather than industrially, motivated. Whatever the cause, though, foreign ownership requirements tend to generate trade disputes.

[90] The State Administration of Radio, Film and Television, The Ministry of Commerce, and the Ministry of Culture, 'Provisional Rules on Foreign Invested Cinemas' [Wai shang tou zi dian ying yuan zan xing gui ding], adopted on 28 September 2003, effective as of 1 January 2004, Art 4(4).

[91] WTO, *China—Publications and Audiovisual Products*, WT/DS363; see also below Chapter 6; J Shi and W Chen, 'The Specificity of Cultural Products versus the Generality of Trade Obligations-Reflecting on "China—Publications and Audiovisual Services"' (2011) 45(1) *Journal of World Trade* 159.

[92] In Germany, the domestic market is characterised by the dichotomy of public and private broadcasting stations of roughly equal sizes. The fee-financed public stations are hardly direct competitors to private stations, but they do reduce viewer numbers for private stations and thus the market size open to foreign investors. See Perino and Schulze, above n 27, 84.

[93] Despite the encouraging policies, the response has been slow, largely due to the limited market size and the bureaucracy faced by domestic and foreign investors alike. See AF Ghoneim, 'The Audiovisual Sector in Egypt', in Guerrieri et al, above n 6, 195–96.

3.3.2.1 The Polygram *Case*

In 1988, Investment Canada[94] issued a directive forbidding foreign distributors from distributing films in Canada for which they did not own proprietary rights. Proprietary rights are deemed to exist when a foreign distributor provides major financing for a film or owns its worldwide distribution rights. The directive exempted Hollywood majors from this requirement and thereby avoided potential disputes between the US and Canada. By 1996, however, the directive and the grandfathering of Hollywood majors resulted in a dispute between Canada and the EC. Polygram, a European media multinational, was excluded from the group of foreign firms exempted from the directive.[95] After its investigation, the EC concluded that Canada's treatment of Polygram was discriminatory and violated the most-favoured nation obligation under the GATS.[96] The EC began the process of registering a formal complaint to the WTO. While Canada was in preliminary discussions with the EC, Seagram, the Canadian owner of Universal Studios, a grandfathered Hollywood major, acquired Polygram, thereby converting the firm to Canadian ownership. The complaint was then shelved.[97] This case indicates the impact of Canada's cultural policies on foreign interests and provides an illustrative example of government policies that affect international trade.

3.3.2.2 Borders Case

One challenge faced with foreign ownership regulations is how to ensure that the minority foreign owner does not manipulate the operation of a joint venture or partnership. Canada is willing to attract investment into certain cultural sectors, provided that foreigners do not control operations. Therefore, foreigners are prohibited from starting a new cultural business in Canada without yielding majority control to Canadian investors.[98]

[94] Investment Canada was established in 1973 (originally named Foreign Investment Review Agency, FIRA) to screen inward investment in Canada. One of its mandates is to retain responsibility for reviewing certain types of investment, including 'cultural businesses', while attracting foreign investment into Canada: Investment Canada Act, s 14 (the definition of cultural business includes the print and broadcast media, films and sound recordings, and investments in a business activity related to 'Canada's cultural heritage or national identity') and s 15 (relating to Canada's cultural heritage or national identity).

[95] On 13 March 1997, the application of Polygram Group Canada Inc to establish a new film production and distribution business in Canada was approved. However, as a new foreign-owned firm, Polygram would only be able to distribute films for which it held proprietary rights and thus was at a disadvantage in competing with the major American firms, which were grandfathered under the then existing policy.

[96] See Acheson and Maule, above n 2, 315–16.

[97] Canada entered a MFN exception for its film and television coproduction agreements under its GATS commitment, but it did not enter an exception for film distribution. Canada contended that a MFN exception for film distribution was not necessary, as grandfathering is allowed under GATS. Ibid, 145, 316.

[98] Ibid, 248.

The lower ratios of foreign investment may nevertheless allow minority foreign investors to effectively control the company through a variety of contractual arrangements. To prevent this from happening, the regulator may look behind the veil of ownership to determine whether the foreigner has effective control over the commercial decision-making of a company.

In *Borders*, the US bookstore chain Borders sought to open a mega-bookstore in Canada. The partnership was submitted to Investment Canada for review and approval. Since Borders only intended to take a minority position in the undertaking, the issue became whether it would have effective control of the arrangement.[99] Investment Canada found that Borders' involvement would lead to a degree of de facto control that was unacceptable. Borders had to withdraw its application and the proposed partnership was dissolved. The US complained that Canada's action was an undue protection of domestic industry.[100] Here the conflict is over Canada's denial of Borders' entry into book retailing on the ground that its contractual relationship with the majority Canadian investors gave it de facto control in the company.[101] The review of a foreign investor's potential degree of control over a company aims to close the loophole in foreign ownership restrictions that is opened by a narrow appraisal of ownership.

These cases are helpful in understanding the actual status of foreign ownership restrictions. It is clear that Canada assumes that domestic ownership makes a difference in the way profit-oriented firms behave, and believes that Canadian-owned firms plough earnings back into the publication and distribution of Canadian authors. However, this belief does not always align with reality. The objective of commercially operated firms, regardless of ownership nationality, is often to produce and distribute products that earn a return on shareholders' investment. The ownership restrictions are not necessarily effective means to achieve the targets set by the government. At the same time, the constraints on foreign investment may restrict trade and shield consumers from the benefits of increased competition. As a result, restricting the level of foreign ownership, despite seeming to be a straightforward policy to administer, involves more complex procedures and policy considerations.

[99] Ibid, 249.

[100] See Browne, above n 28, 2. As the Borders partnership dissolved, another entrant, Chapters Inc, consisting of an American minority investor and Canadian majority investors, was forming. Its proposal was vetted by the Bureau of Competition Policy of Industry Canada. The role of Investment Canada is less clear in this case. See Acheson and Maule, above n 2, 249–51.

[101] For more discussions in this regard, see Acheson and Maule, ibid, 244–57.

3.4. LOCAL CONTENT REGULATIONS

Local content requirements, especially measures regulating radio and television broadcasting, are key components of cultural policy measures in many countries. Those supporting such policies argue that the requirement ultimately leads to more consumption of domestic products. Content-related regulations may take different forms, among which import quotas and screen quotas attract wide attention from policymakers.[102] In practice, regulators generally combine these systems to meet the needs of local markets.

3.4.1 Import Quotas

Import quotas used in countries such as Egypt, India and China are intended to limit the numbers of imported foreign products. For instance, as part of its WTO commitments, China has lowered tariffs for imported films and home videos, and increased the annual quota of foreign films from 10 to 20 films.[103] In India, prior to 1992, there were various restrictions on the import of foreign films; however, the policy has changed significantly in recent years.[104] Egypt imposes a non-binding import quota. Interestingly, given the high rate of illiteracy and the use of subtitling instead of dubbing, there is a de facto 'natural quota' on the foreign films broadcast on public television in Egypt.[105]

[102] In addition to the import quota and screen quota, there is the production quota, acquisition quota, etc. UNESCO, 'Meetings of Experts on Audiovisual Services', above n 4, 15–16.

[103] WTO, 'Trade in Services—The People's Republic of China—Schedule of Specific Commitments', GATS/SC/135, 14 February 2002, available at http://www.wto.org (last accessed on 2 June 2012), 21 (without prejudice to compliance with China's regulations on the administration of films, upon accession, China will allow the importation of motion pictures for theatrical release on a revenue-sharing basis and the number of such imports shall be 20 on an annual basis). It is noted that US and Chinese negotiators announced a film agreement on 17 February 2012, which significantly increased the number of US films allowed to be shown in Chinese cinemas and provided a more equitable share of revenue for American film companies. The agreement was signed during Chinese Vice President Xi Jinping's visit to the US as the Memorandum of Understanding on WTO film-related issues between the US and China. The memorandum includes three main provisions. The first is that China will allow the entry of 14 3-D or large-screen IMAX films in addition to the present 20 films per year from abroad. Secondly, American studios that produce films screened in China will receive, after deducting costs, around 25% of the box-office proceeds, as compared to the previous 13.5–17.5% share. Thirdly, independent companies, rather than the current single, state-backed entity, will be licensed to distribute films imported from the US. For more discussions on this new development, see, eg X Wang, 'Sino-US Film Agreement Tests China's Film Industry', *China Today*, available http://www.chinaculture.org/info/2012–05/28/content_434444.htm (last accessed on 10 June 2012); N Finke, 'Reactions to Today's Sino-US Film Pact', 17 February 2012, available at http://www.deadline.com/2012/02/reaction-to-todays-u-s-china-film-agreement/(last accessed on 10 June 2012).

[104] See Mukherjee, above n 17, 225.

[105] See Ghoneim, above n 93, 201–02.

The import quota is effective at achieving an increase in market share for domestic products, since it directly limits the importation of foreign products into a domestic market. Though import quota is one of the policy measures that most strongly benefit domestic industry, it is a policy that requires complicated negotiation and may still easily lead to trade disputes with other WTO Members.[106] In cultural policymaking, both the benefits and the costs of import quotas should be considered before invoking this policy instrument.

3.4.2 Screen Quotas

The screen quota, a means of government support and protection for domestic cultural industry, obliges exhibitors to set aside a minimum number of screenings for domestic products. The screen quota may be viewed as a kind of cultural exception in trade agreements even though it goes against the principle of national treatment.[107] Despite the US's pressure, screen quota systems still operate in many countries, including Canada, France, Italy, Hungary, Spain and Korea.[108]

In Canada, the CRTC maintains a system of quotas to regulate the quantity of Canadian content that is broadcast. The resulting rules, referred to as 'Cancon', were devised to stimulate Canada's cultural production by ensuring greater exposure for Canadian artists in the domestic marketplace. Applying to radio, television and specialty broadcasting, Cancon rules require television and radio stations to play a certain quantity of domestic programming.[109] A frequently disputed issue regarding the implementation of the Cancon rules is the definition of 'Canadian', which has often appeared arbitrary and is criticised as being consistent more with industrial than cultural objectives.[110] Nevertheless, in general, Cancon

[106] See G Lee, 'A Study of the Effect of Economic Policies on the Domestic Film Market', available at www.M.uky.edu/Capstones_2010/Gyeoreh.pdf (last accessed on 10 June 2012), 22.

[107] See B Lee and H-S Bae, 'The Effect of Screen Quotas on the Self-Sufficiency Ratio in Recent Domestic Film Markets' (2004) 17(3) *Journal of Media Economics* 163, 164–66.

[108] France requires cinemas to screen domestic films five weeks per quarter, while Italy requires 100 days a year to be devoted to the presentation of domestic films. Spain sets a screen quota requiring exhibitors to show one day of EU films for every three days of non-EU films. See ibid, 164. With respect to Korea's screen quota, see below nn 119, 120, and 121 and their accompanying texts.

[109] These rules were established under the Broadcasting Act and are enforced by as a condition of licensing for broadcasters. For more information on Cancon see Media Awareness Network, 'Canadian Content Rules (Cancon)', available at http://www.media-awareness.ca/english/issues/cultural_policies/canadian_content_rules.cfm (last accessed on 12 June 2012).

[110] To qualify as 'Canadian' under Cancon rules, a Canadian production company must retain a financial participation position of at least 50%, and a 50% share of the profits. Critics argue that Canadian content should be defined according to considerations other than 'citizenship' or 'residence', such as theme and subject matter, location of production and post-production, copyright, or rights ownership. See Acheson and Maule, above n 2, 154.

rules have succeeded in replacing foreign product with domestic product; they have not, however, done much to generate national unity.[111]

In Egypt, the Minister of Culture has discretionary power to determine the maximum number of foreign films to be distributed by any domestic firm concurrently involved in the production of Egyptian films. However, this number has serious repercussions on the funding available to Egyptian film producers, who depend on profits from the distribution of foreign firms to finance the production of Egyptian films.[112] Not surprisingly, this regulation has been the subject of endless debate in Egypt. Some producers keep asking for an increase in the ratio, while others are more concerned about its cultural and social implications for domestic cinema.[113]

In economic theory, quotas are considered a major impediment to trade. However, the use of quotas for the specific purpose of protecting domestic cultural content is still permitted under existing trade disciplines. For example, GATT Article IV allows members to impose screen quotas in the form of time limits for showing foreign films in cinemas.[114] In addition to the regulatory exceptions, there are arguments that the screen quota system is necessary to protect domestic cultural industry.[115] The opposite position exists too, though. A study examining the impact of the screen quota system and other determinants on the self-sufficiency ratio[116] indicates that the quota system is not a significant predictor of the ratio. The study also reveals that removing a quota of 100 foreign titles per year in the Indian market did not increase the share of Indian films.[117] This suggests that, in some cases, screen quotas may not be an effective mechanism for limiting the number of foreign film screenings in domestic theatres.[118]

Furthermore, implementing quotas can be problematic when it comes to trade obligations. GATT Article IV clearly anticipates eventual liberalisation through the progressive relaxation of screen quotas. Thus, it seems implausible that this article could be permanently invoked without leading

[111] Ibid, 19.

[112] See Ghoneim, above n 93, 196.

[113] The ratio was originally set at 1:5, whereby a producer of an Egyptian film received the right to distribute five foreign films. There is no economic logic to this ratio; indeed, it is rooted in weak economic interests disguised in cultural format. Ibid, 196.

[114] See GATT Art IV. In 1947, France insisted on introducing GATT Art IV 'Special Provisions Relating to Cinematograph Films'. For more discussions on GATT Art IV, see below Chapter 5.4.

[115] See Lee and Bae, above n 107, 164.

[116] The self-sufficiency ratio is defined as the proportion of domestic film's share in gross box office revenue. It is affected by various factors. See J Oh, 'International Trade in Film and the Self-Sufficiency Ratio' (2001) 14(1) *Journal of Media Economics* 31.

[117] This is because the content of Indian films differs from foreign films and is more appealing to the Indian audience. The solid audience base gives Indian films a natural advantage over external competition. Mukherjee, above n 17, 242–43.

[118] See Lee and Bae, above n 107, 163–76. Note, however, that there are several limitations of this study. Idem, 174.

to a dispute. Another challenging factor is the fact that digital technologies are rendering quotas obsolete in many cases. For these reasons, while quota systems may be invoked for the foreseeable future, there has been a trend to ease screen quotas in recent years.

Some countries have had to abandon quotas in the light of economic globalisation and technological innovation. South Korea provides a case in point. In early 2006, the Korean government announced the reduction of its annual screen quota requirement from 146 to 73 days. The reduction was ostensibly one step towards the successful negotiation of a free trade agreement between the US and Korea.[119] A more fundamental, internal reason for the reduction, however, is that, despite its long history, the screen quota has neither helped the Korean film industry compete against foreign films nor effectively promoted Korean culture. Thus, it is advocated that screen quotas be replaced with other measures in order to build the industry's competitiveness.[120] Korea is not alone in this regard: India now has no local content requirements. There are no minimum quotas for domestic products, nor are there restrictions on the total numbers of films broadcast through either paid or free-to-air channels.[121]

At the same time, however, it should be noted that not all countries are moving away from quotas. Egypt still restricts foreign films to eight prints per title to help support the market share of national films. Since 2009, Argentina has introduced even stiffer exhibition regulations, forcing exhibitors to screen domestic films for at least two weeks in order to secure screen space for domestic films.[122]

It is premature to conclude that local content requirements will soon be a matter of the past. To the extent that significant cultural issues are at stake, there is no doubt that certain means—including quotas—will continue to be used in order to prevent the right to local cultural expression from being compromised.

[119] See the statement by J Goyer, Vice President, International Trade Negotiations & Investment, Coalition of Service Industries, to the International Trade Commission: US–Korea Free Trade Agreement: Benefits to the US Service Sector, 20 June 2007, available at uscsi.org/images/files/press-releases/ITC statement.pdf (last accessed on 1 January 2013), 4 (Korea offers enormous potential for US audiovisual products and services). A week later, the USTR notified Congress of the Administration's intent to initiate negotiations on a free trade agreement with the Republic of Korea.

[120] See CH-K Kim, 'Building the Korean Film Industry's Competitiveness: Abolish the Screen Quota and Subsidize the Film Industry' (2000) 9 *Pacific Rim Law & Policy* 353, 354–55.

[121] See Mukherjee, above n 17, 225.

[122] See Marché du Film, 'Focus 2010: World Film Market Trends', available at http://www.obs.coe.int/oea_publ/market/focus.html (last accessed on 12 June 2012).

3.5 SUBSIDIES AND TAX CONCESSIONS

Lately, some governments have been moving away from quotas; support measures are more often enacted with passive regulatory policies, such as government financial support.[123] Types of government aid for domestic cultural industries vary from country to country, but subsidy and tax concessions are the most frequently used forms of financial support. Subsidy means the direct public funding of or investment in domestic cultural production, most notably audiovisual products. Tax concessions take various forms, such as tax deductions, exemptions or credits for domestic production.

3.5.1 Subsidies and Tax Concessions in Several Countries

Canada promotes the work of Canadian authors and the operations of Canadian-owned publishers by providing grants to authors and subsidies to selected publishers.[124] Canada also offers production subsidies that benefit domestic producers and distributors. For example, a cross-subsidy can be arranged whereby profits from the sale of imported books are intended to fund Canadian-authored works. The fastest growing film and television production firms are private producers whose expansion is fuelled by export sales[125] and subsidies coming from a number of different sources.[126] French subsidies to its film industry are disbursed in two ways, 'automatic support programmes'[127] and 'discretionary support programmes'.[128] However, for various reasons, including insufficient funds and the challenge of objectivity in determining the quality of a film, the objectives of subsidy programmes seem increasingly hard to achieve. In Germany, domestic film production that meets certain requirements is

[123] See Lee, above n 106, 7.

[124] See Acheson and Maule, above n 2, 244.

[125] Canada has been actively seeking to promote culture exports. For more details, see, eg Schwartz, above n 11, 2.

[126] Both the large firms and the niche players of the dynamic private production sectors are dependent on foreign sales and domestic subsidies to sustain their production. The federal government provides subsidies through a specialised agency called Telefilm. In addition, there are other sources of subsidies, such as the Cable Production Fund, other policy-based funding sources, provincial funding, Federal and Provincial Tax Shelters and Production Service Partnerships, Federal and Provincial Tax Credit Programs, etc. See Acheson and Maule, above n 2, 139.

[127] The subsidy is computed as a percentage of the film's total receipts. The objective of this system is to sustain the market share of domestic production. See Guerrieri et al, above n 6, 30.

[128] This aid relies on the advance-on-receipts system and is granted based on the artistic content and the degree to which the film or a distributor meets a set of criteria. It aims to assist the production of more ambitious and innovative French films that would be unable to break even without subsidies. See ibid.

subsidised at both the federal and the state level.[129] Yet the support of domestic production has not led the German film industry to dominance in its home market.[130] The Indian government offers various direct and indirect incentives to support the growth of the audiovisual sector and preserve the nation's rich cultural heritage. Since a large part of the audiovisual sector has been privatised, government incentives are mainly offered in the form of tax concessions.[131]

Egypt is an exceptional case in that its cinema industry enjoys rather minimal protective measures.[132] There is a cultural development fund in Egypt, which, in principle, is a tax-subsidy scheme to help the cinema industry develop. There has been a steep decline, however, in the amount of direct state support for the industry; indirect support has proved ineffective. In contrast, the production of short documentary films receives a substantial amount of direct subsidy.[133] The UK has sought to encourage the development of market-led and commercially oriented audiovisual content producers as opposed to protected or subsidy-driven entities.[134]

3.5.2 The Effectiveness of Subsidies and Tax Concessions

Conventional economic theory holds that subsidies and tax concessions shift the supply curve outward and increase domestic production. Thus, subsidies and tax concessions are likely to stimulate domestic production.[135] The econometric exercise further shows that, at least in the cinema sector, public subsidies have a positive impact on the number of domestic products; similarly tax concessions are strongly correlated with the average budget per film.[136] If subsidies and tax concessions increase the number of domestic films and the average budget per film, they may help protect domestic cultural industry.

The European experience indicates that subsidies are more effective than screen quotas in terms of promoting creativity and innovation in filmmaking and supporting the production of quality film that is commercially viable.[137] In South Korea, a subsidy programme enables the domestic industry to accumulate capital, strengthen its infrastructure and create a competitive film industry that promotes Korean culture.[138]

[129] See Perino and Schulze, above n 27, 78.
[130] American films account for about 80% of the German market. Ibid, 81.
[131] See Mukherjee, above n 17, 227–29.
[132] See Ghoneim, above n 93, 200.
[133] Ibid, 198–99.
[134] See Doyle and Hibberd, above n 41, 142–53.
[135] See Lee, above n 106, 10.
[136] See Andreano and Iapadre, above n 17, 124–27; see also Lee, ibid, 21.
[137] See Kim, above n 120, 372–73.
[138] Ibid, 377–78.

Subsidies and tax concessions mobilise significant financial support for cultural industries and are necessary, given the substantial non-market value of cultural products in promoting national identity. These measures may be justified by cultural arguments, while financial support for merely industrial reasons should be banned. The boundary between these two types of financial support, however, is often murky. In open economics, even if subsidies and tax concessions increase the quantity of domestic products, they may not necessarily guarantee an increased market share for domestic products. An analysis concludes that screen quotas, subsidies and tax concessions have little impact on the market share of domestic films. It thus maintains that subsidies and tax concessions may not be promising tools to improve domestic films' market share.[139] Furthermore, if consumers prefer foreign over domestic products, the domestic product share still does not change. In this situation, subsidies and tax concessions may not even stimulate domestic production.[140] Another concern is that a market-driven trade scheme subjects subsidies and tax concessions to scrutiny under which these measures may be found incompatible with a country's trade obligations.

In brief, a study of the effectiveness of tax concessions and subsidies seems to confirm the need for strategy reform to improve the operation of subsidies and tax concession programmes. In particular, some important issues require further investigation, such as whether and how these measures could be tied to the quality and commercial viability of domestic cultural production.

3.6 OTHER CULTURAL POLICIES AND MEASURES

In addition to foreign ownership requirements, content regulations, and subsidies and tax concessions, many governments implement an array of other cultural policy measures to protect or promote their domestic culture. The following briefly touches upon several of them.

3.6.1 Government Censorship or Content Review

Government censorship, or 'content review', has a long history in print, film and broadcast media. Each society sets its own censorship standards. Traditionally, censorship has focused on sex, obscenity, violence and political views. In recent years, the list has grown to cover new areas in which social values are under pressure to change.[141] For societies that

[139] See Lee, above n 106, 20–21.
[140] Ibid, 12.
[141] See Acheson and Maule, above n 2, 277.

value free expression, the existence of censorship has always aroused public debate. A concern of particular relevance here is the possibility that censorship can serve as a mask for excluding foreign products based on cultural policy considerations.

Cultural policymaking is generally subject to strategic considerations arising out of domestic political concerns. These interact to determine a policy position on censorship to a varying degree. While cultural values are important in determining the incidence of censorship, censorship may balkanise the distribution of content. Whatever the strength and stability of the political support for censorship, the boundaries around what is acceptable are often imprecise. This fuzziness can be exploited for protectionist purposes. For instance, it is hard to find a foreign film that does not offend the religious or social traditions of Egyptian society and will therefore be allowed by the Censorship Authority over audiovisual products.[142] A recent WTO case, *China—Publications and Audiovisual Services*, provides a good illustration of this point as well.[143]

In many countries, censorship has recently been displaced by a content classification system. Nevertheless, given that censoring standards are applied differently to accommodate diverse values in different countries, this substitution raises a more subtle concern with respect to trade: the manipulation of rating systems to discriminate against products of certain origins.[144] Because of the difficulty in determining what rating a programme should receive in a classification scheme, regulations can be manipulated to pursue protectionist goals, thereby magnifying the potential for trade frictions.

3.6.2 Copyright Protection Mechanism and Culture Policymaking

Cultural industries are essentially synonymous with industries that produce copyrighted goods or provide copyrighted services. Copyright law provides a legal framework for contracting in cultural industries. As such, govern-

[142] See Ghoneim, above n 93, 201–02.

[143] WTO, 'China—Measures Affecting Trading Rights and Distribution Services for Certain Publications and Audiovisual Entertainment Products, the Report of Panel', WT/DS363/R (12 August 2009); see also WTO, 'China—Measures Affecting Trading Rights and Distribution Services for Certain Publications and Audiovisual Entertainment Products, the Report of Appellate Body', WT/DS363/AB/R (21 December 2009); see also below Chapter 6; Shi and Chen, above n 91, 159–86; JY Qin, 'Pushing the Limit of Global Governance: Trading Rights, Censorship, and WTO Jurisprudence–A Commentary on *China—Audiovisual Services*', 23 November 2010, available at http://papers.ssrn.com/sol3/papers.cfm?abstract_id=1713886 (last accessed on 12 June 2012), 14–20 (discussing the impact of the case decisions on China's censorship regime and political reform).

[144] It is noted that the most common manipulation of the system appears to be at the trash end of the spectrum, where producers seek a severe rating to exploit the 'forbidden fruit' syndrome. See Acheson and Maule, above n 2, 292.

ments may intervene to benefit domestic cultural industries through legislation relating to copyright, including neighbouring rights. Such legislation confers on authors, artists and content industries the fundamental rights of intellectual property, remunerating them for their work, increasing receipts and making more investment in new creation possible.[145] A number of countries, including Canada, have also adopted neighbouring rights regimes that establish funds to remunerate recording companies, recording artists, owners of audiovisual programmes and broadcasters.

It is beyond doubt that the countries adopting cultural polices pertaining to copyright and neighbouring rights want to reward their own performers and are reluctant to do the same for foreign performers. The lack of conformity of copyright laws and enforcement, together with the increasing trade volume in copyrighted material, has led to a series of trade irritants regarding the treatment of neighbouring rights. For example, the US repeatedly attacked the Canadian and European public performance rights for performers and producers as offending 'fairness'.[146]

On another front, while rights holders are inclined to distribute their copyrighted works on a wide scale, a country may invoke cultural protection to restrict the entry of foreign copyrighted works into domestic marketplace, diminishing the effects of a trade regime. Effective protection of copyright and neighbouring rights involves strict application of international conventions. WTO, via the Agreement on Trade-Related Aspects of Intellectual Property Rights (the TRIPS Agreement), establishes a relatively effective mechanism for enforcing international copyright protection.[147] However, since the TRIPS Agreement focuses on the acquisition, maintenance and transfer of intellectual property rights—instead of authors' rights to exploit their work—it is unlikely that it will, by itself, affect cultural protection in this regard.[148]

The fight against piracy is also a priority in ensuring the sustainable development of cultural industry.[149] It is noteworthy that, in its effort to protect against the illegal reproduction and distribution of American films, the Motion Pictures Association of America (MPAA) faces particular problems in China, a country strongly criticised for its poor record of intellectual property rights protection. It is argued that compounding China's inadequate intellectual property rights enforcement is a supply problem generated by the import quota that China imposes on foreign

[145] UNESCO, 'Meetings of Experts on Audiovisual Services', above n 4, 18.
[146] See Acheson and Maule, above n 2, 258–73.
[147] Ibid, 258–59.
[148] See SI Strong, 'Banning the Cultural Exclusion: Free Trade and Copyrighted Goods' (1993) 4 *Duke Journal of Comparative & International Law* 93, 95–96.
[149] UNESCO, 'Meetings of Experts on Audiovisual Services', above n 4, 19.

films.[150] The MPAA holds that China's low quota for foreign films (20 per annum) has created and strengthened a market for pirated DVDs to satisfy Chinese demand for American films.[151] At the same time, a slow censorship process, a film distribution monopoly, blackout periods and high tariffs have also played a role in creating this situation.[152]

This case highlights the interrelated problems caused by a country that protects its domestic industry by restricting the import of cultural products, particularly American films. The widespread availability of counterfeit Hollywood films, however, hinders the regulations from truly protecting Chinese culture from outside influence. China needs to balance the competing interests of promoting its domestic cultural industry and protecting intellectual property rights.[153] In order to effectively deal with the problem, it is suggested that China reduce its import quota, eliminate the blackout periods, make censorship more efficient to avoid delays, and liberalise its import and distribution system.[154] In particular, China should consider how import quotas, subsidies and other measures can be applied in a manner that protects against the restrictive policies that foster counterfeit networks. In the same vein, the rules need to strike a balance between culturally protective measures and those policies guaranteed in the TRIPS Agreement.

3.6.3 Film Co-Production Arrangement

In 1949, France signed the first intergovernmental co-production treaty with Italy.[155] Canada signed its first co-production treaty with France

[150] See CE Heiberg, 'American Films in China: An Analysis of China's Intellectual Property Record and Reconsideration of Cultural Trade Exceptions Amidst Rampant Piracy' (2006) 15 *Minnesota Journal of International Law* 219, 219–20.

[151] When a state restricts legal importation of foreign films, the restriction is actually countered by increases in unlicensed channels, including pirated DVDs networks and the internet. Ibid, 250–51.

[152] Similarly, as pointed out, due to the slow home-video censorship process and the small number of retail outlets, legitimate copies of video tapes, VCDs and DVDs are typically sold several months after consumers have already bought pirated versions sold upon the film's original release. See US–China Trade: Preparations for the Joint Commission on Commerce and Trade: Hearing before the Subcommittee on Commerce, Trade, and Consumer Protection, of the High Commission Energy and Commerce, 108th Congress 45–55 (2004) (testimony of Fritz E Attaway, Executive Vice President and Wash. General Counsel, MPAA).

[153] See Heiberg, above n 150, 262.

[154] Nevertheless, China's piracy problem is not limited to counterfeit DVDs. Many other goods that are not subject to such quotas are still produced and sold throughout China. Therefore, even if quotas, blackout periods, tariffs and censorship were removed and the distribution monopoly was liberalised, DVD piracy would likely continue to exist for the immediate future. See ibid.

[155] See Jäckel, above n 34, 24.

in 1963.[156] Since then, many such treaties have been created. There are different types of co-production arrangements: official co-productions and twinning arrangements take place within a bilateral treaty; co-ventures are co-productions that do not meet the conditions of an existing treaty or are undertaken with partners outside a treaty country.[157]

The principal purpose of co-production is to give producers access to new sources of funding and to facilitate access to foreign markets. In order to achieve this goal, a complex administrative structure is put in place that permits national authorities to certify co-productions and to monitor them over time.[158] A co-production treaty allows the producers of films to claim dual nationality for better access to different markets. Producers whose films are granted co-production status are also eligible to receive national subsidies and enjoy benefits such as screen quotas in the countries concerned.

Co-production treaties traditionally require that each co-producer's financial participation be matched by an equivalent artistic and technical participation. Recent trends seem to waive such a reciprocity clause and allow the financial involvement from other partners, even those whose countries have not signed co-production agreements. This is a more flexible arrangement, but it may render it more difficult to assess a film's nationality.[159] However, referring to the experience of Canada and France, the implementation of co-production treaties has generated a positive effect in promoting cultural cooperation and exchange.

3.7 PROTECTIVE POLICIES VERSUS EFFICIENT REGULATION?

> The global spread of liberalisation does not result in simple deregulation but rather in varieties of regulatory capitalism.[160]

As noted before, each nation has a desire to preserve its cultural identity—and the US is no exception. Both the cultural sector's increasing

[156] France and Italy signed the first co-production agreement in 1949. It reveals the complexity of interpretations required. For example, details are laid out as to whether a person should be considered a national of the country based on citizenship or residency. See Acheson and Maule, above n 2, 72.

[157] For more details about these arrangements, see ibid, 72–74.

[158] Ibid, 72.

[159] See Jäckel, above n 34, 24–26; see also KF Falkenberg, 'The Audio-Visual Sector' in JHJ Bourgeois et al (eds), *The Uruguay Round Results: A European Lawyer's Perspective* (1999) 429–34 (pointing out that the country of origin of audiovisual products is increasingly difficult to ascertain, given the growing role of international co-production agreements, particularly in the film industry).

[160] CR Way, 'Political Insecurity and the Diffusion of Financial Market Regulation' (2005) 598 *Annals of the American Academy of Political and Social Science* 125.

contribution to national economy and its potential to act as a cultural ambassador[161] readily explain why governments wish to intervene in cultural industries. The pressure caused by economic globalisation on domestic culture provides another compelling reason for governments to act. However, the mixture of industrial support and cultural protection that motivates the relevant policy measures has produced contradictory results. Conflicts often emerge between securing social and cultural goals associated with cultural industries, on the one hand, and the desire to remove regulatory interventions that may stifle or impede the industry's commercial and economic development on the other. The survey in this chapter of a non-exhaustive list of cultural policy measures employed for protecting domestic cultural industry reveals their broad range and wide practical application. Whether these policies or measures have truly achieved their intended goal remains controversial. The problem seems to be that, while protective measures are passionately supported, not much effort has been expended in determining if their outcomes are in line with the expectations of their supporters. As such, the time is ripe to explore the practical effectiveness of protective cultural policy.

3.7.1 From the Perspective of Cultural Specificity

Culture, in its very nature, is particularly nurtured by concepts such as autonomy, spontaneity and criticism. Adorno recognised the difficulty of regulating culture and warned of its possibly detrimental effects, suggesting that culture itself may be negated when it is subject to rigid planning and administration.[162] A culture's survival is not ensured by its insularity but, rather, by its ability to absorb the best of other cultures. All cultures, according to Adorno, comprise a highly complex web of interactions. Accordingly, the popularity of American cultural products is not simply the result of economies of scale or a beneficial trade regime.[163] The Hollywood majors have disparate ownership and have always absorbed creative and marketing talent from everywhere in the world.[164] In contrast, inward-looking cultural protection has done little to lessen the dominance

[161] K Boryskavich and A Bowler, 'Trade and Culture: Hollywood North: Tax Incentives and the Film Industry in Canada' (2002) 2 *Asper Review of International Business & Trade Law* 25, 39–40.

[162] See TW Adorno and JM Bernstein, *The Culture Industry: Selected Essays on Mass Culture* (2001) 123.

[163] See OR Goodenough, 'Defending the Imaginary to the Death? Free Trade, National Identity, and Canada's Cultural Preoccupation' (1998) 15 *Arizona Journal of International and Comparative Law* 203, 226–27.

[164] For example, with Seagram's acquisition of Universal and its purchase of Polygram, the Canadian share of control over the actions of the Hollywood and recording majors exceeds the relative importance of the Canadian market in the world market for films, television programmes, or recorded music. See Acheson and Maule, above n 2, 335.

of American products. Indeed, an improper attempt to protect culture through regulatory schemes is tantamount to freezing culture or confining it to centrally determined legal criteria.

A worthy purpose of cultural policymaking is to foster citizens' awareness of their cultural options.[165] From a practical perspective, a positive and constructive approach to cultural policy should be encouraged. In this regard, India offers a convincing example of successfully sustaining its cultural diversity in spite of the process of globalisation. A country where different cultures coexist and have evolved over the ages, India has been implementing reforms and liberalisation in the cultural sector since the 1990s.[166] Competition from foreign firms has encouraged domestic sectors to improve the quality of productions. Instead of crowding out the domestic firms, opening up cultural industries has led to the growth of audiovisual sectors and increased the country's export of audiovisual products.[167]

3.7.2 From the Perspective of Trade Obligations

The issue remains whether a nation's cultural concerns justify special treatment of cultural products in a world economy that emphasises free trade. Here are several thoughts to address the inquiry.

First, a country can no longer make cultural policy and regulate its industries in isolation. Even countries like Canada that have tried to insulate their policies from trade agreements have only succeeded partially in doing so.[168] It has become evident that trade rules, which constrain domestic regulation, need to be factored into cultural policymaking.

Secondly, the avowal that public intervention in cultural sectors is warranted does not mean that any protective policy can be justified.[169] Market failure itself does not justify trade-restrictive measures in response. In particular, when the source of market failure is domestic and cannot be directly removed, protection is usually not warranted; other policy tools creating less distortion may be better suited to the task. Trade distorting cultural policy measures are justified only to the extent that their costs are lower than those imposed by the market failures identified in the first place.[170]

Thirdly, because culture yields to the profit motive over time, it is encour-

[165] See Schwartz, above n 11, 17.

[166] See Mukherjee, above n 17, 230–32.

[167] International producers operating in India have had to reorient their products to cater specifically to Indian culture and tradition. At the same time, Indian products have secured a niche market abroad. See ibid, 251–52.

[168] See Browne, above n 28, 3.

[169] See Andreano and Iapadre, above n 17, 97.

[170] See Voon, above n 37, 53–54.

aging that growth-inducing institutions, including trade, are resilient and compatible with a range of cultures.[171] It is a long held tenet of trade theory that free trade increases the welfare of nations, and that deviations from trade rules are often politically motivated and should therefore be abolished. Although the economic arguments justifying policy activism and trade protection in cultural sectors are well grounded, departing from free trade principles is often risky. Realignment to a more open domestic trade policy will strengthen the case for integrating cultural industries into global governance. At another level, domestic cultural policymaking is further challenged by the ongoing technological progress marked by digitalisation and the internet, a process that has weakened the effectiveness of cultural protection measures.[172] In this sense, the WTO regime can be beneficial in helping its Members to make necessary reforms, ie to transform cultural protectionism into a genuine cultural policy.

That said, one way to assist domestic cultural industries is to help them compete internationally; the resulting success in foreign markets will allow domestic producers and distributors to develop their capabilities and competitiveness.[173] The Indian government, for example, in a decision based on this belief, has adopted a series of open cultural policy measures.[174] The Indian audiovisual industry has benefited from these measures and continues to grow; a substantial part of this growth is accounted for by exports.[175] On the other hand, protectionist policies may stifle cultural exports and are not always in the best interests of a country and its culture.

3.7.3 An Effectiveness Perspective

In assessing the nascence, evolution and current vitality of cultural policy measures from the perspective of efficiency, one must question whether cultural policies are truly designed to promote expressions of national culture or are merely trade protectionism by another name. Cultural policies may fail not only in producing excessive economic distortions, but also in failing to accomplish their cultural objectives, or

[171] See J Bhagwati, *The Wind of the Hundred Days: How Washington Mismanaged Globalization* (2000) 219–23.

[172] See Guerrieri et al, above n 6, 11.

[173] See Acheson and Maule, above n 2, 332–34.

[174] See Mukherjee, above n 17, 238.

[175] India has transitioned from an importer of television content into an exporter of audiovisual products. Given the availability of highly skilled workers, technical know-how and lower production costs, India has the potential for exporting television content. Indian companies have expanded into global markets. This expansion has been encouraged by the significant demand for Indian programmes. Expatriate Indians maintain close cultural and linguistic ties with their motherland and there is a growing demand for Indian-language programmes from non-resident Indians. Ibid, 240–43.

even jeopardising diversity in the marketplace by discouraging cultural imports.[176] For example, regardless of the high degree of market access restriction mandated by Italian audiovisual policies, the Italian domestic sector still shows weak performance, particularly in regard to competition with foreign producers.[177] It must be emphasised that the effectiveness of any cultural policy measure in promoting national culture depends on its structure and implementation.[178] If the policies do not produce advantageous effects or contribute to domestic culture, there is no rationale for maintaining them.[179]

The next question is whether protection is the ideal way to treat cultural concerns. Two Canadian academics persuasively argue that an open regime would serve domestic interests better than the current protectionist position.[180] They contend that Canada's protectionist policies have only embroiled Canada in trade disputes and retaliatory measures; they suggest that Canadian culture would be more creative and commercially competitive in the absence of such protection.[181] The experience of the Korean film sector also indicates that promotion seems to be a better solution than protection.[182] In Egypt, notwithstanding the importance of protecting Egyptian culture, the evidence and analysis have shown that trade protectionist tools did not serve their aims. It is apparent that the cure for the ills of cultural industry actually lies in regulatory reforms, not in the implementation of protectionist tools.[183]

The important fact remains that cultural policy measures are not always motivated by cultural concerns, even if it is hard to differentiate between protectionist and non-protectionist motives for such measures.[184] Given that the values of trade liberalisation run parallel to those of cultural diversity, trade-restrictiveness should ideally be limited without jeopardising the underlying cultural goals.[185] Accordingly, the challenge for

[176] Ibid, 6–7.

[177] See Andreano and Iapadre, above n 17, 114–24.

[178] See Voon, above n 37, 62–63.

[179] See Pinto, above n 9, 925–26.

[180] See K Acheson and CJ Maule, 'Canadian Cultural Policies—You Can't Have It Both Ways' (1996) 4(3) *Canadian Foreign Policy* 65.

[181] See K Boryskavich and A Bowler, 'Trade and Culture: Hollywood North: Tax Incentives and the Film Industry in Canada' (2002) 2 *Asper Review of International Business & Trade Law* 25.

[182] See Bhagwati, above n 171, 211–13. Given the cultural dissonance between the EU and the US, it is surely a good idea to see if, instead of simply banning the availability of such beef in the EU, it is advisable to accept a labelling solution. That would maintain market access for the American hormone-fed beef and make information available for EU health concerns. Labelling is in this instance a superior solution to outright prohibitions. Bhagwati used this hormone-fed beef case to explain how to wisely deal with protectionism and shore up domestic culture.

[183] See Ghoneim, above n 93, 212–13.

[184] See Voon, above n 37, 60–61.

[185] See C Ezetah, 'Patterns of an Emergent World Trade Organization Legalism: What Implications for NAFTA Cultural Exemption?' (1998) 21(5) *World Competition* 93, 123.

policymakers lies in devising a set of measures and institutions that are able to effectively hit cultural and economic targets without imposing unnecessary restrictions on trade.

3.8 CONCLUSION

> Our biggest problem in cultural policy is not . . . lack of resources, lack of will, lack of commitment or even lack of policy co-ordination to date. It is, rather, a misconstrual or only partial formulation and recognition of the policy object itself: culture.[186]

Culture does not exist by itself. Rather, it is integrally bound up with and shaped by the economic, political and other institutions of the society concerned.[187] Culture changes in response to several other factors, often in a manner that is neither understood nor even recognised. Furthermore, since culture is a source of legitimacy and power, political and economic battles are often fought at the cultural level as well; similarly, cultural struggles often have inescapable political and economic dimensions.[188] For good or bad, cultural matters are now becoming more and more an essential part of foreign policy. Carol Balassa emphasises that cultural issues exhibit broad policy implications and, as such, should be addressed as part of a comprehensive public diplomatic strategy.[189] All these elements highlight the need to design cultural policy measures from a comprehensive perspective, taking a society's political, economic, cultural and other social conditions into account.

The details of cultural policies and measures presented in this chapter convey the complexity of formulating cultural policies and measures. In particular, as the dismantling of trade barriers proceeds, cultural policy measures originally devised for domestic purposes begin to increasingly spill over national boundaries, calling for an adjustment to the global governance system.[190] These concluding remarks seek to set out guidelines for a better cultural regulatory structure.

First, cultural policies should retain the specific objective of cultural development and diversity, which takes precedence over pure economic concerns in certain conditions.[191] An economically efficient policy may in fact be inefficient if it trumps a greater wealth-creating policy. Likewise,

[186] Jeffrey, above n 16, 162.
[187] See Parekh, above n 59, 157.
[188] Ibid, 152–53.
[189] See C Balassa, 'America's Image Abroad: The UNESCO Cultural Diversity Convention and US Motion Picture Exports France', available at: sitemason.vanderbilt.edu/files/../Americas%20Image%20Abroad%20final.pdf (last accessed on 5 June 2011), 3.
[190] See Andreano and Iapadre, above n 17, 96.
[191] UNESCO, 'Meetings of Experts on Audiovisual Services', above n 4, 9.

a seemingly inefficient policy may indeed be necessary if it satisfies public concerns about a controversial matter and thereby prevents a potentially more inefficient outcome.[192]

Secondly, a policy oriented towards free trade does not necessarily stop governments from pursuing cultural objectives. However, in the context of globalisation, any trade restriction may be counterproductive to the achievement of a thriving cultural environment, especially in the classic case of audiovisual services. Thus, governments have to choose intervention methods on the basis of their efficiency and effectiveness, taking into account the need to minimise distortions in international trade.[193]

Taken together, these considerations allow an enhanced understanding of the issues at stake and the appropriateness of any solution proposed in the future. A middle route between the two extremes of protectionist and liberalist policies—termed 'new-style cultural nationalism' or 'weak protectionism'[194]—may allow for protection of cultural values within specified boundaries. While Chapter 8 offers more specifics regarding the design of domestic cultural policy measures, a brief account of this proposal follows.

This middle regulatory path is characterised by several distinct assumptions: the adoption of the rationale of promotion of cultural diversity to anchor the case for cultural sovereignty; a focus on state support for a national framework within which diverse communities can conduct the conversations that make up the many-threaded fabric of the nation, rather than an emphasis on the preservation of a unified national heritage; and an emphasis on the properties and consequences of new digital and multimedia technologies. Technically, this route limits cultural protection through predetermined economic standards, such as allowing trade restrictions only up to a certain monetary limit or to a given percentage of the gross national product. In addition, protections must be implemented through readily transparent systems.

[192] See TM Murray, 'The US–French Dispute over GATT Treatment of Audiovisual Products and the Limits of Public Choice Theory: How an Efficiency Market Solution was "Rent-Seeking"' (1997) 21 *Maryland Journal of International Law & Trade* 203, 203–05.

[193] See Bhagwati, above n 171, 209–13.

[194] It is suggested that people's legitimate interest in limiting their government's power to deny them access to media or cultural products is better considered under human rights law than under trade law. See Baker, above n 44, 1361–63.

4

UNESCO and Cultural Diversity: Theories and Approaches

> In its rich diversity, culture has intrinsic value for development as well as social cohesion and peace. Cultural diversity is a driving force of development, not only in respect of economic growth, but also as a means of leading a more fulfilling intellectual, emotional, moral and spiritual life. UNESCO[1]

4.1 INTRODUCTION

UNESCO WAS ESTABLISHED after World War II with the primary purpose of disseminating knowledge around the world to encourage global peace and the common welfare of mankind.[2] UNESCO's foundation demonstrates a widely held belief that cultural exchange is capable of greatly benefiting the world.[3] This chapter looks at UNESCO's evolving theories and approaches to culture, and analyses how UNESCO has elevated the notion of 'cultural diversity' to a concept recognised in international law. The latest developments in protecting and promoting cultural diversity under the aegis of UNESCO are addressed, as well as the challenges UNESCO is facing in carrying out its cultural mission in the context of economic globalisation.

First, this chapter investigates the springhead of UNESCO's conception of culture and cultural diversity, with a special focus on the impact of historicism and the anthropological notion on UNESCO's conception of

[1] UNESCO, available at http://portal.unesco.org/culture/en/ev.php-URL_ID=34321&URL_DO=DO_TOPIC&URL_SECTION=201.html (last accessed on 14 June 2012).

[2] The establishment of UNESCO is 'for the purpose of advancing, through the educational and scientific and cultural relations of the peoples of the world, the objectives of international peace and of the common welfare of mankind'. Preamble, UNESCO Constitution, adopted in London on 16 November 1945, entered into force on 4 November 1946.

[3] See J Reeves, *Culture and International Relations: Narratives, Natives and Tourists* (2004) 50; see also K Dowler, 'The Cultural Industries Policy Apparatus' in M Dorland (ed), *The Cultural Industries in Canada: Problems, Policies and Prospects* (1996) 338 ('Culture constituted a form of defence against both internal and external threats').

culture. Historicism underscores the unchangeability of certain groups and the impossibility of assimilating smaller groups into larger conglomerates.[4] This is related to the appreciation and respect for local culture and cultural identity. The anthropological notion of culture emphasises the equality of various cultures, a belief that underpins UNESCO's promotion of cultural diversity.

Secondly, this chapter discusses how UNESCO's conception of culture interacts with other social norms, which, to some extent, accounts for why UNESCO values cultural diversity. This chapter also articulates UNESCO's systematic view that the preservation of cultural diversity means maintaining and developing existing cultures while ensuring their openness to other cultures.[5] This serves as a key component in adapting different cultures to the transformations imposed by free trade.

Thirdly, this chapter studies UNESCO's efforts to protect and promot cultural diversity in the recent decade, with a focus on the 2005 UNESCO Convention on Cultural Diversity. It analyses both the Convention's success in accomplishing its mission and its failure in counterbalancing powerful WTO trade rules. The concluding remarks posit the necessity of increased conceptual interaction between cultural protection and free trade.

4.2 HISTORICISM, ANTHROPOLOGY AND UNESCO'S CONCEPTION OF CULTURE

4.2.1 Historicism

UNESCO's notion of culture has been influenced by the theory of historicism.[6] An approach to the study of anthropology and culture dating back to the middle nineteenth- and early twentieth centuries, historicism refers to philosophical theories that claim an organic succession of development. The early historicist position held by Hegel suggests that any human society and all human activities—such as science, art or philosophy—are defined by their history; their essence can be sought only through

[4] Historicism maintains that the characteristics between the members of different cultures, classes and groups are permanent, often resulting from genetic features, and that change is impossible. See, eg MR Cohen, 'Psychology and Scientific Methods' (1914) 11 *Journal of Philosophy* 701, 705, also in, WM Reisman and AM Schreiber, *Jurisprudence: Understanding and Shaping Law: Cases, Readings, Commentary* (1987) 234.

[5] See I Bernier, 'A UNESCO International Convention on Cultural Diversity' in CB Graber et al (eds), *Free Trade versus Cultural Diversity: WTO Negotiations in the Field of Audio-visual Services* (2004) 66–67.

[6] See, eg UNESCO, 'Towards a UNESCO Culture and Development Indicators Suite', Working Document, Dimension No 5: Cultural Dimension in Human Rights and Development (1995) 13 (listing the rights of indigenous people as one indicator for measuring culture and development).

understanding that history.[7] The term 'historicism' has developed different and divergent, though loosely related, meanings, but it generally holds that the basic significance of specific social context is central to human development.[8] In other words, local conditions and peculiarities decisively influence social development.

The shift from nature to culture is a key element in the development of historicism.[9] Historicism produces history as 'tradition' and a series of 'cultural treasures'.[10] In this sense, culture is a historically created system of meaning and significance, or a system of beliefs and practices in terms of which a group of human beings understand, regulate and structure their individual and collective lives.[11] Interestingly, the *Oxford English Dictionary* reiterates this conception by defining 'culture' as 'the civilization, customs, artistic achievement, etc, of a people, especially at a certain stage of its development or history'.[12] This definition does not specify a clear-cut scope for culture, but emphasises the links between history, culture and human development. In fact, culture and cultural differences have always been at the heart of human behaviour, acting as a powerful, underlying force in history.[13] Indeed, human history and experience is one aspect of culture.

However, unlike the differences that spring from individual choices, culturally derived difference is embedded in a shared, inherited system of meaning and significance. To highlight the distinction between these two kinds of difference, the term 'diversity' is used to refer to culturally derived differences.[14] A basic tenet of historicism is that 'the meaning of history does not exist in some universal structure . . . but in the multiplicity of individual manifestations at different cultures'.[15] Accordingly, culture stresses the diversity of life forms and becomes the most frequently cited

[7] Hegelian historicism can be contrasted with reductionist theories, which maintain that all development can be explained by fundamental principles (such as 'economic determinism').

[8] For an understanding of historicism, see generally, AL Kroeber, *The Nature of Culture* (1952); see also CG Ryn, 'Defining Historicism' (1998) 11(2) *Humanitas*; L von Mises, *Theory and History* (1957) ch 10.

[9] In the eighteenth century, theorists tended to think of societies as collections of individuals who acted according to universal laws of human nature. Scholars shifted their attention to culture during the nineteenth century. See M Mandelbaum, *History, Man and Reason* (1971) 163–91.

[10] See A Kapcznski, 'Walter B after the 20th Century: The Future of a Past: Historicism, Progress, and the Redemptive Constitution' (2005) 26 *Cardozo Law Review* 1041, 1059.

[11] See B Parekh, *Rethinking Multiculturalism: Cultural Diversity and Political Theory* (2002) 143.

[12] *Oxford English Dictionary*, 2nd edn (1989) 5(b).

[13] This is a statement in which the 'facts' of culture were seemingly established beyond dispute. See S Murden, 'Culture in World Affairs' in J Bayliss and S Smith (eds), *The Globalization of World Politics: An Introduction to International Relations* (1997) 456–69.

[14] See Parekh, above n 11, 3 (2000).

[15] See H Meyerhoff, 'Introduction' in H Meyerhoff (ed), *The Philosophy of History in our Time: An Anthology Selected, and with an Introduction and Commentary* (1959) 10.

determinant of human behaviour.[16] By emphasising the distinctiveness of a particular group's culture, historicism reveals the differences in human perspective and behaviour that other theoretical approaches to human history might neglect.[17]

The historicist approach has a definitive impact on UNESCO's conception of culture. UNESCO contends that culture is not a spontaneous or unconditional phenomenon, but rather is subject to historical factors; the impact of these factors has to be understood in assessing the content and value of cultural works.[18] At the same time, UNESCO emphasises that culture is changing rather than static, and that cultural dynamics are fluid over time.[19] These ideas support UNESCO's contention that culture has to be analysed in a certain historical context.

4.2.2 The Anthropological Notion of Culture

UNESCO has experienced the creeping influence of anthropology and moved towards accepting the idea of culture in the anthropological sense. This is reflected in the UNESCO's articulation of culture.

Although criticisms of 'cultural imperialism' during the 1980s proved damaging to UNESCO,[20] UNESCO became more sensitive to a broader definition of culture in the following years. In 1995, UNESCO published a key report entitled 'Our Creative Diversity',[21] which drew on the work

[16] See JC Williams, 'Culture and Certainty: Legal History and the Reconstructive Project' (1990) 76 *Virginia Law Review* 713, 730–31.

[17] See WM Reisman, 'Autonomy, Interdependence, and Responsibility' (1993) 103 *Yale Law Journal* 401, 401.

[18] UNESCO, *Cultural Industries: A Challenge for the Future of Culture* (1982) 12.

[19] See E Reichert, 'Human Rights: An Examination of Universalism and Cultural Relativism' (2006) 22(1) *Journal of Comparative Social Welfare* 23.

[20] The US and UK withdrew from UNESCO, alleging the undue politicisation of UNESCO and its financial waste and mismanagement, as well as its anti-Western sentiment. See Reeves, above n 3, 50–53. A more fundamental reason for the US's withdrawal from UNESCO was its strong opposition to developing alternatives—in the name of 'New World Information and Communication Order'—for the 'free flow of information' within UNESCO. For useful information on the US's withdrawal, see HN Weiler, 'Withdrawing from UNESCO: A Decision in Search of Argument' (1986) 30(1) *Comparative Education Review* 132, 132–34; J Smiers, 'The Curiosity of a Cultural Omnivore' in N Obuljen and J Smiers (eds), *UNESCO's Convention on the Protection and Promotion of the Diversity of Cultural Expressions: Making It Work* (2006) 12–13 (claiming that the US's departure is not just a departure from an organisation, but a symbolic expression of the desire of the US to eliminate measures intended to protect and to promote local culture). The withdrawal greatly weakened the function of UNESCO. See S Lee, 'Heritage Conventions Intertwine with the Concept of Cultural Diversity: Asian and European Perspectives', in Obuljen and Smiers, idem, 219–20. The UK rejoined UNESCO in 1997 and the US in 2003.

[21] See S Wright, 'The Politicization of Culture'(1998) 14(1) *Anthropology Today* 7. In 1991, UNESCO adopted a resolution requesting the establishment of an independent World Commission on Culture and Development (WCCD) in charge of preparing a World Report on Culture and Development (WRCD) for both urgent and long-term actions to meet cultural needs in the context of development. This request was endorsed by the General Assembly

of a number of world-renowned anthropologists.[22] In the report, an introductory quote from Marshall Sahlins defines culture as 'the total and distinctive way of life of a people or a society'.[23] The report further offers two definitions of 'culture'. First, it takes up the argument made by development anthropologists that 'culture' is not just one domain of life but is 'constructive, constitutive and creative' of all aspects of life, including the economy and development. Secondly, it holds that the world is made up of discrete 'cultures' or peoples. It concludes that the neglect of 'culture'—in the first sense—by 'cultures'—in the second sense—has caused development efforts to fail.[24] Overall, the report provides anthropologists with an opportunity to overtly influence the concept 'culture' and provides UNESCO with a broad and comprehensive notion of culture.

The shift from the movement for 'multiculturalism' to the concept of 'cultural diversity' put forth by the UNESCO Convention further reflects the impact of the anthropological notion of culture on UNESCO. Unlike the transnational 'cultural diversity', 'multiculturalism' emphasises cultural diversity 'within' a particular society. The world's first national multicultural legislation was adopted in Canada in 1988.[25] An influential movement in the US as well,[26] multiculturalism owes its development to anthropological and political theory.[27] Linked with a wide range of political theories emphasising social justice, multiculturalism in the US aims to promote sociopolitical and economic utility and the pluralistic coexistence of equally valued cultural systems.[28] Within a society, the multiculturalist project is characterised by three objectives: to enhance

of the UN thereafter. The WCCD began its work in the spring of 1993 and produced the report in 1995.

[22] Each member on the Commission was convinced that culture is a central variable in explaining different patterns of change and an essential determinant of sustainable development. See UNESCO, 'Our Creative Diversity: Report of the World Commission on Culture and Development' (finalised by J Pérez de Cuéllar, 1995), Executive Summary, 8–10 (1995).

[23] Ibid, 21.

[24] Ibid, 7.

[25] The Multiculturalism Act acknowledged that cultural diversity is a fundamental feature of Canadian society, and gave impetus to a range of government policies and programmes to preserve and enhance it. See An Act to Promote and Preserve Multiculturalism, cited as Multiculturalism Act. RS, c 294, s 1, available at http://nslegislature.ca/legc/statutes/multicul.htm (last accessed on 14 June 2012).

[26] The US is and has been a multi-ethnic society with a wide range of cultural practices. See L Grossberg, 'Identity and Cultural Studies: Is That All There Is?' in ST Huall and P Du Gay (eds), *Questions of Cultural Identity* (1996) 88.

[27] During the 1990s, multiculturalism (or 'cultural pluralism') was discussed as an alternative model to the assimilation or integration of immigrants who belonged to minority cultures. The promotion of minority cultural expression has been increasingly considered a public policy that can serve to strengthen social cohesion within multi-ethnic societies. See generally, W Kymlicka, *Multicultural Citizenship: A Liberal Theory of Minority Rights* (1996); W Kymlicka, *The Rights of Minority Cultures* (1995).

[28] See J Drimmer, 'Hate Property: A Substantive Limitation for America's Cultural Property Laws' (1998) 65 *Tennessee Law Review* 691, 726. See also G Yúdice, *The Expediency of Culture: Uses of Culture in the Global Era* (2003) 16.

public awareness and tolerance of the nation's pluralistic character;[29] to increase the representative diversity of society's economic, political and educational institutions;[30] and, eventually, to dislodge the unicultural hegemony that has governed these institutions.[31] These goals are informed by the beliefs and ideologies relevant to each, including cultural diversity.[32] Thus, multiculturalism recognises cultural diversity within a political community as an important value, which ought to be accommodated in political structures and legal arrangements accordingly. In this sense, the principle of multiculturalism can be understood as an orienting principle of the political–legal code that values cultural diversity.

In the era of globalisation, cultural diversity 'among' states and societies attracts more attention. A commitment to cultural diversity has become a natural imperative, creating a reality in which a plurality of cultures can coexist across the states.[33] At this level, cultural diversity is regarded as a principle representing the need for balanced cultural exchange across the globe. This approach is characterised by the development of links between culture and trade, or culture and the economy in general, and the ability of nation states to intervene in cultural markets for a balanced cultural exchange.[34]

Amidst the huge body of scholarly contributions, it is hard to single out a clear definition of cultural diversity. In examining the term, one should avoid terminological entrapment and look beyond the term itself, ensuring that variants and adjacent concepts, such as multiculturalism and cultural pluralism, are identified as well.[35] The work of UNESCO in recent decades displays an evolution from multiculturalism as a notion in anthropology to cultural diversity as a principle in international relations. In UNESCO's discourse, it is important to safeguard both multiculturalism and cultural diversity. The Convention on Cultural Diversity is concerned

[29] See, eg GA Martinez, 'Latinos, Assimilation and the Law: A Philosophical Perspective' (1999) 20 *Chicano-Latino Law Review* 1, 14 (today's political discourse often involves the 'demand for recognition', the demand to have one's culture and cultural identity appreciated and respected; minority groups and the 'politics of multiculturalism' often generate this demand).

[30] See PD Carrington, 'Diversity!' [1992] *Utah Law Review* 1105, 1110 (observing that diversity 'appears as an aspect of the larger objective of multiculturalism').

[31] See Drimmer, above n 28, 726.

[32] See SC Idleman, 'Multiculturalism and the Future of Tribal Sovereignty' (2004) 35 *Columbia Human Rights Law Review* 589, 589–90.

[33] See H Rojas, 'Stop Cultural Exclusions (in Chile)!: Reflections on the Principle of Multiculturalism' (2003) 55 *Florida Law Review* 121, 130–31.

[34] See N Obuljen, 'From Our Creative Diversity to the Convention on Cultural Diversity: Introduction to the Debate', in Obuljen and Smiers, above n 20, 22.

[35] Cultural diversity in modern society takes many forms. According to Parekh, three are most common: subcultural diversity, perspectival diversity and communal diversity. The terms 'multicultural society' and 'multiculturalism' are generally used to refer to a society that exhibits these three and other kinds of diversity. For more discussions on the meaning of these different diversities, see Parekh, above n 11, 3–4.

equally with the need to promote diversity within nations and the need to find ways to encourage balanced cultural exchanges among the states.[36]

In short, UNESCO's conception of 'cultural diversity' rests on a broad meaning of 'culture' influenced by the anthropological understanding of the concept. In addition to literature and the arts, it covers modes of life, value systems, traditions and beliefs, as well as ways of living.[37] This conception of culture not only points to a multiplicity of dynamic identities, but also reveals it as the driving force for endlessly fruitful human development.

4.3 CULTURAL DIVERSITY: A CORE CONCEPT OF UNESCO

UNESCO is the only United Nations agency entrusted with a mandate to promote the 'fruitful diversity of cultures'.[38] As such, its regulatory instruments reflect the theory of cultural diversity that UNESCO has articulated.

First, human capacities and values conflict, and no culture can embody all that is valuable in human life.[39] Different cultures correct and complement each other, expand each other's horizon of thought and alert each other to new forms of human fulfilment. Cultural diversity arises from the coexistence of a multiplicity of cultural identities and encourages a healthy interaction between different systems of ideas and ways of life.[40] The differences in cultural traits and the coexistence of distinctive cultures make the world more diversified.[41] In recent decades, a fast-paced process of cultural diversification has been taking place across the world, fed by the new awareness that human civilisation is a mosaic of different cultures.[42] This not only creates a rich, varied and stimulating world, but also increases the range of available options and increases freedom of choice.[43]

Secondly, cultural diversity recognises that differences in human societies are involved in complex systems and relationships.[44] Tolerance and

[36] See Obuljen, above n 34, 23.

[37] K Stenou (ed), *UNESCO and the Question of Cultural Diversity 1946–2007—Review and Strategies: A Study Based on A Selection of Official Documents* (2007) 75; UNESCO, 'Meeting of the Experts Committee on the Strengthening of UNESCO's Role in Promoting Cultural Diversity In the Context of Globalization', Working Document, CLT/CIC/BCI/DC/DOC 5E, 21–22 September 2000, Paris, 2.

[38] See UNESCO, Constitution, Arts I (3) and V(A)(3).

[39] See UNESCO, Universal Declaration of Cultural Diversity (2001), Art 1; UNESCO, Convention on Cultural Diversity, Preamble.

[40] See Parekh, above n 11, 166–67.

[41] See R Benedict, *Patterns of Culture* (1989) 37.

[42] See UNESCO, above n 22, 7.

[43] See Parekh, above n 11, 165–66.

[44] UNESCO & UNEP, 'Cultural Diversity and Biodiversity for Sustainable Development: Background Documents', 3 January 2003, 16.

reciprocal respect for cultural distinctiveness are indispensable conditions for increased mutual understanding among people and the recognition of common humanity. The need for people to live and work together peacefully should result in mutual respect between different cultures.[45] In this sense, diversity is less a function of the isolation of groups than of the relationships that unite them.[46] Cultural diversity creates a climate in which different cultures can engage in a mutually beneficial dialogue. This is inherent in the belief held by the founders of UNESCO that cultural exchange is one of the best guarantees of peace in our world.

Thirdly, cultural diversity as a value to be safeguarded goes beyond the value of a single cultural object and aims to prevent domestic culture from undue foreign influence.[47] In this sense, suggests Parekh, it is regarded as an operative public value, one that 'a society cherishes as part of its collective identity'.[48] To describe cultural diversity as an operative public value signals that it is more than just a guiding interpretive principle for lawmaking or policymaking.[49] Such a description articulates the need to operationalise the notion of cultural diversity, to incorporate it into regulatory structures and ensure that it is meaningfully applied.[50] In looking at the relevant UNESCO documents for an answer to why 'cultural diversity' is worthy of protection, one regularly finds the allusion to UNESCO's role in the protection of identity.

Fourthly, cultural diversity offers a critical link between the tangible and the intangible dimensions of human development. Tangible development can be measured in terms of health, economic capabilities, commodity flows, and physical guarantees of security and productivity. Intangible development consists in the spirit of participation, the enthusiasm of empowerment, the joys of recognition and the pleasures of aspiration. Cultural diversity provides a crucial link between these two dimensions of development, by guaranteeing the survival of multiple visions of the 'good life', and of a range of concrete ties between cultural values and material well-being.[51]

Fifthly, since humans are culturally embedded beings, they have a

[45] See UNESCO, above n 22, 54.

[46] See A Kuper, *Culture—The Anthrologists' Account* (1999) 243.

[47] See A von Bogdandy, 'The European Union as Situation, Executive, and Promoter of the International Law of Cultural Diversity—Elements of a Beautiful Friendship' (2008) 19 *European Journal of International Law* 241, 245–46.

[48] See Parekh, above n 11, 363.

[49] Although the term 'operative public value' is academic in origin, the approach it implies is broadly consistent with that envisaged by a number of standard-setting international texts, which employ different terminology. For instance, cultural diversity is described as 'an essential public interest objective' in the Council of Europe's Committee of Ministers Recommendation (2003) to Member States on measures to promote the democratic and social contribution of digital broadcasting.

[50] See T McGonagle, 'The Promotion of Cultural Diversity via New Media Technologies: An Introduction to the Challenges of Operationalization' (2008) 2008(6) *IRIS-Plus* 1, 1–2.

[51] See UNESCO & UNEP, above n 44, 17.

right to their culture. Cultural diversity is an inescapable and legitimate outcome of the exercise of that right.[52] In recent decades, people have begun asserting the value of their own cultural wealth and the manifold assets that cannot be reduced to money, while simultaneously recognising the universal values of a global ethic.[53] During the 1990s, the promotion of minority cultural expression increasingly came to be considered a public policy that could serve to strengthen social cohesion within multi-ethnic societies. Cultural diversity is further advocated as the *conditio sine qua non* for the provision of the greatest variety of cultural expressions within a common framework available to all people.[54] This contributes to a better understanding of, and dialogue between, the different cultures that provide the true wealth and life in this world.

4.4 UNESCO'S UNDERTAKINGS ON CULTURE AND CULTURAL DIVERSITY: AN OVERVIEW

Since the birth of UNESCO, alongside the rapid growth of global markets, cross-border economic flows and deep technological interdependence, the issues pertaining to culture and cultural diversity have essentially become more and more connected to questions of ethics, freedom, and law.[55] UNESCO fulfils its mission of promoting culture and cultural diversity through various projects and programmes, development work, conferences and publications. In order to keep up with a constantly changing international context, the work of UNESCO in the field of culture has evolved alongside changes in the meaning of 'culture' and in the functions ascribed to it. The following account of a succession of UNESCO's main undertakings provides a series of useful benchmarks for UNESCO's work that reflect the changing consensus of UNESCO Members.[56] A historical survey, this section, largely based on UNESCO's official literature, briefly traces the UNESCO's approach to culture and cultural diversity.[57]

UNESCO's first undertaking, entitled 'culture and knowledge', began in 1945, immediately following World War II. The 1946 UNESCO

[52] See Parekh, above n 11, 165–66.

[53] See UNESCO, above n 22, 7.

[54] See RJ Neuwirth, 'The Fragmentation of the Global Market: The Case of Digital Versatile Discs (DVDs)' (2009) 27 *Cardozow Arts & Entertainments Law Journal* 409, 412–13.

[55] See Stenou, above n 37, 75.

[56] Though the lack of a single definition represents the major obstacle in identifying the most important instruments and fora that have dealt with issues of cultural diversity, 'UNESCO and the Issue of Cultural Diversity: Review and Strategy, 1946–2007' identifies five UNESCO undertakings and instruments in the evolution of the concept of cultural diversity. See ibid.

[57] Since the foundation of UNESCO, the dominant ideas characterising these undertakings have been contained in its official texts. See ibid.

Constitution undertakes to preserve the diversity of cultures,[58] inter alia, by recommending international agreements designed to promote the free flow of ideas by word and image.[59] At this stage, UNESCO saw culture mainly in terms of 'works of art' rather than the 'ways of thinking, feeling, perceiving or being whose entirety'. UNESCO recognised the importance of uniting culture and knowledge as a central factor in the pursuit of world peace.[60]

UNESCO's second undertaking, called 'culture and politics', started with the proliferation of newly independent states resulting from the process of decolonisation in the 1950s and 1960s. During this historical period, culture was an essential element in many countries' search for independence. This historical moment brought a new and different light to the notion of 'culture': it began to be seen as a marker of identity.[61] For instance, the 1966 Declaration of Principles of International Cultural Cooperation states that each culture has a dignity and value which must be respected and preserved; every people has the right and the duty to develop its culture; and all cultures, in their rich variety and diversity, and the reciprocal influences they exert on one another, form part of the common heritage of mankind.[62]

The third undertaking, called 'culture and development', occurred in the years between the 1960s and 1990s, and was a continuation of the previous undertaking with a rebalanced emphasis. In 1982, UNESCO's 'Mexico City Declaration on Cultural Policies' articulated culture with a broad definition based on the fundamental assumption that cultural identity and cultural diversity are inseparable.[63] This declaration linked the notion of 'culture' with that of 'endogenous development', giving it new importance. During this period, UNESCO began to place more emphasis on mutual borrowings between societies as a structure that could open the way to a new form of partnership capable of ensuring real international cooperation.[64]

A fourth undertaking, called 'culture and democracy', emphasised the link between culture and democracy, insisting on the need for tolerance not only among, but also within societies. It drew attention to cultural relations within states as well as between states, and encouraged countries

[58] UNESCO, Constitution, Art I:3.

[59] UNESCO, Constitution, Art I:2 (a).

[60] See Stenou, above n 37, 76, 81–83.

[61] See id., 76, 87–97.

[62] See UNESCO, Declaration of Principles of International Cultural Co-operation, 4 November 1966, Art I.

[63] Mexico City Declaration on Cultural Policies, Art 4 (All cultures form part of the common heritage of mankind. The cultural identity of a people is renewed and enriched through contact with the traditions and values of others. Culture is dialogue, the exchange of ideas and experience and the appreciation of other values and traditions; it withers and dies in isolation) and Art 5 (Cultural identity and cultural diversity are inseparable).

[64] See Stenou, above n 37, 76, 101–10.

to take account of cultural aspirations and foundations in the building of democratic societies.[65]

The fifth and latest undertaking, called 'culture and globalisation', is defined by the accelerating process of globalisation, which has upset not only the economic and technological orders, but also the patterns of thought and ways of viewing the world. The 1995 World Report on Cultural Development (WRCD) highlights, for the first time, the threat of a homogenisation of traditional cultures under the pressure of a globalising media market. It introduces the concept of cultural diversity as 'global public goods' of utmost importance and a precondition for the proper functioning of democratic societies.[66]

Against the changing international background, UNESCO has always sought to offer practical responses to the particular challenges which each age poses to the notion of culture and cultural diversity. In this way, UNESCO reaffirms the intrinsic value of culture in its rich diversity, both for development and for social cohesion and peace. Its overall strategy is to prepare a road map for promoting the central role of culture in international and domestic development arrangements, through an integrated approach that demonstrates the linkages between operational actions at the state level and the principles enshrined in the international normative framework.[67] Notwithstanding these changes, however, the continuity of UNESCO's mandate and mission is evident. As its history proves, the need to study situations of cultural pluralism and, as a political response to the fact of cultural diversity, to engage in managing cultural pluralism at all levels, remains a vital and indispensable landmark for future activities.

Considering that development and globalisation are more relevant to the scope and subject of this book, the following discusses these two undertakings in more detail, with a view to presenting new developments in UNESCO's theory and approach to culture and cultural diversity.

4.5 CULTURE AND DEVELOPMENT

Development is a phenomenon with strong intellectual and moral implications for individuals and communities. The ultimate aim of development is the universal physical, mental and social well-being of every human being.[68] Since the 1980s, culture has gradually increased its visible role in the rhetoric of development policymaking.[69] As Javier Pérez de Cuéllar,

[65] See ibid, 76–77, 113–18.
[66] See UNESCO, above n 22, 9.
[67] See Stenou, above n 37, 137.
[68] See UNESCO, above n 22, 15–16.
[69] See OG Hansen, 'Co-operation for Development: Building Cultural Capacity', in Obuljen and Smiers, above n 20, 114.

the former Secretary-General of the United Nations, observed, the failures in human developments often result from underestimating the importance of culture, which lies at the very heart of the complex web of human relationships.[70] Therefore, redressing those failures would mean rethinking the development process itself and building cultural insights into a broader development strategy, as well as a more effective and practical development agenda.

UNESCO introduced new links between culture and development in the 1995 WRCD. Besides the urgent call to eradicate poverty, the WRCD addresses two important needs: the reformulation of cultural policies in general[71] and a new, improved understanding of the links between culture and development.[72] The report changes the fundamental perception of the role of culture as an important benchmark in building the international movement for cultural diversity.[73] It adopts a new approach to the development of culture and cultural policies, away from a focus exclusively on cultural preservation and towards cultural growth and the reinforcement of the creative potential of humans.

4.5.1 Sustainable Development: Pairing Cultural Diversity with Biodiversity

The 1992 Convention on Biological Diversity transcends the traditional approach based on the conservation of individual species and recognises the interconnected nature of the different components of the global ecosystem.[74] Inspired by this development, the 1995 WRCD recognised cultural diversity as one of the essential elements of sustainable development, and, for the first time, drew a parallel between biodiversity and cultural diversity. Six years later, the UNESCO Declaration on Cultural Diversity maintained that cultural diversity is 'necessary for humankind as biodiversity is for nature'.[75] Just one year later, on 3 September 2002, UNESCO and the United Nations Environment Program (UNEP) jointly convened a high-level roundtable discussion in Johannesburg. This inter-

[70] See UNESCO, above n 22, 7–8.

[71] The report expands the concept of cultural policy from a narrow focus on the arts, and suggests that cultural policy should be directed at encouraging multicultural activities. Ibid, 18.

[72] The report lists the issues at the heart of culture and development, which include the cultural and sociocultural factors that affect development, the cultural impact of social and economic development, and the policies promoting sustainable human development and encouraging the flowering of different cultures. Ibid, 8, 18.

[73] See Obuljen, above n 34, 24–25.

[74] See Convention on Biological Diversity, 5 June 1992, available at www.cbd.int (last accessed on 14 June 2012).

[75] UNESCO, UNESCO Declaration on Cultural Diversity, Art 1 (Cultural diversity: the common heritage of humanity).

disciplinary panel underlined the importance of respecting and integrating the diversity of nature and culture as a prerequisite for sustainable development.[76] One meaningful contribution of the discussion and the ensuing report was to reiterate that cultural diversity is as necessary for the human sphere as biodiversity is for the natural realm.

As the joint report points out, humanity's relation to the natural environment has long been seen in predominantly biophysical terms. However, there has been a growing recognition that cultural diversity unites individuals and societies, and enables them to share cultural heritage: in other words, the experience of the present and the promise of the future.[77] This sharing underpins the sustainability of social development, and has to be taken into serious account if sustainable human development is to become a reality.[78]

The report identifies a mutual dependency between biodiversity and culture. On the one hand, innumerable cultural practices depend upon specific elements of biodiversity for their continued existence and expression. On the other hand, significant quarters of biological diversity are developed, maintained and managed by cultural groups through language and knowledge.[79] Along with biodiversity, cultural diversity ranks as a central means for securing the sustainability of every tangible and intangible form of development. Therefore, human and natural diversity are inseparable; together they hold the key to ensuring resilience in both social and ecological systems.

On another level, cultural diversity guarantees sustainability because it binds universal developmental goals to plausible and specific moral visions. The focus on 'sustainable diversity' assumes that human beings belong to the biological universe while at the same time being privileged to create diverse forms of culture in space and time. This, in turn, places a special obligation on human beings to ensure the proper balance between environmental health and equitable development.[80] This demonstrates that cultural diversity may serve as a powerful guarantee of biodiversity.

It is worth noting that there are those who might find the link between cultural diversity and biodiversity to be inappropriate or unconvincing. I would argue, however, that the concept of 'sustainable development', based on a clear understanding of the role of biological and cultural diversity in jointly maintaining ecological systems, cannot be viewed exclusively through the prism of tangible nature. The primary focus of the link is the idea that each is fundamental to sustainable development and the future of humanity. Meanwhile, the link reminds us that the protection and

[76] UNESCO & UNEP, above n 44, 5.
[77] Ibid, 10.
[78] See UNESCO, above n 22, 17–18.
[79] UNESCO & UNEP, above n 44, 9.
[80] Ibid, 7–8.

promotion of cultural diversity should not be something static, but rather a dynamic process. In any sense, such a comprehensive understanding of the interaction between intangible and tangible elements necessary to achieve sustainable development should be welcome and desirable.

4.5.2 The Role of Culture in Development

Another major contribution of UNESCO's undertaking on culture and development is reflected in its clarification of the precise role of culture in development. A conventional view perceives culture as either a help or a hindrance to development[81] and holds that culture plays an instrumental rather than fundamental role.[82] Without a doubt, this instrumental view of culture is of great importance, given that the process of economic growth is generally highly valued in measuring development progress. Nevertheless, the notion of development has broadened in recent decades, as people realised that economic criteria alone could not provide a programme for human dignity and well-being.[83] The 1995 WRCD argued that human development is a process that enhances the effective freedom of people to pursue that which they have reason to value. This view of development reflects a culturally conditioned view of economic and social progress,[84] and indicates that development can no longer be seen as a single, uniform, linear path; such an attitude would dangerously limit human creative capacity.[85] Put another way, development divorced from its human or cultural context is growth without a soul; the pursuit of purely economic development ignores the development of the self.

According to this broadened concept of development, the significance of culture cannot be fully captured if one understands culture as merely instrumental. The report defines 'culture' in the specific context of economic development as 'a set of activities, sometimes known as cultural industries and, in the functional sense, represented by the cultural sector of the economy'. Taking into account both the positive and negative impacts of economic development on culture, the report suggests that an analysis of foreseeable cultural effects should be built into all development projects.[86] As such, it is important to acknowledge both the far-reaching

[81] See UNESCO, above n 22, 15.

[82] Ibid, 22–23.

[83] For instance, the UNDP elaborates the notion of human development as 'a process of enlarging people's choices'. It measures development in a broad array of capabilities for being healthy, educated, productive, creative and enjoying self-respect and human rights. Culture was implied in this notion, but was not explicitly introduced. Ibid, 8.

[84] See A Sen, 'Culture, Economics and Development', paper contributed to the World Commission on Culture and Development, May 1995, on file with the author; see also M Ul Haq, *Reflections on Human Development* (1995).

[85] See UNESCO, above n 22, 7.

[86] Ibid, 259.

instrumental function of culture in development and the role of culture as a desirable end in itself, ie as a phenomenon that gives meaning to human existence.[87] UNESCO stresses the role of culture in human development and recommends that the cultural dimension be 'mainstreamed' into development policies.

Taken as a whole, contemporary international law has recognised biodiversity as a common concern of humankind. The evolutionary character of culture similarly requires the protection of cultural traditions whose richness and diversity permit fruitful exchange and interaction among different peoples.[88] UNESCO's pairing of cultural diversity with biodiversity for the purpose of achieving sustainable development is an opportune response to the challenges posed by the partly failed development models of the past decades.

4.6 CULTURE AND GLOBALISATION

The emergence of cultural diversity as a key factor in international relations is also related to the intensification of globalisation in recent decades. In particular, economic globalisation creates political tensions in both developed and developing countries, and negatively impacts culture. Countries need stronger local cultures to maintain their senses of belonging. Engaging the challenge of coordinating the protection of cultural diversity and the advancement of economic development remains imperative for international community. It is against this backdrop that UNESCO's undertaking of culture and globalisation seeks to tackle the challenges that economic globalisation brings to cultural diversity: ensuring both that people and groups with a varied and dynamic plurality of cultural identities interact harmoniously and that creative diversity is defended.

UNESCO has been addressing the issue of cultural diversity and trade pressure since the late 1990s. To this end, the cultural diversity introduced by UNESCO aims to remedy economic globalisation's negative impact on culture. The 2001 UNESCO Declaration on Cultural Diversity clearly signalled that all UNESCO Members favoured the idea of putting forward a legally binding international instrument for the protection of cultural diversity in the context of globalisation.[89] It is also noted that cultural diversity is a positively formulated version of '*exception culturelle*'—the slogan that was fervently defended by France and Canada during the

[87] Ibid, 23.

[88] See F Francioni, 'Beyond State Sovereignty: The Protection of Cultural Heritage As A Shared Interest of Humanity' (2004), 25 *Michigan Journal of International Law* 1209, 1221–22.

[89] See Obuljen, above n 34, 28.

Uruguay Round trade negotiations. In contrast to the negativism and the latent anti-Americanism of the rhetoric of cultural exceptionalism, the term 'cultural diversity' has the advantage of being conceptually neutral;[90] as such, it is more acceptable to both trade negotiators and culture advocates. France and Canada championed the 2001 UNESCO Declaration, and their experience has further led to the shape of the subsequent UNESCO Convention on Cultural Diversity.[91] Leaving aside details of the convention for later discussion, the following section addresses UNESCO's attitude towards the free flow of cultural products, a subject closely related to the culture and trade issue.

Despite the influence of historicism, UNESCO's perception of culture is not of a completely unchanging deposit that simply needs preserving. Instead, according to UNESCO, culture may act as a setting for continuous, unifying dialogue among different expressions of identity.[92] Likewise, cultural diversity, as a source of innovation, creativity and exchange, holds the key to a mutually enriching future for humankind. Recognising that the forces of economic globalisation may actually encourage or foster the proliferation of cultural diversity, UNESCO has been attempting to promote a free flow of ideas and information, and to avoid the oppressive inequality caused by disparate economic conditions.

On the one hand, UNESCO recognises the need to encourage the free flow of products and ideas for culture to develop and flourish. As the UN's organ for encouraging peace through cultural exchanges of all kinds, UNESCO was in favour of the role mass media could play in the modern world.[93] Inspired by such considerations, early UNESCO instruments contained some provisions promoting the free flow of cultural information and products. For instance, the 1948 Beirut Agreement required contracting states to exempt the import of films and sound recordings of an 'educational, scientific or cultural character' originating in any other contracting state from customs duties, quantitative restrictions and the requirement of import licences.[94] Similarly, the parties to the 1950 Florence Agreement—including France, Germany, Spain and the US –agreed to eliminate customs

[90] See CB Graber, 'The New UNESCO Convention on Cultural Diversity: A Counterbalance to the WTO?' (2006) 9 *Journal of International Economic Law* 553, 555.

[91] For an in-depth account of Canada's efforts in relation to the CCD, see, eg T Voon, *Cultural Products and the World Trade Organization* (2007) 175–216; see also Obuljen, above n 34, 29–30.

[92] UNESCO & UNEP, above n 44, 7.

[93] See Z Druick, 'International Cultural Relations as a Factor in Postwar Canadian Cultural Policy: The Relevance of UNESCO for the Massey Commission' (2006) 31(1) *Canadian Journal of Communications* 177, 182.

[94] UNESCO, Agreement for Facilitating the International Circulation of Visual and Auditory Materials of an Educational, Scientific and Cultural Character with Protocol of Signature and model form of certificate provided for in Article IV of the above-mentioned Agreement 1948, Beirut, 10 December 1948, entry into force on 12 August 1954, Arts I, II and III:1.

duties and grant unconditional licences for the importation of books and other cultural materials of an educational, scientific or cultural character.[95] The Florence Agreement also provided that the contracting states would 'continue their common efforts to promote by every means the free circulation of educational, scientific or cultural materials, and abolish or reduce any restrictions to that free circulation'.[96]

The 1966 Declaration of the Principles of International Cultural Co-operation asserted that cultural cooperation is essential to the enrichment of cultures.[97] Subject to certain exceptions, the parties to the 1976 Nairobi Protocol agreed to extend this obligation to certain additional materials.[98] The 1976 UNESCO Recommendation on Participation in Cultural Life further stated that

> the mass media can serve as instruments of cultural enrichment, both by opening up unprecedented possibilities of cultural development, and in contributing to . . . the preservation and popularization of traditional forms of culture, and to the creation and dissemination of new forms'.[99]

These provisions resemble in some sense the trade commitments contained in the GATT/WTO agreements.

The spirit of these provisions is carried forward in UNESCO's new instruments on cultural diversity. The 2001 Universal Declaration on Cultural Diversity confirmed that creativity flourishes in contact with other cultures, and suggested that genuine dialogue among cultures should be encouraged and that an unrestrained global exchange of cultural products might be desirable and beneficial.[100] The 2005 UNESCO Convention on Cultural Diversity represents the most effective contribution towards 'preserving the independence, integrity and fruitful diversity of cultures' as well as 'promoting the free flow of ideas by word and image', two fundamental pillars of UNESCO's constitutional mission.[101] The convention acknowledged that cultural diversity is strengthened by the free flow of ideas, and that it is nurtured by constant exchanges and interaction between cultures. This 'principle of equitable access' ensures that cultural

[95] UNESCO, Agreement on the Importation of Educational, Scientific and Cultural Materials, with Annexes A to E and Protocol annexed 1950, Florence, 17 June 1950, entry into force on 21 May 1953, Art I:1, annexes A and C.

[96] Ibid, Art IV.

[97] UNESCO, Declaration of the Principles of International Cultural Cooperation, 14C/Resolution 8, 4 November 1966, Arts IV:1, IV:4 and VII:1.

[98] UNESCO, Protocol to the Agreement on the Importation of Educational, Scientific or Cultural Materials, with Annexes A to H 1976, Nairobi, 26 November 1976, entry into force on 2 January 1982, Art I.

[99] UNESCO, 'Recommendation on Participation by the People at Large in Cultural Life and their Contribution to It', 26 November 1976, Preamble.

[100] UNESCO, UNESCO Declaration on Cultural Diversity, Art 7.

[101] See K Asmal, 'What the Convention Means to Me', in Obuljen and Smiers, above n 20, 357.

diversity is not misunderstood as an excuse to erect barriers for free cultural exchange.[102]

The above instruments and provisions have a common feature: they do not impose concrete obligations on state parties. They do, however, indicate that, although cultural policy measures may have incidental trade-restrictive effects, trade restriction itself need not and should not be their ultimate goal. Instead, minimising the trade-restrictiveness of cultural measures may be an appropriate goal for Member States' cultural policymaking and a guide to evaluating their trade commitments.[103] In other words, UNESCO's insistence on cultural exchange is consistent with an emphasis on free trade. To a certain degree, the objectives of art as ennobling and identity-promoting are thrown together with the promotion of national cultural industry, a tangle of problems embodied in UNESCO's mandate.[104]

On the other hand, while it recognises the importance of the free flow of ideas and cultural exchange, UNESCO regards the commercial intention of cultural industries as antagonistic to cultural development; in fact, UNESCO exhibits an ambivalent feeling towards the concept of 'cultural industries' in general. The 2005 UNESCO Convention on Cultural Diversity defined 'cultural industries' as 'industries producing and distributing cultural goods and services'.[105] The evident conflict is that 'cultural industries' may be used for different policy objectives, so the question is beyond disagreement over which kinds of activities fall under the heading. UNESCO expresses particular concern over both the concentration and the internationalisation of ownership and control in the cultural industries, as well as 'the subordination of creative artists to market forces or to more or less overtly dictated consumer demand'.[106] UNESCO also maintains that market self-regulation alone will not necessarily guarantee an equitable development of trade in cultural products.[107]

[102] UNESCO, Convention on Cultural Diversity, Preamble, Art 2.7.

[103] See Voon, above n 91, 66.

[104] See Druick, above n 93, 185–86.

[105] UNESCO, Convention on Cultural Diversity, Art 4.5.

[106] UNESCO, *Cultural Industries: A Challenge for the Future of Culture* (1982), 21. This concern was originally framed within the New World Information and Communication Order debate during the 1970s and 1980s. In that debate, the protection of national cultural integrity against foreign influence was a major issue, and third world countries were encouraged to develop their own communication and cultural policies. UNESCO thus brought forward the concerns voiced in many countries about 'cultural imperialism' and, in so doing, legitimated the principle of national cultural sovereignty and, hence, policies supportive of domestic cultural industries. See, eg J Sinclair, 'Culture and Trade: Theoretical and Practical Considerations' in EG McAnany and KT Williams (eds), *Mass Media and Free Trade: NAFTA and Cultural Industries* (1996) 33–34.

[107] Similarly, the UN Commission on Human Rights maintains that market forces alone cannot guarantee the preservation and promotion of cultural diversity. UN Commission on Human Rights, 'Promotion of the Enjoyment of the Cultural Rights of Everyone and Respect for Different Cultural Identities', E/CN/4/RES/2002/26, 22 April 2003, ¶13.

In the present context, it is not appropriate to attempt to resolve this problem philosophically; rather, UNESCO seeks to design pragmatic policies and measures in culture protection, industry interests, and trade liberalisation both at international and national level.

4.7 THE UNESCO CONVENTION CULTURAL DIVERSITY

In a landmark development, UNESCO adopted the Convention on the Protection and Promotion of the Diversity of Cultural Expressions (hereinafter UNESCO Convention on Cultural Diversity, or the Convention) on 20 October 2005. The Convention entered into force on 18 March 2007, after a swift ratification process.[108] While Chapter 8 in this book will offer more analysis on the relationship between the UNESCO Convention and WTO rules, this section explains: the Convention's motivation and the negotiation dynamics resulting from the internal politics of UNESCO; the Convention's specific purposes, goals and guiding principles; the rights and obligations of the contracting parties; its operational mechanism; and its core message. In addition, the section provides an assessment of the Convention's strength and weakness in accomplishing its mission: the protection of cultural diversity.

4.7.1 The Background of the Convention and Dynamics of the UNESCO Negotiation

Notwithstanding a fundamental social phenomenon, culture has only recently received protection in international law, because of both the slow evolution of social awareness and the nature of culture itself. International law first extends protection to specific cultural items, such as folklore, crafts and skills.[109] Given that a significant component of culture is presently embodied in the goods and services produced by cultural industries, it is time to revisit the objectives, scope and means of cultural protection in international law.

[108] In addition to the UNESCO instruments mentioned here, there are plenty of other documents associated with the issue of cultural diversity sponsored by UNESCO. For an overview, see, eg Obuljen, above n 34, 23–29.

[109] See R Bernhart et al (eds), *Encyclopedia of Public International Law* (1992) 890.

4.7.1.1 *Two Rationales for Negotiating and Adopting the UNESCO Convention*

There are two rationales with very different roots for the negotiation and adoption of the UNESCO Convention on Cultural Diversity. The first is grounded in concerns of culture and national sovereignty, a perspective from which many countries saw the Convention as a key step in the long battle to promote cultural development and intercultural dialogue. The concept of 'state sovereignty' is central to the substance of international law. Jack Donnelly explains that international relations are structured around the legal fiction that states have exclusive jurisdiction over their territory, occupants and resources, and the events that take place there.[110] Culture and sovereignty are the twin concepts most closely associated with global governance.[111] One traditional conception of sovereignty assumes that, given the pivotal role that culture plays in nation building, a state is identified with a particular national culture. This argument touches upon the sovereign rights of states to maintain effective government and thus protect their very existence: people who know little about their society and state are not ideally suited to responsible roles in state governance.

The conventional view of state power further asserts that culture is pre-political: culture precedes and constitutes the state, and the state exists to protect that culture from negative foreign influences.[112] Internally, culture creates the bond of nationality between the individual and the state; together with territory, nationality defines the bounds of sovereign jurisdiction. Externally, sovereignty justifies the use of appropriate measures in international law to protect national cultural values. The notion of 'cultural diversity' addresses legal institutions of national sovereignty mostly from the perspective of the formation and protection of cultural identity;[113] this is an especially pressing need in the face of globalisation. The UNESCO Convention on Cultural Diversity represents an international legal response to this need, as well as an unprecedented step towards protecting and promoting cultural diversity at the international level.

The second rationale rests on the side of trade, and points to an impetus of real urgency for developing the Convention.[114] It is even argued that the foremost justification of the Convention lies in its opposition to the

[110] Historically, the idea of sovereignty international relations dates back to 1648 with the Treaty of Westphalia, which ended the Thirty Year's War. See, eg J Donnelly, *International Human Rights* (1993) 28–29.

[111] See KY Schooley, 'Cultural Sovereignty, Islam, and Human Rights—Toward A Communitarian Revision' (1995) 25 *Cumberland Law Review* 651, 653.

[112] See JR Paul, 'Cultural Resistance to Global Governance' (2000) 22 *Michigan Journal of International Law* 1, 3–4.

[113] See Bogdandy, above n 47, 247.

[114] See Obuljen, above n 34, 12–13.

liberalisation of trade in cultural products.[115] It is, indeed, beyond a doubt that the WTO has been the main stimulus for a number of states to pursue the Convention.[116] The most legally safe mechanism to reconcile cultural policy measures with trade rules—a cultural exception within the WTO regime—was prevented by the US during the Uruguay Round negotiation. Thereafter, France, Canada and other states embarked on developing an alternative solution to secure their national cultural space. The result of this endeavour, the UNESCO Convention, was charged with addressing the unique problem of preserving and promoting cultural diversity in a context of economic globalisation. Unsurprisingly, it has refocused the limelight on the suitability of applying WTO rules to cultural products.

4.7.1.2 *The Negotiation Dynamics of the UNESCO Convention*

Both culture and trade rationales are important to understanding the clashes that occurred during the negotiations surrounding the UNESCO Convention.[117] France and Canada, as the main advocates of the Convention, attempted to assign to the Convention the ambitious role of filling the lacuna in international law around cultural objectives and serving as a cultural counterbalance to the WTO.[118] In fact, most informed observers of the UNESCO negotiation that led up to adoption of the Convention agree that the initiative was not about the integrity of cultural expressions, but rather represented an attempt by Canada and France to remove any culture-related trade issues from the purview of the WTO. Thus, throughout the whole negotiation, an obvious trade objective was pursued indirectly and advanced not by arguments based in the facts and figures of trade negotiations, but rather in language supporting the creation of an international cultural instrument within UNESCO.[119] France and Canada counted on the support of China, and several African as well as many Latin America countries. Quite a few other large film producing and exporting countries—such as the UK, Japan and India—also finally adopted the Convention.[120]

[115] See, eg M Burri-Nenova, 'Trade versus Culture in the Digital Environment: An Old Conflict in Need of a New Definition' (2009) 12(1) *Journal of International Economic Law* 17, 18; see also Graber, above n 90, 553.

[116] See HR Fabri, 'Reflections on Possible Future Legal Implications of the Convention', in Obuljen and Smiers, above n 20, 73.

[117] For a detailed account of the negotiation of the UNESCO Convention on Cultural Diversity, see, eg Obuljen, above n 34, 29–34; see also G Gómez, 'Threats and Opportunities for Cultural Diversity: WSIS between WTO and UNESCO', socument prepared for Instituto del Tercer Mundo (ITeM), July 2005, 20–25.

[118] See Graber, above n 90, 553.

[119] See C Balassa, 'America's Image Abroad: The UNESCO Cultural Diversity Convention and US Motion Picture Exports France', available at sitemason.vanderbilt.edu/files/../Americas%20Image%20Abroad%20final.pdf (last accessed on 5 June 2012), 2–3.

[120] The US was initially aligned with Japan and India. India later defected and insisted that the Convention related to culture, not trade. See A Lewin, 'Convergences and Divergences:

The US had identified the potentially adverse effects that such a Convention may have on trade, the free flow of information and human rights, and strongly opposed the idea from the beginning.[121] First, the US was concerned that such a Convention would create an a priori exclusion for cultural products and threaten to curtail Hollywood's ability to generate revenue from overseas markets at the current rate. Secondly, the US held that trade regulation falls exclusively under the jurisdiction of the WTO and UNESCO should not be involved.[122] Thirdly, the US castigated the ambiguities in the Convention and claimed that it could be used by states to deny human rights and fundamental freedoms. The US Ambassador suggested a strong likelihood that the Convention would be used as an excuse for imposing WTO-incompatible barriers to free trade.[123] In contrast to the broad appeal of the Convention's vaguely defined 'cultural diversity', the US position—often couched in legalistic trade terminology—was of little interest to most UNESCO delegations. Trade arguments did not resonate with cultural leaders, a disconnection that was especially apparent in the debate over the relationship between the Convention and the WTO rules.[124]

The final failure of the US to prevent, or at least delay, the adoption of the UNESCO Convention can be attributed to a series of complex reasons. In a larger context, an extended postwar period of remarkable US hegemony over the UN system had given way to a much more complicated set of forces and counterforces, and had led to a net loss of influence of the US over the UNESCO decision-making processes.[125]

The internal politics of UNESCO, exemplified by the dominance of France and Canada over the organisation at the time of the debate over the Convention, did not serve US interests. Canada launched its diversity strategy in 1998; negotiation of the Convention was already under way when the US returned to UNESCO in October 2003. By then, the fundamental tenets of the Convention had already been agreed upon. When the US rejoined UNESCO in 2003 after a nineteen-year absence, a number of delegations were uncertain of its loyalty to the institution and looked

The United States and France in Multilateral Diplomacy' (2006) 58 *Maine Law Review* 395, 399.

[121] See A Khachaturian, 'The New Cultural Diversity Convention and Its Implications on the WTO International Trade Regime: A Critical Comparative Analysis' (2006) 42 *Texas International Law Journal* 191, 192.

[122] See WTO, Council for Trade in Services, 'Communication from Hong Kong China, Mexico, The Separate Customs Territory of Taiwan, Penghu, Kinmen and Matsu, and US', TN/S/W/49, 30 June 2005.

[123] See JA Smith and H Dale 'Cultural Diversity and Freedom at Risk at UNESCO', available at http://www.heritage.org/Research/InternationalOrganizations/wm885.cfm (last accessed on 15 June 2012).

[124] See Balassa, above n 119, 19.

[125] See Weiler, above n 20, 134.

suspiciously at US motives in opposing the Convention.[126] It came as no surprise that the US did not have much opportunity to publicly state its position on the Convention.

Furthermore, to ensure that their proposal would receive a warm reception within UNESCO, Canada and France skilfully played on resentment over US dominance in foreign motion picture markets to appeal to growing concerns over national cultural identity. For several years before the Convention was drafted, France and Canada garnered support for their position in a series of unofficial meetings of cultural ministers, a strategy that succeeded in isolating the US negotiating position.[127]

In short, the negotiation of the UNESCO Convention was exceedingly complex. Given the amorphous subject matter of the Convention, the unfavourable negotiation dynamics encountered by the US and other reasons identified,[128] the US was poorly positioned to either prevent or delay the Convention's adoption. Adoption of the Convention revealed strong anti-Hollywood sentiments among many foreign policymakers and film communities—negative opinions based in large part on the overwhelming presence of US films in foreign markets.[129]

In terms of the Convention's practical effect, however, it appears to be minimal as of this writing (June 2011). Canada and France satisfied their constituencies that they had finally created a de facto *exception culturelle*, though neither has shown signs of invoking the Convention to justify further trade restrictions on American films. It is expected that the Convention will have little impact on what is already a globalised market for cultural products, and American films are likely to continue to dominate most foreign film markets for the foreseeable future. For the US, the industry is still one of the most highly competitive around the world; it is one of the nation's most valuable cultural and economic resources.[130]

Perhaps the most significant impact of the Convention—aside from being invoked once by China in *China—Publications and Audiovisual Services*[131]—can be seen in references to the Convention in international agreements pending in other fora. Again, the UNESCO Convention is a

[126] See Balassa, above n 119, 21–22.

[127] Ibid, 2, 6–14.

[128] Ibid, 2 (during 2003–05, when the Convention was under discussion, the US government was deeply concerned about America's declining image abroad; as a policy matter, little serious attention was accorded to cultural issues in the then US).

[129] Ibid, 3–4, 15.

[130] The US did $13.5 billion in audiovisual services exports in 2010, down 2% over 2009 but still up 6% over 2006, and a positive services trade surplus of $11.9 billion, or 7% of the total US private-sector trade surplus in services. The motion picture and television services surplus was larger than the surpluses of the telecommunications, management and consulting, legal, medical, computer and insurance services sectors. Motion Picture Association of America (MPAA), '2012 Economic Contribution Report-Factsheet', available at http://www.mpaa.org/policy/industry (last accessed on 15 June 2012).

[131] See below Chapter 6; see also Shi and Chen, above n 91, 164–66.

response of international law to the culture and trade conundrum. The disputes during the negotiation indicate a concern that such an international culture initiative spearheaded by UNESCO might undermine the economic paradigm for cultural sectors set up in the WTO trade rules.

4.7.2 The Scope and Subject Matter of the Convention

The scope and subject matter of the Convention is broad, applying to all policies and measures adopted by the parties related to the protection and promotion of the diversity of cultural expressions.[132] The scope and subject matter suggest several aspects that merit close attention.

First of all, the Convention describes 'cultural diversity' as 'the manifold ways in which the cultures of groups and societies find expressions';[133] these expressions are passed on within and among groups and societies.[134] Note here that 'cultural expression' is a concept that extends beyond cultural activities, goods and services, and is not restricted to cultural policies either. The concept gives precedence to a substantive approach based on the content of the policies and measures rather than on their formal description, preventing the subject matter of the Convention from being too narrowly confined.[135] Such a definition of cultural diversity ensures that cultures are able to develop independently while simultaneously remaining receptive to valuable input from other cultures. At the same time, the definition of 'cultural expression' is more specific than UNESCO's broad definition of 'culture' in its previous instruments. Such a pragmatic approach makes sense in the international environment, where the diversity of creative expressions is endangered primarily by dominant market forces.[136] The provisions relating to cultural expressions under threat in the UNESCO Convention have received little attention thus far. According to Ivan Bernier, the significance of these provisions in the Convention must not be underestimated, given that, for many countries, particularly in the developing world, this issue has to be dealt with very seriously.[137]

[132] UNESCO, Convention on Cultural Diversity, Art 3.

[133] Ibid, Art 4.1.

[134] Cultural diversity is made manifest not only through the varied ways in which the cultural heritage of humanity is expressed, augmented and transmitted through the variety of cultural expressions, but also through diverse modes of artistic creation, production, dissemination, distribution and enjoyment, whatever the means and technologies. Ibid, Art 4.

[135] See Fabri, above n 115, 75.

[136] See Graber, above n 90, 558.

[137] Four articles in the Convention refer explicitly to cultural expressions under threat: Art 8, which concerns the problem of cultural expressions under threat; Art 12, which concerns international cooperation in general and consideration of the situations mentioned in Art 8; Art 17, which concerns international assistance offered to developing countries in situations where cultural expressions are seriously threatened; and Art 23.6(d), which includes the

Secondly, the scope defined above refers to creations of the mind; in other words, the Convention is essentially concerned with cultural content and the messages transmitted rather than the precise forms or vehicles of expression. In this sense, the Convention covers not only traditional forms of cultural expressions, but also contemporary media, including audiovisual sectors. This is important because it clarifies the meaning of the notion of cultural products, stressing their inclusion 'irrespective of the commercial value they may have'. This echoes the reference to the 'dual nature' of cultural products, which constitute, on the one hand, commodities that can be traded and, on the other hand, vehicles of identity, values and meaning.[138]

The explicit recognition of the inherent duality of cultural products in a binding international legal instrument is a major contribution of the Convention towards filling the lacuna in public international law regarding cultural diversity. This also provides a basis for challenging an exclusively commercial treatment of cultural products.[139] Note that 'cultural industries' are explicitly mentioned in the Convention.[140] In general, it is unusual for a UNESCO instrument to include industries in its scope. This indicates the relevance of cultural products for knowledge-based societies. Moreover, the Convention acknowledges that all modes of artistic creation, production, dissemination and distribution are covered 'whatever the means and technologies used'. In other words, the Convention explicitly recognises the principle of technological neutrality in the age of the internet. Another way of looking at these provisions is to recognise that the Convention negotiators acted with a keen business sense as well as out of a genuine concern for cultural diversity.[141]

Thirdly, the Convention concerns both the protection and the promotion of cultural diversity. The use of the term 'protection' gave rise to bitter disputes during the negotiation, resulting in the addition of an explicit definition.[142] This definition reveals the underlying tensions between an approach that links the maintenance of cultural diversity almost exclusively to the development of the free circulation of cultural products and

power 'to make appropriate recommendations to be taken in situations brought to its attention by Parties, in particular Article 8'. Bernier offers a good review and analysis of these articles. See I Bernier, 'Cultural Expressions under Threat in the UNESCO Convention on the Diversity of Cultural Expressions', available at http://www.diversite-culturelle.qc.ca/index.php?id=133&L=1 (last accessed on 15 June 2012), April 2009, 1.

[138] See UNESCO, Convention on Cultural Diversity, Preamble.

[139] See Fabri, above n 115, 75–76.

[140] UNESCO, Convention on Cultural Diversity, Art 4.5.

[141] See V Wiedemann, 'Empowering Audiovisual Services for the Future', in Obuljen & Smiers, above n 20, 103–04.

[142] 'Protection' means the adoption of measures aimed at the preservation, safeguarding and enhancement of the diversity of cultural expressions. To 'protect' means to adopt such measures. UNESCO, Convention on Cultural Diversity, Art 4.7.

one that allows for the need to intervene to regulate that circulation. As a result, the text invites a subtle reading.

Fourthly, the Convention is focused on the policies and measures adopted by the parties with a view to protecting and promoting the diversity of cultural expressions. In other words, the Convention aims mainly to regulate the actions of states, so as to ensure that they do not inadvertently depart from its strictures in favour of liberalisation commitments whose ramifications they may fail to appreciate.[143] Meanwhile, the Convention is not intended to regulate cultural rights, the legal status of authors and artists, intellectual property rights or the economic structuring of the cultural sector, even though these regulatory areas are essential to the diversity of cultural expressions.

4.7.3 The Imbalance between the Parties' Rights and Obligations

While many new developments in the UNESCO Convention are largely judged to be positive, the Convention suffers from a great deal of criticism, in particular with regard to the imbalance between the unlimited rights granted to the parties and their weak obligations.

Rights and obligations are generally correspondent in international law. However, what is immediately noteworthy about the UNESCO Convention is that it seems to be primarily a rights regime. The normative heart of the Convention lies in the reaffirmation of the sovereign right of the state to formulate cultural policies and implement measures to protect and promote cultural diversity.[144] In explicitly stating that cultural goods transcend their economic values,[145] the Convention grants states the right to determine special situations under which their cultural expressions are at risk of extinction or otherwise in need of urgent safeguarding. In these exceptional cases, parties may take appropriate measures to protect cultural expressions in a manner consistent with the Convention.[146]

The Convention gives unlimited discretion to the parties to decide which cultural policy measures they deem appropriate. This 'all-inclusive' approach signals the Convention's objective 'to endorse forms of market intervention rather than to preclude them and [that,] as such, it is not necessarily in line with the contemporary theory of regulation seeking the slightest possible intervention'.[147] The Convention does not offer a general definition of the measures that parties can take. In order to avoid the trap of being simultaneously too vague and too restrictive, the Convention gives

143 See Fabri, above n 115, 76–77.
144 UNESCO, Convention on Cultural Diversity, Art 5.1.
145 UNESCO, Convention on Cultural Diversity, Preamble, ¶18.
146 UNESCO, Convention on Cultural Diversity, Art 6.2.
147 See, eg Burri-Nenova, above n 115, 23–24.

an illustrative list.[148] However, this gives rise to uncertainty. For instance, although the Convention permits subsidising domestic and selected foreign producers, or setting up local content thresholds and quotas,[149] there are no criteria defined for granting these measures. Overall, the rights granted by the Convention seem very broad.

The Convention's unbridled openness to domestic cultural policies and measures has invited criticism from the US, which regards it as a vehicle for disguised trade protectionism. According to the US, the Convention grants virtual carte blanche to national discrimination in all relevant aspects of commercial activity, as long as they can fit the discrimination into a framework of 'cultural policies'.[150] Although the Convention clearly acknowledges the duality of cultural products, there is no attempt to reduce the trade-distorting effects of cultural policy measures. It is suggested that the Convention could have at least made reference to principles such as proportionality or effectiveness, which might guide the application of these measures and prevent blatant protectionism.[151]

Part IV of the Convention, entitled 'Rights and Obligations of Parties', articulates further rights and obligations. It should be noted that, in this section, the accent is on rights; the obligations are only weakly binding and, in general, act more like incentives. Rights defined by the Convention are lightly conditioned and have no material requirements attached to their exercise. In contrast, there is only one article containing an obligation of binding nature.[152] Overall, the obligations are too generally worded and vague in designating their beneficiaries, or too cautious in their formulation, to constitute real limits.[153] The Convention does not require any real discipline from the states to protect and promote cultural diversity

[148] The list sets out the principal types of measures that parties may use, including support measures, which enable the economic dimension of cultural diversity to be taken into account, as well as content quotas. There is also a reference to public institutions, and measures on behalf of domestic independent cultural industries. Thus, all these measures gain legitimacy, subject to their being applied in a manner consistent with the objectives of the Convention.

[149] UNESCO, Convention on Cultural Diversity, Art 6.

[150] See 'Explanation of the Vote of the United States on the Convention on the Protection and Promotion of the Diversity of Cultural Expressions', Statement by Louise V Oliver, US Ambassador to UNESCO, available at http://www.america.gov/st/washfile-english/2005/October/20051020170821GLnesnoM3.670901e-02.html (last accessed on 15 June 2012); J-B Harelimana, 'Eye on Recent Trade versus Culture Decision Case, USA–China: Clash or Beautiful Friendship between the UNESCO Diversity Convention and International Economic Law?', available at http://www.multipol.org (last accessed on 15 June 2012).

[151] See RC Smith, 'The UNESCO Convention on the Protection and Promotion of Cultural Expressions: Building a New World Information and Communication Order?' (2007) 1 *International Journal of Communication* 24.

[152] Art 16 of the Convention obliges developed countries to facilitate cultural exchange with developing countries by granting preferential treatment to artists and other cultural professionals and practitioners, as well as cultural products from developing countries. This is the only provision in the Convention of binding nature that resembles the preferential treatment for developing countries.

[153] See Fabri, above n 116, 81–82.

beyond some vague 'shall endeavour' obligations that the states can construe and implement as mere discretionary rights to act.[154] As a result, the question of the resources needed to implement genuine policies for the protection and promotion of cultural diversity is by no means settled.

To close this critical glimpse of the Convention, it should be acknowledged that the unsatisfactory imbalance between rights and obligations set in the Convention mirrors a political reality: the majority of negotiators are not ready to accept more far-reaching commitments with regard to domestic cultural policies, nor substantive international cooperation.

4.7.4 Dispute Settlement Mechanism

The Convention provides a mechanism for the settlement of disputes based on negotiation, mediation or conciliation. The mechanism itself is compulsory for all parties, except those that declare at the time of ratification that they do not wish to be bound by such mechanism.[155] This mandatory conciliation procedure can be activated unilaterally, forcing a possible disagreement to be reviewed by a body composed of specialists in cultural matters. The appeal of this mechanism is that it may encourage states to submit their cultural disputes to cultural specialists.[156] The decision, even if not binding, may still be useful for proposing interpretations of the Convention, which has its share of ambiguities. Accordingly, the jurisprudence founded on cultural considerations may be developed over time.[157] This flexibility could be all the more important in that the Convention has to fit in with the rest of international law.

As a whole, the dispute settlement mechanism is more political than legal. The provisions set out in the Convention remain vague and inefficient; of particular note is the lack of a permanent dispute settlement body. If a party violates or abuses the Convention, there is no authoritative evaluation by a quasi-judicial organ. The lack of an effective dispute settlement mechanism is one of the most disappointing aspects of the Convention. Furthermore, the real problem lies in the absence of lock-in implementation mechanisms to promote cultural diversity. Imagine the type of disputes likely to arise out of a Convention with very few obligations: the Convention may not be in a position to cause a genuine conflict of laws, since a legal right can only conflict with a legal obligation if the right that contradicts the obligation can actually be exercised.

[154] See C Germann, 'Towards a Global Cultural Contract to Counter Trade Related Cultural Determination', in Obuljen and Smiers, above n 20, 281–82.

[155] UNESCO, Convention on Cultural Diversity, Art 25.

[156] See I Bernier and HR Fabri, 'Implementing the Convention', in Obuljen and Smiers, above n 20, 173.

[157] See Fabri, above n 116, 83.

This situation is in a sharp contrast with the dispute settlement mechanism set up in the WTO rules. The structure of rights and obligations in the WTO regime both constrains and enables Members' behaviour in important ways, and is given further momentum by its very powerful dispute settlement mechanism, as discussed in Chapter 6. The obligations to resolve disputes are particularly significant because they radiate out to all substantive obligations under the WTO.[158] Given the uneven rigour of dispute settlement, it is likely that the most contentious issues regarding cultural diversity will not arise within the setting of the UNESCO Convention but rather within the WTO framework. If that happens, it will be not only because of the WTO's strong dispute settlement mechanism, but also due to the duality of cultural products, which lays the foundation for the WTO to hear culture-related trade disputes.

4.7.5 A Preliminary Assessment of the Convention

The UNESCO Convention is a response to the urgent need for a cultural counterbalance to the WTO trade rules.[159] The Convention enshrines an unprecedented international consensus on a variety of guiding principles and concepts related to cultural diversity. It forms the basis of a new pillar of world governance in cultural matters. The first of its kind in international relations, the Convention serves the important role of raising awareness and alerting states to the risks and consequences of their commitments, especially in the area of trade liberalisation. The rapid conclusion and entry into force of the Convention demonstrates that it is well accepted in international community. By ratifying the Convention, states demonstrate their conviction that the protection of cultural diversity must be placed in the province of international law.

Reinforcing the focus on culture in the development agenda, the Convention first reaffirms the values established by the international community over the last few decades, particularly in fields of human rights and fundamental freedoms,[160] sustainable development, equal access

[158] See C Carmody, 'Creating "Shelf Space": NAFTA's Experience with Cultural Protection and Its Relevance for the WTO' (2007) 2(2) *Asian Journal of WTO & International Health Law and Policy* 287, 301–02. See also below Chapter 6.

[159] It is a mistake, however, to view the Convention as an instrument whose only goal is to ensure special treatment of culture in a trade framework. Indeed, if the purpose of the Convention were only to carve out culture from the WTO, it would have been a battle lost even before it began. In assessing the possible impacts of the Convention, it is necessary to learn about the broader debates that have been taking place over the past decade or more, which go beyond trade concerns. See Obuljen, above n 34, 20.

[160] One of the guiding principles laid down by the Convention is to respect human rights and fundamental freedoms. It is positively echoed in the general rule regarding rights and obligations, which makes 'universally recognised human rights instruments' one of the foundations on the basis of which states affirm their right to protect cultural diversity. See

and opportunities, and international solidarity and cooperation.[161] The new development lies in the way that the Convention links this value framework with cultural diversity, which, as indicated by the Convention's title, tops the list of its objectives. It is a breakthrough of the concept of cultural diversity as an internationally recognised policy choice—from being a rather obscure soft-law notion to a recognised legal concept. For the first time, the duality of cultural products is formally recognised in an international legal instrument. To achieve its goal of protecting and promoting cultural diversity, the Convention recognises the sovereign right of governments to formulate and implement cultural policy measures.

However, it should also be noted that most of the provisions in the Convention have little normative effect, as they impose neither genuine responsibilities nor binding commitments on the parties and involve no necessity or proportionality test to differentiate between licit and illicit measures.[162] The Convention is weakly binding, in strictly legal terms, with regard to their obligations. The Convention's purpose to serve as a counterbalance to the WTO rules is further undermined by the lack of enforceable substantive provisions and a strong dispute settlement mechanism.[163] Without a mechanism that could generate case law interpreting and defining these terms and concepts, the content of the Convention is likely to remain general and abstract. Even if it is justiciable, it is not sufficiently operational from the legal perspective, at least in a way that would be comparable to the WTO rules.[164] Nor is it clear that the interpretative and legislative solutions will help lessen the tension arising from jurisdictional overlap between the Convention and WTO rules.

Technically, the Convention will only be able to counterbalance the WTO if it acquires universal or quasi-universal status. In order to achieve this, the number of ratifications should at least equal the number of WTO Members. Nevertheless, the US's absence directly affects the standing and persuasive force of the Convention, given that the US is one of the world's leading economies, with a very successful cultural industry. With these deficiencies, one is concerned that the Convention is a mere declaration that lacks much legal effect beyond that already achieved by the Declaration in 2001.

UNESCO, Convention on Cultural Diversity, Art 2. The Convention links cultural diversity to human dignity and expressly states that it may not be used to limit the scope of human rights and fundamental freedoms. Idem, Art 5.

[161] Ibid, Arts 1–4. See also Hansen, above n 69, 116.

[162] For a critique of the Convention, see, eg K Acheson and C Maule, 'Convention on Cultural Diversity' (2004) 28 *Journal of Cultural Economics* 243.

[163] See M Hahn, 'A Clash of Cultures? The UNESCO Diversity Convention and International Trade Law' (2006) 9 *Journal of International Economic Law* 515, 532–33.

[164] See Germann, above n 154, 282–83.

4.8 CONCLUSION

This chapter reviews UNESCO's theories, strategies and approaches towards culture and cultural diversity since its inception. UNESCO constantly renews its theories and approaches with regard to culture and cultural diversity in order to accommodate changing social and political realities. Among its other missions, respect for cultural diversity has been a central cause for UNESCO. In order to accomplish this goal, UNESCO's task has been to define itself as the place where frameworks for thought and action concerning culture can be endlessly reinvented, so as to ensure that culture retains its unique and rightful place on the international scene.[165] Throughout its history, UNESCO has acted in many ways to tackle various aspects of cultural diversity: as a laboratory of ideas, a centre for the exchange of information and a standard-setting body, as well as a real catalyst for international cooperation. Through all of this, UNESCO has worked steadily towards promoting and protecting cultural diversity.

The 2005 UNESCO Convention on Cultural Diversity fills a lacuna in public international law in the sense that it successfully elevates cultural diversity as a valid, legitimate goal. The Convention is intended to function as a frame of reference, a normative instrument for policymaking, and a discussion forum for all countries that consider the preservation of cultural diversity to be an essential aspect of globalisation. Admittedly, objectives, principles and remedies have been formulated and established; that is an achievement. However, the effectiveness of the Convention still depends on how the Members make it work.

The exact impact of the Convention and its ambiguities require further observation and analysis. Whether the Convention will become a dynamic and significant part of international law or fade into irrelevance will largely depend on how it is used, on the monitoring of developments and on the interpretation of its provisions in response to real challenges.[166] UNESCO's ideals of cultural relations and cultural exchange require participation at the national level from Member States. The connection between national cultural practice and international relations has become clear. Therefore, subsequent state practice will show whether the Convention lives up to its mission. One key factor is the seriousness with which Members take their commitment to work together in other fora (especially the WTO framework) to coordinate with the objectives of the Convention. In this sense, the adoption of the Convention has by no means put the culture and trade debate to rest; rather, it has reignited it.

[165] See Stenou, above n 37, 138.
[166] See Obuljen, above n 34, 21.

5

The Treatment of Culture in the GATT/WTO (I): Theoretical and Legislative Framework

There are three ways to control the culture of another country: through political coercion, which is less feasible as the Communist collapse demonstrates; through acquisition, which is expensive; and through flooding . . . Flood the markets of other countries with your slick, cheap, heavily advertised product, swamping the local variety until it ceases to exist. Sylvia Fraser[1]

5.1 INTRODUCTION

AS OUTLINED IN Chapter 2, culture is an amorphous concept and may refer both to the less tangible notions such as 'ways of life' and to the concrete products of artistic endeavour. The idea of protecting cultural identity has existed for a long time, arguably going as far back as the origins of state sovereignty.[2] The modern doctrine of cultural protection, however, did not start to take shape until the establishment of free trade regimes.[3] Given the broad concept of culture, almost all trade policies or systems could have a cultural impact. I submit that the causes for the current conundrum of culture and trade can, to some extent, be attributable to the ambiguous status of cultural products under trade agreements,[4] represented by the gigantic World Trade Organization (the WTO) framework.

[1] S Fraser, 'Canada and the US: Too Close for Comfort?' *World Paper*, March 1992, 12.

[2] See DS Petito, 'Sovereignty and Globalization: Fallacies, Truth, and Perception' (2001) 17 *New York Law School Journal of Human Rights* 1139.

[3] See FS Galt, 'The Life, Death, and Rebirth of the "Cultural Exception" in the Multilateral Trading System: An Evolutionary Analysis of Cultural Protection and Intervention in the Face of American Pop Culture's Hegemony' (2004) 3 *Washington University Global Studies Law Review* 909, 911.

[4] Literally hundreds of trade agreements—bilateral, regional and multilateral—have been negotiated over recent decades, and their treatment of cultural products varies as greatly as

The only global institution endowed with the mission of liberalising trade, the WTO asserts trade rules applicable to cultural products and provides the best opportunity to examine the treatment of culture under a liberal trade regime. Structurally, the WTO regulates goods, services, intellectual property and other issues through different agreements with potential overlap.[5] As cultural products can be bifurcated into cultural goods and cultural services that are subject to different disciplines, this chapter presents separate discussions of the treatment of cultural products under the GATT, GATS, TRIPS and other WTO agreements where necessary. Beyond a textual analysis of treaty clauses, the chapter addresses the history of negotiation and debate around cultural products during the Uruguay Round[6] and the current Doha Round.[7]

Beginning with a description of the 'comparative advantage' theory underlying the GATT/WTO framework, this chapter touches upon the basic rationale for free trade and explores its application to cultural products. It then examines an institutional vicissitude that reveals a shift in *telos* from the Havana Charter to the WTO Agreement on Establishing the WTO. After examining the screen quotas asserted in GATT Article IV, the first article concerning cultural products, this chapter discusses the Uruguay Round negotiation on audiovisual services and the 'agreement to disagree' compromise finally reached. Thereafter, attention shifts to the general exceptions clauses both in the GATT and GATS, and analyses how these exceptions might apply to cultural products. Next, it explores anti-dumping, subsidies, safeguard measures and their applicability to cultural products. In an effort to elaborate a wide view of the treatment of culture in the GATT/WTO, the chapter also delves into several emerging issues, such as investment and intellectual property, and explores extent to which they can be employed to protect culture.

the historical circumstances, national interests and relative negotiating leverage of the parties. See CM Bruner, 'Culture, Sovereignty, and Hollywood: UNESCO and the Future of Trade in Cultural Products' (2008) 40 *International Law and Politics* 351, 366.

[5] WTO 'Understanding the WTO: The Agreements—Overview: A Navigational Guide', available at http://www.wto.org/english/thewto_e/whatis_e/tif_e/agrm1_e.htm (last accessed on 16 June 2012) (addressing the framework and structure of WTO agreements).

[6] The Round was launched in Punta del Este, Uruguay, in September 1986, followed by negotiations in Montreal, Geneva, Brussels, Washington, DC and Tokyo, resulting in over 20 agreements signed in Marrakech—the Marrakesh Agreement—in April 1994, and the establishment of World Trade Organization (WTO).

[7] The WTO Fourth Ministerial Conference held in Doha, Qatar, in November 2001, launched the first round of negotiation under the auspice of WTO. Ministerial Declaration, WTO Doc WT/MIN(01)/DEC/1, 20 November 2001. The Doha Round is also called 'The Development Round', emphasising a development agenda that contemplates the interests of developing countries. See WTO 'Doha Development Agenda: Negotiations, Implementation and Development—Gateway', available at http://www.wto.org/english/tratop_e/dda_e/dda_e.htm (last accessed on 16 June 2012).

5.2 COMPARATIVE ADVANTAGE THEORY AND ITS APPLICATION TO CULTURAL PRODUCTS

Prior to examining the treaty provisions concerning cultural products under the trade regimes, it is helpful to understand basic trade theory. This section studies the 'comparative advantage' theory underlying the modern trade regime and the problems associated with its application to cultural products.

5.2.1 The Theory of 'Comparative Advantage' Underlying Free Trade Regimes

The English economist David Ricardo (1772–1823) applied the simple exchange of 'wine-for-woolens' to illustrate the theory of comparative advantage.[8] The theory privileges economic efficiency[9] and wealth maximisation as its pre-eminent values; it posits that, in order to achieve high efficiency, countries need to trade the products they are most efficient at producing. Free trade permits the best products to flow across national borders at the lowest price, and therefore becomes a means to effectively allocate resources and increase productivity, economic efficiency and total world wealth.[10] From the perspective of global welfare,[11] trade is a positive-sum instead of a zero-sum game.[12] This, in turn, leads to the common claim that free trade benefits all people.[13]

[8] See generally, JR McCulloch, *The Works of D Ricardo* (2002).

[9] Economic efficiency depends on a function of 'factor endowments', including a country's natural resources, industrial base and the size and skills of its workforce. Ibid, 76.

[10] In this way, a country is better off because its lagging sectors' efficiency is improved or, more often, the resources used in comparatively inefficient sectors are moved to economic activities in which it holds a comparative advantage. See CE Baker, 'An Economic Critique of Free Trade in Media Products' (2000) 78 *North Carolina Law Review* 1357, 1381–82 (2000); see also United Nation Commission on Trade and Development (UNCTAD) & World Bank, *Liberalizing International Transactions in Services: A Handbook* (1994) 37; I Kónya, 'Modeling Cultural Barriers in International Trade' (2006) 14(3) *Review of International Economics* 494, 495.

[11] Welfare economics explain why trade liberalisation may enable each country to increase its 'total welfare' through trade. See KC Kennedy, 'A WTO Agreement on Investment: A Solution in Search of Problem?' (2003) 24 *University of Pennsylvania Journal of International Economic Law* 77, 94–95. Although free trade may initially cause some adjustment problems, in the long run, national and global welfare will increase. See generally D Irwin, *Against the Tide: An Intellectual History of Free Trade* (1996); A Sykes, 'Comparative Advantage and the Normative Economics of International Trade Policy' (1998) 1(1) *Journal of International Economic Law* 49.

[12] There will be both winners and losers from trade policy, but the efficiency gains of greater liberalisation can be redistributed to compensate the losers. See Galt, above n 3, 918.

[13] See P Krugman, 'Competitiveness: A Dangerous Obsession' (1994) 73 *Foreign Affairs* 2, 28–44; see also C Prestowitz et al, 'The Fight over Competitiveness: A Zero-Sum Debate?' (1994) 73 *Foreign Affairs* 4, 186–203; J Devlin, 'Canada and International Trade in Culture: Beyond National Interests' (2004) 14 *Minnesota Journal of Global Trade* 177, 197.

In modern times, Ricardo's theory has become a central tenet of international economic relations. It is widely held that the theory of 'comparative advantage' promotes specialisation in production and mutually beneficial exchange,[14] while intervention that distorts trade flow results in a loss of efficiency and a reduction in world welfare. Beginning in the 1980s, free trade policy was repackaged to include deregulation.[15] The end of the cold war marked the beginning of a period during which trade has replaced ideology as the focus of globalisation.[16] Based on the idea of 'comparative advantage', specialisation and economies of scale[17] become possible as the result of wide access to a barrier-free international market. This, in turn, leads to product and process innovation, further reducing costs. The international dominance of American cultural products exemplifies the US's strong comparative advantage in producing and selling cultural products.[18] Despite its complex distributional consequences, both over time and between and within countries and categories of workers, free trade is, by and large, widely understood to be good for consumers.[19]

It is worth noting that free trade is unlikely to produce global welfare

[14] See, eg JH Jackson, *World Trade and the Law of GATT* (1969) 9 (1969) (international trade is beneficial which is partly based on premises such as value of economies of scale, the utility of market exchange, and ideas stemming from the theory of comparative advantage).

[15] This not only ensures greater profits for corporations, but guarantees that there will be little government interference in the conduct of business. See M Wolf, 'Why Trade Liberalization Is a Good Idea' in JM Finger and A Olechowski (eds), *The Uruguay Round: A Handbook on the Multilateral Trade Negotiations* (1987) 14; G Yúdice, *The Expediency of Culture: Uses of Culture in the Global Era* (2003) 216.

[16] The idea behind economic globalisation is free market capitalism—the more market forces rule, the more an economy is open to trade and competition, the more efficient and flourishing the economy will be. See D Goulet, 'The Evolving Nature of Development in the Light of Globalization' (2004) 6 *Journal of Law & Social Challenges* 1, 11–13. See also Baker, above n 10, 1357–435; J Mandle, 'Globalization and Justice' (2000) 570 *Annals* 126.

[17] The notion of 'comparative advantage' relates to the theory of economies of scale. When nations specialise, they become more efficient in producing a product. If they can trade their products or services for the different products or services that other countries specialise in producing, then all parties involved will be better off. See, eg JH Jackson, *The Jurisprudence of GATT and the WTO: Insights on Treaty Law and Economic Relations* (2000) 418.

[18] Wildman and Siwek specify several factors that account for the international dominance of American cultural products, including a natural advantage in the domestic market, high-quality production values that travel well, and language. They refer to this advantage as a 'domestic opportunity advantage'. See SS Wildman and SE Siwek, *International Trade in Films and Television Programs* (1988) 68; Baker, above n 10, 1389–79. Furthermore, the US government has actively supported the domestic film industry in bilateral and multilateral trade agreements because of Hollywood's importance to the US economy, and also because of the MPAA's influential lobbying efforts. The MPAA has even intervened directly in bilateral trade relations to advance its interests. See K Lee, 'The Little State Department: Hollywood and the MPAA's Influence on US Trade Relations' (2008) 28 *Northwestern Journal of International Law & Business* 371. See also WM Shao, 'Is There No Business Like Show Business? Free Trade and Cultural Protectionism' (1995) 20 *Yale Journal of International Law* 105, 127–29 (discussing the US government–industry alliance).

[19] See P Sauvé and K Steinfatt, 'Towards Multilateral Rules on Trade and Culture: Protective Regulation or Efficient Protection?' in *Achieving Better Regulation of Services*, Conference Proceedings, AusInfo, Canberra (Productivity Commission and Australian National University, November 2000) 326.

without the institutional support of the GATT/WTO trade regime. The GATT/WTO has played a significant role, based on the theory of 'comparative advantage',[20] in fostering and enhancing trade, in particular by reducing protectionism and freeing up global markets.[21] A principal engine behind economic integration, trade will continue to be justified in terms of utilitarian economics and politics. Accordingly, trade regimes remain an essential feature of the international community and merit much of the credit for global transformation.

5.2.2 'Comparative Advantage' Applied to Cultural Products

Notwithstanding its theoretical contribution to world economy, it is worth noting that there are some limits to the theory of 'comparative advantage'. While the theory is attractive when considered from a strictly economic perspective, when it is examined more broadly, and difficult-to-quantify social concerns are taken into account,[22] the theory's potential repercussions give cause for a reassessment of its application and outcome. The pronounced orientation towards efficiency retained by the WTO often leads to a purely economic attitude towards the theory. However, there is an array of non-economic concerns that should be factored into international policy making.

The duality of cultural products gives rise to special considerations when 'comparative advantage' theory is applied to cultural products. Cultural products are characterised by initial high production costs paired with extremely low reproduction and distribution costs. This creates a strong incentive for marketing cultural products on a wider scale and is a market logic that has been exploited by producers to maximise their audience. However, cultural products exhibit both 'private' and 'public' characteristics.[23] The drive for efficiency through trade raises the question of

[20] Efficiency is clearly referred to in the Preamble of the WTO Agreement, which mentions improved living standards—'full employment and a large and steadily growing volume of real income and effective demand'—as policy objectives to be achieved through 'optimal use of the world's resources'. See generally the Marrakesh Agreement Establishing the World Trade Organization, in Final Act Embodying the Results of the Uruguay Round of Multilateral Trade Negotiations, 15 April 1994, 33 ILM 1125 (1994).

[21] For classical and contemporary arguments in support of free trade and the arguments for protectionism, see, eg R Bhala, *International Trade Law: Theory and Practice* (2001) 1–123; RB Stewart, 'International Trade and Environment: Lessons from the Federal Experience' (1992) 49 *Washington & Lee Law Review* 1329, 1330.

[22] See C Carmody, 'When "Cultural Identity Was Not At Issue": Thinking about Canada—Certain Measures Concerning Periodicals' (1999) 30 *Law & Policy International Business* 231, 234.

[23] See Baker, above n 10, 1377 (pointing out that markets work well only with respect to 'private goods', but because cultural products have a substantial public goods aspect, markets fail to produce enough, and sometimes favour less-desired products).

equality in cultural industries, since the economics of cultural products are different from those of conventional goods.[24]

Meanwhile, the theory of comparative advantage cannot adequately account for cultural production and consumption. On the one hand, cultural production is rooted in a particular culture. Inefficient producers of such cultural products may still be motivated to produce them, despite possible economic loss. On the other hand, price is not always the determinant factor in a consumer's purchasing decision.[25] Furthermore, cultural consumption is a social activity conducted in an informational setting. Culture products are prone to becoming transmitters of cultural values in the form of symbols, and have a considerable impact on combined individual and collective human behaviour. Free trade is not always capable of giving consumers more choices, since cultural premium is likely to diminish with increased exposure to foreign cultural products.[26] In this sense, free trade may even thwart the free choice of some citizens.

Comparative advantage theory also fails to consider 'externalities' generated by cultural products and the associated 'adjustment costs' problem. As W Ming Shao explains, 'externalities' occur when the market price of a product does not reflect all the benefits and costs associated with its production and consumption.[27] Cultural products generate both positive and negative externalities. Trade policies, however, remain 'producer driven', which serves the interests of powerful producers while tending to leave the just distribution of gains from trade and social adjustment problems to governments.[28]

In sum, free trade in cultural products based on the theory of 'comparative advantage' does not stand up well to scrutiny, given these products' value in a broader social context that is far beyond their immediate physical qualities.

[24] See F Pinto, 'Book Review—Blockbusters and Trade Wars: Popular Culture in a Globalized World' (2004) 7 *Journal of International Economic Law* 922.

[25] See, eg D Irwin, *Against the Tide: An Intellectual History of Free Trade* (1996) 51 (discussing the theory of comparative advantage); see also M Braun and L Parker, 'Trade in Culture: Consumable Product or Cherished Articulation of a Nation's Soul?' (1993) 22 *Denver Journal of International Law and Policy* 155, 174 (explaining that cultural products do not fit well within the theory of comparative advantage).

[26] Cultural premium refers to consumers' preference for local products, products in the local language or products concerning local issues. See Baker, above n 10, 1435.

[27] See Shao, above n 18, 137.

[28] There is an emerging anti-globalisation movement aimed at the irresponsibility of trade institutions that are not subject to oversight by any electorate. See P Sutherland et al, 'Challenges Facing the WTO and Policies to Address Global Governance' in GP Sampson (ed), *The Role of the World Trade Organization in Global Governance* (2001) 84.

5.3 AN INSTITUTIONAL EVOLUTION AND A SHIFT IN *TELOS*[29]

5.3.1 A Historical Narrative: From GATT to WTO

The dawn of modern global trading system dates back to 1947, when a group of countries, spearheaded by the US, undertook to rebuild the stagnant post-war economy.[30] A critical historical lesson from wars is that trade might facilitate and sustain peace by interlocking states in businesses, as Immanuel Kant observed.[31] The GATT was initially tied to the Havana Charter for International Trade Organization (ITO),[32] launched as one of the three pillars of a new post-war international economic order established by the Bretton Woods System.[33] Unfortunately, the Havana Charter remained as paper and ink in the archives.[34] Instead, the GATT, then negotiated and drafted within a United Nations Committee, was completed and approved in 1947 at a UN Conference on Trade and Employment in Havana.[35] Lacking the institutional support of the ITO, the first GATT Secretariat was staffed by the UN.[36]

[29] A *telos* (originating from the Greek, for 'end', 'purpose' or 'goal') means an end or purpose, in a fairly constrained sense used by philosophers such as Aristotle. It is the root of the term 'teleology', roughly the study of purposiveness, or the study of objects with a view to their aims, purposes or intentions.

[30] The absence of a regulatory framework of international trade was mentioned as one of the causes that led to two world wars, though the precise causal link between trade and politics is yet to be established. This view crystallised that the world's political organisations must keep pace with its economic organisations. See, eg JH Jackson, *The World Trading System: Law and Policy of International Economic Relations* (1989) 31; L Baudin, *Free Trade and Peace* (1939) 77–79; P Mavroidis, *The General Agreement on Tariffs and Trade: A Commentary* (2005) 3 (pointing out that the international community thought that the promotion of trade was one of the key ways to avoid conflict).

[31] See I Kant, 'Perpetual Peace: A Philosophical Sketch (1795)' in H Reiss (ed), *Kant's Political Writings* (1991) 93, 114; see also FR Tesón, 'The Kantian Theory of International Law' (1992) 92 *Columbia Law Review* 53, 76–77.

[32] UN Conference on Trade and Employment, Havana Charter for an International Trade Organization and Final Act and Related Document (hereinafter Havana Charter), UN Doc ICITO/1/4/1948, Havana, 11 November 1947.

[33] The 1944 United Nations Monetary and Financial Conference, commonly known as the "Bretton Woods Conference", was a gathering of 730 delegates from 44 nations at Bretton Woods, New Hampshire in July 1944, to regulate the international monetary and financial order after the conclusion of World War II. This conference envisaged three pillars towards the establishment of postwar economic order, including the International Monetary Fund (IMF), the International Bank for Reconstruction and Development (IBRD) and the International Trade Organization (ITO). For more on the background of GATT's birth and its early history, see, eg Jackson, above n 17, 20–34 (discussing the GATT and its troubled origin).

[34] See JH Jackson, 'National Treatment Obligations and Non-Tariff Barriers' (1989) 10 *Michigan Journal of International Law* 207, 207 (noting that the ITO did not come into existence).

[35] United Nations: General Agreement on Tariffs and Trade, 30 October 1947, 58 UNTS 187 (entered into force 1 January 1948).

[36] See, eg K Annan, 'Laying the Foundations of a Fair and Free World Trade System' in GP Sampson (ed), *The Role of the World Trade Organization in Global Governance* (2001) 20.

The GATT operated for almost half a century as a de facto international economic organisation, notwithstanding its birth as a merely provisional agreement. From 1948 to 1994, the GATT held eight rounds of trade negotiation and greatly facilitated international trade.[37] The last one, the Uruguay Round (1986–1994), created the WTO to succeed GATT in January 1995. The principal source of WTO law, the Marrakesh Agreement Establishing the World Trade Organization (hereinafter the WTO Agreement)[38] launches a legally formal institutional framework and overcomes GATT's birth defect.[39] More importantly, the WTO Agreement establishes a regime of 'single undertaking' by integrating all the agreements and associated legal instruments.[40] The old GATT is incorporated into this framework and forms a key part of it as GATT 1994.[41] The evolution from the Havana Charter to GATT 1947 and then to the WTO regime reveals two elements related to the discussions about the culture and trade conundrum to be described below.

The ITO was originally designed as a specialised agency under the auspice of the UN Charter to provide expertise in the field of trade. This design would have directly linked the ITO with other specialised UN agencies, including UNESCO.[42] Nevertheless, the proposed ITO never came into existence. Instead, the GATT had to enter into force on a provisional arrangement without institutional support. Neither was the GATT able to fulfil those requirements of a specialised agency contained

[37] The GATT/WTO created trade policy through negotiations called "Rounds". For more information on these rounds, see generally, TW Zeiler, *Free Trade, Free World* (1999); P Demaret, 'The Metamorphoses of the GATT: From the Havana Charter to the World Trade Organization' (1995) 34 *Columbia Journal of Transnational Law* 123.

[38] The Marrakesh Agreement Establishing the World Trade Organization, in Final Act Embodying the Results of the Uruguay Round of Multilateral Trade Negotiations, 33 ILM 1140 (1994). The WTO Agreement consists of a basic agreement and other agreements and understandings included in the annexes to the basic agreement. The substantive rules of WTO law are found in the agreements contained in Annex 1 and consist of three parts. Annex 1A contains 13 multilateral agreements on trade in goods, including General Agreement on Tariffs and Trade 1994 (GATT 1994), Annex 1B contains the General Agreement on Trade in Services (GATS), and the Agreement on Trade-Related Aspects of Intellectual Property Rights (the TRIP Agreement) constitutes Annex 1C.

[39] See, eg E-U Petersmann, 'The Transformation of the World Trading System through the 1994 Agreement Establishing the World Trade Organization' (1995) 6 *European Journal of International Law* 161, 189 (noting that the WTO Agreement 'completes the original design of the Bretton Woods system' and 'reduces the existing fragmentation of international economic law, by a 'global integration law' for international movements of goods, services, persons, investments and payments').

[40] WTO Agreement, Art II:1 and II:2.

[41] General Agreement on Tariffs and Trade 1994, 15 April 1994, Marrakesh Agreement Establishing the World Trade Organization, Annex 1A, Legal Instruments—The Results of the Uruguay Round, 1867 UNTS 187, 33 ILM 1153 (1994) (hereinafter GATT 1994).

[42] The other relevant UN agencies include the World Health Organization (WHO), the International Labor Organization (ILO), the World Intellectual Property Organization (WIPO) and the United Nation Commission on Trade and Development (UNCTAD).

in the UN Charter.[43] As a result, the GATT is founded in a legal vacuum within the UN system.

The WTO continues to retain this autonomy and remains outside the UN's direct institutional reach.[44] This institutional setting presents several difficulties, one of which is the challenge posed by more and more 'trade and . . .' issues.[45] More broadly, this concerns the 'policy discord' between trade and non-trade values, the accommodation among those competing norms,[46] the relationship between WTO rules and other international legal systems,[47] and the coherence in global economic policymaking.[48] It has become apparent that these trade linkage issues, including trade and culture, cannot be addressed by the WTO alone. Instead, the responsibility is incumbent on all WTO Members, which are often UN Members as well, to foster and strengthen more coherence of international law. In response to this challenge, the WTO has already realised and underscored the necessity to cooperate with the UN system.[49] Likewise, there must be cooperation between the WTO and UNESCO to effectively cope with the culture and trade issue.

[43] UN, Charter of the United Nations, 59 Stat 1031, TS 993, 26 June 1945, entered into force on 24 October 1945, Art 57.

[44] Relations of the GATT with the UN, UNGA-Doc A/AC 179/5, 9 March 1976. The autonomy mainly results from the unique efficiency of GATT in dealing with trade disputes, while the UN system as a whole is relatively inefficient in this regard. The International Court of Justice (ICJ), for instance, heard only 74 cases and delivered 61 judgments between 1946 and 1996, whereas the GATT accepted over 200 cases during the same period; and since it began work in early 1995, the WTO has so far accepted over 400 cases.

[45] The missions of many UN specialised agencies correspond to the present 'trade linkage debate' or 'trade and . . .' problems. See generally JP Trachtman, 'Trade and . . . Problems, Cost–Benefit Analysis and Subsidiarity' (1998) 9 *European Journal of International Law* 32; DP Steger, 'The Boundaries of the WTO: Afterword: The "Trade and . . ." Conundrum—A Commentary'(2002) 96 *American Journal of International Law* 135; RJ Neuwirth, 'The Fragmentation of the Global Market: The Case of Digital Versatile Discs (DVDs)' (2009) 27 *Cardozo Arts & Entertainments Law Journal* 409, 411–13 (pointing out the institutional separation and lack of coherence between UN system and WTO system which is manifest in their ability to tackle with trade linkage problems).

[46] John H Jackson discussed 'policy discord' issue between trade liberalisation and environmental protection and also pointed out that there are many similar policy discords at both the national and international levels that the governments must confront. See Jackson, above n 17, 414–18.

[47] See J Pauwelyn, 'The Role of Public International Law in the WTO: How Far Can We Go?' (2001) 95 *American Journal of International Law* 535.

[48] See GP Sampson, 'Greater Coherence in Global Economic Policymaking: A WTO Perspective' in AO Krueger (ed), *The WTO as an International Organization* (1998) 257.

[49] See, eg WTO 'Arrangement for Effective Cooperation with other Intergovernmental Organizations between the WTO and the UN: Communication from the Director-General', WTO Doc WT/GC/W/10 (3 November 1995).

5.3.2 The Transformation of the *Telos*

Sungjoon Cho aptly analyses the transformation of the *telos* of the global trading system through two constitutional moments:[50] the birth of the GATT and the launch of the WTO.[51] This shift in objective tends to explain the ever-changing ideological balance between trade value and social concerns.

The GATT focused its mission on tariff reduction and embraced a built-in pro-trade bias and an anti-protectionist *telos*.[52] Non-trade concerns were treated as mere exceptions to general obligations. In contrast, the WTO extends beyond the conventional, narrow anti-protectionist purpose to cover a broader range of matters relating to 'integration' and 'sustainable development'.[53] This integrationist *telos* assumes that the pro-trade bias will yield to a more mature and nuanced approach with a view to achieving the dual objectives of free trade and non-trade concerns.

The transformation of the *telos* from anti-protectionist to integrationist results from the need to respond more effectively to the challenges presented by the contemporary global economy. Coincidentally, this transformation aligns with a striking continuity between the general objectives embraced by the Havana Charter and those of the WTO Agreement.[54] Over six decades ago, the proposed Havana Charter was inscribed not only with free trade policy, but also with policies that have a wider social reach.[55] While the GATT focused on tariff reduction, the WTO is directed once more towards enhancing the Members' trading relations and mutual

[50] According to Professor Ackerman, every single polity or institution has its own critical moments of creation, transformation, and evolution. Those moments may be dubbed 'constitutional moments' in that they dictate the very identity of the polity or institution. See BA Ackerman, 'The Storrs Lectures: Discovering the Constitution'(1984) 93 *Yale Law Journal* 1013, 1071.

[51] In the case of a global trading community, Cho regards the creation of the GATT 1947 and the Uruguay Round culminating in the birth of the WTO in 1986–95 as two constitutional moments. See S Cho, *Free Markets and Social Regulation: A Reform Agenda of the Global Trading System* (2003) 3, 11.

[52] Concerning the use of the term 'pro-trade bias', see HL Schloemann and S Ohlhodd, 'Constitutionalization and Dispute Settlement in the WTO: National Security as an Issue of Competence' (1999) 93 *American Journal of International Law* 424, 451. With regard to the *telos* of anti-protectionism, see Cho, ibid, 3, 11.

[53] The WTO Agreement, Preface (addressing the optimal use of the world's resources in accordance with the objective of sustainable development and entering into reciprocal and mutually advantageous arrangements).

[54] See RJ Neuwirth, 'The Cultural Industries and the Legacy of Art IV GATT: Rethinking the Relation of Culture and Trade in Light of the New WTO Round', paper presented at the Conference 'Cultural Traffic: Policy, Culture, and the New Technologies in the European Union and Canada', Carleton University, 22–23 November 2002, 5.

[55] Havana Charter, Art 19 (concerning tariffs reduction, elimination of quantitative restrictions, etc). Compare Arts 2, 3, 7, 8, 11, 24 and 46 (addressing rules on employment and economic activity, economic development and reconstruction, monetary issues, and restrictive business practices, etc).

advantage and benefit.[56] This transformation of *telos* displays a coherent effort on the part of the proposed ITO and the WTO in delimiting both free trade and non-trade concerns.

In addition to the jurisprudential evolution of the GATT/WTO regime, the clash between trade and social values has also been addressed through legislative initiatives. According to Cho, a set of WTO side agreements has been developing a derivative jurisprudence in this area.[57] For instance, the Agreement on Sanitary and Phytosanitary Measures (SPS)[58] and the Agreement on Technical Barriers to Trade (TBT)[59] no longer marginalise legitimate domestic regulatory concerns as mere exceptions, but redefine them as 'rights'.[60]

It is particularly relevant that both the redefined *telos* and the derivative jurisprudence being developed by the WTO agreements provide a favourable environment to deal with trade and non-trade concerns, including the issue of trade and culture protection. The challenge becomes finding a way to take advantage of this development by designing suitable mechanisms to address the issues of concern. The following section examines the treatment of cultural products in the current regime and identifies the problems with the regime.

5.4 TRADE IN CULTURAL GOODS: GATT ARTICLE IV AND ITS LEGACY

To the extent that traded items are cultural goods, they are subject to GATT obligations,[61] the most important of which are most-favoured

[56] See, eg Jackson, above n 17, 17.

[57] See Cho, above n 51, 5–6.

[58] Agreement on Sanitary and Phytosanitary Measures, Annex 1A, Marrakesh Agreement Establishing the World Trade Organization, 15 April 1994, Final Act Embodying the Results of the Uruguay Round of Multilateral Trade Negotiations, Legal Instruments—Results of the Uruguay Round, 33 ILM 1140 (1994).

[59] Agreement on Technical Barriers to Trade, Annex 1A, Marrakesh Agreement Establishing the World Trade Organization, 15 April 1994, Final Act Embodying the Results of the Uruguay Round of Multilateral Trade Negotiations, Legal Instruments—Results of the Uruguay Round, 33 ILM 1140 (1994).

[60] The preambles to both the SPS and TBT preemptively emphasise that no country should be prevented from taking measures for the protection of human health or the environment. SPS Agreement, Art 2.1 (specifying that 'Members have the right to take sanitary and Phytosanitary measures necessary for the protection of human, animal or plant life or health . . .'). Such autonomous rights are juxtaposed with various obligations, such as SPS Arts 3.3 (scientific justification requirement) and 5.1 (risk assessment requirement).

[61] Annex IA (Multilateral Agreements on Trade in Goods) to the WTO Agreement deals with trade in goods and includes the GATT and 12 other agreements. Note that not all the agreements in Annex IA are equally applicable to trade in cultural goods. Some should be excluded as they deal with specific sectors of economic activity having nothing to do with culture or problems not frequently associated with culture.

nation (MFN) treatment,[62] national treatment[63] and prohibition against quantitative restrictions.[64] Exceptions apply to the extent determined by the relevant rules. The GATT does account for culture in a few ways, but on the whole addresses the subject little.[65] Culture is addressed principally in Article IV, which allows WTO Members, subject to certain conditions, to derogate from national treatment obligations by maintaining screen quotas for cinematograph films.[66] Article IV represents the first and only directly culture-related provision in trade agreements thus far; it serves as a convenient starting point to examine the treatment of culture under the GATT/WTO regime.

5.4.1 The Origin and Background of Article IV

The text of Article IV first appeared in Article 19 of the Havana Charter,[67] which survived the failure of the ITO. A mix of political, commercial, and cultural factors motivated the drafting of this article. During the early years of World War I, many countries imposed limitations on the importation of foreign films or reserved screen time for domestic films.[68] The late 1920s witnessed an overwhelming dominance of American films abroad,[69] an imbalance perceived as a vital threat to domestic producers and an infringement on access to the locally produced films which promote national culture. A series of actions were taken to restrict market access for foreign films.[70] Years later, after the end of World War II, the film

[62] GATT, Art I (General Most-Favored-Nation Treatment).

[63] GATT, Art III (National Treatment on Internal Taxation and Regulation).

[64] GATT, Art XI (General Elimination of Quantitative Restrictions).

[65] In light of the era in which the GATT came into being, it is fair to assume that the drafters had no intent to homogenise all culture through comparative advantage; they could not have foreseen the tremendous power of trade to reshape cultures. See Carmody, above n 22, 255–56.

[66] GATT Art IV(a) reads: If any contracting party establishes or maintains internal quantitative restrictions relating to exposed cinematographic films, such regulations shall conform to the following requirements: (a) Screen quotas may require the exhibition of cinematographic films of national origin during a specified minimum proportion of the total screen time actually utilised, over a specific period of not less than one year, in the commercial exhibition of all films of whatever origin, and shall be computed on the basis of screen time per theatre per year or the equivalent thereof. Compare GATT, Art III and Art XI.

[67] Final Act of the United Nations Conference on Trade and Employment: Havana Chapter for an International Trade Organization, Art 19 (Special Provisions Relating to Cinematograph Films).

[68] See Neuwirth, above n 54, 3.

[69] American films dominated theatrical screens throughout Europe after 1918, leading these countries to devise measures to restore the viability of their film industries and to promote the production and exhibition of locally made films. See K Acheson and C Maule, *Much Ado about Culture: North American Trade Disputes* 56 (1999).

[70] For instance, some governments provided funding to assist local production and used quotas and taxes to restrict trade, while some private actors boycotted foreign films. In the

industry in Europe faced a renewed surge of Hollywood films that could not been released during the war years.[71]

Accordingly, when the GATT was negotiated in 1947, one conflict that occupied the drafters' minds was the treatment of 'cinematograph films', the dominant film medium of the time. The underlying conceptual problem was whether films fell within the regulatory scope of trade or cultural policy. Eventually, a compromise was reached that brought films into a particular regime provided in Article IV. According to Professor Jackson, the objections of negotiators to the subordination of films to national treatment were based on the consideration that 'its regulation was more related to domestic cultural policies than to economic and trade [policies]' and that 'films are distinct from other goods, because their values is not in the film itself, but in its earning power'.[72] A review of the negotiation around Article IV indicates that the early negotiators took note of the potential cultural impact of trade regime and tried to mitigate that impact through Article IV.

5.4.2 The Scope of Article IV: Is an Evolutionary Interpretation Feasible?

The scope of Article IV is limited to cinematograph films and does not extend to other cultural products, such as television programmes, books and magazines.[73] Article IV explicitly calls on contracting parties to negotiate the limitation, liberalisation or elimination of screen quotas.[74] These negotiations have failed thus far, and the scope of Article IV remains unchanged. Since the adoption of GATT 1947, however, the importance of screen quotas has waned and the initial teleological reasoning behind

1940s, the UK imposed a 75% ad valorem duty on imported films. In response, the American distributors organised a boycott of the UK market. The positions taken by various parties at the time of the boycott illustrates the way in which interest groups lined up in connection with this cultural trade dispute. For more analysis on this dispute, see ibid, 56–59.

[71] See H Galperin, 'Cultural Industries in the Age of Free Trade Agreements' (1999) 24 *Canadian Journal of Communications* 49, 68.

[72] Jackson, above n 14, 293.

[73] The reason arguably lies in the limited tradability of printed materials and television programmes when the GATT was drafted. Historically, the first manifestations of the industrialisation of cultural production were in printed media. However, due to their lack of appeal to a critical mass of foreign consumers, the tradability of printed materials remained relatively low during the first half of the twentieth century. By contrast, film production and distribution as early as the 1920s revealed film's potential to reach a wider audience and highlighted its tradability. See WTO, *GATT Analytical Index: Guide to GATT Law and Practice* (1994) 191–93; see also ME Footer and CB Graber, Trade Liberalization and Cultural Policy' (2000) 3 *Journal of International Economic Law* 115, 116–17.

[74] GATT, Art IV(d).

Article IV seems to have been superseded by reality.[75] The rapid technological innovations and social changes of recent decades have subjected Article IV to renewed debates over its scope.

The growing international importance of television, beginning in the 1960s, first forced the question of whether Article IV should have purview over the television screening of motion pictures.[76] Textually, Article IV applies specifically to 'commercial exhibition' of films and should not apply to televised films, let alone made-for-television programming.[77] Furthermore, even if trade in television programmes constitutes trade in goods subject to GATT, it remains to be determined whether Article IV was written broadly enough to cover such types of trade.

A closer examination of the historical meaning of 'cinematograph films' might help address this line of inquiry. This hermeneutic challenge requires an understanding of the treaty interpretation rules contained in the authoritative Vienna Convention on the Law of Treaties (VCLT).[78]

One methodological issue that arises in relation to the interpretation of international law is the delineation of 'ordinary meaning' in regards to treaty terms.[79] Should it be the meaning intended when the treaty was concluded ('contemporaneous interpretation') or that at the moment the treaty is interpreted ('evolutionary interpretation')? The traditionally accepted resolution is the former, called 'the principle of contemporaneity'.[80] Joost Pauwelyn, however, maintains that the meaning of WTO terms should be determined at the time of interpretation—ie evolutionary interpretation.[81] This argument seems to reflect some part of

[75] See, eg H-KC Kim, 'Building the Korean Film Industry's Competitiveness: Abolish the Screen Quotas and Subsidize the Film Industry' (2000) 9 *Pacific Rim Law & Policy Journal* 71.

[76] Technological innovations introduced commercial television to people's life early in the 1950s. Ever since then, the US has attempted to amend the GATT to address restrictions imposed by other countries on television programming. JH Jackson, *World Trade and the Law of GATT* (1969) 294. A working group and several proposals for draft resolutions have yielded no result. See WTO, above n 73, 192; Harpen, above n 74, 168–70 (discussing the historical treatment of cultural industries under GATT).

[77] See S Cahn and D Schimmel, 'The Cultural Exception: Does it Exist in GATT and GATS Frameworks? How Does it Affect or is it Affected by the Agreement on TRIPS?' (1997) 15 *Cardozo Arts & Entertainments Law Journal* 281, 287–89.

[78] Vienna Convention on the Law of Treaties, 23 May 1969, entered into force on 27 January 1980. United Nations, Treaty Series, vol 1155, 331.

[79] VCLT, Art 31(1). It reads: 'A treaty shall be interpreted in good faith in accordance with the ordinary meaning to be given to the terms of the treaty in their context and in the light of its object and purpose'.

[80] See I Sinclair, *The Vienna Convention of the Law of Treaties* (1984) 124–25; see also GG Fitzmaurice, 'The Law and Procedure of the International Court of Justice 1951–4: Treaty Interpretation and Other Treaty Points' (1957) 33 *British Yearbook of International Law* 203, 212.

[81] Pauwelyn made three arguments in support of evolutionary interpretation as the rule, rather than the exception, when it comes to interpreting the WTO treaty. See J Pauwelyn, *Conflict of Norms in Public International Law—How WTO Law Relates to Other Rules of International Law* (2003) 268; see also J Pauwelyn, 'The Nature of WTO Obligations',

the recent WTO practice. For example, in *US—Shrimps*,[82] the Appellate Body interpreted the term 'exhaustible natural resources' in an evolutionary manner, invoking contemporary instruments in the place of those drafted more than 50 years ago.[83] The Appellate Body also frequently refers to the latest editions of dictionaries in identifying the 'ordinary meaning' of particular WTO terms.[84]

Alongside the challenge posed by rapid technological advancement, the issues surrounding the term 'cinematograph films' over 60 years ago have been further transformed into a broader question about the appropriate treatment of other cultural products under the WTO regime. Even if the issue of including television programmes within the scope of Article IV can be resolved through an 'evolutionary interpretation', the decision to extend the scope of Article IV to other cultural products may still be too ambitious to stand. Notwithstanding the plethora of interpretative tools, the question of whether to include other products under the aegis of 'cinematograph films' has no clear answer.

5.4.3 The Legacy Value of Article IV

The discussion above seems to lead to the dismaying expectation that the legacy of Article IV is a political mandate rather than a legal reality with regard to cultural protection. One might arrive at a different conclusion, though, through an analysis of the actual spirit and value of the Article.

In accordance with VCLT Article 31(1), the contemporary significance of Article IV can be better understood through an interpretation that accounts for its objective and purpose. Beyond its technical ramifications, Article IV reflects the original drafters' intention to exempt the film sector from trade disciplines in order to leave certain room for cultural objectives. In this sense, Article IV functions as a safety net for domestic films, and also establishes an authoritative precedent to deal with the issues arising from the conflict between culture and trade. It remains a convincing example of regulation that grants special treatment to certain types of cultural products.

available at http://www.jeanmonnetprogram.org/papers/02/020101-02.html#P303_88290 (last accessed on 16 June 2012).

[82] WTO, *United States—Import Prohibition of Certain Shrimp and Shrimp Products* (hereinafter WTO, *US—Shrimps*), complaints by India, Malaysia, Pakistan and Thailand (WT/DS58), Panel and Appellate Body Reports adopted on 6 November 1998.

[83] WTO, *US—Shrimps*, Report of Appellate Body, ¶¶129–131. The complainants in this case, however, expressed concern about the Appellate Body's use of an evolutionary interpretative approach, suggesting that this would lead to unpredictable results not anticipated in the pertinent agreements. See WTO, 'Minutes of Meeting Held in the Center William Rappard on 6 November 1998', WT/DSB/M/50 (14 December 1998) ¶¶3–14.

[84] See T Voon, *Cultural Products and the World Trade Organization* (2007) 137.

With a hermeneutic transformation that parallels the technological advancements in question, an evolutionary argument suggests that the balance between economic and cultural policies achieved in 1947 may provide some reference to deal with parallel issues in today's highly globalised world. In this interpretation, Article IV establishes a mandate for WTO Members to carefully consider the cultural industries' position within a trade regime.[85] Notably, this interpretation cannot lead to cultural products' exemption from trade obligations, though it can cautiously extend Article IV to apply to other cultural products and, as a possible first step, to the television broadcasting of films.

In short, GATT Article IV presents an example of negotiators' efforts to achieve a balanced trade regime. Despite a rapidly evolving media, the spirit of Article IV has not ceased to exist. We need to develop a feasible methodology for maximising its legacy value in addressing the current culture and trade conundrum.

5.5 TRADE IN CULTURAL SERVICES: AN OBSERVATION ON THE AUDIOVISUAL SECTOR

The Agreement on Trade in Services (GATS)[86] offers the first set of global legal rules for regulating trade in services. The audiovisual sector constitutes one sub-sector of communication services.[87] This section begins with a discussion of the negotiation on audiovisual sectors and the compromise finally reached during the Uruguay Round. It then briefly reviews the GATS's framework and its members' audiovisual commitments, followed by a comment on the treatment of culture under the GATS framework.

5.5.1 Understanding the Schism: A Tale of Two Histories

The conflict between trade and culture presented itself during the GATT Tokyo Round negotiation (1973–79) when the US complained that many countries subsidised domestic cinema and television production.[88] Indeed, the debate eventually gave way to an explicit negotiation about the specificity of cultural products in trade regimes. During the Uruguay Round, the prevailing arguments were over the treatment of audiovisual service,

[85] See Neuwirth, above n 54, 20.

[86] General Agreements on Trade in Services, 15 April 1994, Marrakesh Agreement Establishing the World Trade Organization, Annex 1B, Legal Instruments—The Results of the Uruguay Round, 1869 UNTS 183, 33 ILM 1167 (1994).

[87] WTO, 'GATS Services Sectoral Classification List, Note by the Secretariat', MTN. GNS/W/120 (10 July 1991).

[88] See I Bernier, 'Cultural Goods and Services in International Trade Law' in D Browne (ed), *The Culture/Trade Quandary: Canada's Policy Options* (1998) 108–09.

its relation to GATT Article IV,[89] and the inclusion of the audiovisual sector into trade regimes. The main actors in this battle are well identified: the request for an unfettered, open market comes from the US, while Canada and the EU—particularly France—are the main proponents of cultural protection.[90]

Both Canada and the EU contend that trade agreements should consider 'cultural exception' in order to achieve more coherence in trade policymaking.[91] Canada is itself a consistently vigorous proponent of free trade and actively promotes market liberalisation through trade agreements, including the WTO and NAFTA. When it comes to culture, however, Canada persistently tries to preserve certain room for protectionist measures.[92] Likewise, the EU generally views 'cultural exception' as a necessary measure to protect European identity. Both lobbies from European cultural industries and French political movements make concession in this regard difficult.[93] In contrast, the US challenges the French and Canadian position, calling it an excuse for economic protection of domestic industries, and advocates the inclusion of the audiovisual sector in the GATS.[94]

5.5.2 A Compromise: Agreement to Disagree

The EU and Canada define three strategies to protect their audiovisual industry. 'Cultural exclusion', or 'off-the-table exemption of culture', is seen as the most radical approach. It was mentioned but deemed unrealistic and never seriously pursued. Two other options—the 'cultural specificity' approach and a 'cultural exception' to trade—were discussed within the scope of the GATS.[95] Neither of them succeeded.

In the final stage of negotiations, the audiovisual sector remained

[89] This question mainly concerns whether trade in television programmes constitutes trade in goods or trade in services. Different countries hold divergent views. The US, for instance, applies a 'real purpose of the transaction' test and believes that trade in television programmes constitutes trade in goods. See Shao, above n 18, 111–13; *American Multi-Cinema, Inc v City of Westminster*, 910 P 2d 64, 65–66; *May Broad Co v Boehm*, 490 NW 2d 203, 207–09. In the EU, on the other hand, such trade is classified as trade in services.

[90] See Bernier, above n 88, 108–11.

[91] See JD Donaldson, 'Television without Frontiers: The Continuing Tension between Liberal Free Trade and European Cultural Integrity' (1996) 20 *Fordham International Law Journal* 90.

[92] See B Schwartz, 'Canadian Cultural Policy in a World Context' (2002) 2 *Asper Review of International Business & Trade Law* 1, 1.

[93] See JB Prowda, 'US Dominance in the "Marketplace of Culture" and the French "Cultural Exception"' (1997) 29 *New York University Journal of International Law & Policy* 193, 199–205 (French cultural identity versus the US movie business).

[94] See, eg J Sinclair, 'Culture and Trade: Theoretical and Practical Considerations' in EG McAnany and KT Williams (eds), *Mass Media and Free Trade: NAFTA and Cultural Industries* (1996) 39; see also Braun and Parker, above n 25, 187–88.

[95] See Cahn and Schimmel, above n 77, 293.

on the table and no consensus was reached among negotiators.[96] The impasse even threatened to derail the GATS negotiation, which would have unavoidably endangered the entire Uruguay Round.[97] The failure to conclude the GATS would hurt the American economy hugely and be a painful loss for the US[98] Likewise, neither Canada nor the EU could afford to unravel many years of negotiation. The political will of the negotiators again proved strong enough to overcome this impasse. The negotiators finally shelved their differences and sought a common resolution to the GATS deal.[99] The outcome, euphemistically hailed as the 'agreement to disagree',[100] pulls audiovisual sector into the GATS regime, but allows WTO Members to maintain exclusions in market access and national treatment.[101] The cultural exception, excluded in principle, was accepted de facto on a temporary basis.

The Uruguay Round failed to produce any substantive agreement concerning cultural sectors. On the one hand, it left the text and scope of GATT Article IV untouched. On the other hand, no cultural exception per se emerges from the text of the GATS. The victory that the EU and Canada won constitutes a temporary exclusion of the sector from the GATS liberalisation process. The compromise does not offer a long-term solution to the trade and culture contest.

[96] See CR Karpe, 'European Cultural Protectionism and the Socioeconomic Forces that will Defeat it' (1995) 5 *Indiana International & Comparative Law Review* 425, 425–26.

[97] The situation was also partly attributable to some negotiating mistakes, such as the late submission of the EC's final position and the lack of preparation by both side. See KF Falkenberg, 'The Audio-Visual Sector' in JHJ Bourgeois et al (eds), *The Uruguay Round Results: A European Lawyer's Perspective* (1995) 429, 432.

[98] The entertainment industry is the US's second largest export sector and generates billions of dollars annually. JM Grant, '"Jurassic" Trade Disputes: The Exclusion of the Audiovisual Sector from the GATT' (1995) 70 *Indiana Law Journal* 1333, 1334–35. In the meantime, GATS as a whole is unquestionably more crucial for the US than any single industrial sector. As former US President Bill Clinton rightly put it, 'removing audiovisual from the negotiations was certainly better than leaving a weak agreement intact or catering the whole round over it, because there is just too much aggregate economic benefit to the US from the overall tariff reductions to not trying to keep the round intact'. 'Clinton Says Emerging Uruguay Round Pact is in the US Interest Despite Shortcomings', *International Trade Daily*, 16 December 1993, D5.

[99] See T W. Chao, 'GATT's Cultural Exemption of Audiovisual Trade: The United States May Have Lost the Battle but not the War' (1996) 17 *University of Pennsylvania Journal of International Economic Law* 1127, 1152–53; see also J Smiers, The Curiosity of A Cultural Omnivore, in N Obuljen and J Smiers (eds), *UNESCO's Convention on the Protection and Promotion of the Diversity of Cultural Expressions: Making It Work* (2006) 13–15.

[100] This formula was used by Sir Leon Brittan and Mickey Kantor at a joint press conference held on 13 December 1993. See Cahn and Schimmel, above n 77, 291–301 (addressing the status of culture in the Uruguay Round). See also StE Palka, 'Canada's Cultural Industries, the United States, and Trade Law: Tension, Conflict, and Possibilities' (2000) 10 *Windsor Review of Legal and Social Issues* 105, 121.

[101] See KL Kessler, 'Protecting Free Trade in Audiovisual Entertainment: A Proposal for Counteracting the European Union's Trade Barriers to the US Entertainment Industry's Exports' (1995) 26 *Law & Policy International Business* 563, 574–79 (providing an overall review on the Uruguay Round negotiations concerning audiovisual trade particularly between the EU and the US).

5.5.3 The Treatment of the Audiovisual Service under the GATS

While heavily influenced by the GATT, the GATS has a different normative set-up and creates its obligations more modestly.[102] Unlike the obligations in the GATT, market access[103] and national treatment[104] are not general obligations, and they are only granted if and to the extent that the specific commitments are listed in a member's particular schedule of commitments.[105]

An analysis of WTO Members' commitments reveals that audiovisual services is one of the sectors with the lowest number of Members with commitments (30, as of 31 March 2011). Commitments tend to be more numerous in film-related services than in TV and radio-related services.[106] This implies that most WTO Members feel the necessity to exempt themselves from the GATS obligations in audiovisual sectors. The audiovisual sector is also characterised by a high number of exemptions to MFN treatment through which they may discriminate between other Members, provided such differential treatment is listed in the Annex on Article II MFN Exemptions. There are over 30 MFN exemptions covering the audiovisual sector, which relate, for example, to film co-productions.[107]

In short, though the GATS does not contain any specific exception for cultural products, it leaves existing domestic trade-restricting measures untouched. WTO Members are thus able to secure most aspects of its cultural policy measures under the regime.

[102] For an analysis of the GATS structure, see, eg R Leal-Arcas, 'The Resumption of the Doha Round and the Future of Services Trade' (2007) 29 *Loyola of Los Angeles International and Comparative Law Journal* 339, 349–77.

[103] GATS, Art XVI (Market Access).

[104] GATS, Art XVII (National Treatment).

[105] See, eg R Adlung, 'Services Negotiations in the Doha Round: Lost in Flexibility?' (2006) 9 *Journal of International Economic Law* 865, 879–81. A modification of the specific schedules of commitment is possible but burdensome. It is thus argued that GATS is not flexible enough to absorb the need for change resulting from technological developments. See CB Graber, 'The New UNESCO Convention on Cultural Diversity: A Counterbalance to the WTO?' (2006) 9 *Journal of International Economic Law* 553, 568–70.

[106] As of now, only Albania, the Central African Republic and the US have entered full commitments with regard to all six sub-categories of audiovisual services. Twenty-one other Members have entered some commitments, most notably the major film producers, such as India, Hong Kong and New Zealand. For consolidated information on countries' commitments and exemptions related to audiovisual services, go to http://tsdb.wto.org/default.aspx (last accessed on 16 June 2012). For the commitments of a specific WTO Member, go to 'Jump to a specific sector for a given Member', select 'Audiovisual services' from the sector dropdown list, select the Member of interest and click 'Go'. To see a table showing which Members have made commitments in audiovisual services, choose 'See which Members have made commitments in a specific sector', select 'Audiovisual services' and click 'Go'. For a summary of this issue, see WTO Council for Trade in Services, 'Audiovisual Services, Background Note by the Secretariat', S/C/W/40 (15 June 1998), ¶¶24–68 and Table 9.

[107] GATS, Art II. See also Adlung, above n 105, 868–70.

5.5.4 Doha Services Negotiation: Culture Has Not Been a Focal Point

The GATS mandates that its members enter into successive rounds of negotiations 'with a view to achieving a progressively higher level of liberalisation' in a built-in agenda.[108] Debate about the regulatory position of audiovisual services was part of the new services negotiations, which began in January 2000. The principles of trade in audiovisual services are contained, as for all services, in the GATS. The Doha Ministerial Conference held in November 2001 made the service negotiations part of 'single undertaking' under the Doha Development Agenda.[109]

The GATS provides that 'process of liberalisation shall take place with due respect for national policy objectives in future negotiations'.[110] This is of particular relevance to national policies directed towards cultural protection. However, although the WTO rules applying to the technologically sophisticated audiovisual sector lag somewhat behind the fast pace of change in a digitally networked society, this sector has not been a hot topic in the Doha negotiation. The Doha Round has seen no clear mention of either general cultural concerns or specific culture-related issues. Nor has there been any sign of juridical recognition of cultural specificity during the Doha negotiations.

Thus far, only four proposals on audiovisual services have been submitted by Member States.[111] These proposals generally recognise that audiovisual services have both commercial and cultural components. They try to reconcile governments' economic and cultural considerations within the GATS framework. While the US paper acknowledges the special cultural characteristics of audiovisual media and the public concern for preserving and promoting cultural values and identity, it also attempts to seek clear, dependable and predictable trade rules for this sector.[112] The Swiss paper is of a more general nature, and calls for both a cultural diversity safeguard and an annex to the GATS on audiovisual issues.[113] The Brazilian paper stresses the goal of promoting progressive liberali-

[108] GATS, Art XIX (Negotiation of Specific Commitments).

[109] Most information on the current services negotiation can be found at http://www.wto.org/english/tratop_e/serv_e/s_negs_e.htm (last accessed on 16 June 2012). For a review of service negotiations, see, eg Adlung, above n 105, 865.

[110] GATS, Art XIX(2). Note that the Preamble to GATS also mentions 'giving due respect to national policy objectives'.

[111] WTO Council for Trade in Services Special Session, 'Communication from Switzerland—GATS 2000: Audio-visual Services', S/CSS/W/74 (4 May 2001); WTO Council for Trade in Services Special Session, 'Communication from Brazil—Audiovisual Services', S/CSS/W/99 (9 July 2001); WTO Council for Trade in Services Special Session, 'Communication from Hong Kong China, Japan, Mexico, The Separate Customs Territory of Taiwan, Penghu, Kinmen and Matsu, and United States—Joint Statement on the Negotiation on Audiovisual Services', TN/S/W/49 (30 June 2005).

[112] WTO Council for Trade in Services Special Session, 'Communication from the United States—Audiovisual and Related Services', S/CSS/W/21 (18 December 2000).

[113] WTO Doc S/CSS/W/74, above n 111.

sation of the audiovisual sector while ensuring governmental autonomy to preserve and promote cultural identity and diversity.[114] The joint statement by several other Members urges all WTO Members to include audiovisual commitments in their offers.[115]

These proposals and the discussions that followed their introduction touch on a number of classification and regulatory issues, but they focus mostly on the issue of market access. Delegations calling for further liberalisation lament the low number of Members with commitments in the audiovisual sector and highlight the key barriers that they wish to see reduced: content quotas, economic needs tests, ownership restrictions, and nationality–residency requirements. MFN exemptions, which are particularly numerous in this sector, are also raised in these discussions.

In recapitulating the status quo of cultural services featuring audiovisual sectors under the WTO regime, we must first note that the treatment of audiovisual services was debated as an 'all-or-nothing' issue, an attitude which fails to reflect its whole reality. The facts remain that very few WTO Members have made commitments despite the growing economic importance of audiovisual sectors. In the current Doha Round, the specificity of cultural products remains an unsolved question, an impasse that was inherited from the previous Round. The battle during the Uruguay Round may have left the negotiators with too much pressure to deal with the issue again so soon.[116] Members might now be wise to temporarily shelve the disputes and wait for an opportune time to resume the discussion.

5.6 GENERAL EXCEPTION CLAUSES

The dichotomy between trade-related obligations and regulation-related exceptions reflects one of the GATT's fundamental characteristics.[117] Given that unfettered trade may be at odds with essential societal values, the WTO law provides for general exceptions to reconcile trade with

[114] WTO Doc S/CSS/W/99, above n 111.

[115] WTO Doc TN/S/W49, above n 111.

[116] In order to reserve policy space for domestic cultural policy, the EC/EU has refused to table any proposals for further liberalisation of audiovisual services in the realm of the WTO. In its resolutions of 1 December 2005 and 4 April 2006 on the Doha Round and on the WTO Ministerial Conference, the European Parliament called for basis public services—such as audiovisual services—to be excluded from liberalisation under the GATS negotiations. For more discussion, see, eg M Roy, 'Audiovisual Services in the Doha Round: Dialogue de Sourds, The Sequel?' (2005) 6(6) *Journal of World Investment and Trade* 923.

[117] Professor Donald McRae described this pro-trade dichotomy as a 'hierarchy' between substantive obligations and exceptions to those obligations. See DM McRae, 'GATT Article XX and the Appellate Body' in M Bronckers and R Quick (eds), *New Directions in International Economic Law: Essays in Honor of John H Jackson* (Kluwer Law International, 2000) 232.

non-trade concerns.[118] Both GATT Article XX—drafted in the 1940s as a revision of the Havana Charter[119]—and GATS Article XIV include broadly worded exception clauses, which may provide certain linkages between trade and cultural protection. In addition to a chapeau, these two articles both contain a list of concrete exceptions to a member's trade obligations, which allow the members to deviate from their obligations in pursuit of certain social values.[120]

Though none of these exceptions explicitly refers to cultural protection, the exceptions of particular relevance to culture are contained in GATT Article XX(a), (d) and (f), and GATS Article XIV(a) and (c). The following section explores whether and how these exceptions can apply to cultural products.

5.6.1 Public Morals Exception

GATT Article XX(a) and GATS Article XIV(a) allow members to take measures 'necessary to protect public morals', subject to compliance with the chapeau.[121] The term 'public morals' is not defined, but *US—Gambling*[122] provides some guidance. In this case, a WTO panel recognises the potential relevance of cultural concerns to this exception.[123]

The 'public morals' exception may provide certain room to preserve domestic cultural values, since a cultural measure is often motivated by both cultural and moral concerns. At the same time, however, this makes it difficult to establish that such a measure is necessary to protect public morals alone. However, if a cultural concern were itself deemed to reflect the standards of public morality, this exception would allow

[118] As Trachtman has pointed out, a variety of 'trade-off devices' such as general exception clauses may assist in resolving 'trade and . . .' problems. See Trachtman, above n 45, 35.

[119] Final Act of the United Nations Conference on Trade and Employment: Havana Chapter for an International Trade Organization, Art 23 (Exceptions to the Non-Discrimination Principle).

[120] GATT, Art XX (general exceptions); GATS, Art XIV (general exceptions). Note that the list of GATS exceptions contains fewer public interests serving as grounds for justification. For a survey of GATS exception clauses, see P Van Den Bossche, 'Free Trade and Culture: A Study of Relevant WTO Rules and Constraints on National Cultural Policy Measures', Maastricht Faculty of Law Working Paper No 2007-4 (2007) 116–24.

[121] GATT, Art XX(a). With slight differences, the GATS exception also includes those measures 'necessary to maintain public order', which may be invoked only when a genuine and sufficiently serious threat is posed to one of the fundamental interests of society. GATS, footnote 5.

[122] WTO, *United States—Measures Affecting the Cross Border Supply of Gambling and Betting Services* (hereinafter *US—Gambling*), WT/DS285/R, 10 November 2004.

[123] WTO, *US—Gambling*, Report of the Panel, WT/DS285/R, ¶6.461 (We are well aware that there may be sensitivities associated with the interpretation of the terms 'public morals' and 'public order' in the context of Art XIV. In the Panel's view, the content of these concepts for Members can vary in time and space, depending upon a range of factors, including prevailing socials, cultural, ethical and religious values).

a WTO Member to ban the import of products considered offensive to local cultural values or traditions.[124] In a recent case, *China—Publication and Audiovisual Products*, the Panel recognises that a WTO Member has sovereign rights to determine the appropriate level of protection of the values and objectives covered by Article XX(a).[125]

In one way or another, though, WTO tribunals would have to interpret this exception broadly enough to cover cultural measures. They may be reluctant to do so because of the risk of abusing the exception, not only in relation to cultural products, but also in other unanticipated areas.[126] In consideration of this risk, it is advised that international human rights law fill the gap and furnish a valuable basis for understanding the notions of 'public morals' and 'public order'. As discussed in Chapter 2, culture is an essential component of human rights. Although there is no consensus that the UDHR and the ICESCR reflect customary international law,[127] these human rights instruments do indicate that cultural rights represent a fundamental interest of society.[128] In the same vein, the UN High Commissioner for Human Rights has contended that, although 'human rights should not be used as disguised barriers to trade', 'any judgment of the trade-restrictiveness of a measure should take into account States' obligations under human rights law'.[129] This includes the obligation to full realisation of cultural rights.[130] A UN High Commissioner for Human Rights report calls for a 'human rights approach to trade' which, among other things, sets the promotion and protection of human rights as objectives, rather than exceptions, of trade liberalisation.[131]

Scholarly contributions offer a corresponding response to these documents. Petersmann holds that human rights and free trade serve complementary functions and that, accordingly, there is no conflict

[124] See C Feddersen, 'Focusing on Substantive Law in International Economic Relations: The Public Morals of GATT's Article XX(a) and "Conventional" Rules of Interpretation' (1998) 7 *Minnesota Journal of Global Trade* 75, 115.

[125] See below Chapter 6.3.

[126] See Voon, above n 84, 106.

[127] See, eg E-U Petersmann, 'Time for a United Nations "Global Compact" for Integrating Human Rights into the Law of Worldwide Organizations: Lessons from European Integration' (2002) 13(3) *European Journal of International Law* 619, 619; see also P Alston, 'Resisting the Merger and Acquisition of Human Rights by Trade Law: A Reply to Petersmann' (2002)13(4) *European Journal of International Law* 815, 820.

[128] See Voon, above n 84, 158.

[129] UN Commission on Human Rights, Sub-Commission on the Promotion and Protection of Human Rights, 'Liberalization of Trade in Services and Human Rights: Report of High Commissioner', E/CN.4Sub.2/2002/9 (25 June 2002), annex 14, 58.

[130] More specifically, the High Commissioner states that the application of national treatment provisions should not reduce states' capacity to use local content requirements in the interests of promoting cultural rights. UN Commission on Human Rights, Human Rights, Trade and Investment, 'Report of the High Commissioner for Human Rights', E/CN.4/Sub.2/2003/9, ¶3 (2 July 2003).

[131] UN Doc E/CN.4/Sub.2/2002/9, above n 129.

between them in principle.[132] Voon suggests that the connection between cultural products and cultural rights might assist in demonstrating the necessity of invoking the measures.[133] This may also reduce some of the suspicion that cultural policies represent nothing but protectionism. However, before the 'public morals' exception can provide an avenue for human rights to influence the interpretation of WTO law,[134] we need first to deal with the difficulties in identifying the specific human rights that might be encapsulated within 'public morals'. 'Public morals' and 'public order' are precisely the types of concept that are evolutionary by definition;[135] current international law on culture may cause uncertainty about the ordinary meaning of these words under Article 31(1) of the VCLT. The ambiguity of the terms may lead to little hope of solving the problem associated with cultural products.

5.6.2 Securing Compliance with Laws or Regulations

The exceptions provided in GATT Article XX(d) and GATS XIV(c) allow the members to maintain measures 'necessary to secure compliance with laws or regulations which are not inconsistent with GATT (or GATS) provisions'. WTO cases have demonstrated a two-step approach in justifying a measure under the exception. First, the measure must be designed to 'secure compliance' with laws or regulations that are not themselves inconsistent with WTO provisions. Secondly, the measure must be 'necessary' to secure such compliance.[136]

Two issues may arise from applying this exception to cultural measures. First, the challenge of defining 'compliance' presents itself. In *Canada—Periodicals*,[137] the US claimed that Canada violated GATT Article XI

[132] See E-U Petersmann, 'The "Human Rights Approach" Advocated by the UN High Commissioner for Human Rights and by the International Labor Organization: Is It Relevant for WTO Law and Policy?' in E-U Petersmann (ed), *Reforming the World Trading System: Legitimacy, Efficiency, and Democratic Governance* (2005) 365–79.

[133] See Voon, above n 84, 149.

[134] United Nations, Office of the United Nations High Commissioner for Human Rights, Human Rights and World Trade Agreements, 'Using General Exception Clauses to Protect Human Rights', HR/PUB/05/5 (9 June 2005) ¶4. Regarding the relationship between human rights and liberalising trade in services, the UN High Commissioner for Human Rights issued a report stating that the protection of public morals, life and privacy are familiar themes to human rights law and their inclusion in GATS could be seen as a link to the promotion and protection of human rights. This link could be relevant in determining the appropriate sources of international law relevant to the interpretation of the provisions of GATS in future rulings by the WTO Dispute Settlement Body. UN Doc E/CN.4/Sub.2/2002/9, above n 129.

[135] See Sinclair, above n 80, 139; UN Doc HR/PUB/05/5, ibid, ¶¶ 7–8.

[136] See, eg WTO, *Korea—Measures Affecting Imports of Fresh, Chilled and Frozen Beef* (hereinafter *Korea—Beef*), Appellate Body Report, ¶157; WTO, *Dominican Republic—Import and Sale of Cigarettes*, Appellate Body Report, ¶65.

[137] WTO, *Canada—Certain Measures Affecting Periodicals* (hereinafter *Canada—Periodicals*), complained by the United States on 11 March 1996, WT/DS31.

because Tariff Code 9958 imposes quantitative restrictions on the importation of foreign split-run periodicals. Canada argued that this measure could be justified as it intended to secure the attainment of the objectives of Section 19 of the Income Tax Act. These two measures are an integral part of a package of measures with a single objective: diverting advertising expenditures to Canadian periodicals.[138] The Panel, however, decided that, while both measures share the objective of promoting Canadian periodicals, they are not a single, indivisible package.[139] In explaining its narrow reading of Article XX(d), the Panel raised the concern that a broad interpretation would open a loophole whereby virtually any internal regulation could be justified on this basis. The Panel noted that it was not 'passing judgment on the policy objectives of the Canadian measure regarding periodicals'.[140] Consistent with the way that Article XX(d) has been interpreted in past rulings, this decision indicates that, in general, it is hard to claim that two measures are intended to secure 'compliance' with each other merely on the grounds that they share a single legislative objective.

Secondly, the task of determining the scope of 'laws and regulations' arises. Is its scope limited to domestic laws or regulations, or does it include 'regional or international laws or regulations' and 'domestic laws or regulations implementing non-WTO international obligations'? The answer to this question determines how other international laws might relate to this exception. In *Mexico—Tax on Soft Drinks*,[141] the US alleged that Mexico's tax on the import and transfer of soft drinks and syrups violates national treatment.[142] Mexico responded that the tax is justified as a measure necessary to secure US compliance with its NAFTA obligations.[143] This raises an interesting question: can a WTO Member justify a WTO-inconsistent policy measure by claiming that its intent is to secure another Member's compliance with an obligation under an international convention, such as the UNESCO Convention? The Appellate Body made it clear that the 'laws or regulations' in Article XX(d) include both rules that form part of the domestic legal system of a WTO Member and rules deriving from international agreements that have been incorporated into the domestic legal system of a WTO Member or have a direct effect according to that Member's legal system.[144] This is a necessary clarification, especially given states' common practice of implementing an

[138] WTO, *Canada—Periodicals*, Report of the Panel, ¶3.5.

[139] Ibid, ¶5.9.

[140] Ibid, ¶¶5.9, 5.11.

[141] WTO, *Mexico—Tax Measures on Soft Drinks and Other Beverages* (hereinafter *Mexico—Beverages*), WT/DS308, complained by the United States, request for consultation received on 14 March 2004, Panel Report circulated on 7 October 2005, and Appellate Body Report circulated on 6 March 2006.

[142] WTO, *Mexico—Beverages*, Report of the Panel, ¶3.1.

[143] Ibid, ¶8.162.

[144] WTO, *Mexico—Beverages*, Appellate Body Report, ¶79.

international convention either by granting it direct effect or by incorporating it into their domestic legal system.

In the context of cultural protection, a Member might wish to invoke this exception to justify domestic laws or regulations that implement aspects of the UNESCO Convention. At first glance, the Appellate Body's decision seems to indicate that Article XX(d) could play an important role in justifying a Member's cultural measure as necessary to secure its own compliance with non-WTO international obligations.[145] This may open the door to the widespread use of public international law in justifying WTO-inconsistent obligations. Nevertheless, a closer reading of the report indicates that the Appellate Body is not contemplating this scenario; instead, it appears to indicate that 'securing compliance' refers to compliance with a Member's domestic laws and regulations, not to compliance with its international obligations.[146] This is understandable: in the WTO parlance, what matters is the consistency of a Member's domestic laws with the WTO rules, not the consistency of a Member's non-WTO obligations with its WTO obligations. Therefore, the WTO tribunals are not equipped to determine whether Members are complying with their international obligations outside the WTO.[147] By the same token, they would presumably be equally reluctant to determine whether a Member's cultural measure is necessary to secure its compliance with the UNESCO Convention.[148]

A Member invoking this exception to justify a WTO-inconsistent cultural measure—claiming that it is necessary to secure its compliance with other domestic laws or regulations that implement the UNESCO Convention—might succeed on two conditions. First, the measures implementing the UNESCO Convention should be incorporated into the Member's domestic laws, or have direct legal effect within its territory. Secondly, the measure implementing the UNESCO Convention should itself be WTO-consistent. One may understand that, in this situation, the UNESCO Convention is irrelevant because it would not influence the WTO-consistency of domestic laws or regulations, or the availability of an Article XX(d) defence.

[145] See T Voon, 'UNESCO and the WTO: A Clash of Cultures?' (2006) 55 *International & Comparative Law Quarterly* 635, 648–49.

[146] WTO, *Mexico—Beverages*, Appellate Body Report, ¶75.

[147] Ibid, ¶78.

[148] See Voon, above n 84, 170. The EC stated, when the DSB adopted the reports in this case, that interpreting and applying non-WTO law and ruling on non-WTO obligations, where legally relevant for deciding a WTO dispute, did not mean 'adjudicating' a non-WTO dispute. WTO, 'Minutes of Meeting Held in the Center William Rappard on 24 March 2006', WT/DSB/M/208 (28 April 2007), ¶7.

5.6.3 National Treasures of Artistic, Historic or Archaeological Value

GATT Article XX(f) provides that 'nothing in the GATT shall prevent the adoption or enforcement of any measure imposed[149] for the protection of national treasures of artistic, historic or archaeological value'. This exception finds no equivalent in the GATS and has not been subjected to interpretation in any case.

Although this exception clearly recognises the relationship between culture and national identity,[150] it is widely held that it aims to protect the objects of high culture typically found in museums, as the term 'national treasures' generally refers to outstanding works of visual arts or archaeological artifacts of a certain age.[151] This understanding leaves Article XX(f) with little practical value in terms of the contemporary expressions of art and culture that constitute modern cultural products.[152] As Graber declares, this exception cannot be cited when trade in audiovisual media is concerned.[153] It is also important to note that the exception does not mention 'cultural value'; many cultural products are not of sufficient artistic, historic or archaeological value to be described as national treasures.[154]

On the other hand, some authors read this exception aggressively and consider it to include 'copyrightable goods'.[155] Voon has explained how international law on culture could assist in interpreting Article XX(f) and perhaps render it more useful for justifying cultural measures.[156] The words 'national treasures of artistic value' originally refer only to a narrow category of cultural items. However, if a WTO tribunal is willing to adopt the type of 'evolutionary interpretation' mentioned above, the term might include the broader range of cultural items declared by the UNESCO Convention to be under protection. Given that the definitions of 'treasure' and 'artistic, historic or archaeological value' are often subject to human beings' shifting tastes and priorities,[157] an evolutionary interpretation is not unwarranted. In any sense, as in the case of GATT Article IV, the mere existence of such an exception demonstrates that the GATT acknowledges

[149] Whereas other specific exceptions listed in GATT Art XX require that the measures are 'necessary' for the protection of the societal value at issue, Art XX(f) merely requires that the measure be 'imposed' for the protection of 'national measures of artistic value'. This might make it easier for a measure to meet the requirement.

[150] See Bernier, above n 88, 114.

[151] See Carmody, above n 22, 256.

[152] See Galt, above n 3, 913.

[153] See C Graber, 'Audiovisual Media and the Law of the Law' in CB Graber et al (eds), *Free Trade versus Cultural Diversity: WTO Negotiations in the Field of Audiovisual Services* (2004) 200.

[154] See T Voon, 'A New Approach to Audiovisual Products in the WTO: Rebalancing GATT and GATS' (2007) 14 *UCLA Entertainment Law Review* 1, 13.

[155] See, eg Cahn and Schimmel, above n 77, 284–85.

[156] See Voon, above n 84, 137.

[157] Ibid, 143–44.

the nexus between cultural items and national identity. Indeed, it offers a framework to protect them, although the practical value of its operation is subject to future judicial practice.

5.6.4 The Chapeau of General Exceptions: An Emerging Jurisprudence?

WTO tribunals have developed a two-tier test to determine whether a WTO-inconsistent measure can be justified under general exceptions. First, the measure should be provisionally justified under one of the specific exceptions listed in the articles. Secondly, the application of the measure has to meet the requirements set by the introductory paragraph (or chapeau) of the articles.[158] The purpose of the chapeau is to avoid situations where the application of the measures constitutes an abuse of general exceptions.[159] Here it is important to understand that the chapeau does not itself prohibit discrimination per se, but rather prohibits arbitrary or unjustifiable discrimination.[160]

According to the chapeau, a Member trying to justify a WTO-inconsistent measure relating to cultural products may have to use case law to prove several points: first, that the measure has been applied with due regard to different conditions between Members; secondly, that the design of the measure does not reveal a protectionist objective; and thirdly, that the Member has made serious, good faith efforts to negotiate a multilateral solution to the problem that the measure is said to address.[161]

As noted before, the old GATT regime featured a pro-trade bias, which may lead to both 'regulatory failure' and 'trade failure' under certain circumstances.[162] Recent years have seen the culmination of the WTO's strength and power, which has provoked a crisis of legitimacy for the trade system and a widespread fear that the WTO cares only about free

[158] The chapeau of Art XX GATT reads: 'Subject to the requirements that such measures are not applied in a manner which would constitute a means of arbitrary or unjustifiable discrimination between countries where the same conditions prevail, or a disguised restriction on international trade, nothing in this Agreement shall be construed to prevent the adoption or enforcement by any contracting party of measures'. GATS Art XIV contains the same language (except changing the term 'contracting party' into 'Member').

[159] WTO, *United States—Standards for Reformulated and Conventional Gasoline* (hereinafter *US—Gasoline*), Report of the Panel, WT/DS2/R, 29 January 1996, ¶22.

[160] Ibid, ¶23.

[161] See Bossche, above n 120, 66–67.

[162] In this regard, the famous asbestos saga eloquently demonstrates the dilemma associated with a pro-trade dichotomy between general obligations and exceptions. See WTO, *European Communities—Measures Affecting Asbestos and Asbestos-Containing Products* (hereinafter *EC—Asbestos*), Report of the Panel, WT/DS135/R and Add 1, 18 September 2000; WTO, *EC—Asbestos*, Report of Appellate Body, WT/DS135/AB/R, 12 March 2001; Cho, above n 51, 63–68.

trade.[163] This has emerged as one of the greatest challenges facing the WTO regime.

The WTO needs to locate a novel jurisprudence to address the conflicts between trade and non-trade values.[164] Cho suggests that the chapeau of general exceptions has the potential to serve as the origin for this jurisprudence. He observes that the chapeau has gradually begun to play a more positive, teleological role that extends beyond its textual meaning within the WTO system.[165] A new jurisprudence (dubbed 'chapeau test') tends to promote both the goals of free trade and regulatory autonomy. Under this jurisprudence, social values are not merely exceptionalised by or subordinated to trade dogma. This jurisprudence tends to redeem a non-protectionist, yet discriminatory measure as a right rather than an exception, and further emphasises the manner or application of the measure instead of its content.[166] The jurisprudence may lead the WTO tribunals to grant more room for general exceptions, including the protection of cultural diversity. Nevertheless, despite its theoretical attraction, the practical implication of the proposed jurisprudence demands a sober evaluation.[167]

In sum, the relationship between general exceptions and cultural policy remains ambiguous for the time being. Flexibilities exist, though their real effect is questionable. Justifying a measure under general exceptions largely depends on the importance that a WTO tribunal attaches to the non-trade values involved. Given that the regulatory texts live in a dynamic reality, it is hard to firmly assess the odds of successfully invoking general exceptions to justify a cultural measure. However, these exceptions may at least serve as a political mandate for future negotiations on the specificity of cultural sectors.[168]

[163] See A Rosas, 'Non-Commercial Values and the World Trade System: Building on Article XX' in K Van Der Borght et al (eds), *Essays on the Future of the WTO: Finding a New Balance* (2004) 83–84.

[164] See, eg J P. Trachtman, 'Unilateralism, Bilateralism, Regionalism, Multilateralism, and Functionalism: A Comparison with Reference to Securities Regulation' (1994) 4 *Transnational Law and Contemporary Problems* 69, 116 (arguing that at every level, especially at the multilateral level, it seems necessary to combine the trade perspective with the regulatory perspective).

[165] See Cho, above n 51, 45–46.

[166] Ibid, 62.

[167] On the one hand, the jurisprudence fails to address the pro-trade bias symbolised by the fundamental dichotomy of trade obligations and non-trade exceptions. On the other hand, the Achilles' heel of this jurisprudence is that it may invite an influx of 'regulatory unilateralism', leading to market disintegration and regulatory heterogeneity. Ibid, 68.

[168] See J Loisen, 'Can the Existing WTO Legal Framework Take into Account the Cultural Specificity of the Audiovisual Sector' in N Obuljen and J Smiers (eds), *UNESCO's Convention on the Protection and Promotion of the Diversity of Cultural Expressions: Making It Work* (2006) 276.

5.7 TRADE REMEDY MEASURES WHICH MAY INVOLVE CULTURAL PRODUCTS

Anti-dumping policies, subsidies and safeguard measures are trade remedy measures designed to ensure fair trade. This section examines how these measures might be applied to cultural products. It is important to note that the GATS currently contains no equivalent to the GATT provisions on these measures; the following discussion focuses mainly on the provisions contained in the GATT and other relevant WTO agreements.

5.7.1 Anti-dumping

One argument advanced by Canada in *Canada—Periodicals* contended that American publishers were engaged in dumping editorial content that had already been cost-recovered in the US, leaving them an unfair advantage over Canadian publishers.[169] The same argument has been made on other occasions about American film producers.[170] Before discussing how anti-dumping provisions may apply to cultural products, it is helpful to understand the essence of WTO rules on dumping.[171] In a nutshell, the WTO does not prohibit dumping as such. However, the importing Member is allowed to take action when dumped goods cause 'material injury' to competing industries in the domestic market.[172] The basic requirement for claiming 'material injury' is that the product's export price be less than the 'normal value' or 'comparable price' of the like product destined for consumption within the exporting country.[173] Anti-

[169] The practice regarding split runs of magazines is invoked as 'cultural dumping'. See, eg J Liss, 'The Impact of Technology Change on Canada's Affirmative Policy Model in the Cultural Industry and New Media Sectors' (1999) 25 *Canada—US Law Journal* 379, 379; Canadian Magazine Publishers Association, 'Split-Run Editions: The Danger to the Canadian Magazine Publishing Industry and Implications for Tariff Item 9958', 12 December 1992, 3. See also V Ross, 'Sports Illustrated Tackles Canada: Time Warner Plan Assailed as Dumping', *The Globe and Mail*, 13 January 1993, C1–C2.

[170] It has been argued that American cultural goods such as films are 'dumped' on the European market. It has been questioned whether the imposition of anti-dumping duties on these cultural products might be an appropriate and lawful response. See Shao, above n 18, 122; see also C Hoskins et al, 'Television and Film in a Freer International Trade Environment: US Dominance and Canadian Responses' in EG McAnany and KT Williams (eds), *Mass Media and Free Trade: NAFTA and Cultural Industries* (1996) 70; 'Culture and Trade: Cola v Zola', *The Economist*, 16 October 1993, 78 (employing the term 'cultural dumping').

[171] The relevant rules are set out in GATT Art VI (Anti-dumping and Countervailing Duties) and the WTO Agreement on Implementation of Art VI of the GATT 1994 (hereinafter WTO, Anti-dumping Agreement).

[172] WTO, GATT, Art VI; WTO, Anti-dumping Agreement, Art 1(Principles).

[173] WTO, Anti-dumping Agreement, Art 2.1.

dumping duties can only be imposed after demonstrating that the dumped imports are causing 'injury' to the domestic production of like products.[174]

While almost any goods can be subject to anti-dumping procedures, cultural goods stand in a special category because of both their particular 'public goods' characteristic and the 'cultural discount' that characterises trade in such products.[175] Although the possibility of initiating an anti-dumping procedure against cultural products should not be ruled out,[176] such a procedure is subject to a series of questions without clear answers.

First, how can one determine 'normal value' and calculate 'dumping margins' in the case of cultural products?[177] In this particular circumstance, the reference cost may not be the production cost of the original product, but rather the incremental cost of supplying additional markets.[178] Secondly, to what extent do dumped products cause 'injury' to 'domestic industry'? It appears difficult to practically demonstrate injury exacted by dumped cultural products. Thirdly, how can one establish that the imported and domestic goods are 'like products'? Cultural products such as films, books, magazines and television programmes are characterised by their artistic and intellectual content. Even if they are in the same category of goods, they might differ from one to another.[179] In addition to these difficulties, the requirement of a 'causal link' between dumping and injury also generates tough questions about invoking anti-dumping procedures against foreign cultural products.

There are no disciplines for anti-dumping in services sectors. In the Doha Round negotiations, it was suggested that WTO Members should develop disciplines to regulate service dumping in response to the alleged dumping of American audiovisual services.[180] Opponents to this suggestion, however, claim that extending anti-dumping measures to services would be

[174] Ibid, Art 3.5 and 3.6.

[175] See Bernier, above n 88, 120; Shao, above n 18, 121–23.

[176] See Bernier, ibid, 119–20.

[177] Hoskins and Mirus discuss 'cultural discount', which asserts that audiovisual products rooted in one culture will have diminished appeal in others because they portray non-native values, behaviours, institutions and the like. Therefore, they contend, the imported products are sold at a discounted price in order to compete with local productions. See EG McAnany and KT Williams (eds), *Mass Media and Free Trade: NAFTA and Cultural Industries* (1996) 18.

[178] The production and sale of cultural products is universally characterised by high fixed and low marginal cost with frequent price discrimination between markets. Therefore, the case for dumping is based on the incremental cost of supplying additional markets at prices below those charged in the domestic market rather than on the simple fact of selling below cost. See Hoskins et al, above n 170, 70.

[179] See I Bernier, 'Cultural Goods and Services in International Trade Law' in D Browne (ed), *The Culture/Trade Quandary: Canada's Policy Options* (1998) 119–211 (presenting an excellent overview of the prevailing views and literature on the relevance of dumping of cultural products).

[180] See WTO Doc S/CSS/W/99, above n 111, ¶10; WTO Council for Trade in Services, 'Report of the Meeting Held on 19–22 March 2002: Note by the Secretariat', TN/S/M/1 (5 June 2002), ¶316.

a retrograde step.[181] The economic justification, the difficulties associated with imposing anti-dumping measures and other related issues were also discussed. Overall, there seems to be little prospect of formulating an anti-dumping procedure for trade in services in the foreseeable future.

5.7.2 Subsidies

Subsidy is a highly sensitive matter in international trade relations.[182] As discussed in Chapter 3, cultural products in many countries benefit from a wide array of subsidy programmes. The WTO provides an intricate set of rules for subsidies,[183] according to which some subsidies—eg export subsidies—are strictly prohibited, while others are allowed, but should be withdrawn if they adversely affect the interests of other Members.

The granting of subsides must conform to the requirements of the Agreement on Subsidies and Countervailing Measures (hereinafter SCM Agreement). The Agreement sets out a broad definition of 'subsidy' that leaves very few governmental financial contributions outside its scope, provided that they are 'specific' in law or in fact.[184] Inspired by a 'three baskets' or 'red–green–yellow' approach,[185] the SCM Agreement groups subsidies into three types: those that are prohibited,[186] those that are nonactionable[187] and those that are actionable.[188]

If the traded items in question are cultural goods, then GATT Article

[181] See P Sullivan, 'Antidumping Law and the Dumping of Services' (1992) 24 *New York University Journal of International & Policy* 1677, 1708.

[182] On the one hand, subsidies are used to pursue and promote important objectives of economic, social and cultural policy. On the other hand, subsidies may have adverse effects on the interests of trading partners whose industries may suffer from unfair competition from the subsidised products. See Bossche, above n 120, 76. For more about international subsidies rules and policy underpinnings of countervailing duties, see generally Jackson, above n 30.

[183] GATT Art VI (Anti-dumping and Countervailing Duties) permits countervailing duties by national governments. GATT Art XVI (Subsidies) provides substantive international law rules that prohibit certain kinds of government subsidies. In addition, complete subsidies rule also include the 1979 Subsidies Code from the Tokyo Round. WTO Agreement on Subsidies and Countervailing Measures provides more detailed rules on subsidies.

[184] WTO, SCM, Art I.1.

[185] The approach was initially suggested during the Tokyo Round, but was blocked and failed to become the basis for the 1979 Subsidies Code. One basic idea of this approach is to clearly and directly specify which type of subsidy can result in countervailing duties and which cannot. See, eg Jackson, above n 17, 95–96.

[186] Prohibited subsidies are those that are contingent on export performance or the use of domestic over imported goods. WTO, SCM, Art III.

[187] Nonactionable subsidies are those that are termed not specific and do not restrict the subsidy to certain enterprises. WTO, SCM, Art VIII. While it may be argued that many cultural programmes are non-specific, or specific to a degree unlikely to cause prejudice, the audiovisual sector might be different in view of the limited number of producers and the serious imbalances in market share. See Footer and Graber, above n 73, 140–41.

[188] Actionable subsidies are those that are specific or have adverse effects on other WTO Members by causing injury or serious prejudice to their domestic industry. WTO, SCM, Art V.

III.8(b) also applies. This provision permits 'the payment of subsidies exclusively to domestic producers'. The scope of this provision is limited, as demonstrated in *Canada—Periodicals*. In the case, Canada supported its domestic periodicals through, inter alia, the use of subsidised postal rates; when challenged, Canada invoked Article III:8(b) as a defence. The Appellate Body concluded that postal subsidy was incompatible with Article III:8(b) because it was not paid directly to periodical publishers.[189]

This is of particular significance to the interpretation of Article III:8(b) in cases concerning cultural products: the conclusion represents the triumph of form over substance. It is also important to understand the practical consequences of this interpretation. After the decision of this case, Canada immediately began resorting to simple, specific subsidies for magazines that appear to be consistent with Article III:8(b).[190] For other Members, this decision signals that financial assistance to industries must be carefully considered and assessed for its compatibility with Article III:8(b).[191]

It is also relevant to determine whether subsidised products are categorised as goods or services, as the current WTO regime regulates subsidies for goods and services differently. As it stands, the GATS sets no constraints on subsidies. The current negotiations on services are being conducted under GATS Article XV,[192] and are expected to develop multilateral disciplines for avoiding the trade-distortive effects of subsidies. Interestingly, most submissions pertaining to audiovisual services propose to consider subsidies as a mechanism by which to achieve cultural policies.[193] However, although GATS may impose potentially powerful disciplines in this area,[194] subsidies of any type can be offered to cultural services even before such disciplines are put in place.

[189] WTO, *Canada—Periodicals*, Report of the Appellate Body, ¶34.

[190] See Bernier, above n 179, 117.

[191] Generally, subsidies can be granted in a number of ways, including direct grants, loans on favorable terms, loan guarantees, equity investments, government purchases, tax credits, deductions, and remissions. See Acheson and Maule, above n 69, 82. The WTO Members shall carefully structure their subsidy programmes in order for them to be compatible with WTO rules.

[192] Subsidies as they relate to services are provided in Art XV of the GATS, which notes that they may distort trade. GATS, Art XV (subsidies). The further disciplines in this area are still under the construction. See below n 218 and its accompanying text.

[193] WTO Doc S/CSS/W/21, above n 112 (developing an understanding on subsidies for audiovisual services that will respect the Members' need to foster cultural identity by creating an environment to nurture local culture); WTO Doc S/CSS/W/74, above n 111 (maintaining that a common understanding on subsidies would represent a positive precondition for the negotiation of specific commitments); WTO Doc S/CSS/W/99, above n 111 (advising subsides mechanism in the audiovisual sector).

[194] WTO Working Party on GATS Rules, 'Communication from Argentina and Hong Kong, China: Development of Multilateral Disciplines Governing Trade Distortive Subsidies in Services', S/WPGR/W/31 (16 March 2000); WTO Working Party on GATS Rules, 'Subsidies and Trade in Services: Note by the Secretariat', S/WRGR/W/9 (6 March 1996).

5.7.3 Safeguard Mechanism (or the Escape Clause)

Free trade may be difficult to sustain if it creates a severe hardship for an importing Member's domestic economy; this is the rationale for establishing safeguard mechanisms in trade systems. When confronted with a surge in importation that causes or threatens to cause serious injury to domestic industry, a WTO Member is allowed to take safeguard measures.[195] Unlike anti-dumping measures and countervailing duties that target unfair trade, safeguard mechanisms furnish a temporary escape hatch for domestic producers. The relevant disciplines are set out in the GATT[196] and the Agreement on Safeguards (AOS). GATT Article XIX requires that the injury should occur 'as a result of unforeseen developments and the effect of the obligation incurred'. However, the AOS does not impose this requirement,[197] which makes the safeguard mechanism easier for Members to invoke.

GATT Article XIX and the AOS do not treat cultural goods differently from other goods with regard to safeguard measures. Theoretically, therefore, a cultural measure may be justified under these provisions if the competition is so fierce that a domestic cultural sector's survival is in jeopardy. The WTO Members shall apply safeguard measures subject to several conditions.[198] The requirements, such as 'increased imports', 'serious injury', and a 'causal link' between importation and injury[199], may raise special problems in the case of cultural products. For instance, given that the intellectual content of these products cannot easily be separated from its material support, it is hard to prove 'like or directly competitive products'.

GATT/WTO practice further paints an unpromising picture for invoking safeguard measures in cases relating to cultural products. Thus far, there have been no safeguard cases involving cultural products, but a review of the past cases concerning other products reveals that it is almost impossible for defendants to win a safeguard measure case before the

[195] See generally AO Sykes, 'The Persistent Puzzles of Safeguards: Lessons from the Steel Dispute' (2004) 7 *Journal of International Economic Law* 523, 526–38 (laying out the key provisions of WTO law on safeguards along with their history and noting the most important interpretive issues).

[196] WTO, GATT, Art XIX (Emergency Action on Imports of Particular Products).

[197] WTO, Agreement on Safeguard, Art 2.1.

[198] See WTO, Agreement of Safeguards, Art 1 (General Provision), Art 2 (Conditions); GATT, Art XIX. These provisions require that in order to resort to safeguard measures, an invoking Member shall demonstrate that such product is being imported into its territory in such increased quantities, absolute or relative to domestic production, and under such conditions as to cause or threaten to cause serious injury to the domestic industry that produces like or directly competitive products.

[199] See C Ledet, 'Causation of Injury in Safeguards Cases: Why the US Can't Win' (2003) 34 *Law & Policy International Business* 713, 717–43 (illustrating how hard to satisfy the WTO's stringent requirement to utilise safeguard measures).

WTO.[200] Indeed, the real question is not how to win a safeguard measure case, but whether winning such a case is possible.[201] Trade protection measures such as safeguard mechanisms often cause unintended negative consequences.[202] The WTO tries to encourage its Members to bear this in mind before invoking such a measure.

The other side of the coin is that, when challenged, a defendant has little hope of winning; nevertheless, the Member may still want to invoke such measures to protect domestic industry. Under the current regime, doing so can provide domestic industry with a period of adjustment without the need to pay compensation. To this end, it might be tempting for a Member to resort to a safeguard mechanism to protect its domestic cultural industry. With regard to the safeguard mechanism for trade in services, the GATS contains a built-in mandate to negotiating emergency safeguard measures (ESM) on a non-discrimination principle.[203] Nevertheless, the negotiation, which began in 1998, involves so many complicated issues that is has yet to be completed.[204] Consequently, a WTO Member may rely on safeguard measures to protect its audiovisual services industry until more detailed rules emerge.

5.8 THE TREATMENT OF CULTURE IN EMERGING AREAS

The WTO framework integrates trade in goods, trade in services, trade-related investment, trade-related intellectual property and other issues into a 'single undertaking' for the first time. This makes it necessary to examine culture protection in several emerging trade-related areas.

[200] The experience of US provides the best reference. See ibid, 714, 744 (2003).

[201] A case study reveals that the Appellate Body's current stance signals an obvious lack of deference to the decisions of the Members in this area. See Sykes, above n 195, 526–38 (making the point that WTO rules pose nearly insurmountable hurdles to the legal use of safeguard measures).

[202] See BH Liebman and KM Tomlin, 'Safeguards and Retaliatory Threats' (2008) 51 *Journal of Law & Economics* 351, 373 (the article surveys the response of shareholders to the threat of retaliatory tariffs authorised by the WTO in the aftermath of the US Steel Safeguard dispute).

[203] GATS, Art X (Emergency Safeguard Measures).

[204] As the unfinished agenda remaining after the Uruguay Round, the GATS granted mandates to conduct negotiations on ESM and government procurement and subsides, together referred to as 'rules-making negotiations'. These negotiations not have resulted in any significant progress, especially in the case of ESM. See, eg A Warouw, 'Realistic and Prospects of the Current Services Negotiations: Indonesia Perspectives' (2006) 1 *Asian Journal of WTO & International Health Law & Policy* 141, 150–53.

5.8.1 Investment

Unlike in the province of trade, there are no global rules currently in place governing international investment.[205] Given the complementarity of investment and trade in the international economy, the barriers to investment may easily restrict or distort trade, and vice versa.[206] It thus comes as no surprise that the WTO expanded its portfolio to include investment issues during the Uruguay Round. It is widely held that the GATS is an investment agreement in the sense that one of the four modes of service supply regulated by GATS is 'commercial presence', which constitutes a typical category of investment in service areas.[207] The Uruguay Round also concluded the Agreement on Trade Related Investment Measures (hereinafter the TRIMs Agreement),[208] which provides a patchwork of regulation to reinforce GATT rules regarding national treatment and the prohibition of import quotas.[209] Note that the TRIMs Agreement does not apply to services.[210] Notwithstanding its limited scope, the TRIMs Agreement can be used to challenge investment measures related to cultural industries. For instance, it includes a general ban on local content requirements. If a Member imposes such a requirement on cultural enterprises with foreign investment, the measures are subject to the scrutiny of the TRIMs Agreement. Theoretically speaking, direct foreign investment that is larger than annual foreign trade may lead to a greater assault on local culture. In many countries, however, such as China, the cultural industry

[205] The OECD's attempt to negotiate a multilateral agreement on investment (MAI) failed after several years of negotiations. See EM Burt, 'Developing Countries and the Framework for Negotiations of Foreign Direct Investment in the World Trade Organization' (1997) 12 *American University Journal of International Law & Policy* 1015, 1040–58 (reviewing the origins, particulars, benefits and limitations of the MAI); see also UNESCO, *World Culture Report 2000* (2000) 76–78 (discussing the negotiation of MAI and the assertion of cultural diversities). NAFTA does contain a chapter on investment but only applies regionally.

[206] Regarding the interaction between international trade and investment, see generally UN Conference on Trade and Development, Investment-Related Trade Measures (IRTMs), UNCTAD Series on Issues in International Investment Agreements, 1999.

[207] The GATS covers investment by defining trade in services as encompassing the supply of service through the establishment of a 'commercial presence' in the territory of another WTO Member. WTO, GATS, Art 1.2(c), Art XXVIII, ¶2(d) (defining 'commercial presence' as 'any type of business or professional establishment', including through (i) the constitution, acquisition or maintenance of a juridical person, or (ii) the creation or maintenance of a branch or a representative office, within the territory of a member for the purpose of supplying a service). See also TL Brewer and S Young, 'The Multilateral Agenda for Foreign Direct Investment: Problems, Principles, and Priorities for Negotiations at the OECD and WTO', *World Competition*, June 1995, 67–72; Kennedy, above n 11, 77.

[208] WTO, Agreement on Trade-Related Investment Measures, 15 April 1994, Marrakesh Agreement Establishing the World Trade Organization, Annex IA, Legal Instruments—Results of the Uruguay Round, 33 ILM 81 (1994) (hereinafter WTO, TRIMs Agreement).

[209] WTO, TRIMs Agreement, Art 2.1. An Illustrative List annexed to the TRIMs Agreement lists measures that are inconsistent with para 4 of Art III and para 1 of Art XI.

[210] Ibid, Art 1 (Coverage, the Agreement applies to investment measures related to trade in goods only).

is generally closed to foreign investment. This may reduce the effect of foreign investment on local cultures. In this case, the TRIMs Agreement may not function in a complete sense.

5.8.2 Telecommunication and Audiovisual Services

A survey of the GATS's impact on cultural industry would not be complete without addressing telecommunication services. The members negotiated their commitments on telecommunications services under the GATS framework,[211] which generates a salient impact on the audiovisual sector.

Telecommunication service is a broad concept:[212] although the GATS Annex on Telecommunications excludes cable or broadcast distribution of radio or television programming,[213] it is still hard to distinguish between telecommunication services and audiovisual services in many cases. As a general rule of thumb, it has been accepted that commitments involving programming content are classified as audiovisual services, while those involving only the transmission of information are classified as telecommunications.[214] However, as the boundaries between different media blur, this rule of thumb is under increasing pressure to change.[215] Accordingly, a clearer definition of telecommunication services and its distinction from audiovisual services is needed in order to identify the Members' specific commitments and their corresponding obligations.

5.8.3 Intellectual Property Rights Protection and Culture Diversity

The issue of intellectual property rights is particularly vital to the discussion of the culture and trade nexus. The WTO has intervened around the growing global concern about the implementation of intellectual property rights. The Agreement on Trade-Related Intellectual

[211] At the conclusion of the Uruguay Round in December 1993, approximately one-half of the participants scheduled specific commitments on value-added telecommunication services. Negotiations on basic telecommunication services were extended through 1996 and concluded in 1997. Sixty-seven participants also reached the GATS Annex on Telecommunications that allows access to other participating Members' basic telecommunication networks.

[212] It includes voice telephone services, electronic mail, online information and database retrieval, online information or data, etc. WTO, 'Note by the Secretariat, Services Sectoral Classification List', MTN.GNS/W/120 (10 July 1991) 2.c.

[213] GATS, Annex on Telecommunications, 2(b).

[214] The WTO Secretariat has observed that it can be difficult to distinguish 'radio and television transmission services' characterised as 'telecommunications' from those characterised as 'audiovisual services'. WTO Council for Trade in Services, above n 106, 5. The US, however, has disagreed with this suggestion. WTO Council for Trade in Services, 'Communication from the United States—Audiovisual Services', S/C/W/78 (8 December 1998).

[215] See Loisen, above n 168, 270.

Properties (hereinafter the TRIPS Agreement)[216] pulls intellectual property protection into the purview of trade regimes, and puts in place international norms and standards with which the WTO Members are obliged to comply.[217] The Agreement lays the foundation for global protection of intellectual property rights, a move that has implications for cultural protection. The TRIPS Agreement defines 'intellectual property rights' as including copyright,[218] trademarks, geographical indications, designs and patents. The protection of patents plays a crucial role in audiovisual equipment, while copyright is generally more relevant to trade in culture since cultural products are almost all copyrighted materials.

The implication of the TRIPS Agreement on cultural protection is somewhat different from that of the GATT and the GATS. The interaction between intellectual property rights and culture protection raises the question of whether an intellectual property rights regime is conducive to safeguarding culture. It is argued that copyright protection has become too strong and begun to threaten cultural diversity instead of nurturing it. The commodification of intellectual property products and the blurring of the private and public spheres of cultural works and their attendant rights exemplify this phenomenon.[219]

On the other hand, although the trade and culture problem pits free trade and cultural protection against one another to some extent, the goal of cultural diversity is in line with the TRIPS Agreement.[220] The rules pertaining to protecting intellectual property rights protect cultural

[216] WTO, Agreement on Trade-Related Aspects of Intellectual Property Rights, 15 April 1994, Marrakesh Agreement Establishing the World Trade Organization, Annex IC, Legal Instruments—Results of the Uruguay Round, 33 ILM 81 (1994) (hereinafter WTO, TRIPS Agreement).

[217] See M Agdomar, 'Removing the Greek from Feta and Adding Korel to Champagne: The Paradox of Geographical Indications in International Law' (2008) 18 *Fordham Intellectual Property, Media & Entertainment Law Journal* 541, 544.

[218] The provisions of TRIPS concerning copyright and related rights incorporate most of the provisions of the Berne Convention, and can be found in Arts 9–14 of the TRIPS Agreement. World Intellectual Property Organization (WIPO), Berne Convention for the Protection of Literary and Artistic Works of 9 September 1886, completed at Paris on 4 May 1896, last amended on 28 September 1979.

[219] See J Curtis, 'Culture and the Digital Copyright Cinema: Assessing the International Regulatory System of the Music Industry in Relation to Cultural Diversity' (2006) 13(1) *International Journal of Cultural Property* 59, 80; J Bosland, 'The Culture of Trade Marks: An Alternative Cultural Theory Perspective' (2005) 10(2) *Media & Arts Law Review* 99, 101. See also J Gibson, *Community Resources: Intellectual Property, International Trade and Protection of Traditional Knowledge* (2005) 186–90 (discussing the globalised environment and the privatised intellect).

[220] Both cultural rights and intellectual property rights seek to 'strike a balance between promoting general public interests in accessing new knowledge as easily as possible and in protecting the interests of authors and inventors in such knowledge'. See United Nations Commission on Human Rights, Sub-Commission on the Promotion and Protection of Human Rights, 'The Impact of the Agreement on Trade-Related Aspects of Intellectual Property Rights on Human Rights: Report of the High Commissioner', E/CN.4/Sub.2/2001/13 (27 June 2001).

values as well. This is particularly true in the domain of copyright,[221] since cultural rights and authors' rights often go hand in hand. For example, the TRIPS Agreement makes creative ideas more profitable and brings consumers a wider menu of cultural choice. This is evidenced by WTO disputes, including *Japan—Sound Recordings*[222] and *EC—Intellectual Property Rights.*[223] In a digital world, domestic cultural policy, trade obligations and the protection of intellectual property rights intersect to generate increased friction. Despite the discord, however, free trade and intellectual property protection should not only complement cultural diversity, but also constitute a necessary component of its promotion and protection.

5.8.4 Geographical Indications (GIs) and Culture Protection

The TRIPS Agreement includes geographical indications (GIs) as one of its protected subject matters.[224] GIs are defined as 'indications that identify a product as originating in the territory of a Member, or a region or locality in that territory, where a given quality, reputation, or other characteristic of the product is essentially attributable to its geographical origin'.[225] The GIs that qualify for protection in the TRIPS Agreement are place-related names often associated with food and beverage products. Developed countries, especially those in Europe, traditionally hold most formally protected GIs, though recent years have witnessed a growing interest from other countries.[226]

[221] See P Samuelson, 'Implications of the Agreement on Trade Related Aspects of Intellectual Property Rights for the Cultural Dimension of National Copyright Laws'(1999) 23 *Journal of Cultural Economics* 95.

[222] WTO, *Japan—Measures Concerning Sound Recordings: Request for Consultations by the United States*, WT/DS28/1, 14 February 1996. The US and Japan resolved their dispute over Japan's protection of American sound recordings. Japan adopted amendments to its Copyright Law and provided protection to American recordings produced between 1946 and 1971. *Japan—Measures Concerning Sound Recordings: Notification of a Mutually Agreed Solution*, WT/DS42/4, 17 November 1997.

[223] WTO, *European Communities—Enforcement of Intellectual Property Rights for Motion Pictures and Television Programs: Request for Consultations by the United States* (hereinafter WTO, *EC—IP*), WT/DS124/1, 7 May 1998. In this case, the US claimed that a significant number of television stations in Greece regularly broadcast copyrighted motion pictures and television programmes without the authorisation of copyright owners, which violated TRIPS Arts 41 and 61. Greece finally passed legislation that provides an additional enforcement remedy for copyright holders whose works were infringed by television stations operating in Greece. WTO, *EC—IP, Notification of Mutually Agreed Solution*, WT/DS124/2, 26 March 2001.

[224] Three articles in the TRIPS Agreement, Arts 22, 23 and 24, are devoted to the GIs issue.

[225] WTO, TRIPS Agreement, Art 22.1.

[226] See, eg MJ Calaguas, 'A Rose by Any Other Name: Protecting Geographical Indications for Wines and Spirits in China' (2006) 3 *Loyola University of Chicago International Review* 257, 264–66.

GIs issues have been hotly debated since the Uruguay Round, with a focus on the scope of protected GIs.[227] For historical reasons, the TRIPS Agreement establishes stronger protections for wines and spirits than for other goods.[228] During the Doha negotiation, one debate has been whether the 'additional protection' provided for wine and spirits should be extended to other goods. The EU represents traditional ally to this convention, claiming that GIs are 'key to EU and developing countries' cultural heritage, traditional methods of production and natural resources'. In contrast, the US is concerned that too much GI protection constitutes trade protectionism and therefore opposes their extension.[229] In *EC—GIs*,[230] the only case concerning GIs thus far, the US and Australia argue that the EC's regulations fail to provide national treatment or sufficient protection for pre-existing trademarks that are similar or identical to GIs. The Panel found the substance of the EC system of GIs protection is consistent with WTO obligations, but that part of the regulation is TRIPS-inconsistent because it provides no national treatment to the rights holders and products of other Members.[231]

The GIs debates and the *EC—GIs* case bring up the question of whether GI protection is an effective way to achieve cultural diversity. There is an argument that the primary goal of GIs is not to achieve cultural diversity, but rather to protect consumer interests. GIs do not appear to have an inherent value beyond their role in the perfection of market information and thus cannot provide cultural protection.[232] I would maintain that GIs might serve as one of the mediums for cultural protection for several reasons.

First, the cultural backdrop of GIs—ie they are required for the preservation of local traditions and cultural diversity—is necessary to justify their inclusion in the TRIPS Agreement, which generally intends to encourage innovation and individual creativity through the means of

[227] WTO, 'TRIPS: Geographical Indications—Background and the Current Situation', 11 November 2005, available at http://www.wto.org/english/tratop_e/trips_e/gi_background_e.htm (last accessed on 16 June 2012). See also D Rangnekar, 'The Pros and Cons of Stronger Geographical Indication Protection', www.iprsonline.org/ictsd/docs/RangnekarBridges-Year6N3MarchApril2002.pdf (last accessed on 16 June 2012); Calaguas, ibid, 264–66 (discussing the reasons for the GIs debates).

[228] WTO, TRIPS Agreement, Art 23. This article goes a step further by granting nearly absolute exclusivity to GIs, which prevents others from using them even when measures have been taken to prevent confusion.

[229] See J Hughes, 'Champagne, Feta, and Bourbon: The Spirited Debate about Geographical Indications' (2006) 58 *Hastings Law Journal* 299, 311–21 (examining the TRIPS provisions on geographical indications).

[230] WTO, *EC—Protection of Trademarks and Geographic Indications for Agricultural Products and Foodstuffs* (hereinafter WTO, *EC—GIs*), Report of the Panel, WT/DS/174/R, 15 March 2005.

[231] Ibid, ¶7.573.

[232] See T Broude, 'Culture, Trade and Additional Protection for Geographical Indications', available at http://www.iprsonline.org/ictsd/Bridges%20Monthly.htm (last accessed on 16 June 2012).

temporary monopoly. According to the definition contained in the TRIPS Agreement, GIs embody unique expressions of place and culture. These cultural components partly account for the authenticity, quality, belonging and attribution of GI products. This illustrates the inseparability of GIs and cultural protection, and explains why the protection of GIs can morph into the role of cultural guardian.

Secondly, protection of GIs provides an exceptional opportunity to utilise market power to recognise and reward the products that convey the uniqueness of local culture and place.[233] GIs establish communal rights and are maintained to protect traditional knowledge. Particularly in the case of wine and spirits, consumer protection, which was the original rationale for integrating GIs in the TRIPS Agreement, no longer serves as the sole basis for protection and is replaced by such considerations as the protection of local tradition and cultural heritage.

Thirdly, GIs protection actually adds value to the goods by creating a monopoly for the GI brand. Thus, culture is protected not only by distinguishing cultural widgets from the non-cultural, but also by valorising the cultural expression embodied in the widget and converting it into a commercial premium. In this sense, GIs provide a good example of combining culture protection with trade interests. Accordingly, if the EU's position prevails in this negotiation, the extension of the scope of protected GIs may equip them with more strength to undertake a cultural mission.

5.9 CONCLUDING REMARKS

This chapter offers a full-scale survey of the treatment of culture in the GATT/WTO framework, finding that the global trade regime contains no cultural exception, nor does it grant cultural products a special status except for very limited cases. In seeking a solution to the trade and culture conundrum, this survey hints at several starting points.

First, the evolution from the Havana Charter to GATT 1947 and then to the WTO regime highlights the necessity of cooperation between the WTO and UN agencies in dealing with non-trade concerns arising in the legitimacy crisis that has faced the WTO. It also indicates that the culture issue should be addressed in a broader context, and that the WTO is not the sole organisation to tackle this task.

Secondly, cultural products are treated differently under the GATT and the GATS, depending on whether the traded items are classified as goods or services. GATT Article IV was designed to recognise the film's importance to the contracting parties' cultural identity. The inclusion of film merits some reconsideration in the information age, but the original rationale

[233] See Agdomar, above n 217, 560.

behind Article IV is certainly still valid today in a legacy sense. The GATS regime generally offers more flexibility with respect to Members' obligations in liberalising cultural services and leaves more room for the protection of audiovisual sectors. These sectors are, however, subject to further liberalisation through future negotiations.

Thirdly, general exception clauses aim to accommodate trade and non-trade concerns. The 'public morals', 'securing compliance of WTO-consistent laws and regulations' and 'historic, archeological value' exceptions are of clear relevance to cultural protection. However, as they currently stand, there are various difficulties in invoking these exceptions to justify a domestic cultural policy measure, both theoretically and practically.

Fourthly, trade remedy measures, including anti-dumping, subsidies and countervailing duties, and safeguard measures, may apply to protect culture to some extent. Nevertheless, just as with general exception clauses, the special nature of cultural products presents an array of thorny issues with regard to such measures.

Fifthly, the ever-widening scope of the GATT/WTO regime adds more dimensions to the culture and trade issue. Trade-related investment measures, trade-related intellectual property, the blurring of the telecommunication and audiovisual sectors, and GI protection touch upon different aspects with regard to culture protection and offer some emerging ideas on the relationship between trade regimes and cultural diversity.

In one way or another, the examination of trade in culture within the GATT/WTO regime tends to raise more questions than answers, but it does shed some light on the subject. One can clearly conclude, however, that the trade regime is oriented for promoting trade instead of culture. It is not realistic to depend on WTO rules to provide desirable protection to national culture. While recognising the virtue of free trade, non-economic objectives such as culture have to be accommodated in order to mitigate the crisis facing the WTO in recent years because of its intrusion into areas traditionally regulated by national governments. Taking all these concerns into account, one concludes that breaking the impasse between trade and culture calls for an open trade policy tempered by appropriate culture safeguard mechanisms.

6

The Treatment of Culture under the GATT/WTO (II): Case Study and Identification of Problems

Rather than attempt once again to decide what is 'in' or 'out of' of the WTO, we should try to mould the rules and their interpretation to structure the interaction of the trading regime with other powers and authorities, both domestic and international, in a legitimate manner. Robert Howse[1]

6.1 INTRODUCTION

As observed in Chapter 5, the WTO framework shows noteworthy shortcomings and ambiguities in relation to the treatment of cultural products. This not only requires the assessment and clarification of current treaty provisions conducted in Chapter 5, but also an analysis of the related judicial practice and identification of pertinent problems.

Following an introduction about the WTO dispute settlement mechanism, this chapter studies two important WTO cases involving cultural products: *Canada—Periodicals*[2] and *China—Publications and Audiovisual Products.*[3] In addition to an examination of the case background and procedural posture, and reflections on the findings of the WTO tribunals, this chapter analyses several key issues in settling trade disputes concerning cultural

[1] R Howse, 'From Politics to Technocracy–and Back Again: The Fate of the Multilateral Trading Regime' (2002) 96 *American Journal of International Law* 94, 112.

[2] WTO, *Canada–Certain Measures Affecting Periodicals* (hereinafter WTO, *Canada—Periodicals*), complained by the US, WT/DS/31, request for consultations received on 11 March 1996, Panel Report circulated on 14 March 1997, Appellate Body Report circulated on30 June 1997.

[3] WTO, *China—Measures Affecting Trading Rights and Distribution Services for Certain Publications and Audiovisual Entertainment Products* (hereinafter WTO, *China—Publications and Audiovisual Products*), complained by the US, WT/DS/363, request for consultations received on 10 April 2007, Panel Report circulated on 12 August 2009, the Appellate Body Report circulated on 21 December 2009. DSB adopted the reports on 19 January 2010.

products, including: the possibility of invoking UNESCO instruments as a cultural defence; the applicability of the 'public morals' exception to cultural products; the incoherence among WTO agreements that rises from the overlap of cultural goods and services; and the extent to which cultural content may be used to distinguish 'like products'. In an effort to present a holistic picture, the chapter also cross-references other cases decided under the GATT/WTO regime, such as *Japan—Leather Goods*[4] and *Japan—Alcoholic Beverages II*.[5]

This chapter relies largely on case studies, but tries to be analytical and to identify relevant problems instead of merely stating cases facts. It also reiterates the challenges faced by the WTO in solving the culture-related trade disputes.

6.2 A BRIEF ACCOUNT OF GATT/ WTO DISPUTE SETTLEMENT

Described as a 'central international economic institution',[6] the WTO is vitally characterised by a dispute settlement mechanism derived from decades of experiment and practice in the GATT[7] and elaborately set forth in the Dispute Settlement Understanding (DSU).[8] The DSU serves to preserve the rights and obligations of WTO Members under the covered agreements, and to clarify the existing provisions in accordance with the customary rules of interpretation of public international law.[9] A separate Dispute Settlement Body (DSB) was established to administer dispute settlement. The DSU underlines the DSB's central role and lays down the rules governing its work. In its simplest form, the DSB is composed of three-person panels and a standing Appellate Body of seven members. The

[4] WTO, *Japan—Measures on Imports of Leather* (hereinafter WTO, *Japan—Leather*], complained by the US, L/4789-26S/320, Panel Report adopted on 8 November 1979.

[5] WTO, *Japan—Taxes on Alcoholic Beverages II*, complained by the European Communities, WT/DS8 (WT/DS/10, complained by Canada; WT/DS/11, complained by the US), request for consultations received on 7 July 1995, Panel Report circulated on 11 July 1996, Appellate Body Report circulated on 4 October 1996.

[6] See, eg L Bierman et al, 'The General Agreement on Tariffs and Trade from a Market Perspective' (1996) 17 *University of Pennsylvania Journal of International Economic Law* 821, 845.

[7] Petersmann examined a series of cases under the GATT/WTO to demonstrate the progressive development of GATT/WTO law through its dispute settlement system. He particularly discusses the contribution of GATT's dispute settlement jurisprudence to the clarification and development of GATT law, using the topical example of the relationship between international trade and environmental law. See E-U Petersmann, *The GATT/WTO Dispute Settlement System—International Law, International Organizations and Dispute Settlement* (1997) 92–130.

[8] DSU contains a set of reformulated dispute settlement rules. See WTO, Understanding on Rules and Procedures Governing the Settlement of Disputes (hereinafter WTO, DSU), 15 April 1994, WTO Agreement, Annex 2, 33 ILM 1226 (1994).

[9] WTO, DSU, Art 3.2.

panels hear disputes and suggest resolutions. Unless parties agree otherwise, the terms of reference given to the panels are standard,[10] limiting what they may consider in deliberations. The Appellate Body takes appeals and can uphold, modify or reverse conclusions made by a panel.[11] Despite the limited jurisdiction of the Appellate Body, this additional layer of adjudication effectively transforms WTO dispute resolution into a two-tiered review system.[12] It was desirable for the Uruguay Round negotiation to make DSB decisions binding in the absence of a consensus against them.[13] This principle, known as the 'negative consensus' rule, has been hailed as a move away from 'power-oriented' trade relations to a 'rule-oriented' adjudication system.

Dispute resolution procedures are provided in GATT Articles XXII[14] and XXIII[15] and GATS Articles XXII[16] and XXIII;[17] a number of other provisions are sprinkled throughout the WTO agreements as well. The dispute settlement mechanism plays a significant role in the GATT/WTO system, rendering trade rules effective and adding an essential measure of predictability to the whole system.[18] The Appellate Body, as a permanent body with a comparatively fixed complement of judges, has significantly shaped WTO law more effectively than a series of ad hoc tribunals. It is beyond the scope of this chapter to consider WTO dispute settlement procedures in detail.[19] Instead, I will focus on two disputes decided under this set of rules to illustrate WTO attitudes towards the treatment of cultural products.

[10] WTO, DSU, Art 7 (Terms of Reference of Panels). See also DSU, Art 6.2 (in case the applicant requests the establishment of a panel with other than standard terms of reference, the written request shall include the proposed text of special terms of reference).

[11] For more discussions about the work of DSB, see, eg C Reitz, 'Enforcement of the General Agreement of Tariffs and Trade' (1996) 17 *University of Pennsylvania Journal of International Economic Law* 555, 580–84 (describing the WTO panels and Appellate Body).

[12] The Appellate Body can only hear 'issues of law covered in the panel report and legal interpretation developed by the panel'. WTO, DSU, Art 17 (Appellate Review).

[13] See WTO, DSU, Art 16 (Adoption of Panel Reports), Art 17.14 (Adoption of Appellate Body Report).

[14] WTO, GATT, Art XXII (Consultation).

[15] WTO, GATT, Art XXIII (Nullification or Impairment).

[16] WTO, GATS, Art XXII (Consultation).

[17] WTO, GATS, Art XXIII (Dispute Settlement and Enforcement).

[18] See generally, JH Jackson, *The World Trading System: Law and Policy of International Economic Relations*, 2nd edn (1997).

[19] The literature on the GATT/WTO dispute settlement mechanism has received a boom. See, eg JJ Jackson, *World Trade and the Law of GATT* (1969); Petersmann, above n 7; GC Shaffer and R Meléndez-Ortiz (eds), *Dispute Settlement at the WTO—The Developing Country Experience* (2010); K Kulovesi, *The WTO Dispute Settlement System-Challenges of the Environment, Legitimacy and Fragmentation* (2011); AD Mitchell, *Legal Principles in WTO Disputes* (2011).

6.3 *CANADA—PERIODICALS*

Canada—Periodicals led to the first DSB decision involving cultural products and generated numerous thought-provoking comments regarding the treatment of culture under the WTO. Subsequent to an overview of the case background and procedural posture, this section discusses the WTO's prism of economic efficiency,[20] and the culture and trade policy issues reflected in this case.

6.3.1 The Case Background and a Procedural Posture

The tension between Canada and the US over cultural products is part of a wider conflict concerning trade and culture. Canadians consider their culture particularly susceptible to American influence, due to linguistic overlap and geographic proximity.[21] Early in the 1920s, the US became increasingly active in trade in cultural products since the products represent a larger portion of export earnings. In stark contrast, the magazine industry in Canada has been only marginally profitable and has benefited from various government policies.[22] Responding to political pressures from an outraged domestic intelligentsia and a beleaguered publishing industry, Canada has maintained a series of measures designed to exclude foreign periodicals from the domestic marketplace, including a high tax on imported split runs[23] imposed by Tariff Code 9958.[24]

Canada—Periodicals is an emblematic cultural spat between the US and

[20] See JR Paul, 'Cultural Resistance to Global Governance' (2000) 22 *Michigan Journal of International Law* 1, 54.

[21] See M Braun and L Parker, 'Trade in Culture: Consumable Product or Cherished Articulation of a Nation's Soul?' (1993) 22 *Denver Journal of International Law and Policy* 155, 162–64.

[22] See A Scow, 'The *Sports Illustrated Canada* Controversy: Canada "Strikes Out" In Its Bid to Protect Its Periodical Industry from US Split-Run Periodicals' (1998) 7 *Minnesota Journal of Global Trade* 245, 248–50 (addressing the Canadian and US periodical industries).

[23] Magazines generally consist of advertising content and editorial content and, accordingly, revenues accrue to publishers from the sale of space to advertisers and magazines to readers. The term 'split run' or 'regional editions of magazines', refers to the separation of editorial and advertising content, a commercial technique and marketing strategy widely used to combine common editorial content with advertisement tailored to particular markets. The American edition of *Sports Illustrated* sold in Canada is classified as a split-run when the edition has largely the same editorial content but different advertising content that targets a Canadian audience. See, eg K Acheson and C Maule, *Much Ado about Culture: North American Trade Disputes* (1999) 187.

[24] See A de Fazekas, 'Free Trade and Culture: An Alternative Approach' (1993) 2 *Dalhousie Journal of Legal Studies* 141, 154–55 (noting that Canada relied on a series of policies to encourage the development of Canadian cultural industries); CP James, 'Trade, Culture and Technology: A Test of Canada's Cultural Mettle' (1997) 8(7) *Entertainment Law Review* 253, 253–64.

Canada.[25] The sequel of a 1960s dispute involving *Time* and *Reader's Digest*,[26] this case involves *Sports Illustrated*, a magazine published by Time Warner. During the 1990s, new technology enabled American publishers to circumvent Canada's traditional protectionist measures.[27] In this case, Time Warner exported a split-run edition of *Sports Illustrated* to Canada via satellite; no hard copy physically crossed the border, thereby bypassing the tariff on imported split runs.[28] In response, Canada adopted an Excise Tax that made it prohibitively expensive for Time Warner to continue publishing a split-run edition of *Sports Illustrated* in Canada.[29]

On 11 March 1996, the US requested consultations with Canada over two measures prohibiting or restricting the importation of periodicals into Canada: the tax treatment of split-run periodicals and the application of favourable postage rates to Canadian periodicals.[30] The consultations were held on 10 April 1996, but did not result in a satisfactory resolution to the matter. The US requested that the DSB establish a panel to examine the matter;[31] the panel was established and submitted a report to the parties on 21 February 1997.[32] Both the US and Canada appealed the case, and the Appellate Body circulated its report on 30 June 2007.[33]

[25] See J Devlin, 'Canada and International Trade in Culture: Beyond National Interests' (2004) 14 *Minnesota Journal of Global Trade* 177, 179–82 (discussing the history of trade in cultural commodities between Canada and the US, mentioning several disputes arising from Canada's protection measures).

[26] The disputes over Time and Reader's Digest reflect the issues associated with split runs in an early stage. For a recount of these stories, see, eg Acheson and Maule, above n 23, 187–91.

[27] See R Eberschlag, 'Culture Clash: Canadian Periodical Policies and the World Trade Organization' (1998) 26 *Manchester Law Journal* 65, 66; JH Thompson, 'Canada's Quest for Cultural Sovereignty: Protection, Promotion, and Popular Culture' in SJ Randell et al (eds), *North America without Borders?* (1992) 269, 272.

[28] See H Loeb, The Management and Resolution of Cross Border Disputes As Canada/US Enter the 21st Century: Telecommunication and Culture: Transborder Freedom of Information or Cultural Identity?' (2000) 26 *Canada—US Law Journal* 303, 303–11.

[29] Many studies address this historical context of *Canada—Periodicals* disputes. See, eg Scow, above n 22, 256–59; J Liss, 'The Impact of Technology Change on Canada's Affirmative Policy Model in the Cultural Industry and New Media Sectors' (1999) 25 *Canada—US Law Journal* 379 (arguing that, despite technological innovations, the rationale for Canada's affirmative cultural industries modes did not change).

[30] WTO, *Canada—Periodicals*, Request for Consultations by the United States, WT/DS31/1, 14 March 1996.

[31] WTO, *Canada—Periodicals*, Request for the Establishment of a Panel by the United States, WT/DS31/2, 24 May 1996.

[32] At its meeting on 19 June 1996, the DSB established a panel to hear the matter. The panel was constituted on July 25. The panel met with the parties on 11 October 1996 and 14–15 November 1996. WTO, *Canada—Periodicals*, Constitution of a Panel Established at the Request of the United States—Note by the Secretariat, WT/DS31/3, 29 July 1996. The Panel report was circulated to WTO Members on 14 March 1997.

[33] WTO, *Canada—Periodicals*, Report of the Appellate Body, WT/DS31/AB/R, 30 June 1997.

The decisions made by the panel and Appellate Body support most of the US argument.[34]

6.3.2 Lessons from *Canada—Periodicals*

A central issue in this case is the competition for advertising revenues between Canadian-owned magazines and split runs of American magazines. Trade issues arise from Canadian measures designed to bar foreign split runs, which fall into the realm of the WTO.[35] Canada argued that domestic periodicals promote national identity, which justifies enacting protective measures on their behalf. The US, in contrast, intended to use this case to demonstrate its hard line against trade barriers based on cultural measures.[36] As such, this case presents a conflict between economic value and cultural concern.

As noted above, although the cultural industry is a business, cultural products contain non-commercial values that distinguish them from other products. The question to be asked is whether the WTO tribunals neglect the constitutive role of culture and draw an equivalency between conventional goods and cultural products. Critics argue that the approach taken by the WTO tribunals in *Canada—Periodicals* does not grasp the duality of cultural products. They claim that the tribunals fail to fully appreciate Canada's dilemma in safeguarding its cultural autonomy in the face of an overwhelmingly one-way trade flow. The decisions are arguably at

[34] It was decided that the tariff item is inconsistent with GATT Art XI, as it is a quantitative restriction applying to a good instead of a service. The excise tax is inconsistent with Canada's WTO obligations because it does not provide national treatment under GATT Art III: the postal rate structure is inconsistent because it fails to provide national treatment, and the funding of postal rate scheme is not an allowable subsidy because the payments are not made directly from government revenues to publishers. WTO, *Canada—Periodicals*, Report of the Panel; WTO, *Canada—Periodicals*, Report of the Appellate Body.

[35] In a broad sense, all the measures at issue are relevant to cultural protection. Canada claims that domestic periodicals are necessary to assure that Canadian writers are read and Canadian readers have the opportunity to choose their work, contending that, because over 80% of English-language periodicals distributed in Canada are foreign, Canadian periodicals could not survive without protection. Canada further claims that split-run editions of American magazines involve unfair competition due to the dumping of editorial content into the Canadian market. See generally, WTO, *Canada—Periodicals*, Report of the Panel; WTO, *Canada—Periodicals*, Report of the Appellate Body.

[36] The US could have chosen to challenge Canadian measures under the North America Free Trade Agreement (NAFTA). In that forum, the complaint would have been a Chapter 20 dispute concerning the general applicability of NAFTA to cultural trade; the US did not choose this route because of the Canadian cultural exemption contained in the NAFTA. By placing the dispute before the WTO, the US could use the precedent as a lever to alter similar policies of Canada and other WTO Members. Canada was left holding a worthless note in the NAFTA exemptions, which seems to have evaporated under the WTO regime. See Eberschlag, above n 27, 90; see also Acheson and Maule, above n 23, 201. This raises an interesting question about the possibly overlapping jurisdictions of the WTO and NAFTA, and the resulting potential for forum shopping in trade disputes. See Scow, above n 22, 246.

variance with the overall objectives of the WTO Agreement, as well as international law that recognises that cultural autonomy is inherent to a global legal order.[37]

Canada—Periodicals is not an isolated example of GATT/WTO scepticism toward the claim of cultural exception.[38] One can explain the WTO tribunals' position by noting that, as it stands, the WTO is foremost a trade agreement concerned with opening markets. The WTO rules are made and perceived mainly through an economic prism.[39] By the same token, it is economic thinking that shapes how problems are understood and drives the WTO tribunals' analysis in resolving disputes. The recognition of culture's special nature may run counter to the key premise of free trade.[40] As a result, cultural justifications for deviating from trade rules are often ignored, sidestepped or belittled in the name of economic efficiency.

In another sense, the decisions in *Canada—Periodicals* provide certain guidance as to how governments should act to protect local culture and, at the same time, conform to trade rules; this is especially significant in an era where international treaties increasingly intrude into areas previously considered to be purely domestic. Canada—indeed any WTO Member—can no longer avoid addressing the conflict between domestic cultural policies and international trade obligations. Canada's challenge becomes how to both support national culture and remain in compliance with its trade obligations. Simply favouring one commitment over the other will not eliminate this tension. Rather, new WTO-consistent instruments for supporting domestic cultural industries and mediating the interplay between trade and culture must be creatively developed.

The Canadian government faces certain political difficulties in complying with the WTO decisions in light of the fact that cultural protection enjoys widespread support in Canada. Dismantling protective measures at the behest of WTO would expose the Canadian government to criticism citing its inability in protecting domestic culture and its cession of sovereignty to trade bureaucrats in Geneva.[41] It must be noted, however, that these results in the case of Canada do not mean that trade liberalisation spells the end of cultural policies.

The WTO panel in this case expressly stated that it was not judging

[37] See C Carmody, 'When "Cultural Identity Was Not At Issue": Thinking about Canada—Certain Measures Concerning Periodicals' (1999) 30 *Law & Policy International Business* 231, 304.

[38] For example, in 1984, a GATT panel rejected a similar argument advanced by Japan in defence of certain quotas on leather imports. See WTO, *Japan—Measures on Imports of Leather* (hereinafter WTO, *Japan—Leather*), Report of the Panel, L/5623-315/94, ¶44, 15 May 1984. *Japanese—Alcoholic Beverages II* presents another similar picture.

[39] See Loeb, above n 28, 308–09; Devlin, above n 25, 177–98.

[40] See Paul, above n 20, 43.

[41] See Eberschlag, above n 27, 86.

Canada's right to protect its culture, but rather the instruments it used to achieve that goal.[42] This suggests that Canada can continue to pursue its cultural goal, but must do so through innovative means, through which cultural policies and trade principles can be brought into conformity with each other. In other words, Canada needs to reformulate its approach to protecting culture in light of trade obligations and changing technologies. In particular, these cultural policies should be modernised to fit within the range of what is acceptable under the WTO. In fact, on 29 July 1998, Canada announced that it was taking four specific actions to comply with the DSB rulings, including the elimination of the excise tax on foreign split runs. At the same time, it also announced its intention to introduce a new measure limiting the sale of advertising to Canadian publishers.[43]

6.4 *CHINA—PUBLICATIONS AND AUDIOVISUAL PRODUCTS*

The first WTO case concerning audiovisual products, *China—Publications and Audiovisual Products*, provides an unparalleled opportunity to examine the WTO's attitudes towards the conflict between trade and culture in this new era, especially after the UNESCO Convention on Cultural Diversity entered into effect on 18 March 2007.

6.4.1 Case Background and China's Audiovisual Sectors

As the media serves as an essential instrument in disseminating government policy and shaping public opinions, foreign engagement in this area may pose a threat to governmental control of information. Prior to its WTO accession, China's audiovisual sector was exclusively state-owned and a general ban was applied to foreign investment in this field. A licensing system was also widely used to control market access in cultural sectors. These restrictions were considered necessary because the Chinese audio-

[42] The panel in *Canada—Periodicals* stated obiter that, in order to avoid any misunderstanding as to the scope and implications of the findings, it would like to stress that the ability of any Member to take measures to protect its cultural identity was not at issue in the present case. See *Canada—Periodicals*, Report of the Panel, ¶5.45; see also T Knight, 'The Dual Nature of Cultural Products: An Analysis of the World Trade Organization's Decisions Regarding Canadian Periodicals' (1999) 57 *University of Toronto Faculty of Law Review* 165, 167.

[43] On the same day, the USTR denounced the Canadian initiative as "every bit as inconsistent with Canada's international trade obligations as its current discriminatory practices". See Scow, above n 22, 277–78.

visual sector performs multiple political, economic, social and cultural functions.[44]

The integration of the Chinese economy into the world market since 1980s, however, has gradually rendered it impossible for China to insulate its audiovisual sectors from foreign participation. Indeed, China made one of the most ambitious GATS commitments when it formally became a WTO Member in late 2001.[45] Its commitments on audiovisual sectors, while limited, appear to constitute a bold undertaking, given that this is a heavily regulated field in China. WTO membership greatly enhances access to the Chinese market for foreign cultural products, including audiovisual products.[46] China's means of fulfilling its WTO commitments has naturally attracted wide attention from other WTO Members. To this end, China overhauled domestic laws and regulations, and began to allow foreign involvement in cultural sectors.[47]

The US is keen on the prospect of an open Chinese market and expanded commercial opportunities for its highly competitive cultural products.[48] However, a close reading of China's WTO commitments reveals that a large part of its cultural sectors remains closed to foreign investment, with additional restrictions introduced in politically and economically sensitive areas.[49] Despite China's changing regulatory landscape since its accession to the WTO, information flow remains heavily censored and media distribution channels are still tightly controlled.[50] Although content review

[44] With respect to more discussion on China's media, see generally, S Donald, M Keane and Y Hong (eds), *Media in China: Consumption, Content, and Crisis* (2002).

[45] See A Mattoo, 'China's Accession to the WTO: The Services Dimension' (2003) 6 *Journal of International Economic Law* 299, 299. China became a WTO Member on 11 December 2001 after the WTO's Ministerial Conference had approved the text of agreement for China's entry into the WTO on 10 November 2001. See WTO, 'WTO Ministerial Conference Approves China's Accession', Press/252 (10 November 2001), available at http://www.wto.org/english/news_e/pres01_e/pr252_e.htm (last accessed on 16 June 2012).

[46] China's market access commitments on audiovisual sectors cover distribution services of audiovisual products and Internet service, creating an opening for international media companies in this huge market. See WTO, The Schedules of Specific Commitments of the P. R. of China, available at http://www.wto.org/english/thewto_e/acc_e/protocols_acc_membership_e.htm (last accessed on 16 June 2012).

[47] These take place particularly in the area of co-production and wholesaling and retailing of publications and audiovisual products. See Z Niu, 'The Door Is Wedged Open: China's Regulation on Foreign Access to Audiovisual Markets' (2007) 18(8) *Entertainment Law Review* 265, 265.

[48] WTO, *China—Publications and Audiovisual Products*, First Submission of the United States, May 13, 2008, ¶1.

[49] See, eg The Several Opinions on Introducing Foreign Investment Into the Cultural Sector, jointly issued by the Ministry of Culture (MOC), State Administration of Radio, Film and Broadcast (SARFB), General Administration of Press and Publication (GAPP), National Development and Reform Commission (NDRC) and the Ministry of Commerce (MOFCOM), Order [2005] 10 of the Ministry of Culture, 6 July 2005, Art 4 (prohibiting foreign investment into some specific cultural sectors).

[50] China retains a tight regime of content review associated with ideological control, which addresses the concerns of China's regulators over the political impact of foreign

for each sub-sector varies, the language employed is generally vague and directed towards political and economic needs.[51] This regulatory landscape severely limits the ability of foreign producers and distributors to benefit from the world's fastest growing market.

6.4.2 A Procedural Posture and the Summary of Case Decisions

On 10 April 2007, the US brought a case before the WTO regarding an array of Chinese measures affecting trading rights[52] and distribution services for certain publications and audiovisual home entertainment (AVHE) products.[53] After two unsuccessful consultations, the US requested the establishment of a panel.[54] The panel circulated its final report on 12

participation. See Niu, above n 47, 268. Under China's existing practices, 'content review'—in other words, 'censorship'—is tied to the importation and distribution of publications and audiovisual products. The state-approved companies may review the materials they import and decide what to reject.

[51] For a critique of censorship, see, eg N Mei, 'China and the Prior Content Requirement: A Decade of Invasion and Counter-Invasion by Transfrontier Satellite Television' (2003) 25 *Hasting Communications & Entertainment Law Journal* 265.

[52] Trading rights is one of the central issues in this case. China joined the WTO after it was founded in 1995 and thus had to accept disciplines on the right to import and export as part of the price of accession imposed by other WTO Members. These disciplines are included in China's Accession Protocol and Working Party Report, which constitute an integral part of WTO agreements. See WTO, 'Protocol on the Accession of the People's Republic of China', WT/L/432 (23 November 2001); WTO, 'Working Party on the Accession of China—Report of the Working Party on the Accession of China', WT/ACC/CHN/49 (1 October 2001). For more analysis on these WTO-plus provisions, see JY Qin, 'The Challenge of Interpreting "WTO-Plus" Provisions' (2010) 44(1) *Journal of World Trade* 127.

[53] The US requested consultations with China pursuant to Arts 1 and 4 of the Understanding on Rules and Procedures Governing the Settlement of Disputes (DSU), Art XXII of the GATT 1994 and Art XXII of the GATS regarding certain measures that restrict trading rights pertaining to reading materials, audiovisual home entertainment (AVHE) products, sound recordings and films for theatrical release, and that restrict market access for, or discriminate against, foreign suppliers of distribution services for reading materials, foreign suppliers of audiovisual services (including distribution services) for AVHE products, and foreign suppliers of distribution services for sound recordings. See WTO, *China—Publications and Audiovisual Products*, Request for the Consultations by the United States, 16 April 2007. On 10 July 2007, the US requested supplemental consultations with China with regard to certain national treatment concerns related to sound recording distribution services, as well as the distribution of sound recordings and films for theatrical release. See WTO, *China—Publications and Audiovisual Products*, Request for the Consultations by the United States—Addendum, WT/DS363/Add.1, 16 July 2007. The EC, Japan, Australia, Korea and Chinese Taipei reserved their third-party rights.

[54] The US and China held consultations respectively on 5–6 June and 31 July 2007. The consultations failed to resolve the dispute. The Panel was established by the DSB on 27 November 2007 and constituted on 27 March 2008. See DSB, 'Minutes of the Meeting Held on 19 November 2007', WT/DSB/M/242 (11 February 2008), ¶67; Constitution of the Panel Established at the Request of the United States: Note by Secretariat, WT/DS363/6, 28 March 2008.

August 2009;[55] both China and the US appealed its findings,[56] and the Appellate Body circulated its report on 21 December 2009.[57] The DSB adopted the Appellate Body's report and the modified panel report on 19 January 2009.[58] On 18 February 2010, China notified the DSB of its intention to implement its recommendations and rulings in this dispute and stated that it would need a reasonable period of time for implementation.[59] On 12 July 2010, China and the US agreed that this reasonable period of time should be 14 months from their adoption, a period which expired on 19 March 2011.[60]

In a series of China's status reports regarding the enforcement of DSB decisions, China expresses its respect for the rulings and reiterates its intention to implement the recommendations. China also emphasised that, because this dispute concerns a number of Chinese administrative measures on cultural products and is both complex and sensitive, it needs additional understanding from the WTO Members with regard to implementation. According to China's last status report, submitted on 13 April 2012, China has taken necessary measures to implement the DSB rulings and recommendations, and has ensured full implementation by amending or repealing most measures at issue,[61] except those concerning films for theatrical release.[62]

[55] WTO, *China—Publications and Audiovisual Products*, Report of the Panel, WT/DS363/R, 12 August 2009.

[56] On 22 September 2009, China notified the DSB of its intention to appeal certain issues of law covered in the Panel Report and certain legal interpretations developed by the panel, and filed a Notice of Appeal. On 29 September 2009, China filed an appellant's submission. The US announced its intention to appeal on 5 October 2009 and filed another appellant's submission on 7 October 2009. On 19 October 2009, China and the US each filed an appellee's submission. The oral hearing in this appeal was held on 2 and 3 November 2009.

[57] See generally WTO, *China—Publications and Audiovisual Products*, Report of the Appellate Body, WT/DS363/AB/R, 21 December 2009.

[58] WTO, *China—Publications and Audiovisual Products*, Action by the Dispute Settlement Body, WT/DS363/14, 21 January 2010.

[59] WTO, *China—Publications and Audiovisual Products*, Communication from China and the United States concerning Art 21.3(c) of the DSU, WT/DS363/15, 9 March 2010.

[60] WTO, *China—Publications and Audiovisual Products*, Agreement under Art 21.3(b) of the DSU, WT/DS363/16, 13 July 2010.

[61] The repealed or expired measures include Measures for Administration of Foreign-Invested Book, Periodical and Newspaper Distribution Enterprises, Measures for Administration of Sino-Foreign Distribution Contractual Joint Ventures of Audiovisual Products, Provisions on the Administration of Publishing Electronic Publications, etc. The amended measures include Regulations on the Management of Publications, Regulations on the Management of Audiovisual Products, and Provisions on the Administration of the Publications Market, Catalogue of Industries for Guiding Foreign Investment, etc. See WTO, *China—Publications and Audiovisual Products*, Status Report by China, WT/DS/363/17/Add.15, 13 April 2012.

[62] Regarding this part, note that China and the US made preliminary arrangements set forth in a Memorandum of Understanding, which were notified to the WTO. With respect to the key elements in the arrangements, see WTO, *China—Publications and Audiovisual Products*, Joint Communication from China and the United States, WT/DS/363/19, 11 May 2012. The Communication mentioned that the opportunities provided by these elements are available to all WTO Members.

In this case, the US claimed that China had failed to live up to its WTO commitments on trading rights[63] and distribution services involving certain cultural products.[64] The US also argued that some Chinese measures reduced the competitiveness of American media products and created pirating opportunities in the Chinese market.[65] These measures are contained in a series of administrative regulations issued by various Chinese government agencies.[66] The US held this to be inconsistent with China's obligations under the Accession Protocol, GATT Articles III:4 and XI:1, and GATS Articles XVI and XVII.[67]

China invoked the UNESCO instruments and GATT Article XX(a) to defend its measures as necessary to protect culture and maintain public morals. China also argued that some products at issue were not goods and therefore not subject to trading rights commitments or national treatment obligations. Though some of these efforts failed, China did

[63] With respect to trading rights, the US identifies a group of measures through which China only allows a handful of state-owned enterprises to import cultural products into China. The US alleges that these measures restrict the trading rights of foreign enterprises and individuals, as well as private Chinese enterprise, with respect to imported films for theatrical release, AVHE products, sound recordings and publications. WTO, *China—Publications and Audiovisual Products*, Request for Consultations by the United States, WT/DS363/1, 16 April 2007.

[64] Regarding the distribution service of pertinent cultural products, the US maintains that China limits market access for, or discriminates against, foreign suppliers of distribution services for publications and foreign suppliers of audiovisual services for AVHE products. Furthermore, the US submits that the imported products are placed in a less advantageous position than Chinese products. See ibid. Interestingly, it has been predicted that distribution services are likely to remain fertile ground for conflict between trade and culture, both in the audiovisual and print and media sectors. See ME Footer and CB Graber, Trade Liberalization and Cultural Policy' (2000) 3 *Journal of International Economic Law* 115, 137. With respect to China's commitments on the trading rights and distribution services, see Protocol on the Accession of the People's Republic of China, WT/L/432, 23 November 2001, ¶¶5.1–2; Working Party on the Accession of China–Report of the Working Party on the Accession of China, WT/ACC/CHN/49, 1 October 2001, ¶¶83–84.

[65] The US maintains that because of censorship and distribution restrictions, American products fail to obtain approval to enter Chinese markets. When legitimate copyright-intensive products face high market barriers, consumers have to resort to other channels of dissemination, settling for black market products or pirated goods. Pirates can readily gain footholds in the protected marketplace. As time passes, the Chinese market becomes saturated with unauthorised substitutes. This, in turn, causes the added unfortunate effect of undermining intellectual property protection for the goods being supplied. WTO, *China—Publications and Audiovisual Products*, First Submission of the United States, 13 May 2008, ¶ 9. However, from the perspective of information control, it is argued that stronger copyright protection may help control the flow of information and is likely to help legitimise China's information control policy. See, eg PK Yu, 'Three Questions That Will Make You Rethink the US–China Intellectual Property Debate' (2008) 7 *John Marshall Review of Intellectual Property Law* 412, 426–29.

[66] These include the State Council, the Ministry of Culture, the General Administration of Press and Publication, the State Administration of Radio, Film and Television, the Ministry of Commerce and other relevant government bureaus.

[67] WTO, *China—Publications and Audiovisual Products*, Request for Consultations by the United States, WT/DS363/1, 16 April 2007.

succeed in removing several measures from the panel's terms of reference on procedural grounds.

The panel found that China acted inconsistently with its WTO obligations in a number of ways. In particular, China unfairly restricted trading rights and market access, as well as failing to provide national treatment in certain areas.[68] The appeal mainly involved three issues: China's trading rights commitments,[69] the GATT Article XX(a) 'public morals exception'[70] and China's GATS obligations.[71] The Appellate Body upheld most of the panel's rulings.[72] Although the US did not get the maximum possible benefit out of this case,[73] the rulings handed a significant victory to America's creative industries, marking a key step towards ensuring Chinese market access both for American products and for American exporters and distributors.[74] Moreover, the rulings may complement American efforts to

[68] WTO, *China—Publications and Audiovisual Products*, Report of the Panel, WT/DS363/R, 12 August 2009.

[69] This concerns whether the panel erred in finding that China's measures pertaining to films for theatrical release and unfinished audiovisual products are subject to China's trading rights commitments. *China—Publications and Audiovisual Products*, Report of the Appellate Body, ¶124.

[70] This concerns whether Art XX(a) of the GATT 1994 may be invoked by China as a defence for violations of its trading rights commitments, and whether the panel erred in finding that China had not demonstrated its measures could be justified under Art XX(a). A related question is whether the Appellate Body can complete the analysis under Art XX(a) and the chapeau of Art XX should it find that the panel erred in its analysis of the 'necessity' within the meaning of Art XX(a). See ibid.

[71] This concerns whether the panel erred in finding that the entry 'Sound recording distribution services' in China's GATS Schedule extends to the distribution of sound recordings in non-physical forms and in finding, as a consequence, that the provisions prohibiting foreign-invested entities from engaging in the distribution of sound recordings in electronic form are inconsistent with Art XVII of the GATS. See ibid.

[72] See generally, *China—Publications and Audiovisual Products*, Report of the Appellate Body, ¶¶414–16.

[73] The US's failure to establish a number of those claims softens the impact of this case on China. In the majority of claims where inconsistency was not established, the panel notes that the US did not adequately establish their arguments in the first place, but merely indicated that the alleged inconsistency existed.

[74] See USTR, 'Finding is a Victory for America's Creative Industry', available at http://www.ustr.gov/about-us/press-office/press-releases/2009/december/wto-appellate-body-confirms-finding-against-china (last accessed on 16 June 2012). The US record and film companies hail the decision as a major victory and call upon China to use this occasion to adopt measures across the board that will expand opportunities for creators regardless of nationality and to abandon all practices that hinder legitimate commerce. Neip Turkewitz, vice president of the Recording Industry Association of America, said this in a statement. Citing from J Lynn, 'WTO Dispute Panel Paps China on Audiovisual Goods' (12 August 2009), available at http://www.reuters.com/article/industryNews/idUSTRE57B5YP20090812 (last accessed on 16 June 2012).

combat intellectual property piracy in China.[75] Interestingly, the rulings even met with a favourable response in some Chinese quarters.[76]

Notwithstanding the argument that this case is more about the conflict between economic liberalisation, political censorship and ideological control in China,[77] China's much-maligned censorship of cultural products was not addressed either in the panel report or in the Appellate Body report. Therefore, the case does not imply that China will open its market to more products but, rather, only to more providers dealing with the same quantity of products.[78]

Note that there are other cases concerning cultural products initiated within the WTO dispute settlement system, such as *Turkey—Taxation of Foreign Film Revenue*[79] and *Canada—Measures Affecting Film Distri-*

[75] Dan Glickman, President of the Motion Picture Association of America, called the panel finding 'a major victory in the MPAA's years-long battle to open the Chinese movie market'. (In spite of all the restrictions we face, there is no shortage of US filmed entertainment in China. Unfortunately far too much of it is pirated.) But the MPAA noted that the ruling did not affect a quota that allows no more than 20 foreign films to be released in Chinese cinemas each year. See 'WTO Rules against Chinese Restrictions on Foreign Books, Movies, Music', *Bridges Weekly*, 7 September 2009, available at http://ictsd.org/i/news/bridgesweekly/54713/(last accessed on 16 June 2012).

[76] The President of Huayi Brothers, China's largest privately owned media company, welcomed the ruling and called it 'good news for private companies'. See ibid.

[77] See H Gao, 'The Mighty Pen, the Almighty Dollar, and the Holy Hammer and Sickle: An Examination of the Conflict between Trade Liberalization and Domestic Cultural Policy with Special Regard to the Recent Dispute between the United States and China on Restrictions on Certain Cultural Products' (2007) 2 *Asian Journal of WTO & International Health Law & Policy* 313, 313.

[78] Although China's censorship rules were only a subtext in this case, the panel's findings about national treatment could have ramifications for China's Internet censorship policies. In fact, the California First Amendment Coalition, a freedom of expression advocacy group, has petitioned the USTR to initiate WTO dispute proceedings with China over its Internet censorship rules. They argue that the so-called 'great firewall' is a market access barrier. The USTR's office is currently considering this petition. See 'CFAC Taking on the Great Firewall of China', 14 June 2009, available at http://www.firstamendmentcoalition.org/2009/06/chinawto/(last accessed on 16 June 2012); see also N Rahaim, 'Using Free Trade to Force China to Permit More Free Speech', available at http://www.firstamendmentcoalition.org/2009/06/commentary23/(last accessed on 16 June 2012). Since 19 October 2011, the United States, under the WTO rules, has been seeking detailed information on the trade impact of Chinese policies that may block US companies' websites in China, creating commercial barriers that especially hurt America's small business, available at http://www.ustr.gov/about-us/press-office/press-releases/2011/october/united-states-seeks-detailed-information-china%E2%80%99s-i (last accessed on 16 June 2012).

[79] In June 1996, the US initiated this case concerning Turkey's taxation of foreign film revenues. At times, Turkey imposed a 25% tax on box office receipts generated from showing foreign films, while no such tax was due for receipts from showing locally produced films. GATT Art III (national treatment) was at the root of this complaint. The issue whether GATS was applicable was not touched upon. Following unsuccessful consultations, a panel was established in February 1997. During the panel's hearings, both parties notified the DSB of a mutually agreed upon solution in July 1997. Turkey acknowledged that its tax measure is incompatible with GATT Art III and agreed to equalise the box office tax imposed on the showing of both domestic and foreign films. See WTO, *Turkey—Taxation of Foreign Film Revenues*, complained by the US, WT/DS43, the request for consultations received on 17 June 1996, notification of mutually agreed solution received on 24 July 1997.

bution Services.[80] Some of these cases are relevant to culture through the media of legal, social or political traditions. Carmody examined several results of GATT decision-making where parties raised policy arguments based on cultural concerns,[81] which help us understand more about the treatment of culture under the multilateral trade regime. In the following sections, I will analyse several key issues involving cultural aspects—mainly in *Canada—Periodicals* and *China—Publications and Audiovisual Products*—in order to explore the WTO attitude towards the treatment of cultural products from the perspective of dispute settlement. These issues include the possibility of invoking UNESCO instruments as a general cultural defence, the overlap between cultural goods and services, and culture in 'like products' analysis.

6.5 HOW LIKELY IS A PARTY TO INVOKE UNESCO INSTRUMENTS AS A GENERAL CULTURAL DEFENCE?

In *Canada—Periodicals*, Canada's cultural arguments were not endorsed by the WTO tribunals. *China—Publications and Audiovisual Products* involves exclusively cultural products; China understandably chose to defend its measures by, among other arguments, claiming the need for cultural protection and diversity.

China held that the US was essentially attempting to obtain enhanced market access and greater commercial opportunity in China, while ignoring the unique nature of the products concerned. China tried to justify its measures by invoking the UNESCO Convention and UNESCO Universal Declaration on Cultural Diversity. Citing the definitions of 'culture' and the nature of cultural products articulated in these instruments, China intended to prove that cultural goods fall under a specific category of goods.[82] China emphasised that cultural goods are 'vectors of identity, values and meaning' and have a strong impact on public morals, and that, as such, they 'must not be treated as mere commodities or consumer

[80] On 20 January, 1998, the EC requested consultations with Canada concerning certain measures affecting film distribution services, including the 1987 Policy Decision on Film Distribution and its application to European companies. The EC contended that these measures violate GATS Art II (MFN treatment) by treating US competitors more favorably than European companies and GATS Art III (transparency). There was no panel established, nor was a settlement reached in this case. In fact, because the EC company most affected by the Canadian legislation was taken over by a Canadian company, this case was dropped. See WTO, *Canada—Measures Affecting Film Distribution Services*, complained by the European Union, WT/DS117, request for consultations received on 20 January 1998.

[81] For more discussion on these cases, see Carmody, above n 37, 261–76.

[82] WTO, *China—Publications and Audiovisual Products*, First Written Submission of the People's Republic of China, ¶¶129–34; Report of the Panel, ¶¶4.89, 4.276.

goods'.[83] Imported cultural goods, China further argued, may collide with standards of right and wrong conduct specific to China.[84] This, China argued, legitimates its regulatory framework and relevant measures.[85]

The US pointed out that the UNESCO Convention expressly provides that nothing in the Convention shall be interpreted as modifying the rights and obligations of the parties under any other treaties to which they are parties. Likewise, nothing in the text of the WTO agreements provides an exception in terms of cultural products.[86] Australia agreed that cultural values could contribute to public morals but did not think that China could rely on the cited UNESCO instruments to demonstrate such a relationship, not only because of the aspirational status of the UNESCO Declaration, but also due to the provision of the UNESCO Convention.[87] Korea considered that China's argument in this regard was misplaced not only because the UNESCO Convention itself precludes a situation where it can be used as a ground to justify alleged violations of the WTO agreements, but also because the relevant provisions of the DSU explicitly prohibit a panel from accepting such an argument.[88]

The panel did not address this sensitive issue, avoiding a direct answer as to whether there was a general cultural concern that China might invoke. Instead, the panel noted that China's defence questioned whether the regulatory measures could be maintained on the grounds that they are covered by China's right to regulate trade in a WTO-consistent manner and, further, that this right takes precedence over the relevant obligations.[89] In so doing, the panel actually transformed the cultural concern into a discussion of China's concrete WTO obligations. On appeal, China again stressed that cultural products have a specific nature and requested that the Appellate Body be mindful of this.[90] Like the panel, the Appellate Body did not conclusively decide whether cultural concern could serve as a general defence for China.

This is somewhat disappointing to people who would like to observe how the WTO tribunals directly copes with a cultural defence. The methodology adopted by this panel is similar to that adopted by the panel in *Canada—Periodicals* and may suggest again that cultural concern is not within the WTO tribunals' direct reach. This is due not only to

[83] WTO, *China—Publications and Audiovisual Products*, Oral Statement of the People's Republic of China to the First Meeting of the Panel, 22 July 2008, ¶2.

[84] WTO, *China—Publications and Audiovisual Products*, Report of the Panel, ¶7.712.

[85] Ibid, ¶4.387.

[86] Ibid, ¶4.207.

[87] Ibid, ¶5.13. See also UNESCO, Convention on Cultural Diversity, Art 20 (2) (nothing in this Convention shall be interpreted as modifying rights and obligations of the parties under any other treaties to which they are parties).

[88] WTO, *China—Publications and Audiovisual Products*, Report of the Panel, ¶5.61.

[89] Ibid, ¶7.721.

[90] WTO, *China—Publications and Audiovisual Products*, Report of the Appellate Body, ¶25.

the sensitivity of the issue itself, but also to the panel's standard term of reference, which may prevent it from considering outside conventions.[91]

6.6 APPLYING THE 'PUBLIC MORALS' EXCEPTION TO CULTURAL PRODUCTS

Recognising the difficulties in invoking the UNESCO instruments, China attempted to justify its measures with a general exception clause, specifically GATT Article XX(a), which relates to the measures 'necessary to protect public morals'.[92] Prior to this case, the 'public morals exception' was only applied once, in *US—Gambling*.[93] The findings in that case provide the WTO tribunals with seasoned guidance for the applying this exception in the present case. Both the panel and the Appellate Body discussed this issue in great detail, which furnishes us with a practical illustration of how the exception may be applied to cultural products.

6.6.1 The Availability of GATT Article XX(a) as China's Defense

China's invocation of GATT Article XX(a) as its defence for trading rights commitments contained in the Accession Protocol presents an interesting legal issue: can a GATT general exception clause be directly invoked as a defence to a breach of non-GATT obligations?

6.6.1.1 The Parties' Arguments and DSB's Findings Based on Different Approaches

China argued that the term 'WTO agreements' includes the WTO Agreement and all its Annexes. Hence, China claimed, it is entitled to take trade-regulating measures that are authorised by any WTO agreement. In accordance with this argument, China may take measures to pursue policy objectives in a manner consistent with GATT Article XX.[94] China further held that the measures at issue primarily aim at regulating, instead

[91] The panel is directed to consider 'covered agreements or agreements cited by the parties to the dispute'. DSU, Art 7. As a result, the more informal contexts in which cultural concerns arise might not be taken into account by the panels.

[92] WTO, *China—Publications and Audiovisual Products*, First Written Submission of the People's Republic of China, 22 July 2008, ¶16.

[93] WTO, *United States—Measures Affecting the Cross-Border Supply of Gambling and Betting Services* (hereinafter WTO, *US—Gambling*), WT/DS285, Report of the Panel, WT/DS285/R, adopted on 20 April 2005, as modified by Report of the Appellate Body, WT/DS285/AB/R.

[94] WTO, *China—Publications and Audiovisual Products*, Report of the Panel, ¶¶4.239, 7.735–38.

of restricting, the import of foreign cultural products, and could therefore be justified by GATT Article XX(a).[95]

Both the EC and Australia (third parties) submitted that GATT Article XX is not directly applicable to China's trading rights obligations since China's Accession Protocol is not part of GATT.[96] The US considered the relationship between GATT Article XX(a) and the Accession Protocol to be a question of broad systemic import.[97] In regard to the measures at issue, the US argued that they reside well outside of the parameters of Article XX(a). Moreover, their application fails to meet the requirements set forth in the chapeau of Article XX. It is thus unnecessary for the panel to determine whether Article XX(a) is available as an affirmative defence to China's trading rights commitments.[98]

After identifying the measures that China tried to justify under Article XX(a),[99] the panel examined whether this exception is available for China to invoke. The panel first recognised that China's trading rights obligations should be understood without prejudice to China's right to regulate trade in a WTO-consistent manner.[100] The panel found it appropriate to follow the approach taken by the Appellate Body in *US—Customs Bond Directive* to examine the issue.[101] Under the approach, the panel first assumed that Article XX(a) is available to China as a defence. Based on this presumption, the panel then examined whether the relevant measures satisfy the requirements of Article XX(a). If so, the panel would revert to the availability issue.[102] Note that a strict logic dictates that the panel should first examine the availability issue and then decide whether the measures can pass the two-tier test. The panel, however, inverted the order of analysis to avoid ruling on an issue that it might not want to grapple with. In fact, the panel concluded that China had not demonstrated that its measures are 'necessary' to protect public morals. This makes it unnecessary to revert to the availability issue.[103]

[95] Ibid, ¶7.708.

[96] WTO, *China—Publications and Audiovisual Products*, Third Party Oral Arguments by the European Communities, 23 July 2008, 2; Report of the Panel, ¶5.9.

[97] WTO, *China—Publications and Audiovisual Products*, Report of the Panel, ¶7.739.

[98] Ibid, ¶7.741.

[99] The panel understands that the measures China claims are justified under Art XX(a) concern reading materials and finished audiovisual products. China is not seeking to defend under Art XX(a) any of the relevant measures concerning films for theatrical release. This is because of China's position that these measures are not subject to China's trading rights commitments under the Accession Protocol. Ibid, ¶¶7.725–34.

[100] Ibid, ¶¶7.721–22.

[101] WTO, *United States—Customs Bond Directive for Merchandise Subject to Anti-dumping/Countervailing Duties*, WT/DS345/AB/R, 16 July 2008, ¶310. In this case, the Appellate Body was presented with an appeal concerning an affirmative defence under GATT Art XX(d) to justify a measure found to be inconsistent with the Anti-dumping Agreement. The Appellate Body inverted the order of analysis suggested by India, which indicated the Appellate Body's explicit unwillingness to rule on the issue.

[102] WTO, *China—Publications and Audiovisual Products*, Report of the Panel, ¶7.745.

[103] Ibid, ¶¶7.913–14.

The panel's approach may constitute the more far-reaching exercise of judicial economy,[104] but the Appellate Body did not consider it appropriate to employ such a method in the present case. The Appellate Body held that assuming *arguendo* that China can invoke Article XX(a) could be at odds with the objective of promoting security and predictability through dispute settlement, and may not assist in resolving disputes. The Appellate Body thus decided to first examine the availability issue and concluded that the provisions that China sought to justify have a clearly discernible, objective link to China's trade regulation. In light of this close relationship, the Appellate Body found that China might seek to justify those provisions as necessary to protect public morals in China.[105]

6.6.1.2 A Commentary on the Availability Issue

Altering the order of analysis for strategic reasons or to avoid undesired issues or claims is arguably an exercise of substantive judicial economy called 'judicial avoidance',[106] which takes place when a tribunal does not wish to deal with a particular issue raised by a party and takes steps to avoid it in a way that still allows the tribunal to adjudicate the dispute. This is not uncommon in international adjudication.[107] The International Court of Justice, for instance, used the same methodology in a case concerning an arrest warrant.[108]

Although reliance upon an assumption *arguendo* is a legal technique that an adjudicator may use in order to enhance simplicity and efficiency in decision-making, there are several problems associated with this approach identified by the Appellate Body. First, the tribunals may choose to employ

[104] See A Alvarez-Jiménez, 'The WTO Appellate Body's Exercise of Judicial Economy' (2009) 12 *Journal of International Economic Law* 393, 410.

[105] WTO, *China—Publications and Audiovisual Products*, Report of the Appellate Body, ¶¶215–35.

[106] The difference between the this type of substantive judicial economy and judicial economy regarding issues unnecessary to resolve a controversy lies in the fact that, in the latter, the Appellate Body deems that it does not need to address the given substantive issue to resolve the dispute. In the former, in addition to judicial economy, there is also judicial avoidance: the Appellate Body feels the need to resolve the controversy without addressing a particular substantive issue. See Alvarez-Jiménez, above n 104, 407.

[107] Ibid, 409.

[108] See International Court of Justice, *Case Concerning the Arrest Warrant of 11 April 2000 (Democratic Republic of the Congo v Belgium)* [2002] ICJ Rep 3, ¶¶45–46. The facts in this case are associated with the legality of the arrest warrant in absentia issued by a Belgian judge against Abdulaye Y Ndombasi, then Minister of the Democratic Republic of Congo (DRC), for crimes against humanity that took place in the DRC and that did not involve Belgian citizens or interests. Belgium was trying to exert universal jurisdiction to prosecute crimes of this nature; the DRC claimed that Belgium lacked jurisdiction to issue the arrest warrant and that this warrant violated the international law principle according to which foreign ministers enjoyed criminal immunity. The Court considered it necessary not to deal with the complex issue of universal criminal jurisdiction and concentrated only on the less complex subject matter of diplomatic immunity.

this technique in particular circumstances, but it may not always provide a solid foundation upon for legal conclusions. Secondly, use of the technique may detract from a clear enunciation of the relevant laws and create difficulties for implementation. Thirdly, recourse to this technique may be problematic for certain types of legal issues, such as those that go to the jurisdiction of a tribunal or preliminary questions on which the substance of a subsequent analysis depends.[109]

In the present case, the approach adopted by the Appellate Body may reduce uncertainty with respect to the WTO Members' implementation obligations. For those who seek to have Article XX apply outside the GATT context, this is clearly a positive result. However, the Appellate Body did not offer a general guidance on the relationship of GATT Article XX to non-GATT agreements. As a result, the full scope of the Appellate Body's conclusions in this regard is likely to be the subject of much debate.[110]

6.6.2 Applying Article XX(a) to China's Measures

Successful justification of its measures requires that China demonstrate that they comply with the requirements of GATT Article XX; in other words, China must prove that they constitute an exercise of its right to regulate trade in a manner consistent with the WTO Agreement.

6.6.2.1 The Concept of 'Public Morals'

China maintained that the preservation of public morals is a crucial policy objective and forms 'a central element of social cohesion and the capacity

[109] WTO, *China—Publications and Audiovisual Products*, Report of the Appellate Body, ¶213.

[110] One noteworthy recent development on this issue was reflected in *China—Measures Related to the Exportation of Various Raw Materials*. In this case, the Panel found that the wording of China's Protocol of Accession did not allow China to use the general exceptions in Art XX of the GATT 1994 to justify its WTO-inconsistent export duties. The Appellate Body concluded that a proper interpretation of para 11.3 of China's Accession Protocol does not make available to China the exceptions under Art XX of the GATT 1994 to justify export duties that are found to be inconsistent with China's obligations under para 11.3. See WTO, *China—Measures Related to the Exportation of Various Raw Materials*, the Report of Appellate Body, WT/DS/394/AB/R, WT/DS395/AB/R, and WT/DS398/AB/R, 30 January 2012, ¶¶270–307. These decisions provoked widespread discussions on a systemic issue. See, eg F Piérola, 'The Availability of a GATT Article XX Defence with Respect to a Non-GATT Claim: Changing the Rules of the Game?' (2010) 5 *Global Trade and Customs Journal* 172; JY Qin, 'The Predicament of China's "WTO-Plus" Obligation to Eliminate Export Duties: A Commentary on the *China–Raw Materials* Case' (2012) 11 *Chinese Journal of International Law* 239; M Tyagi, 'Flesh on a Legal Fiction: Early Practice in the WTO on Accession Protocols' (2012) 15 *Journal of International Economic Law* 398; M Matsushita, 'Export Control of Natural Resources: WTO Panel Ruling on the Chinese Export Restrictions of Natural Resources' (2011) 3 *Trade, Law and Development* 286.

of communities to live together'. The concept of 'public morals' covers a wide range of issues, from the depiction or vindication of violence or pornography to the protection of Chinese culture and the traditional values to which China grants the utmost importance. China alleged that there was a close link between the import entities, the content review mechanism for imported cultural products and the protection of public morals.[111]

The US did not challenge China's assessment of the importance of public morals, nor did it argue that the measures at issue were not designed to protect public morals. Instead, the US challenged the means through which China had chosen to achieve its objectives.[112] Australia, as a third party, held that not all items having genuine cultural value to a Member are automatically encompassed by the term 'public morals'.[113] China had to show a relationship between the cultural value of the products at issue and the standards of right and wrong conduct maintained in China.[114]

The panel agreed that the term 'public morals' denotes standards of right and wrong conduct maintained by or on behalf of a community or nation, a definition adopted by the WTO tribunals in *US—Gambling*.[115] Moreover, the panel noted that the content of 'public morals' can vary in time and space, depending upon a range of factors including prevailing social, cultural, ethical and religious values.[116] The panel recognised that a WTO Member has the sovereign right to determine the level of protection for values and objectives covered by Article XX(a).[117] Based on these considerations, the panel concluded that China enjoyed some freedom to define its own concept of 'public morals'.[118]

[111] WTO, *China—Publications and Audiovisual Products*, Report of the Panel, ¶¶7.711–16.

[112] Ibid, ¶¶7.717–20.

[113] Consider the example of books, which have cultural value. The fact that books have cultural value in Australia would not automatically give Australia the right to control the import of all books to protect public morals in Australia. Rather, Australia would have to show a relationship between the cultural value of books to Australia and the standards of right and wrong conduct maintained in Australia. Ibid, ¶5.12.

[114] Ibid, ¶¶5.12–13.

[115] WTO, *US—Gambling*, Report of the Panel, ¶6.465; Report of the Appellate Body, ¶299.

[116] WTO, *US—Gambling*, Report of the Panel, ¶6.461.

[117] See WTO, *China—Publications and Audiovisual Products*, First Written Submission of the People's Republic of China, ¶192. See also WTO, *European Communities—Measures Affecting Asbestos and Products Containing Asbestos* (hereinafter WTO, *EC—Asbestos*), Report of Appellate Body, WT/DS135/AR/R, 12 March 2001, ¶168; WTO, *Korea—Measures Affecting Imports of Fresh, Chilled and Frozen Beef* (hereinafter *Korea—Beef*), Report of Appellate Body, WT/DS161/AB/R, 11 December 2000, ¶176. An example of such measure is an import ban on cultural goods with specific characteristics, such as foreign X-rated films, music CDs containing songs with racist lyrics, etc. See P Van Den Bossche, 'Free Trade and Culture: A Study of Relevant WTO Rules and Constraints on National Cultural Policy Measures', Maastricht Faculty of Law Working Paper No 2007-4 (2007) 64–65.

[118] WTO, *China—Publications and Audiovisual Products*, Report of the Panel, ¶7.817.

6.6.2.2 *The Parties' Arguments on the 'Necessity' Test*

The 'necessity' test is of extreme importance in determining whether China's defence could succeed on the ground of public morals; as such, the parties to the disputes always lay much emphasis on this issue.

In this case, China argued that, in considering the potential impact of cultural goods on public morals, its long-standing policy had been highly protective, completely prohibiting both cultural goods with content deemed inappropriate and the possible dissemination of cultural goods with content that could have a negative impact on public morals.[119] China considers this prohibition essential to ensuring that traditional cultural values are not damaged by imported cultural goods.[120] To achieve this goal effectively and efficiently,[121] China applies a content review to the importation of cultural goods, enacted through the careful selection of importation entities.[122] Although this system may result in limiting the right to trade, it is consistent with China's 'right to regulate trade'.[123] Overall, China emphasised that the content review is 'necessary' to protect public morals and that the selection of import entities is 'necessary' to avoid any possible circumvention of the content review process.[124]

Invoking the Appellate Body's opinion in *US—Gambling*, the US contended that China's measures lie far outside the scope of 'indispensability' that defines a measure as 'necessary'.[125] In particular, the US submitted that denying trading rights to all foreign importers and privately owned Chinese importers cannot be justified under Article XX(a).[126] Furthermore, according to the US critique, China never explained why the entities involved in content review need to be granted a monopoly over the importation process.[127]

[119] Ibid, ¶¶4.277, 7.713. WTO, *China—Publications and Audiovisual Products*, First Written Submission of the People's Republic of China, ¶ 135.

[120] WTO, *China—Publications and Audiovisual Products*, First Written Submission of the People's Republic of China, ¶190.

[121] WTO, *China—Publications and Audiovisual Products*, First Written Submission of the People's Republic of China, ¶¶173–234; Report of the Panel, ¶4.107–109, 4.413, 7.743–45.

[122] Ibid, WTO, *China—Publications and Audiovisual Products*, Report of the Panel, ¶4.278.

[123] Id., ¶¶7.713–14.

[124] According to China, the selection of import entities is a decisive element of its content review mechanism. Specifically, China argues that its selection criteria—(i) an appropriate organisational structure of the selected entities; (ii) a reliable, competent and capable personnel within the selected entities; (iii) appropriate geographical coverage by the selected entities; and (iv) a limited number of selected entities—contribute to an efficient and effective content review and to the fulfilment of its objective.

[125] WTO, *China—Publications and Audiovisual Entertainment Products*, Report of the Panel, ¶7.718, which reads: 'a necessary measure is . . . located significantly closer to the pole of "indispensable" than to the opposite pole of simply "making a contribution to"'.

[126] Ibid, ¶¶4.210–12.

[127] Ibid, ¶¶7.717, 7.752–75.

6.6.2.3 *The Analytical Approach to the 'Necessity' Test under Article XX(a)*

In this case, the panel was required to assess 'necessity' within the meaning of the multiple provisions in Article XX(a) that it had found to be inconsistent with China's trading rights commitments. To this end, the panel first considered the relationship between the measures at issue and the protection of public morals.[128] The panel assumed that each of the types of prohibited content in China's measures could have a negative impact on public morals in China. The panel then identified the importance of the protection of public morals and the level of protection sought by China.[129] Up to this point, the panel's analysis dealt with all the measures that China sought to justify. In the next stage, the panel addressed each individual measure that it had found to be inconsistent with China's obligations.

On appeal, the US raised issue with this 'two-step' analytical approach taken by the panel. The US pointed to the fact that the text of Article XX(a) sets out 'necessary' as a single criterion—which suggests a 'single, integrated, yet multifaceted inquiry'—and requested clarification, claiming that an Article XX analysis should be approached in a integrated fashion.[130] The Appellate Body summarised the approach used by the panel, but did not think that the approach amounted to an error.[131] In essence, the panel undertook an analysis that was aggregated and relevant to all measures and, at the same time, disaggregated and specific to each individual measure. In this way, the panel may have created some confusion. However, given that the difficulty faced by the panel in deciding how to tackle the series of factors to be weighed and balanced in its analysis of 'necessity' was heightened by the large number of challenged measures, it is understandable that the panel grouped all of the relevant provisions together for the purpose of certain analytic steps while analysing measures individually for the purposes of other steps.

6.6.2.4 *The Key Elements of the 'Necessity' Test*

The panel recognised that the protection of public morals ranks among the most important values or interests as a matter of public policy. Thus, in reviewing the 'necessity' test, the panel considered the high level of public morals protection that China had determined to be appropriate

[128] Ibid, ¶¶7.751–93.
[129] Ibid, ¶¶7.817–19.
[130] WTO, *China—Publications and Audiovisual Products*, Report of the Appellate Body, ¶¶236–38.
[131] Ibid, ¶¶239–49.

for its territory with respect to cultural products.[132] At the same time, the panel referred to the relevant jurisprudence in making its decisions.[133]

The panel examined three different groups of relevant provisions in the content review system: criteria provisions, discretion provisions and exclusion provisions. For each measure, the panel performed three analytic steps: (i) identifying the contribution made to the protection of public morals; (ii) identifying the restrictive impact on trade; and (iii) 'weigh[ing] and balanc[ing]' three factors—that is, the extent of the contribution, the restrictive impact on trade and 'the fact that the protection of public morals is a highly important interest in China'.[134] After a thorough analysis, the panel characterised the 'suitable organization and qualified personnel requirement' and 'the state plan requirement' as 'necessary', in the absence of available measures, to protect public morals in China.[135]

If a panel reaches the preliminary conclusion that a challenged measure is 'necessary', this result must be confirmed by comparing the measure with possible alternatives, which may have a less trade-restrictive effect.[136] The US contended that China had numerous alternatives at hand to achieve its content review objectives without restricting trading rights.[137] After analysing the US's proposal that the Chinese government be given sole responsibility for conducting content review, the panel found that China had not demonstrated that the proposed alternative was not a genuine alternative or was not reasonably available.[138] These findings led the panel to conclude that none of the measures at issue was 'necessary' within the meaning of Article XX(a).[139]

At this point, the panel had completed all steps involved in a 'necessity' analysis. According to the well-established WTO dispute settlement practice, it must subsequently examine whether the measure satisfies the requirements of the chapeau of Article XX.[140] This approach equips the WTO tribunals with sufficient latitude to prevent the excessive use or

[132] WTO, *China—Publications and Audiovisual Products*, Report of the Panel, ¶7.819.

[133] Some previous Appellate Body Reports provide more details in analysing the 'necessity' test. See, eg WTO, *Brazil—Measures Affecting Imports of Retreaded Tires*, Report of the Appellate Body, WT/DS22/AB/R, 3 December 2007; WTO, *Korea—Beef*, Report of Appellate Body; WTO, *US—Gambling*, Report of the Appellate Body.

[134] WTO, *China—Publications and Audiovisual Products*, Report of the Panel, ¶¶7.820–28.

[135] Ibid, ¶¶7.821–68.

[136] WTO, *Korea—Beef*, Report of Appellate Body, ¶166; WTO, *US—Gambling*, Report of the Appellate Body, ¶308.

[137] WTO, *China—Publications and Audiovisual Products*, Report of the Panel, ¶¶4.320, 7.719.

[138] Ibid, ¶¶7.897–908.

[139] Ibid, ¶7.911.

[140] See, eg *Brazil—Retreaded Tires*, Report of the Appellate Body, ¶139; *United States—Restrictions on Importation of Certain Shrimp and Shrimp Products* (hereinafter *US—Shrimps*), Report of the Appellate Body, WT/DS58/AB/R, adopted 6 November 1998, ¶147. This test was also confirmed by the Appellate Body to apply mutatis mutandis for the general exceptions clause under the GATS. See WTO, *US—Gambling*, Report of the Appellate Body, ¶292.

abuse of general exceptions.[141] Here, given the panel's conclusion that China had not demonstrated that its measures were 'necessary' to protect public morals, there was no need to examine whether they satisfied the requirements of the Article XX chapeau.[142]

On appeal, China challenged the panel's analysis under Article XX(a), as well as its ultimate finding with respect to the 'necessity' test. China also requested that the Appellate Body complete the analysis of 'necessity'. The US, on the other hand, requested that the Appellate Body uphold its findings and reverse an intermediate finding that China's mandate for conformity to its 'state plan' was 'necessary'.[143] In its report, the Appellate Body individually addressed these issues and finally upheld the panel's conclusion that China had not demonstrated 'necessity'.[144]

Note that both the panel and the Appellate Body laid their analytical emphasis on whether the measures at issue could meet the 'necessity' test when they made decisions on GATT Article XX(a). In order to render judgment on 'necessity', the panel first assumed that the measures fell within the purpose of protecting public morals, and then evaluated those measures on the basis of their trade-restrictiveness and their contribution to the purported goals. The Appellate Body revised the *arguendo* approach but employed a similar technique in analysing the 'necessity' test. In so doing, the WTO tribunals sidestepped the highly sensitive issue of censorship. The approach used by the tribunals to analyse 'necessity' in this case also shows that they may be receptive to non-trade concerns that underlie trade-restrictive measures. When it came to cultural concerns, however, China and the tribunals avoided the debate on whether cultural diversity is conducive to the substantive purpose of a 'public morals' exception.

6.7 DISTINGUISHING CULTURAL GOODS FROM CULTURAL SERVICES

Under the WTO framework, the treatment of cultural products depends on the different regulatory disciplines that result from the products' categorisation as either goods or services. Because the GATS provides more flexibility and less stringent disciplines than the GATT, the current level of protection is relatively low for cultural goods, but high for cultural services. Therefore, for example, the classification of a film download as

[141] See NF Diebold, 'The Morals and Order Exception in WTO Law: Balancing the Toothless Tiger and the Undermining Mole' (2008) 11 *Journal of International Economic Law* 43, 74; see also above ch 5.6 (General Exception Clauses).

[142] WTO, *China—Publications and Audiovisual Products*, Report of the Panel, ¶7.912.

[143] WTO, *China—Publications and Audiovisual Products*, Report of the Appellate Body, ¶¶234–35.

[144] Ibid, ¶¶250–337.

a good or as a service results in a starkly different regulatory discipline. The difference also affects the applicability of a number of other WTO agreements regulating the use of contingent instruments—principally anti-dumping and countervailing measures, given that these instruments have not been applied to cultural services.

6.7.1 Identifying the Issue and its Associated Difficulties

The problem of differentiation between a cultural good and a service arises both in theory and in practice. As culture becomes an increasingly profitable business and technology makes international dissemination of cultural products easier, the classification of these activities for the purpose of trade regulation has become a key issue. It is often impossible to categorise a cultural product neatly as either a good or a service.[145] Some cultural products—such as CDs, books and paintings—are obvious goods, while a cultural performance more closely resembles a service. Many cultural products, however, have both service and good components,[146] which has caused a long-standing controversy within the GATT/WTO regime.[147]

Take digital cultural products as an example. The US conceivably favours classifying digital products as goods in order to trigger stricter GATT disci-

[145] See Braun and Parker, above n 21, 187–88.

[146] For instance, although cinema is specifically mentioned in GATT Art III (National Treatment) and Art IV (Special Treatment for Cinematographic Films), cinema may be considered a service in the GATS and some other international instruments. See, eg OECD, Code of Liberalization of Current Invisible Operations 2008, Annex V to Annex A, Films (Art 1 provides that for cultural reasons, systems of aid to the production of printed films for cinema exhibition may be maintained provided that they do not significantly distort international competition in export markets).

[147] In 1961, a Working Party was established at the request of the US to examine the application of GATT 1947 to television programmes. The US argued that television programmes are goods under the GATT, but that Art IV should not extend to these programmes because of the different nature of television programmes from cinematographic films. Other members of the Working Party suggested that Art IV should apply equally to television programmes, or that television programming is a service not covered by the GATT. The Working Party made draft recommendations but did not resolve the issue. For the background and development of this issue, see GATT, Application of GATT to International Trade in Television Programs, L/1615, 16 November 1961; GATT, Application of GATT to International Trade in Television Programs: Statement Made by the United States Representative on 21 November 1961, L/1646, 24 November 1961; GATT, Application of GATT to International Trade in Television Programs: Revised United States Draft Recommendations, L/1908, 10 November 1962; GATT, Application of GATT to International Trade in Television Programs: Report of the Working Party, Annex 1, L/1741, 13 March 1962, ¶¶6–10; GATT, Application of GATT to International Trade in Television Programs: Proposal by the Government of the United States, L/2120, 18 March 1964; Uruguay Round Group of Negotiations on Services, Working Group on Audiovisual Services, Note on the Meeting of 27–28 August 1990, MTN. GNS/AUD/1, 27 Sepember 1990, ¶8.

plines and the resulting liberalisation of electronic commerce.[148] In stark contrast, the European Union sticks to the view that electronic delivery constitutes a service and thus falls within the scope of the GATS.[149] This categorisation would ensure that the EU's exclusion of audiovisual service from its GATS commitments applies to music, films and similar electronically delivered products.[150] Trade in materials, sound recordings, films and other apparatus used to diffuse television signals, however, is subject to rules related to the free movement of goods.[151] Some cases that have been heard by the European courts mirror this view.[152]

Along with the increasingly arbitrary substantive separation between goods and services,[153] the traditional classification of audiovisual services under the GATS no longer reflects reality.[154] Technological development and media convergence have further blurred the distinction: satellites and

[148] WTO, Work Programme on Electronic Commerce: Submission by the United States, ¶7, WT/COMTD/17; WT/GC/16; G/C/2; S/C/7; IP/C/16, 12 February 1999. See also S Wunsch-Vincent, *The WTO, the Internet and Trade in Digital Products: EC–US Perspectives* (2006) 52.

[149] WTO Council for Trade in Services, 'Communication from the European Communities and their Member States: Electronic Commerce Work Programme', S/C/W/183 (30 November 2000), ¶6(a).

[150] See W Drake and K Nicolaidis, 'Global Electronic Commerce and GATS: The Millennium Round and Beyond' in P Sauvé and R Stern (eds), *GATS 2000: New Directions in Services Trade Liberalization* (2000) 399–408.

[151] For instance, in the Cinéthèque case, the importation of audiovisual material in the form of videocassettes was ruled to involve goods instead of service. Common Market Reporter, *Cinéthèque SA v Fédération Nationale des Cinémas Francais*, Case 60–61/84 (1986), Court Decisions, 1985–86, ¶¶14.220, 16.344. In another case involving favourable treatment given to French newspaper printers, the Court ruled that 'printing work cannot be described as a service, since it leads directly to the manufacture of a physical article which, as such, is classified in the Common Customs Tariff'. See Common Market Reporter, *EEC Commission v France*, Case 18/84 (1986), Court Decisions, 1985–86, ¶¶14.207, 16.259.

[152] For example, in the *Sacchi* case, it was ruled that the transmission of television signals, including those containing advertising, comes under the rules of the Treaty of Rome related to services. The Court of Justice of the European Communities, Case C-155/73 *Italian v Guiseppe Sacchi* [1974] ECR 409, 427. This finding is used by the EC/EU to argue that broadcasting does not fall under the scope of GATT during the Uruguay Round negotiation. Interestingly, the Motion Picture Export Association of America (MPEAA) later used the *Sacchi* case to argue that television programmes and films are goods within the meaning of Art XI:1 of the GATT. The MPEAA argument is made 'in the request of the MPEAA for Designation of the EC as a Priority Country Under Section 182 of the Omnibus Trade Act of 1988', filed by Jane K Albrecht, 15 February 1991.

[153] Hahn observes that it is largely arbitrary, from a policy standpoint, that a Hollywood blockbuster would be subjected to a completely different legal regime if it were projected onto foreign screens not from a cinematographic film (a good governed by the GATT), but rather by using digitally transmitted data sent from a central distribution point (a service governed by the GATS). See M Hahn, 'A Clash of Cultures? The UNESCO Diversity Convention and International Trade Law' (2006) 9 *Journal of International Economic Law* 515, 527.

[154] WTO Council for Trade in Services, 'Communication from the United States—Audiovisual and Related Services', S/CSS/W/21 (18 December 2000) [3], [10(i)]. Moreover, audiovisual services may also overlap with other service sectors, such as 'recreational, cultural and sporting services', given the fact that some WTO Members have included 'cinema theatre operation services' in this sector.

the internet allow cultural products to reach wide audiences without being packaged and shipped across borders.[155] This increase in the complexity of the distinction between goods and services is paralleled by a gradual expansion of trade rules beyond services to intellectual property rights.[156] These issues are currently the subjects of a work programme on electronic commerce.[157]

In summary, the imprecision of the goods–service distinction remains an unsettled subject for the culture and trade issue. The radical divergence among central negotiators calls for greater efforts to harmonise the treatment of audiovisual products within the WTO regime.[158] Until a line is established, conflicts of this nature are bound to multiply and may pose a threat to cultural policy measures,[159] as indicated by *China—Publications and Audiovisual Products*.

6.7.2 The Practice of WTO Tribunals

The line between what constitutes an audiovisual good and a service has been left largely unclear by the WTO agreements. In practice, this thorny issue was examined in both *Canada—Periodical* and *China—Publications and Audiovisual Products*. In *Canada—Periodicals*, the Appellate Body ruled that periodicals are goods comprising two components: editorial content and advertising content. Both components can be viewed as having service attributes, but they combine together to form a physical product—the periodical itself.[160] *China—Publications and Audiovisual Products* offers a recent illustration of how WTO tribunals classify 'films distributed for theatrical release' and 'audiovisual products used for publication'.

[155] As digital technology advances, cultural products may take physical forms, such as film reels, DVDs and audiotapes, which can be purchased at a store and online, but can also be delivered directly in digitalised form via cable or the internet. See Braun and Parker, above n 21, 187–88.

[156] See RJ Neuwirth, 'The Cultural Industries and the Legacy of Art IV GATT: Rethinking the Relation of Culture and Trade in Light of the New WTO Round', paper presented at the Conference 'Cultural Traffic: Policy, Culture, and the New Technologies in the European Union and Canada', Carleton University, 22–23 November 2002, 20.

[157] WTO Secretariat, 'Fifth Dedicated Discussion on Electronic Commerce under the Auspices of the General Council on 16 May and 11 July 2003: Summary by the Secretariat of the Issues Raised', WT/GC/W/509 (31 July 2003); WTO, 'Work Program on Electronic Commerce Adopted by the General Council on 25 September 1998', WT/L/274 (30 September 1998), ¶¶2.1, 3.1.

[158] See, eg Voon, above n 156, 17–18, 31 (advocating the application of GATS to digital audiovisual products, though with invigorated MFN and national treatment obligations and subject to a limited exception for discriminatory subsidies).

[159] For further analysis of the problematic distinction between goods and services, see F Smith and L Woods, 'A Distinction without Difference: Exploring the Boundary between Goods and Services in the World Trade Organization and the European Union' (2005) 12(1) *Columbia Journal of European Law* 1.

[160] WTO, *Canada—Periodicals*, Report of the Appellate Body, ¶463.

In this case, China argued that films for theatrical release, unfinished AVHE products and unfinished sound recordings are not goods, and that, as services, their importation is subject to China's GATS Schedule of Commitments.[161] China listed several reasons to support this argument, including the intangibility of motion pictures, the nature of tangible film as a mere accessory of a service and international classification instruments that classify motion pictures as services.[162] China argued that a 'tangible good' is undeniably involved. A physical copy of the film, whether in celluloid or digital form, is a good that has to pass through customs clearance and falls under a specific tariff heading. However, China argued, the essential nature of a film which is being distributed for a theatrical release, the tangible good itself, is merely the vehicle to transport a bundle of intellectual property rights, on which a distribution contract between the film's producers and distributors and theatre owners is based. The distribution contract represents the essential commercial value, while the actual tangible good, the celluloid or digital copy of the film, is a mere accessory.

On the opposing side, the US invoked the GATT text, the Appellate Body's guidance on the issue and China's own treatment of films as goods, and contended that its claims concerned goods. The US warned that China's reasoning, if accepted, would transform all goods commercially exploited through associated services into services themselves.[163]

The EU did not support the US's line of argument on this issue. The EU held that if a film were traded as a good, it would be copied to a DVD or to a videocassette, and would be sold to private individuals for their own personal use and viewing. Such copies of films are generally not intended for public viewing in theatres, while the showing of films in theatres for the general public cannot be treated as anything but a service.[164] Australia maintained that films for theatrical release are goods.[165] Korea tended to agree that the main characteristics of motion pictures for theatrical release are somewhat closer to those of services, but was not persuaded that motion pictures as goods can be separated from the associated services.[166]

In considering this issue, the panel found several regulatory factors to be relevant: heading 3706 of the Harmonized Commodity Description and

[161] WTO, *China—Publications and Audiovisual Products*, First Written Submission of the People's Republic of China, ¶29.107.

[162] WTO, *China—Publications and Audiovisual Products*, Report of the Panel, ¶4.302.

[163] Ibid, ¶4.301.

[164] WTO, *China—Publications and Audiovisual Products*, Third Party Oral Arguments by the European Communities, 23 July 2008, 3.

[165] Australia suggests, however, that the panel may consider that the items at issue are not necessarily physical goods. In that event, Australia does not consider content separate from its carrying media to be a good. WTO, *China—Publications and Audiovisual Products*, Report of the Panel, ¶¶5.2–5.

[166] Ibid, ¶5.57.

Coding System (HS),[167] China's Schedule of Concessions and China's levy of customs duties on the importation of exposed and developed cinematographic film. The panel also found the explanatory note accompanying heading 3706 of the HS to be instructive.[168] In the light of these factors, the panel concluded that 'films for theatrical release'—that is, hard-copy cinematographic films in any tangible form—should be classified as goods for the purpose of China's trading rights commitments.[169]

The US also claimed that some measures regulating 'unfinished audiovisual products' are inconsistent with China's trading rights commitments, because they inject qualifying criteria and government discretion into a process that China has committed to make 'non-discretionary'.[170] China held that these products are not goods and that the challenged measures that regulate the importation of 'audiovisual products used for publication' constitute the licensing of the right to make copies of audiovisual content rather than the importation of goods.[171]

The panel's analysis began by noting that the challenged measures apply to both hard-copy sound recordings and other audiovisual products. The panel continued by pointing out that the US claim concerns 'master copies'—such as videocassettes, VCDs and DVDs, or physical sound recordings—intended to be used to publish and manufacture copies for sale in China. As to whether these master copies are goods, the panel employed the same methodology used earlier to decide that 'films for theatrical release' belong to goods or services. The panel found relevant heading 8542 of the 1996 HS,[172] China's Schedule of Concessions and China's confirmation of charging customs duties on the importation of

[167] The Harmonized Commodity Description and Coding System (HS) of tariff nomenclature is an internationally standardised system of names and numbers for classifying traded products developed and maintained by the World Customs Organization (WCO) (formerly Customs Co-operation Council), an independent intergovernmental organisation with over 170 member countries based in Brussels. Heading 3706 defines as a separate good 'cinematographic film, exposed and developed, whether or not incorporating sound track or consisting only of sound track'.

[168] The explanatory note provides that 'this heading covers developed standard or substandard width cinematographic film for the projection of motion pictures, negative or positive . . .'. The panel considers that this indicates that exposed and developed cinematographic films are 'films for theatrical release', and that both negative and positive cinematographic films are considered goods. It further indicates that, despite the fact that cinematographic films are used to provide a service, they are considered goods. Furthermore, the explanatory note shows that a physical carrier containing content is treated as a good. WTO, *China—Publications and Audiovisual Products*, Report of the Panel, ¶7.525.

[169] Ibid, ¶7.527.

[170] Ibid, ¶7.612.

[171] Ibid, ¶¶7.615–16.

[172] Heading 8542 of 1996 HS defines as goods 'records, tapes and other recorded media for sound or other similarly recorded phenomena, including matrices and masters for the production of records, but excluding products of Chapter 37'. Similarly, heading 8523 of the 2007 HS defines as goods 'discs, tapes, solid-state non-volatile storage devices, smart cards and other media for the recording of sound or of other phenomena, whether or not recorded, including matrices and masters for the production of discs'. In the panel's view,

these products.[173] The panel concluded that the 'audiovisual products intended for publication'—tangible master copies—are goods for the purpose of China's trading rights commitments.[174] China challenged these findings on appeal. The Appellate Body supported the panel's analysis and upheld its conclusion.[175]

6.7.3 The Overlap of the GATT and the GATS in Application to Cultural Products

Although there is a provision on how to resolve conflicts between the GATT and other agreements regarding trade in goods,[176] the WTO Agreement contains no indication regarding the general relationship between the GATT and the GATS. The jurisprudence developed from dispute settlement practice reveals that classifying an item as a good or a service does not mean that it is only subject to the GATT or the GATS.

One legal issue that arises from *Canada—Periodicals* involves the treatment of services (advertising) when combined with goods (periodicals). Canada claimed that the provision of the Excise Tax Act challenged by the US was not a measure regulating trade in goods but rather a measure regulating trade in services (access to the advertising market). Since Canada made no commitments regarding trade in advertising service, this measure did not contravene its WTO obligations. The US countered that the GATS does not take primacy over the GATT, and that, furthermore, GATT Article III (national treatment) prohibits discrimination by services attached to goods, such as distribution and transportation.

The panel decided that GATT Article III applies to the excise tax, which affects trade in periodicals. Although Canada held that 'it is necessary to interpret the scope of application of each so as to avoid overlap', the panel referred to Article II:2 of the WTO Agreement[177] and found that Members cannot choose to abide by only those parts of the agreements that suit their interests. The Appellate Body ruled that the tax affects both

both descriptions are sufficiently broad to cover master copies, such as master videocassettes, VCDs and DVDs as well as master sound recording discs. Ibid, ¶7.640.

[173] Ibid, ¶7.641.

[174] Ibid, ¶7.642.

[175] WTO, *China—Publications and Audiovisual Products*, Report of the Appellate Body, ¶¶159–74.

[176] The general interpretative note to Annex 1A of the WTO Agreement provides that, in the event of conflict between a provision of the General Agreement on Tariffs and Trade 1994 and a provision of another agreement in Annex 1A to the Agreement Establishing the World Trade Organization (referred to in the agreements in Annex 1A as the 'WTO Agreement'), the provision of the other agreement shall prevail to the extent of the conflict.

[177] WTO Agreement, Art II:2 (stating that 'The agreements and associated legal instruments included in Annex 1, 2, and 3 are integral parts of this Agreement, binding on all members').

service and goods and the absence of Canada's commitments under the GATS could not overrule its GATT obligations.[178] A similar issue was raised in *EC—Bananas III*.[179] The Appellate Body more fully explained its view on the subject:

> Given the specific scope of the two agreements, they may or may not overlap, depending on the measures at issue. Certain measures could be found to fall exclusively within the scope of GATT 1994, when they affect trade in goods as goods. Certain measures could be found to fall exclusively within the scope of GATS, when they affect the supply of services as services. There is yet a third category of measures that could be found to fall within the scope of both the GATT and GATS. These are measures that involve a service relating to a particular good or service supplied in conjunction with a particular good. In all such cases in this third category, the measure in question could be is scrutinized under the GATT or the GATS . . . Whether a certain measure affecting the supply of a service related to a particular good is scrutinized under the GATT 1994 or the GATS, or both, is a matter that can only be determined on a case-by-case basis.[180]

In *China—Publications and Audiovisual Products*, China maintained that, because the challenged measures regulate services, its trading rights commitments do not apply to them.[181] The panel invoked the opinion quoted above and concluded that the mere fact that the measures regulate a service does not remove them from the scope of China's trading rights commitments.[182] By the same token, China's trading rights commitments are applicable, *mutatis mutandis*, to 'audiovisual products used for publication'. The panel thus found that the challenged measures should be examined under both the GATS and China's Accession Protocol.[183]

The Appellate Body noted that these findings concern the relationship between the GATS and the GATT, but do not directly address the relationship between China's trading rights commitments and its GATS commitments. They nevertheless provide assistance in analysing whether a measure can be simultaneously subject to obligations relating to trade in goods and those relating to trade in services. The Appellate Body reiterated that a measure can regulate goods and services, and that there is no clear distinction between 'content' and 'goods'. The Appellate Body did not agree that content and goods, and the regulation thereof, are

[178] WTO, *Canada—Periodicals*, Report of the Appellate Body, ¶463.

[179] WTO, *European Communities—Regime for the Importation, Sale and Distribution of Bananas* (hereinafter *EC—Bananas*), WT/DS27, complained by Ecuador, Guatemala, Honduras, Mexico and the United States. Request for consultations received on 5 February 1996, Panel Report circulated on 22 May 1997, and Appellate Body Report circulated on 9 September 1997.

[180] Ibid, *EC—Bananas*, Report of Appellate Body, ¶221.

[181] WTO, *China—Publications and Audiovisual Products*, Report of the Panel, ¶¶7.618–20.

[182] Ibid, ¶¶7.527, 7.541–42.

[183] Ibid, ¶¶7.642–52.

mutually exclusive. Invoking the same finding in *Canada—Periodicals*, the Appellate Body shared the view that China's arguments are premised on an artificial dichotomy between films as content and the physical carrier in which content may be embedded.[184]

Thus far, regarding the Members' obligations under different WTO agreements, all findings made by the WTO tribunals have coherently indicated that the WTO agreements involved coexist and that one obligation cannot override the other. However, this leaves open the possibility that the exercise of a right under one agreement may negate a right under another. For example, a Member's limitations on film distribution, though in full conformity with the GATS, might be vulnerable to a GATT challenge. Furthermore, the defendant cannot hide behind that part of the agreement providing the desired protection, since GATT and GATS must be considered as part of whole WTO agreements. Consequently, to the extent that services are combined with goods, the GATS may not provide the protection for services that some Members expected. WTO Members, including China, should bear this in mind when they make future commitments involving cultural products.

6.8 FACTORING CULTURAL ELEMENTS INTO DECIDING THE 'LIKENESS' OF CULTURAL PRODUCTS

The 'likeness' of imported and domestic products is crucial to determining the competitive relationships that exist among them for the purpose of trade regulation (particularly with respect to MFN treatment and national treatment). This section studies how much cultural elements count in judging 'likeness' among cultural products, using 'like products' in GATT Article III[185] to illustrate the treatment of culture under the WTO.

[184] WTO, *China—Publications and Audiovisual Products*, Report of the Appellate Body, ¶¶193–95.

[185] The term 'like products' appears in several different GATT provisions and other WTO agreements. For example, Professor Jackson lists 10 GATT provisions containing 'like products': I:1, II:2(a), III:2, III:4, VI:1(a,b), IX:1, XI:2(c), XIII:1, XVI:4. See JH Jackson, *World Trade and the Law of GATT* (1969) 259. As noted widely, the meaning of 'like products' is likely to vary from one GATT provision to another because the term is employed to serve a variety of different purposes, with the result that individual precedents often differ due to their different contexts. For more research on 'like products' in GATT see, eg W-M Choi, *'Like Products' in International Trade Law: Towards a Consistent GATT/WTO Jurisprudence* (2005); NF Diebold, *Non-discrimination in International Trade in Services: Likeness in WTO/GATS* (2010); RE Hudec, '"Like Products": The Differences in Meaning in GATT Article I and III' in T Cottier and P Mavroidis (eds), *Regulatory Barriers and the Principle of Non-discrimination in World Trade Law* (2000) 101 (hereinafter Hudec, 'Like Products'); RE Hudec, 'GATT/WTO Constraints on National Regulation: Requiem for an "Aim and Effects" Test' (1998) 32 *International Lawyer* 619 (hereinafter Hudec, '"Aim and Effects" Test'); GC Berg, 'An Economic Interpretation of "like Products"' (1996) 30 *Journal*

6.8.1 GATT/WTO's General Jurisprudence on 'Like Products'

GATT Article III challenges national legislative sovereignty by calling into question the legality of domestic taxation and regulations that fail to grant foreign products national treatment.[186] Other than the general policy stated in Article III:1,[187] Article III contains two pivotal provisions: Article III:2 deals with internal taxation[188] and Article III:4 deals with internal regulations.[189] One of the key issues addressed by GATT Article III is whether domestic products and imported products are 'like products'.[190] More relevantly, how has the interpretation of 'likeness' worked to shape WTO attitudes towards culture? To what extent may WTO tribunals distinguish cultural products from each other based on their cultural content?

Notwithstanding the term's powerful scope, GATT Article III has been functioning without a clear definition of 'like products' since its inception.[191] This has generated a number of disputes and made it especially relevant to examine pertinent cases. For most purposes, a meaningful comparison of 'like products' definitions requires specifying the criteria by which

of World Trade 195; RJ Zedalis, 'The Theory of GATT "like" Product Common Language Cases' (1994) 27 *Vanderbilt Journal of Transnational Law* 33.

[186] See JH Snelson, 'Can GATT Artcle III Recover From Its Head-On Collision With United States Taxes on Automobiles?' (1996) 5 *Minnesota Journal of Global Trade* 467, 467 (explaining the similarity between the GATT and the Dormant Commerce Clause doctrine of the US Constitution).

[187] GATT Art III:1 reads: 'Parties recognize that internal taxes and other internal charges, and laws, regulations and requirements affecting the internal sale, offering for sale, purchase, transportation, distribution or use of products, and internal quantitative regulations requiring the mixture, processing or use of products in specified amounts or proportions, should not be applied to imported or domestic products so as to afford protection to domestic regulation'.

[188] GATT Art III:2 reads: 'The products of the territory of any contracting party imported into the territory of any other contracting party shall not be subject, directly or indirectly, to internal taxes or other internal charges of any kind in excess of those applied, directly or indirectly, to like domestic products. Moreover, no contracting party shall otherwise apply internal taxes or other internal charges to imported or domestic products in a manner contrary to the principles set forth in paragraph 1.' Ad Art III:2: 'A tax conforming to the requirements of the first sentence of paragraph 2 would be considered to be inconsistent with the provisions of the second sentence only in cases where competition was involved between, on the one hand, the taxed products and, on the other hand, a directly competitive or substitutable product which was not similarly taxed'.

[189] GATT Art III:4 reads: 'The Products of the territory of any contracting party imported into the territory of any other contracting party shall be accorded treatment no less favorable than that accorded to like products of national origin in respect of all laws, regulations, and requirements affecting their internal sale, offering for sale, purchase, transportation, distribution or use'.

[190] The Appellate Body has clarified that three elements must be satisfied to establish a violation of Art III: (i) the imported and domestic products at issue are 'like products'; (ii) the measure at issue is a 'law, regulation, or requirement' affecting their internal sale, offering for sale, purchase, transportation, distribution, or use; and (iii) the imported products are accorded 'less favourable treatment' than that are accorded to like domestic products. See, eg WTO, *Korea—Beef*, Report of the Appellate Body, ¶133.

[191] See WJ Snape III and NB Lefkowitz, 'Searching for GATT's Environmental Miranda: Are "Process Standards" Getting "Due Process"?' (1994) 27 *Cornell International Law Journal* 777, 792.

'likeness' is to be measured.[192] In this regard, although far from uniform in their application, the panels defining 'like products' have relied on one set of factors to determine whether imported and domestic products are sufficiently 'like' in order to secure national treatment.

Based on an announcement made by a GATT Working Party in 1970,[193] the WTO tribunals have confirmed that the analysis of 'like products' should be done on a case-by-case basis.[194] Their approach to determining 'likeness' consists of four general criteria:[195] (i) the properties, nature and quality of the products; (ii) the end-uses of the products; (iii) consumers' tastes and habits—more comprehensively termed 'consumers' perceptions and behaviour'—with respect to the products; and (iv) the tariff classification of the products.[196] This can be referred to as 'traditional criteria' for establishing the 'likeness' of products involved. WTO jurisprudence also supports the view that, when origin is the sole criterion distinguishing products, demonstrating that there can or will be domestic and imported products that are 'like' is sufficient to satisfy the 'like products' requirement.[197] This is referred to as the 'alternative route' for establishing the 'likeness' of products.

Thus far, there are only two cases involving cultural products, ie *Canada—Periodicals* and *China—Publications and Audiovisual Products*. The sub-sections below focuse on the analysis of 'like products' in these two cases and try to pinpoint the WTO's past practice in this regard.

[192] See Hudec, 'Like Products', above n 185, 103.

[193] GATT, Report of the Working Party on Border Tax Adjustments, adopted on 2 December 1970, BISD 18S/97, ¶18. See also WTO, *Canada—Periodicals*, Report of the Panel, ¶3.73. There have been only a few GATT legal rulings on the meaning of 'like products'. See, eg GATT, *EEC—Measures on Animal Feed Proteins*, BISD 25S/49; GATT, *Japan—Taxes and Labeling Practices on Imported Wines and Alcoholic Beverages*, BISD 34S/83. A number of those rulings have been seriously questioned. It is perhaps for this reason that most GATT/WTO rulings on 'like products' issue start their analysis by quoting from the above Working Party Report. On the whole, the principal legal value of the quotation seems to be its legitimisation of the case-by-case approach. See Hudec, 'Like Products', above n 185, 111–12.

[194] WTO, *EC—Asbestos*, Report of the Appellate Body, ¶102.

[195] WTO, *Japan—Taxes on Alcoholic Beverages*, Report of the Appellate Body, WT/DS8/AB/R, WT/DS10/AB/R, WT/DS11/AB/R, 1 November 1996, ¶113; WTO, *United States—Gasoline*, Report of the Panel, ¶6.8 (where the approach set forth in the Border Tax Adjustment case was adopted in a dispute concerning GATT Art III:4).

[196] The fourth criterion, 'tariff classification', was not mentioned by the Working Party on Border Tax Adjustments, but was included in the subsequent cases. See, eg WTO, *Japan—Taxes on Alcoholic Beverages*, Report of the Appellate Body, ¶114.

[197] See WTO, *Indonesia—Certain Measures Affecting the Automobile Industry*, Report of the Panel, WT/DS54/R, WT/DS55R, WT/DS64R, 23 July, 1998, ¶14.113; WTO, *Argentina—Measures Affecting the Export of Bovine Hides and Import of Finished Leather*, Report of the Panel, WT/DS155/R, 16 February 2001, ¶11.168–70; WTO, *Canada—Certain Measures Affecting the Automobile Industry*, Report of the Panel, WT/DS139R, WT/DS142R, 19 June 2000, ¶10.74; WTO, *India—Measures Affecting the Automotive Sector*, Report of the Panel, WT/DS146/R, WT/DS175/R, 5 April 2002, ¶¶7.714–16. In these cases, the WTO tribunals found that the 'like products' requirement could be established if the measures distinguished between imported and domestic products solely based on the origin.

6.8.2 'Like Products' Analysis in *Canada—Periodicals*

The decision in *Canada—Periodicals* is instructive with regard to the application of GATT Article III:2. This case demands whether domestic magazines and imported split runs are 'like products' when the 'likeness' has to do with both editorial and advertising content. The US tried to broadly define national treatment obligations,[198] while Canada sought to draw distinctions between imported split runs and domestic magazines based on their cultural content. In Canada's opinion, the end-use of periodicals is intellectual consumption: the reader is looking for the message rather than the medium. In this sense, cultural content matters and plays a role in the case of cultural products that is analogous to the physical properties of conventional goods. For this reason, Canada claimed, imported split runs and domestic magazines are not 'like products'.[199]

The panel rejected the argument that a cultural component may distinguish goods.[200] The Appellate Body did not agree with the panel's comparison of imported and domestic periodicals and reversed this part of the Panel Report. However, for procedural reasons, the Appellate Body failed to complete a binding 'like products' analysis. After overturning the panel's decision that imported split runs and domestic periodicals are 'like products', the Appellate Body referred to the second sentence of GATT Article III:2[201] to determine whether periodicals could be distinguished on the basis of their intellectual content.[202] The answer was that news magazines, like *Time*, *Time Canada* and *Maclean's*, are 'directly competitive or substitutable' products despite the Canadian content of *Maclean's*.[203] The Appellate Body thus found that imported split runs and

[198] See RL Matheny, 'In the Wake of the Flood: "Like Products" and Cultural Products After the World Trade Organization's Decision in Canada Certain Measures Concerning Periodicals' (1998) 147 *University of Pennsylvania Law Review* 245, 247 (noting that in *Canada—Periodicals*, the Canadian Government suffered a great blow to its authority to legislate safeguards for cultural industries).

[199] WTO, *Canada—Periodicals*, Report of the Panel, ¶3.68.

[200] Ibid, ¶5.23.

[201] Note that, with regard to internal taxes but not to other internal regulations, Art III offers a second line of attack. The second sentence of Art III:2 states, in effect, that differential taxes based on product distinctions between 'not-like' but 'directly competitive or substitutable' products are also invalid if the tax difference results in protection of domestic production.

[202] As with 'like products' under the first sentence of Art III:2, the determination of the appropriate range of 'directly competitive or substitutable products' under the second sentence must be made on a case-by-case basis. See WTO, *Japan—Taxes on Alcoholic Beverages*, WT/DS8/AB/R, WT/DS10/AB/R, WT/DS11/AB/R, 1 November 1996, 25. The Appellate Body also found it appropriate to look at competition in the relevant markets as one among a number of means of identifying the broader category of products that might be described as 'directly competitive or substitutable', as the GATT is a commercial agreement and the WTO is concerned, after all, with markets. WTO, *Canada—Periodicals*, Report of the Appellate Body, 27.

[203] WTO, *Canada—Periodicals*, Report of the Appellate Body, 28. At the same time, the Appellate Body also pointed out that the conclusion that imported split-run periodicals and

domestic periodicals are 'directly competitive or substitutable' insofar as they are part of the same segment of Canada's periodicals market. The Appellate Body ruled that, since imported and domestic products were treated differently, Canada violated its GATT obligations.[204]

Canada—Periodicals was read as an allegory for the increasingly contentious relationship between culture and trade.[205] In the case, both the panel and the Appellate Body applied the type of reasoning applied to foreign vodka and Japanese vodka in *Japan—Alcoholic Beverages* II to periodicals, without regard for the value of intellectual information in deciding likeness-related issues. Their analysis showed a tendency to look at the commercial aspects and physical qualities of periodicals rather than the specificity of cultural products as the vehicles of information. The result thus avoided any scrutiny of a product's intangible cultural character or the broader social context in which it is created. When cultural legislation that implicates an entire industry is subject to WTO scrutiny, the WTO tribunals tend to focus more on the objective side of their analysis than on the subjective, culturally determined features.[206] Culture, in this context, is seen as inherently suspect and is therefore judiciously eschewed. A plausible explanation is that, in a quantitative analysis demanded by economics, qualitative measures taken for cultural protection are hard to assess, because they have none of the comfortable absoluteness of numbers.[207]

The WTO tribunals' findings in *Canada—Periodicals*, in leaving no room to evaluate the cultural content of periodicals or the cultural purposes behind domestic laws, suggest that the informational content of cultural products is not considered in judging 'likeness'. Trying to distinguish cultural products based on 'cultural' as opposed to 'commercial' aspects seems unlikely to get a positive reception as long as the measures to protect such products have an effect on competitive commercial relationships.

domestic non-split-run periodicals are 'directly competitive or substitutable' does not mean that all periodicals belong to the same relevant market. A periodical containing mainly current news is not 'directly competitive or substitutable' with a periodical dedicated to gardening, chess, sports, music or cuisine.

[204] WTO, *Canada—Periodicals*, Report of the Appellate Body, 29.

[205] See, eg Matheny, above n 198, 269–70.

[206] See Carmody, above n 37, 269–77 (examining *Japan—Custom Duties, Taxes and Labeling Practices on Imported Wines and Alcoholic Beverages*).

[207] See ibid, 303.

6.8.3 'Like Products' Analysis in *China—Publications and Audiovisual Products*

In this case, the US charged that three sets of Chinese measures, concerning reading materials, sound recordings and films for theatrical release, violated GATT Article III:4. A determination of 'likeness' under Article III:4 is fundamentally a decision about the nature and extent of a competitive relationship between and among products.[208] According to the well-established jurisprudence on establishing a violation of GATT Article III, the panel examined whether the US had demonstrated that the relevant products are 'like', whether the measures are 'laws, regulations, and requirements' that affect one or all of the enumerated transactions, and whether the measures provide for 'less favourable treatment'.[209] As stated above, the US could have established that the imported and domestic products are 'like' via 'traditional criteria' or the 'alternative route'.[210]

6.8.3.1 Reading Materials

The US presented claims under GATT Article III:4 regarding Chinese measures pertaining to all of the products at issue. However, the panel only found violation with respect to reading materials. The US argued that two of China's measures, specifically the *Imported Publications Subscription Rule*[211] and the *Publication (Sub-)Distribution Rule*,[212] are inconsistent with GATT Article III:4 because they afford 'less favourable treatment' than that given to 'like' domestic products by significantly restricting the distributors, distribution channels[213] and consumers available to imported reading materials.[214]

The panel noted that, aside from its assertion that the imported and

[208] WTO, *EC—Asbestos*, Report of the Appellate Body, ¶99; WTO, *India—Measures Affecting the Automotive Sector*, Report of the Panel, ¶¶7.174–7.176; WTO, *China—Measures Affecting Imports of Automobile Parts*, Report of the Panel, WT/DS339/R, WT/DS340/R, WT/DS342/R, 12 January 2009, ¶7.216.

[209] WTO, *China—Publications and Audiovisual Products*, Report of the Panel, ¶¶7.1442–43.

[210] Ibid, ¶7.1447.

[211] Measures for Administration of Subscription of Imported Publications by Subscribers (Order of the General Administration of Press and Publication (GAPP) of PR of China, No 27, 2004), effective as of 1 January 2005.

[212] Measures for Administration of Foreign-Invested Book, Periodical and Newspaper Distribution Enterprises, jointly promulgated by the GAPP in December 2002 and MOFTEC (Ministry of Foreign Trade and Economic Cooperation, the predecessor of MOFCOM, the Ministry of Commerce) in March 2003, effective as of 1 May 2003.

[213] The US maintains that imported reading materials only find themselves blocked from distribution channels in China that are foreign-invested enterprises. WTO, *China—Publications and Audiovisual Products*, Report of the Panel, ¶7.1499.

[214] Ibid, ¶7.1474.

domestic products share the same physical characteristics and commercial uses, the US had not provided any evidence to demonstrate that imported reading materials are 'like' domestic reading materials. The US had not established the physical characteristics and commercial uses of reading materials, nor had it addressed how imported reading materials are 'like' domestic reading materials. The panel therefore concluded that the US had failed to establish 'likeness' between imported and domestic reading materials via 'traditional criteria'.[215]

Turning its attention to whether the US had established 'likeness' via the alternative route, the panel first examined how the Imported Publications Subscription Rule applies to imported reading materials. The subscription requirements contained in this Rule only apply to imported newspapers and periodicals. This constitutes a difference in treatment between imported and domestic products based exclusively on origin. China did not dispute that domestic newspapers and periodicals are not regulated alike, nor that there can be domestic and imported newspapers and periodicals that are the same except for origin. Therefore, the panel concluded that, with regard to newspapers and periodicals, the 'like' products requirement in Article III:4 was satisfied.[216]

For books, however, the situation is somewhat different. Not all imported books require subscriptions; rather, only those with prohibited content do. In other words, a factor other than the origin of books is used as the basis for different treatment. The panel found that the US had not established that imported books are 'like' domestic books via the 'alternative route'.[217]

Although the panel did not consider that the US had established 'likeness' between imported and domestic reading materials via the 'traditional criteria', it did find that the challenged measure—the Publication (Sub-) Distribution Rule—creates a difference in treatment between domestic and imported reading materials by regulating the types of enterprises that may distribute them, based exclusively on the origin of the reading materials. Likewise, China did not dispute that there can be domestic and imported reading materials that are the same except for origin. Therefore, the panel considered that, with regard to the inconsistency of the Publications (Sub-) Distribution Rule with GATT Article III:4, the 'like products' requirement was satisfied.[218]

[215] Ibid, ¶7.1481.

[216] Ibid, ¶¶7.1487–91.

[217] The panel notes that, as imported books without prohibited content are treated in the same way as domestic books, the difference in treatment between imported books in the 'limited' category and domestic books is not exclusively based on the foreign origin of the imported books, but rather is based on whether the imported book contains prohibited content. Ibid, ¶¶7.1433–98.

[218] Ibid, ¶¶7.1501–06.

6.8.3.2 Sound Recordings Intended for Electronic Distribution

The US maintained that all sound recordings, whether domestic or imported, are fundamentally the same in all relevant aspects: they can contain the same kinds of music, appeal to the same audience or target markets, and be equally suitable for digital distribution. China did not present any argumentation on whether imported and domestic hard-copy sound recordings intended for electronic distribution are 'like' within the meaning of Article III:4.[219] The US further argued that China's measures imposed a more onerous content-review regime on imported sound recordings than on 'like' domestic recordings.[220] National origin is the only criterion for determining whether a sound recording intended for electronic distribution must go through the onerous content review process. This means that China accords 'less favourable treatment' to imports of these products than to domestic 'like products'.[221]

China argued that the distribution of sound recording imported in hard copy and intended for so-called 'electronic distribution' does not refer to distribution in the sense of GATT Article III:4, insofar as it does not involve the distribution of physical goods. Thus, China contended, it cannot be scrutinised under the rules governing trade in goods.[222] China further maintained that the formally different treatment identified by the US does not affect the 'distribution' of hard copies and therefore cannot be scrutinised under Article III:4.[223]

The panel held that the US had not established that imported and domestic hard-copy sound recordings are 'like' based on the traditional 'like products' criteria due to lack of further elaboration.[224] In determining whether the US had established 'like products' via the 'alternative route', the panel limited its analysis to the Internet Culture Rule[225] and the Network Music Opinions,[226] which were properly identified in the US panel request. Because it is unclear from the argumentation presented by

[219] Ibid, ¶7.1556.

[220] Ibid, ¶7.1553.

[221] Ibid, ¶¶7.1546–47.

[222] Ibid, ¶7.1548.

[223] China points out that doing so would mean that GATT rules apply to any measure regulating services related to intangible content as long as there exists a physical carrier capable of being traded, since such a measure would always have the alleged effect on its carrier. Ibid, ¶7.1552.

[224] Ibid, ¶7.1560.

[225] Interim Provisions on the Administration of Internet Culture, promulgated by the Ministry of Culture on 3 March 2003, effective as of 1 July, 2003. Note that, as part of China's efforts to implementing DSB rulings and recommendations in *China—Publications and Audiovisual Products*, China replaced these provisions with the No 51 Order of Ministry of Culture, Interim Provisions on the Administration of Internet Culture, promulgated on 11 February 2011, effective as of 1 April 2011.

[226] Several Opinions of the Ministry of Culture on Development and Administration of Network Music, promulgated by the Ministry of Culture and came into effect on 11 December, 2006.

the parties whether or not the challenged measures apply to hard-copy sound recordings, the panel deferred its analysis and proceeded on the assumption that the challenged measures apply to imported hard-copy sound recordings. A definitive determination on 'likeness' is only necessary if the US establishes that the measures affect the distribution of the imported products in a manner that accords 'less favourable treatment'.[227] The panel finally found that the US had not demonstrated that the challenged measures affect the distribution of imported hard-copy sound recordings, which rendered it unnecessary to return to the previous 'likeness' analysis.[228]

Note here that the panel again reversed its order of analysis and deferred its 'like products' analysis. This methodology does not accord with general logic[229] and can be viewed as judicial avoidance by the panel. It seems that the panel did not want to first address whether the challenged measures apply to hard-copy sound recordings because it is not easy to draw a conclusion from both parties' argumentation and evidence. At the same time, the panel realised that this is an essential question that could not be avoided. Therefore, the panel changed the order of analysis for strategic reasons that allowed it to finally adjudicate the dispute. Because the panel's findings in this regard were not appealed by the parties, there is no opportunity to learn the attitude of the Appellate Body towards this strategy.

The Panel Report centres its discussion on Article III:4 with regard to films for theatrical release around whether there is a film distribution 'duopoly' in China which results in discriminatory treatment of imported products. The panel examined whether China's rules and regulations create a *de jure* distribution 'duopoly' or a de facto distribution 'duopoly', and concluded in favour of China. It is worth noting that the panel made it clear that 'duopoly' is not a 'measure' that can be challenged before the WTO.[230] Neither the parties nor the panel engaged in a 'like products' analysis similar to that employed with regard to reading materials and sound recordings.

This case also involves the issue of 'like service suppliers' under GATS Article XVII:1, which requires that treatment be assessed between domestic and foreign services or service suppliers that are 'like'. Since the

[227] WTO, *China—Publications and Audiovisual Products*, Report of the Panel, ¶¶7.1570–71, 7.1584–85.

[228] Ibid, ¶¶7.1652–53.

[229] Strict logic dictates that the order of the analysis should be different: first, whether the US has established that the imported and domestic hard-copy sound recordings intended for electronic distribution are 'like products'; second, whether the challenged measures are 'law, regulation, or requirement' affecting their internal sale, offering for sale, purchase, transportation, distribution or use of hard-copy sound recordings; and third, whether the imported hard-copy sound recordings are accorded 'less favourable treatment' than that accorded to like domestic products.

[230] WTO, *China—Publications and Audiovisual Products*, Report of the Panel, ¶¶7.1655–57, 1659–63.

US focused its claims on the treatment of suppliers rather than services, the panel likewise centred its analysis on the 'likeness' of the service suppliers at issue.[231] In this respect, the panel noted that the challenged measures contain prohibitions on the right to establish and supply the services at issue exclusively on the basis of origin. At the same time, there will, or can, be domestic and foreign suppliers that fall under the measure and are the same in all material respects. The 'like service suppliers' requirement is thus met.[232] It seems safe to conclude from the panel's reasoning that the 'alternative route' for establishing 'likeness' among goods involved can also be applied to establish the 'likeness' among services and service providers. Nevertheless, due to the fundamental difference between goods and services, the 'traditional criteria' for establishing the 'likeness' of goods involved may not be directly transplanted to establish 'likeness' among the services and service providers involved.

6.8.3.3 A Commentary: Factoring Cultural Elements into Deciding the 'Likeness' via the Traditional Route Establishing 'Like Products'

National treatment is presented as one of the key issues in *China—Publications and Audiovisual Products*. The panel's findings in this regard were not appealed. Accordingly, China is obliged to follow the panel's recommendation and accord foreign newspapers and periodicals national treatment. In my view, this is a big loss for China, which might have been avoided if China had seized the opportunity to defend its measures at issue. Further analysis follows.

In this case, the US held that imported and domestic reading materials share the same physical characteristics and commercial uses and are therefore 'like products'. By the same logic, domestic and imported sound recordings are fundamentally the same in all relevant aspects. Aside from noting that there are no domestic publications that contain prohibited content in China, China did not offer any argument on this point.[233] Nor did China argue that the products involved are not 'like' as defined by GATT Article III:4, which discharges the WTO tribunals from fully examining this issue. In fact, notwithstanding China's failure to present argumentation, the panel found that only the measures affecting newspapers and periodicals violate China's national treatment obligations.

One might argue that a similar question—whether domestic periodicals and imported split runs are 'like' products—was presented and discussed in *Canada—Periodicals*. The tribunals in that case gave affirmative answers to this inquiry and did not factor cultural content into its analysis of the 'likeness' issue. One may speculate that the conclusion in *Canada—*

[231] Ibid, ¶7.1283.
[232] Ibid, ¶¶7.1284–85.
[233] Ibid, ¶¶7.1475–78, 7.1553–56.

Periodicals is one of the factors that prevented China from claiming that imported reading materials, sound recordings and films are not 'like' in *China—Publications and Audiovisual Products*. It should be noted, however, that the situations in these two cases are somewhat different.

First, recall that in *Canada—Periodicals* the Appellate Body reversed the panel's finding that imported split runs and domestic periodicals are 'like' products and concluded that they are 'directly competitive or substitutable' products according to the guidelines set out in GATT Article III:2. In *China—Publications and Audiovisual Products*, the US's claims only concerned GATT Article III:4, under which China had no obligations to extend national treatment to 'directly competitive or substitutable' products.[234] It follows that, had China successfully argued that the products at issue did not present 'direct competitiveness or substitutability', it would have dispensed with its national treatment obligations. Yet the core question remains: what argument is available for China to defend its measures?

Canada—Periodicals concerns only the 'likeness' between Canadian domestic periodicals and imported American split runs. The Appellate Body's finding that they are 'directly competitive or substitutable products' makes sense because these two kinds of products contain roughly the same editorial content, differing only in their targeted advertising. *China—Publications and Audiovisual Products* concerns more general cultural products, including books, newspapers, periodicals, sound recordings and films. Neither the parties nor the panel touched upon whether this generality of cultural products had any bearing upon deciding 'likeness'.

I subscribe to the view that this issue should not be ignored in any sense. Applying the findings in *Canada—Periodicals* to the scenario of this case, it seems indisputable that imported *TIME Asia* (regional edition in English, assuming that there is such an edition, or split runs available in the market) and China's domestic periodicals covering current news, eg *Global Times*, are 'directly competitive or substitutable products' rather than 'like' products. However, under GATT Article III:4, China has no obligation to extend national treatment to imported products. As a result, China may invoke this provision to defend its measures. In the meantime, in accordance with the findings in *Canada—Periodicals*, various editions of *TIME* and other periodicals covering different subjects (for example, *Sports Illustrated*, *Fictions Monthly*) are not 'directly competitive or substitutable'.

[234] Note that the national treatment obligation was broadened to cover 'directly competitive or substitutable' products only in regard to fiscal measures contemplated in the second paragraph of Art III of the GATT and the accompanying Addendum. Measures other than fiscal measures are still governed by the term 'like products' in GATT Art III:4. This seeming imbalance brings up one of the most difficult interpretative problems in the GATT. Compare above nn 188 and 189 and the accompanying texts. For more analysis on this issue, see Choi, above n 185, 110–14.

Taking the current situation of China's periodicals market into account, there are several different scenarios to be addressed in dealing with the 'likeness' between imported and domestic periodicals. First, are *TIME USA* imported directly from the US and *Global Times* (English version, published in China) 'like' products? Secondly, are *TIME Asia* (in English) and *Global Times* (English version, published in China) 'like' products? Thirdly, would *TIME China* (in Chinese), assuming that there will be such a version in the future, and *Global Times* (in English) be 'like' products? Fourthly, are *TIME USA* imported directly from the US and *Global Times* (Chinese version) 'like' products? Fifthly, are *TIME Asia* and *Global Times* (in Chinese) 'like' products? Sixthly, what about the 'likeness' between *TIME* (Chinese version) and *Global Times* (English version)?

The scenarios outlined above present questions regarding not only the 'direct competitiveness or substitutability' between products of different origins, but also products in different languages. Does language count in deciding 'likeness' or 'direct competitiveness or substitutability' among cultural products? In *Canada—Periodicals*, because of the linguistic overlap between the US and Canada (excepting Quebec), this issue was not on the table. Nevertheless, language, a key component of culture, should not be neglected in judging the 'likeness' or 'direct competitiveness or substitutability' of cultural products.

Most Chinese people are currently not able to read English; or at the very least, they are not used to reading materials in English. As a consequence, it can be very controversial to define *Time America* imported from the US and *Time China* (regional version in Chinese, assuming there is such one version) as 'directly competitive or substitutable products', even if they share the same overage or editorial content. Among the four 'traditional criteria' establishing 'likeness'—at least two—'the end-uses of the products' and 'consumers' perceptions and behaviour'—may be used to distinguish between imported and domestic products. One can even explore whether imported and domestic sound recordings are 'like' or 'directly competitive or substitutable' products by the same logic.

This may help explain why the US failed to provide further elaboration on the 'likeness' between imported and domestic reading materials and sound recordings based on 'traditional criteria'. The fact is that, even though China did not argue this issue, the panel still found that the US failed to establish such 'likeness' based on 'traditional criteria'. However, when the panel examined whether the US had established 'likeness' via the 'alternative route', it found in favour of the US.

This outcome, which appears to greatly expand China's national treatment obligations, might have been avoided if China had argued that the imported and domestic products at issue were not 'like' or 'directly competitive or substitutable' based on 'traditional criteria'. With respect to whether the US can establish 'likeness' between the imported and domestic products involved via the 'alternative route', China should have further argued that such products will not be, nor can be, 'like' products as defined by GATT Article III(4), or 'like' service suppliers as defined by GATS Article XVII. Beyond the simple criterion of national origin, the difference in treatment is based on such elements as language and content. Whether the WTO tribunals can endorse these arguments, enmeshed with cultural elements as they are, remains an open question.

Looking beyond this case, the WTO's disregard of cultural content as a factor in determining 'likeness' is likely to render void the cultural policy measures taken under the UNESCO Convention. One can also note, however, that the Convention may generate some impact on the WTO tribunals' judgment with regard to the elements contained in the *Border Tax Adjustment* test.[235] For instance, the concept of 'consumers' tastes and habits' is of particular relevance for intellectually consumed products, including films or television productions. Therefore, in *China—Publication and Audiovisual Services*—assuming that China argues that imported and domestic cultural products are not 'like' because of the differences in the audience's cultural background, language ability and consumption genre—it is not impossible that the WTO tribunals may be willing to offer some flexibility in considering the issue. This possibility is supported by the fact that both the panel and the Appellate Body in this case clearly recognised that China enjoys the freedom to define the protection of public morals in its territory.

In accordance with the WTO tribunals' decisions, China is obliged to grant national treatment not only to newspapers and periodicals which have regional editions in China, but to all imported products of these types as well. This is a big challenge for China to grapple with, considering the substantial gap between this obligation and its current regulation.

6.8.4 The 'Aim and Effect' Approach: Another Possibility of Factoring Cultural Elements into Deciding 'Likeness'?

The GATT/WTO practice on the issue of 'like products' articulates that, under GATT Article III, the analysis first turn to which factors are to be taken into account in determining the 'likeness' of imported and domestic products, and then how to balance these factors to arrive at a tenable conclusion.

As stated above, the traditional analysis by which 'likeness' is decided focuses mainly on the physical characteristics and end-uses of the products involved; it is often characterised as mechanical and textualist.[236] This

[235] See GATT, Report of the Working Party on Border Tax Adjustments, above n 193.
[236] See Snelson, above n 186, 480.

approach is in contrast to a more intent-based 'likeness' analysis, termed the 'aim and effect' test, under which imported and domestic products are deemed 'like' only when the measures at issue are applied 'so as to afford protection to domestic production'.[237] In other words, only if the aim or the effect of a certain trade measure is protectionist should it be questioned or reversed. The panel interpreted this language as meaning that the legitimacy of internal taxation and regulation should be determined primarily based on its purpose and market effects, that is, on whether it has a bona fide regulatory purpose and whether its effect on the competition is protective.

Two GATT panels applied the 'aim and effect' test in the context of GATT Article III:2.[238] However, the decision regarding 'like products' in *Border Tax Adjustments* aimed to establish a bright-line rule to avoid discrimination. The WTO Appellate Body, in an effort to avoid situations where its authority might be endangered, later affirmatively rejected the so-called 'aim and effect' test, for the purpose of both GATS Article XVII and GATT Article III:2.[239] The Appellate Body explained that a GATT Article III inquiry is not about the intent of the measures at issue. If a measure is applied to imported products 'so as to afford protection to domestic production', it does not matter whether there is any desire to engage in protectionism.[240] The 'aim and effect' test is to ensure that trade rules do not impinge unnecessarily on the legitimate policy choices of WTO Members by specifically targeting protectionist measures. The obvious policy consideration underlying the Appellate Body's refusal of this test lies in the belief that such a balancing approach would invite abuse. *Canada—Periodicals* demonstrated the abandonment of the 'aim and effect' test. In this case, Canada submitted that the excise tax was intended to secure the survival of the Canadian periodical industry, a 'vital element of Canadian cultural expression', without any discriminatory intent.[241] The WTO tribunals did not evaluate the cultural considerations behind Canada's legislation. This indicates that, when the aim of a measure is to protect a particular domestic industry, it violates Article III regardless of whether the desire to protect that industry is merely a step towards a primary goal of promoting or preserving other values, including culture.

The answers to whether imported and domestic products are 'like' often

[237] Ibid, 487, 495 (1996) (discussing the intent-based approach to Art III analysis).

[238] See GATT, *United States—Measures Affecting Alcoholic and Malt Beverages*, Report of the Panel, DS23/R-39S/206, 19 June 1992, ¶¶5.25–5.26; GATT, *United States—Taxes on Automobiles*, Report of the Panel (unadopted), DS31/R, 11 October 1994.

[239] WTO, *EC—Bananas*, Report of the Appellate Body, ¶240.

[240] See WTO, *Japan—Taxes on Alcoholic Beverages*, Report of the Panel, ¶6.16; WTO, Report of the Appellate Body, ¶¶27–28; WTO, *EC—Bananas*, Report of the Panel, ¶¶216, 241.

[241] WTO, *Canada—Periodicals*, Report of the Appellate Body, 21.

differ if the 'aim and effect' of relevant measures is considered in addition to the 'traditional criteria'. This may provide a path by which to allow legitimate discrimination while simultaneously singling out disguised protectionism.[242] A similar argument might be made with regard to a measure that aims to protect local culture.[243] For instance, had the Appellate Body taken cultural goals and criteria into account in determining 'likeness' of cultural products and adhered to the 'aim and effect' test in analysing Canada's policy, Canada might well have prevailed by arguing that its cultural policies did not aim to protect domestic production but, rather, sought to preserve some medium for the expression of cultural identity.[244]

Under the currently leading interpretation of GATT Article III, however, the criterion of legislative intent provides an insufficient basis for drawing distinctions on the treatment of cultural grounds. Whether an imported product qualifies for national treatment depends not on the cultural value but on how closely the imported products physically resemble the domestic products.[245] Therefore, in the case of cultural products, even if a Member were successful in convincing the WTO that it taxes imported products in the name of a broader public policy to promote national culture rather than as a means of protecting domestic production, the Member would probably still be unable to defeat the national treatment principle.

Canada—Periodicals reiterates the WTO's departure from the 'aim and effect' test, which indicates that the criteria for establishing 'likeness' cannot offer an escape from the core disciplines of national treatment by allowing cultural policy measures that legitimately discriminate on cultural grounds.[246] When Canada formally signalled its intention to meet its GATT obligations on 2 September 1997, it reaffirmed its 'intention to continue to pursue its cultural policy objectives'.[247] At the same time, the importance that the international community has gradually placed on culture, as well as the recognised demand of protecting culture in international trade, must be appropriately considered in parsing the 'likeness' of cultural products. It remains necessary to mediate the legislative interest in safeguarding domestic cultural content with the WTO's regulatory enforcement of trade obligations.

The refusal of the 'aim and effect' test suggests a strict attachment to the exact words of the WTO treaty provisions without regard for

[242] The Appellate Body has indicated that neither Art II nor Art XVII of GATS contains 'specific authority . . . for the proposition that the "aims and effects" of a measure are in any way relevant in determining whether that measure is inconsistent with those provisions'. See, eg *EC—Bananas*, Report of Appellate Body, ¶231.

[243] See T Voon, *Cultural Products and the World Trade Organization* (2007) 82.

[244] See Matheny, above n 198, 252; see also Voon, ibid, 75.

[245] See M Matsushita, et al, *The World Trade Organization, Law, Practice, and Policy* (2006) 239.

[246] See Voon, above n 243, 75, 89.

[247] WTO, *Canada—Periodicals*, Communication from Canada to the World Trade Organization, 2 September 1997.

a Member's domestic cultural policy. It may be the very sensitivity of this issue that explains the Appellate Body's choice to shelter itself from political criticism by staying as close as possible to the legal texts accepted by governments.[248] Such textual literalism in defence of legal predictability is desirable, but it is somewhat disappointing to see the Appellate Body follow such an approach when these issues go to the very core of the WTO's role in policing domestic regulatory policy, a mandate which calls for certain flexibility.

There has been much discussion about whether the WTO would return to an 'aim and effect' analysis of domestic policy. While some commentators maintain that it is unlikely that the WTO tribunals will return to such an intent-sensitive analysis,[249] others hold that the 'aim and effect' test might offer desirable decision room for the WTO tribunals on sensitive issues involving crucial legislative purposes.[250]

In its commentary, the Appellate Body explained that the 'like products' concept was an accordion that can be expanded or contracted depending upon the particular legal and factual context in which an issue is being decided. Likewise, the application of the 'aim and effect' test would always involve an irreducible degree of subjective discretion on the part of decision-makers.[251] Structurally, the architecture of the 'aim and effect' test does not really try to change the underlying criteria of decisions regarding 'like products'. Instead, it tries to bring a covert analysis into the open, where the quality of decisions might be improved. More importantly, the eventual political acceptance of the WTO's policing function over domestic regulatory measures will continue to depend not on the persuasiveness of the legal standards being applied, but on the ability of WTO tribunals to find the right balance, that is, on their ability to know when to prohibit regulatory measures viewed as illegitimate by the larger community and when to accept those measures viewed as bona fide regulation.[252]

Whenever a tribunal is asked to decide whether a particular regulatory measure is or is not playing by the rules, it will instinctively want to know whether the measure has a bona fide regulatory purpose and to what extent its market effects are protective.[253] In this sense, the refusal of the Appellate Body does not mean that the 'aim and effect' approach will be forever precluded; rather, it remains underground and still more

[248] For more discussion on this issue, see Hudec, '"Aim and Effects" Test', above n 185, 631–33.

[249] See D Beppu, 'When Cultural Value Justifies Protection: Interpreting the Language of the GATT to Find a Limited Cultural Exception to the National Treatment Principle' (2008) 29 *Cardozo Law Review* 1765, 1777.

[250] See Hudec, '"Aim and Effects" Test', above n 185, 632–35.

[251] WTO, *Japan—Taxes on Alcoholic Beverages*, Report of the Appellate Body, 20–22.

[252] See Hudec, '"Aim and Effects" Test', above n 185, 629–35.

[253] Ibid, 634–35.

or less affects the decision-making of the WTO tribunals.[254] In *EC—Asbestos*, the Appellate Body made its decisions to allow the policy to treat asbestos-containing products differently from other fibre-containing products for the sake of public health.[255] This may offer some room to take cultural content into account in determining the 'likeness' of products involved in trade disputes.

On all accounts, the 'aim and effect' test offers the possibility for those measures intended to protect culture to stand in line with the national treatment principle. Under the 'aim and effect' inquiry, any legitimate policy objective supporting the measures at issue would have the salutary effect of curing the measure's potential inconsistency with national treatment obligations.[256] Consequently, the criteria of decision called for by the 'aim and effect' approach raises an important question concerning how the WTO ought to police national regulatory autonomy.

As noted earlier, the granting of national treatment depends primarily on whether the imported goods are 'like' domestically produced goods. However, both 'traditional criteria' and the 'alternative route' to establish 'likeness' developed through GATT/WTO practice do not currently seem flexible enough to accommodate the specificity of cultural products. One author suggests that we should rely on the different terms used in GATT Articles III:2 and III:4 to find some room for cultural consideration. Note that Article III:2 refers to similar domestic goods as 'like domestic products', while Article III:4 refers to them as 'like products of national origin'.[257] An examination of the 'ordinary meanings' of these two terms based on the *Oxford English Dictionary* reveals that, despite the arguments that they share the same meaning and are interchangeable, the terms 'domestic' and 'of national origin' have different meanings; the latter has more to do with cultural identity.[258] Consequently, it is possible to interpret 'like domestic products' as meaning 'like products whose properties are related to the nation where they were produced because they were physically produced there'; 'like products of national origin' can be interpreted to mean 'like products whose source of character is their nation of origin itself'.[259]

This textual difference is worth noting to the extent that it allows

[254] Professor Hudec discussed several WTO rulings on the 'aim and effect' approach and analysed where the 'like product' test stands. In his view, the criteria used by the WTO tribunals to apply a 'smell test' to regulatory measures are likely congruent with those suggested by the 'aim and effect' test. Ibid, 629–35.

[255] See M Oesch, 'Commentary on *EC—Asbestos*' (2003) 6 *International Trade Law Reports* 441, 455.

[256] One version of 'aim and effect', however, focuses on the objective aim of the measure as evidenced by the measure and the statute itself rather than on the subjective aims of the legislators. See Hudec, '"Aim and Effects" Test', above n 185, 631–32.

[257] See respectively, above nn 188 and 189.

[258] See Beppu, above n 249, 1783–87.

[259] Ibid, 1777–79.

an interpretation of 'like products of national origin' broad enough to include 'cultural products'. Assuming that 'of national origin' refers to some kind of close connection with a nation's culture, there would be some room to consider whether 'like products of national origin' possess some cultural value that would allow for protectionist treatment. The fact that this 'cultural' value is something that cannot be copied by an importing nation might preclude the claim that the imported product is similar enough to the cultural product 'of national origin' to receive protection under Article III:4. A Member may further use the 'cultural' value of products 'of national origin' to differentiate them from imported products, thereby exempting them from the national treatment principle. Following this approach, an importing Member would not be able to use culture as an excuse to apply internal taxes or other charges on imports under Article III:2. Nevertheless, it could apply laws and regulations to protect its cultural products under Article III:4. By specifically analysing the distinction between the phrases 'like domestic products' and 'like products of national origin', it is concluded that the latter is broad enough in scope to allow for a consideration of 'culture'.[260]

Tempting though this suggestion is, I have some doubt about its acceptability in practice. As discussed in Chapter 2, culture may be viewed as a component of national identity that distinguishes one nation from others. Whether culture equates with 'national origin', however, requires further consideration. It remains to convince the Appellate Body that 'like products of national origin' does not equate with 'like domestic products', and, further, that this difference is essential in determining whether to grant national treatment. Indeed, even if culture is viewed as a source of national origin, provisions granting universal preferential treatment to 'like products of national origin' over imported products carry a great risk for abuse.

6.9 CONCLUDING REMARKS

There has been no surge of cases involving cultural products thus far within the GATT/WTO framework. The two cases discussed in this chapter—*Canada—Periodicals* and *China—Publications and Audiovisual Products*—cannot form a solid basis for predicting the future of this field. Nevertheless, what is clear from studying these cases is that the WTO tribunals have not subscribed to a clear-cut belief that cultural products should be treated differently from other products. Although the WTO rules may theoretically provide Members with a limited degree of freedom

[260] Ibid, 1765.

to pursue cultural objectives, the Members must first subject their domestic policy to the scrutiny of trade obligations.

After a quick survey of WTO adjudication, it does not seem to be true that the WTO tribunals would take cultural protection or diversity into account in their process. The reasons for this status quo can be attributed in part to the fact that a cultural quality has not been on the radar of any trade regime heretofore. Though the WTO tribunals in both cases recognise that a Member is entitled to protect culture or maintain its public morals, the measures to achieve this goal have to be subject to the scrutiny of trade rules. WTO rules contain virtually no explicit recognition of culture or the legitimacy of Members' cultural interests. Thus it comes as no surprise that the measures are often found to be inconsistent with trade obligations.

The overlap between cultural goods and services and the corresponding disciplines set forth respectively in the GATT and GATS add another layer of difficulty in identifying a clear-cut treatment for cultural products. The research on 'like products' further reveals that the content distinction is not reflected in the WTO rules available to distinguish domestic and foreign products. It would be difficult to define workable distinctions between products based on their particular cultural content however the term is defined. Judging by its absence from WTO frameworks, cultural content seems to be suffering a crisis of representation.

In brief, WTO dispute settlement involving cultural products is far from being satisfactory to advocates of cultural protection. If trade liberalisation continues on this course, the current framework will not offer adequate room to allow for necessary cultural policies. In the long run, given the role of culture in nation building and identity construction, this issue should be of concern to many WTO Members. In order for the global trade regime to register the complexity of cultural products, developing an acceptable and effective jurisprudence through the WTO tribunals' practice is required. During this process, a high degree of sensitivity to the balance of interests involved and creativity in fashioning solutions hold the key to striking a desirable balance.

7

Culture under Regional Agreements: The Perspectives from the EC/EU and NAFTA

The danger is that the [Mickey] mouse will kill all the other animals in the kingdom.

Jacques Toubon[1]

7.1 INTRODUCTION

THE CLASH BETWEEN trade and culture is not confined to the global context; it afflicts regional polities and institutions as well. Having examined the treatment of culture under the GATT/WTO framework, it is necessary to pinpoint how culture is treated under regional trade agreements. The central argument in favour of regional trade arrangements is based on greater efficiency.[2] The WTO recognises the legitimacy of its Members' deviations from MFN obligations through arrangements such as custom unions, free trade agreements (FTAs) and other eligible instruments. Generally, such deviations are acceptable under the WTO only if they fulfil certain criteria.[3]

This chapter examines the treatment of culture under two key regional

[1] Former French Minister of Culture and French Language, quoting from P Klebnikov, 'Meet General Gamelin' (1995) 155(11) *Forbes* 292.

[2] Regionalism allows a higher degree of both political and economic integration, which supports the idea of subsidiarity and the fact that some tasks can be better achieved on the local level. A principal issue related to regional trade agreements (RTAs) is whether their effect on the global system is trade creating or merely trade diverting. A possible answer is that it can be both, depending on the will and objectives pursued by such RTAs. For more discussion on RTAs see, eg R Blackhurst and D Henderson, 'Regional Integration Agreements, World Integration and the GATT' in K Anderson and R Blackhurst (eds), *Regional Integration and the Global Trading System* (1993) 409; see also JS Puche, 'Regionalism and the WTO' in The WTO Secretariat (ed), *From GATT to the WTO: The Multilateral Trading System in the New Millenium* (2000) 123.

[3] For the conditions to establish a WTO-compatible RTAs, see GATT, Art XXIV (Territorial Application—Frontier Traffic-Customs Unions and Free-Trade Areas). GATS mirrors the principles in this Article. See GATS, Art V (Economic Integration); see also P Guerrieri et al (eds), *Cultural Diversity and International Economic Integration: The Global Governance of the Audio-Visual Sector* (2005) 24–25.

arrangements, EC/EU[4] and NAFTA,[5] and the interface between WTO and regional regimes. Together with Chapters 5 and 6, this chapter constitutes a trend analysis, which lays the foundation for mapping out reform proposals to tackle the trade and culture issue at international and domestic levels in Chapter 8.

7.2 THE EUROPEAN COMMUNITY/ EUROPEAN UNION

The EC/EU, as a supranational entity carrying out a project of open-ended economic and political integration, escapes the traditional categories of international organisation.[6] Part of Europe's self-portrayal,[7] cultural diversity is spoken of as a constitutional value.[8] This section studies the treatment of culture at the Community/Union level based on diverse legal instruments, including the EC/EU treaties and related EC directives, as well as the pertinent practice by the European Court of Justice (ECJ), to better understand how the EC/EU deals with the issue of cultural protection in its integration process.

[4] The European Union (EU) refers to a union of 27 independent states based on the European Communities (EC) and founded to enhance political, economic and social cooperation, formerly known as the EC or the European Economic Community (EEC). The EU was established by the Treaty Establishing the European Union (hereinafter 'TEU'), which came into effect on 1 November 1993. See Treaty Establishing the European Economic Community, 25 March 1957, 298 UNTS11 (hereinafter EEC Treaty), amended by Treaty on Establishing the European Union, [1992] OJ C224, 1 (1992) (hereinafter 'TEU'), amended by Treaty of Amsterdam Amending the Treaty on European Union, [1997] OJ C340, 1 (hereinafter Treaty of Amsterdam). The Treaty is now known as the European Union: Consolidated Versions of the Treaty on European Union and of the Treaty Establishing the European Community, [2006] OJ C321 E/1 (hereinafter EC Treaty). The Treaty of Lisbon amending the Treaty on European Union and the Treaty establishing the European Community entered into force on 1 December 2009. After that date, any reference to the European Community shall be read as the European Union. Unless otherwise indicated, throughout this chapter, the term 'EC' is used in the period up to the ratification of the TEU and 'EU' is used thereafter, and 'EC/EU' is used to refer generally to the whole period before and after the TEU.

[5] North America Free Trade Agreement, 17 December 1992, Can-Mex-US, 32, ILM 296 (1993).

[6] See, eg M Lickova, 'European Exceptionalism in International Law' (2008) 19 *European Journal of International Law* 463, 463.

[7] See J Richardson, 'The European Union in the World—A Community of Values' (2002) 26 *Fordham International Journal* 12, 14.

[8] See C Piciocchi, 'Europe Faces Cultural Diversity: Towards a European Multicultural Model?' in F Palermo and GN Toggenburg (eds), *European Constitutional Values and Cultural Diversity* (2003) 25.

7.2.1 Culture in the EC/EU: A Unique Situation

It is worth noting that the EC/EU faces a unique situation in terms of preserving cultural diversity. The EU is influenced and characterised by various circles of values, such as founding values, European ideas and common legal principles. The degree of consensus in European societies regarding these values differs, as do the means to control respect for these values.[9] The tortuous evolution of EC/EU cultural policies is shaped by a series of tensions. Internally, tension is caused by the conflicting roles that culture plays in creating a united Europe. The integrative force of the EC/EU has created the parallel need to preserve the individuality of its Member States. From the beginning of the integration process, the attempt to apply a melting-pot approach and foster a European identity to replace national identities has failed. While American sociological and legal scholars had to shift from the 'melting pot' to the 'cultural pluralism' perspective, scholars in the EU have moved towards a perspective based on cultural diversity. This is the main difference between American and European models of multiculturalism.[10]

As European integration brings nations closer, the threat to individual nations' cultures increases. Accordingly, it is imperative to maintain the cultural diversity of Member States and allay fears of cultural degradation to prevent rising nationalism from derailing integration.[11] Yet, the question whether cultural policy should promote unity or diversity within Europe provokes heated debates. For instance, cinema carries a strong symbolic weight and has enormous influence on the development of other means of communication. Because of its strong cultural implications, the film sector does not lend itself easily to the trend towards uniformity inherent in the process of economic integration. This conflict is clearly seen in the relationship between domestic cinematographic legislation seeking to protect national, constitutionally grounded cultural identities and the free market philosophy pursued through the European economic integration process.[12]

Externally, the EC/EU has been trying to cement its common values and interests to tackle the American cultural threat for decades. A large portion of the US entertainment industry's overseas revenue is derived

[9] See GN Toggenberg, 'Cultural Diversity at the Background of the European Debate on Values—An Introduction' in Palermo and Toggenberg, ibid, 19.

[10] See Piciocchi, above n 8, 33–34.

[11] See, eg N Horst, 'Creating an Ever Closer Union: The European Court of Justice and the Threat to Cultural Diversity' (2008) 47 *Columbian Journal of Transnational Law* 165, 170–71; see also S Lee, 'Heritage Conventions Intertwine with the Concept of Cultural Diversity: Asian and European Perspectives' in N Obuljen and J Smiers (eds), *UNESCO's Convention on the Protection and Promotion of the Diversity of Cultural Expressions: Making It Work* (2006) 219–20.

[12] See A Herold, 'Between Art and Commerce: Constitutional Contradictions within the Framework of the EU Film Policy', in Palermo and Toggenberg, above n 8, 72–73.

from the European market. The importance of the EU market for the US also stems from its rapid expansion. US programmers can offer low prices because they have a large domestic market and can recoup most of their investment costs.[13] European shows, on the other hand, are generally only broadcast to a small national audience, which leads to less advertising revenue and, consequently, higher prices for these programmes.[14] This issue has attracted a great deal of attention in the EC/EU, and Member States have different views towards the extent of this threat and how to cope with it.[15] The UK and Italy, for instance, differ from France. They are marked by their advocacy for a system of quotas, primarily as a means to protect commercial concerns. Cultural protection is only a secondary goal, perhaps even incidental to this commercial purpose.[16] In other words, paralleling the 'open versus interventionist' argument at the national level are similar opposing opinions within the bureaucracy of the EC/EU. This further complicates the scenario.

In short, European culture[17] is not only threatened by outside forces, but also susceptible to internal erosion from its integration process. This situation gives rise to a unique challenge in the EC/EU's pursuit of cultural diversity, that is, to maintain the individual Member States' cultures and at the same time mediate the American cultural threat.[18]

[13] See CN Smith, 'International Trade in Television Programming and GATT: An Analysis of Why the European Community's Local Program Requirement Violates the General Agreement on Tariffs and Trade' (1993) 10 *International Tax & Business Law* 97, 102.

[14] In the meantime, American programme producers have come to depend upon the EU market as well. Production costs have increased so significantly that many shows would not break even without the additional sales abroad. Profits from the international market are no longer just a bonus, but instead have become a necessary means of meeting expenses. See KL Kessler, 'Protecting Free Trade in Audiovisual Entertainment: A Proposal for Counteracting the European Union's Trade Barriers to the US Entertainment Industry's Exports' (1995) 26 *Law & Policy International Business* 563, 566; M Hahn, 'A Clash of Cultures? The UNESCO Diversity Convention and International Trade Law' (2006) 9 *Journal of International Economic Law* 515.

[15] Some states (eg France) prefer to introduce more interventionist cultural policies while others (eg UK) do not. See J Middleton, 'The Effectiveness of Audiovisual Regulation Inside the European Union: The Television without Frontiers Directives and Cultural Protectionism' (2003) 31 *Denver Journal of International Law & Policy* 607, 615.

[16] Ibid, 615.

[17] Note that what is meant by European culture is not exactly clear. It could refer to the cultural heritage of individual Member States or to some conglomeration of common aspects of their diverse cultures. The notion of a synthesised European culture seems repugnant to the very concepts of individual expressionism and cultural diversity that the EU claims to be furthering. Therefore, though early Community attempts at cultural policy were characterised by their efforts to create a European culture, the desirability of this policy was questioned. See CB Cunningham, 'In Defense of Member State Culture: The Unrealized Potential of Article 151(4) of the EC Treaty and the Consequences for EC Cultural Policy' (2001) 34 *Cornell International Law Journal* 119, 162.

[18] The Culture Ministers meeting in Thessaloniki in May 2003 stated that 'Europe as a continent of culture can neither accept the threat of cultural homogeneity, nor the threat of the clash of civilisations. The European answer to all this is to insist on safeguarding and promoting cultural diversity'. See Toggenberg, above n 9, 20–21; see also Commission of the European Communities, Communication from the Commission to the Council and

7.2.2 Culture Clause in the EC Treaty: Article 151

Culture is a relatively new sphere of activity in the process of European integration. From the outset, the EC/EU's roots run most deeply in economic grounds. The 1958 Treaty Establishing the European Economic Community (hereinafter the Treaty of Rome, or the EEC Treaty) sought to tear down trade barriers and create a free market to promote economic prosperity among its constituents. Culture did not figure in its objectives at that time. Later in the process of building closer economic relations among Member States, however, it was realised that the elimination of trade barriers would unavoidably affect culture. This called for a response from the Community, since measures taken at the national level had often led both to the distortion of market mechanisms and the devaluation of cultural objectives.[19] In addition, a changing cultural ecosystem marked by new technologies and fragmented audiences also began to render national measures less effective.

Culture issues remained at the periphery of European integration until the early 1990s. When the EEC Treaty was amended by the Maastricht Treaty of European Union (TEU) in 1992, the EEC was transformed into the EU. In seeking a comprehensive approach to boosting European culture, despite the fact that the initial suggestions were met with controversy,[20] the TEU introduced two general, transversal identity or diversity clauses: a clause on 'identity preservation' in Article 6 and a cultural diversity impact clause in Article 128.[21] Article 6 states that 'the Union shall respect the national identities of its Member States'. Article 128 obliges the Community to 'take cultural aspects into account in its action under other provisions of this Treaty, particularly in order to respect and to promote the diversity of culture'. Article 128 was amended and renumbered by the 1997 Treaty of Amsterdam, and currently appears as Article 151 of the Consolidated Version of the EC Treaty.[22]

Referred to as the 'culture clause', Article 151 aims to support cultural endeavours and create avenues for disseminating European culture

the European Parliament: 'Towards an International Instrument on Cultural Diversity', COM(2003) 520 final, 27 August 2003.

[19] See M Burri-Nenova, 'The New Audiovisual Media Services Directive: Television without Frontiers, Television without Cultural Diversity' (2007) 44 *Common Market Law Review* 1689, 1721.

[20] Some critics argued that the regulation of culture was not included in the EC Treaty and fell outside the purview of the Community. See D Goldberg, et al, *EC Media Law and Policy* (1998) 12.

[21] TEU Title IX (as in effect 1993) (now Title XII). This title contained one article on culture: Art 128. This chapter refers to the article as currently numbered.

[22] European Union, Consolidated Versions of the Treaty on European Union and of the Treaty Establishing the European Community, [2006] OJ C321 E/1.

throughout the world. Complementing the policy on the free movement of goods, persons, services and capital (hereinafter the Four Freedoms),[23] Article 151 asks the Community to 'contribute to the flowering of the cultures of the Member States, while respecting their national and regional diversity and bringing the common cultural heritage to the fore'.[24] The wording of Article 151 reflects the compromise struck between advocates of unity and diversity. The article recognises the protection of cultural values as one of the constitutional tasks of the Community. To this end, it provides, at least partially, 'constitutional' resources to deal with the dual nature of cultural sectors. The Community is required, under Article 151(4), to 'take the cultural aspects of its actions into account under other provisions of the EC Treaty'. This clear statement of the significance of cultural diversity establishes a formal recognition of culture in the EC/EU; the European Commission's decision to challenge a Member State's practice as restricting the Four Freedoms must now recognise cultural value as a possible justification for that practice.[25]

Notwithstanding its positive bearing on cultural diversity, Article 151 leads to a contradiction in European cultural policy between the economic objectives of market integration and the obligations to preserve cultural diversity; both are constitutionalised within the EU legal order. It cannot eliminate the tension that exists between free market and cultural diversity within the EU legal order.[26] As a result, Article 151 raises many questions, key among them being the dilemma of how cultural values should be considered when they appear to collide with other, more immediately compelling objectives of the EU, such as economic growth or market integration.

A common concern is that this article is not a measure to defend national cultural diversity but a means of cultural integration. The measures taken by the Member States to protect their cultural diversity may affect the operation of the common market, especially the Four Freedoms. If the 'enhancement of cultural roots and current common to Europeans' is undertaken without due regard to national individuality, Member States' individual cultures may face a slow but steady process

[23] Ibid, Title I (focusing on free movement of goods) and Title III (focusing on free movement of persons, services and capital). The Four Freedoms are the bedrock of the common market.

[24] Ibid, Title XII, Culture, Art 151(1). Acting under the authority of Art 151, the Community administers an extensive funding programme to support cultural undertakings in the Member States. This financing scheme has represented the bulk of the Community's cultural policy in the years since the signing of the TEU. The current one is the 'EU Cultural Programme of 2007–2013'. European Commission, 'Cultural Programme Guide (2007–2013)', available at http://eacea.ec.europa.eu/culture/programme/about_culture_en.php (last accessed on 17 June 2012). See also Cunningham, above n 17, 123.

[25] See Cunningham, ibid, 122–23.

[26] See Herold, above n 12, 73–75.

of erosion.[27] Meanwhile, Article 151(5) limits Community actions in the cultural sphere to recommendations and financing incentives; the direct harmonisation of laws is expressly excluded.[28] By contrast, it is far easier for the EU to take actions on economic matters.[29]

In practice, the European Commission has not altered its evaluation of Member States' practice in response to Article 151(4). For instance, in May 2002, the European Commission asked France for a justification of the law prohibiting certain retail groups from advertising on television. France couched its argument on the premise of cultural exception, holding that the prohibition was necessary to protect local press. Citing concerns about the impact it might have on non-French advertising agencies, the EC took action against this law.[30] Likewise, in an influential dispute over cross-border fixed book prices, the Commission did not recognise any cultural benefit stemming from the price-fixing system and ordered the system dismantled.[31]

The inclusion of a culture clause marks how far the EC/EU has advanced from its initial focus on economic matters such as coal and steel. However, as the result of its inherent weakness, Article 151 has not become a sufficient safeguard for cultural diversity. Outside the Community, the EC/EU has played an active role in the work of UNESCO, notably contributing to the exploratory discussions and the ensuing drafting of the UNESCO Convention on Cultural Diversity. As parties to the Convention,[32] the Member States and the EU have already taken active engagement regarding the protection and promotion of cultural diversity.[33] It remains to be seen whether and how the relevant programmes will be implemented in practice.

[27] European Commission, Bulletin of the European Communities, Culture: Policy Objectives, No 11-2007, point 1.21.14 (2007). See also Horst, above n 11, 181.

[28] EC Treaty, Art 151(5) ('excluding harmonization of the laws and regulations of the Member States').

[29] Compare EC Treaty, Arts 94, 95 and 151.

[30] See FS Galt, 'The Life, Death, and Rebirth of the "Cultural Exception" in the Multilateral Trading System: An Evolutionary Analysis of Cultural Protection and Intervention in the Face of American Pop Culture's Hegemony' (2004) 3 *Washington University Global Studies Law Review* 909, 929–30.

[31] See Cunningham, above n 17, 153–57. For more details on the case see V Kitz, 'The Difference between Books and Chocolate Bars—How EC Treaty Art 151(4) Affects Community Actions' (2004) 32 *AIPLA Quarterly Journal* 361, 367–68.

[32] The EC itself is a party to the Convention. In its resolution of 27 April 2006, Parliament supported the UNESCO Convention. The Council Decision of 18 May 2006 on the conclusion of the Convention on the Protection and Promotion of the Diversity of Cultural Expressions approved the UNESCO Convention on behalf of the Community.

[33] The first steps toward the fulfilment of the commitment are in the European Commission's communications on a European Agenda for Culture in a Globalizing World. See European Commission, 'Commission Communication on a European Agenda for Culture in a Globalizing World', COM(2007) 242 final (10 May 2007); European Commission, 'Inventory of Community Actions in the Field of Culture, Accompanying Document to the Communication on a European Agenda for Culture in A Globalizing World', SEC(2007) 570 (10 May 2007).

7.2.3 Culture in the EC Directives: From TVWF to AVMS

The European Commission maintains that the audiovisual industry is unlike any other that produces goods merely to be sold on the market. Instead, as a cultural industry *par excellence*, audiovisual sectors hold the key to the transmission, development and construction of cultural identities.[34] Cultural diversity has thus been defined as one of the vital justifications for European audiovisual policy. Television in particular has played a significant role in shaping public opinion throughout the history of Europe.[35] This section traces the cultural regulation of television in Europe by studying two important EC directives concerning the subject.

7.2.3.1 TVWF[36]

Several factors led to the adoption of TVWF. First, when trade protections were slowly phased out and the movement towards a unified Europe gained real traction, the benefits of efficiency, competition and greater choice for consumers outweighed the negative effects of integration. The 'American culture threat' developed in Europe alongside this removal of trade barriers in the mid- and late 1980s. American media exports, particularly television, began to appear frequently in Europe. At that time, many European countries initiated and operated their television broadcasting services under a public model. They had little experience with commercial broadcasting and were wary of American-style commercialism.[37]

Secondly, mass media has the power to influence human thought and behaviour, and played an extraordinary role in twentieth-century Europe. Its power can be used for good or evil; those who control the mass media can control the masses. In other words, mass media, as a cultural industry, may systematically indoctrinate individuals with the ideology and

[34] See Council Resolution of 21 January 2002 on the role of culture in the development of the European Union, [2002] OJ C32/2; Council Conclusions of 19 December 2002 on the 'Television without Frontiers' Directive, [2003] OJ C13/1, Recital 3. See also LL Garrett, 'Commerce versus Culture: The Battle between the United States and the European Union Over Audiovisual Trade Policies' (1994) 19 *North Carolina Journal of International Law and Commercial Regulation* 553, 554–55.

[35] After the World War II, television swiftly conquered all other forms of media in the competition for people's attention as nations' storytellers and transmitters of culture. See ML Landsman, 'Restricting Foreign Television Programming in Europe: The European Community's Television Quota Reappraised' (1999) 8 *Media Law & Policy* 29, 48–49.

[36] Council Directive of 3 October 1989 on the Coordination of Certain Provisions Laid Down by Law, Regulation or Administrative Action in Member States Concerning the Pursuit of Television Broadcasting Activities (89/552/EEC), [1989] OJ L298/23, amended by Directive 97/36/EC of the European Parliament and of the Council of 30 June 1997 amending Council Directive 89/552/EEC, [1997] OJ L202. In this chapter, the TVWF refers to the consolidated version of Directive 89/552/EEC and Directive 97/36/EC.

[37] See generally, K Segrave, *American Television Abroad: Hollywood's Attempt to Dominate World Television* (1998).

ways of life of an established society.[38] Since World War II, television has swiftly and decisively conquered all other forms of media in the competition for people's attention. Indeed, television assumes the dominant role as national storyteller and transmitter of culture.[39] Two theories, termed 'all-powerful television' and 'cultural uniformity', embrace the practical strengths of television and emphasise the cultural link between television and the masses and the connection between cultural domain and political sovereignty.[40] In particular, given the television's role in solidifying national identity and European citizenship,[41] it became imperative to regulate television broadcasting in Europe.

Thirdly, EC Member States were technically able to regulate the content of television broadcasting prior to the 1980s, because the transmissions of local companies could only reach local citizens.[42] As transmission capabilities developed with satellite and cable technology, however, it became harder for nations to regulate television signals sent from foreign countries.

Combined, these elements pushed the EC to consider regulating television broadcasting. In response to the American television programming's growing dominance of European networks and its perceived threat to European culture, the European Council stressed that the proposed regulation should ensure the richness and diversity of European culture and substantially strengthen European cultural identity.[43] The 1984 Green Paper on the Establishment of Common Market for Broadcasting[44] marked the beginning of the EC's television regulation. Years later, on 3 October 1989, the EC adopted the Television without Frontiers Directive (TVWF).[45] The TVWF stands as an example of important effects on cultural diversity and market integration, and merits special examination.

First, the TVWF reflected the long-established stance of the Council of Europe (CoE) on media matters[46] and provided an essential regulatory

[38] See generally, ES Herman and N Chomsky, *Manufacturing Consent: The Political Economy of the Mass Media* (1988).

[39] See Landsman, above n 35, 48–49.

[40] See LGC Kaplan, 'The European Community's "Television without Frontiers" Directive: Stimulating Europe to Regulate Culture' (1994) 8 *Emory International Law Review* 255, 257–60.

[41] European Commission, 'Green Paper on the Development of A Common Market for Telecommunication Services and Equipment', COM(1987) 290 final (30 June 1987) 2.

[42] European Commission, 'Interim Report Realities and Tendencies in European Television: Perspectives and Opinions', COM(1983) 229 final (25 May 1983) 13–14, 151–60.

[43] See European Council Decisions of 2 and 3 December 1988, Rhodes, in Bulletin of the European Communities, No 12/1988.

[44] European Commission, 'Television without Frontiers: Green Paper on the Establishment of the Common Market for Broadcasting, Especially by Satellite and Cable', COM(84) 300 final (14 June 1984).

[45] Council Directive 89/552/EEC, [1989] OJ (L298) 23. For the developments leading to the adoption of the TVWF, see, eg DAL Levy, *Europe's Digital Revolution: Broadcasting and Regulation: The EU and the Nation States* (1999) 41–43; Garrett, above n 34, 553–70.

[46] The TVWF mirrors to a great extent the structure and the basic provisions of the Convention on Transfrontier Television (CTT) adopted by the Council of Europe. The

framework for television broadcasting at the Community level. The TVWF addressed three different fields: the protection of minors, the regulation of advertising and the protection of European culture through quotas for the broadcasting of 'European works'.[47] In particular, the TVWF provided the impetus for establishing a single broadcasting market among Member States. Its Preamble describes the right to freely broadcast and distribute television services as a manifestation of freedom of expression.[48] In order to establish a single market for television broadcasting within Europe, the TVWF facilitated the integration and harmonisation of the various broadcasting laws already in place in the individual Member States. Amended in 1997,[49] the directive is a concretisation of the freedom to provide services under specific conditions necessary and sufficient to consolidate a single market for media services.[50] As the only tool at the Community level to serve cultural goals per se, the TVWF overcame the fragmentation of national laws and facilitated the free circulation of television broadcasts.[51] In this sense, the TVWF can be best described as a liberalisation measure relating to television broadcasting within the EC.

The TVWF preserved specific public interest objectives, such as protecting minors, consumers, cultural diversity and European industry. In particular, the TVWF set an aggressive course to protect European audiovisual sectors and stimulate diversity in television content by introducing, inter alia, a 'European content requirement': where practical, television stations must reserve a majority of their airtime for broadcasting 'European works' and 'independent productions'.[52] The content requirement ensured a balance

CTT was opened for signature by the CoE Member States and other states party to the European Cultural Convention (ETS No 018), Paris, 19 December 1954. See Explanatory Report to the European Convention on Transfrontier Television (ETS No 132), Strasbourg, 5 May 1989, as amended by the Provisions of the Protocol (ETS No 171), entered into force on 1 March, 2002.

[47] Council Directive 89/552/EEC, [1989] OJ L298, 23, Arts 4–22.

[48] Freedom of expression is enshrined in the Convention for the Protection of Human Rights and Fundamental Freedoms. See Convention for the Protection of Human Rights and Fundamental Freedoms, 4 November 1950, Art 10(1) (ETS No 5).

[49] Council Directive 97/36, [1997] OJ L202, 60.

[50] See BJ Drijber, 'The Revised Television without Frontiers Directive: Is it Fit for the Next Century?' (1999) 36 *Common Market Law Review* 87, 92; see also M Wheeler, 'Supranational Regulation: Television and the European Union' (2004) 19(3) *European Journal of Communication* 349, 351–57.

[51] See M Burri-Nenova, 'Cultural Diversity and the EC Audiovisual Media Services Directive: Beyond the Handsome Rhetoric', NCCR Trade Regulation Working Paper No 2009/09 (2 April 2009) 4–5.

[52] TVWF, Art 4(1). It provides that Member States ensure 'where practicable and by appropriate means, that broadcasters reserve for European works a majority proportion of their transmission time, excluding the time appointed to news, sports events, games, advertising, teletext services and teleshopping', and where practicable and by appropriate means, broadcasters reserve at least 10% of their transmission time, or alternatively, 10% of their programming budget, for European works created by producers who are independent of broadcasters. 'European works' are defined pursuant to criteria set out by Art 6, TVWF.

of offerings in the European markets and created a cultural safety net to foster the European television industries and preserve common European values.[53] A study shows that the measures to promote European and independent productions generated considerable impact.[54]

However, every coin has a flip side. The TVWF faced both internal and external challenges, and it fell far short of achieving its ultimate objective. Both the US audiovisual industry and the European cultural industry questioned the effectiveness and the purpose of the TVWF. Internally, while the TVWF was a 'victory for commercial forces', it did not do much to achieve cultural goals. One of the objectives of the TVWF was to develop cross-border trade in audiovisual programmes among European countries. Due to the tensions between its economic aims and cultural concern, the TVWF failed to protect the distinct cultures of individual Member States. Furthermore, although certain flexibility is permitted with this provision, the vague phrase 'where practicable' indicates that each Member State may decide autonomously whether to mandate the 51% programming requirement.[55] Externally, the European content requirement has always been a thorn in US–EU relations.[56] The US held that the EC's real concern was to guarantee European industries a substantial share in a burgeoning market, and even placed the EC on its 'Special 301 Priority Watch List'. Indeed, the US later initiated a consultation under the GATT.[57]

Another challenge at both the internal and external levels was posed by rapid technological developments not envisioned by the TVWF. Digital

[53] See Kessler, above n 14, 563; R Collins, 'The Screening of Jacques Tati: Broadcasting and Cultural Identity in The European Community' (1993) 11 *Cardozo Arts & Entertainments Law Journal* 361, 365–66.

[54] The study suggested that TVWF Arts 4 and 5 achieved their cultural aims inasmuch as they have increased the proportion of European works and independent productions broadcast by channels in the EU. See David Graham & Associates, 'Impact Study of Measures (Community and National) Concerning the Promotion of Distribution and Production of TV Programs Provided for under Article 25(a) of the TV without Frontiers Directive', Final Report prepared for the Audiovisual, Media and Internet Unit of DG Information Society, 24 May 2005, 181 and s 4.6.3.

[55] See TVWF, Art 5(1) (this proportion was to be achieved progressively, on the basis of suitable criteria.) The TVWF was largely drafted at France's insistence in line with the main aspects of French audiovisual policy. However, the use of 'where practicable' represents a compromise between France and its European partners. French regulations tend to be much more protectionist in nature than the 'average' European regulation. Indeed, a report regarding the effects of the TVWF Directive indicated that certain European channels did not apply the 51% requirement. See A Forrest, 'Can Community Support Measures Have A Decisive Impact on European Film and Television Production?' (1996) 8 *European Business Journal* 36, 39.

[56] See JD Donaldson, 'Television without Frontiers: The Continuing Tension between Liberal Free Trade and European Cultural Integrity' (1996) 20 *Fordham International Law Journal* 90, 92–93.

[57] See N Garnham, *Capitalism and Communication* (1990) 154; J Filipek, 'Culture Quotas, The Trade Controversy over the European Community's Broadcasting Directive' (1992) 28 *Stanford Journal of International Law* 323, 328–31.

technology, such as television on demand and webcasting, threatens to obliterate the function of European content quotas. The increased convergence within the audiovisual sectors has also radically and irreversibly transformed the media landscape and continues to affect both the context and the content of media consumption.[58] Regulation in this realm has lagged far behind technological progress.

These challenges raise the question of how the protection of European culture can best be accomplished: will it be by strengthening the TVWF or by liberalising regulation? In addition to questioning the effectiveness of the TVWF in practice, there is a further argument that liberalising audiovisual regulatory policies is necessary to develop a more competitive European audiovisual sector.[59] In fact, TVWF quotas and ambiguity around what constitutes 'European works' made it difficult for European audiovisual sectors to form alliances and reach parity with Hollywood.

7.2.3.2 *AVMS:*[60] *An Improvement to Promote Cultural Diversity?*

Both the exogenous transformation of the legal model and the endogenous development of audiovisual sectors, as addressed above, prompted another round of review of the TVWF. The review addressed a number of key issues, including scope of application, cultural quota mechanism, the rules relating to advertising and product placement. As a result of the review, the European Commission proposed the EC Audiovisual Media Services Directive (AVMS) on 13 December 2005. Member States had transformed the AVMS into national law by 19 December 2009.[61]

The AVMS proffers a fresh approach to regulating media in a complex and dynamic environment and presents a new case study of protecting cultural diversity in digital era. It demonstrates the significance that the EU has placed on sweeping technological advancement.[62] With respect to scope, the AVMS includes the entire range of audiovisual media services, irrespective of the technology delivering them.[63] This is in stark contrast to the regulatory asymmetries that predominated before, under which different delivery modes received different treatment. The AVMS also endeavours to create a level playing field for both linear and non-linear

[58] See Middleton, above n 15, 625–26.

[59] For a vivid discussion on the history of the GATT and the Television without Frontiers Directive, see Garrett, above n 34, 553–70.

[60] Directive 2007/65/EC of the European Parliament and of the Council of 11 December 2007 amending Council Directive 89/552/EEC on the Coordination of Certain Provisions laid down by law, regulation or administrative action in Member States Concerning Pursuit of Television Broadcasting Activities, [2007] OJ L332/27 (hereinafter AVMS).

[61] Directive 2007/65/EC, Art 3.

[62] See V Little, 'Audiovisual Media Services Directive: Europe's Modernization of Broadcast Services Regulations' [2008] *University of Illinois Journal of Law, Technology & Policy* 223, 236.

[63] AVMS, Art 1.

services.[64] In consideration of the fact that the regulation of non-linear services may be onerous for smaller providers, and may in turn create a barrier to emerging creativity and digital content distribution,[65] the AVMS introduces a unique two-tiered method of regulation.[66]

Cultural diversity and promoting European and independent production are still priorities in the AVMS.[67] To this end, the AVMS is meant to sustain the balance between the free circulation of audiovisual media and the preservation of European cultural diversity in the digital realm, while respecting the principles of subsidiarity and proportionality inherent in the Community.[68] In order to achieve this goal, the AVMS incorporates adaptations necessary to embrace technological developments, while at the same time upholding many previous provisions.[69] Among other measures, the European content quotas remain the same. The AVMS creates an obligation for Member States to ensure that media service providers 'promote, where practicable and by appropriate means, production of and access to European works'.[70] Also unchanged is the percentage mandated for content produced by independent European sources.

The European content requirement continues to serve as a bulwark against American domination of cultural markets, but it hardly defends against the homogenising effects of regulatory competition within the EU.[71] At the same time, in its cultural policy endeavours, the EU tends

[64] AVMS, Art 1(e) and (g). The rule-of-thumb for delimiting the categories of linear/non-linear services is the possibility of choice and control the user can exercise, as well as the impact they may have on society. AVMS, Recital 42. When the TVWF was drafted, television broadcast was primarily 'linear' in nature. See COM(84) 300 final, above n 44, 332.

[65] See Burri-Nenova, above n 51, 23.

[66] In contrast to the relatively heavy regulatory burden on traditional television broadcasters ('second tier regulations'), the regulatory scheme governing new on-demand services only lays out certain basic rules ('first tier regulations'). This reflects the European Commission's intention to lower entry costs for new market entrants in order to create a vibrant EU industry and open national markets to more competition from other EU countries. See T Gibbons, 'The Impact of Regulatory Competition on Measures to Promote Pluralism and Cultural Diversity in the Audiovisual Sector' (2006–07) 9 *Cambridge Yearbook of European Legal Studies* 239, 257.

[67] European Commission, 'Fourth Report on the Application of Directive 89/552/EEC Television without Frontiers', COM(2002) 778 final (6 January 6 2003). The European Parliament was insistent on the amendment of Recital 3, which held that audiovisual media services are as much cultural services as economic services. Their growing importance for societies, democracy, diversity of opinion and media pluralism justifies the application of specific rules to these services. See AVMS, Recital 3.

[68] See Art 5(3) of the EC Treaty and the Protocol on the application of the principles of subsidiarity and proportionality attached to the Treaty of Amsterdam amending the Treaty of European Union, the Treaties Establishing the European Communities and related acts, [1997] OJ C340/1.

[69] See Little, above n 62, 223.

[70] AVMS, Art 3(i)(1). It is further clarified that such promotion could relate, inter alia, to the financial contribution to the production and rights acquisition of European works or to the share and/or prominence of European works in the catalogue of programmes. AVMS, Art 3(i)(1) and Recital 48.

[71] See Gibbons, above n 66, 257.

to stress the competitiveness between nations as the primary governance problem.[72] Meanwhile, the channel proliferation brought about by digital technology leads to further market fragmentation,[73] making it harder for European producers to compete with American imports. As a result, an odd relationship emerges between 'European' and 'non-European' culture, and between 'European' and national identities.[74] It is advocated that the EU abandon its 'Europe against the rest of world' strategy because it seems difficult to justify both in economic and in cultural terms.[75]

Another criticism of the European content requirement has to do with the definition of 'European work', which is neither based on originality and quality criteria nor requires a particular expression of national and European themes. Instead, it is based on the requirement that a majority of its authors and workers reside in one or more Member State.[76] This definition does little to prevent the increasing homogenisation of content and deteriorating quality of programmes.

The AVMS tries to secure preferred access for European productions. The question is whether a higher share of European productions truly reflects an increased diversity of cultural expressions. Another question concerns whether the quota mechanism can be translated into the domain of non-linear services. As pointed out, the effects of the quota mechanism on non-linear services are uncertain and may even have diametrically opposed outcomes. One possible result is that consumers would simply not choose 'European works' and thus render any quota virtually ineffective. A better option suggested is that consumer selection can constantly generate new products in the digital age, such as archived European works. This may ultimately lead to a greater share of available and effectively consumed European works, and could represent a genuine expression of cultural diversity.[77]

In sum, the AVMS is an update on the TVWF that takes into account an intrinsically dynamic and complex new media environment. The overall effect intended by the reform is increased consumer choice, diversity

[72] See T O'Regan and B Goldsmith, 'Making Cultural Policy: Meeting Cultural Objectives in a Digital Environment' (2006) 7(1) *Television New Media* 68, 69.

[73] The growth in channel choice reduces the total audience share of the primary channels and the share of individual primary channels in each Member State. Furthermore, new media distribution channels continue drawing consumers away from traditional media, further reducing the audience share of primary channels. See David Graham & Associates, above n 54, ss 3.5.1, 3.5.4 and 3.5.5.

[74] See, eg T Risse, 'A European Identity? Europeanization and the Evolution of Nation-State Identities' in MG Cowles et al (eds), *Transforming Europe: Europeanization and Domestic Change* (2001) 198–216.

[75] See Burri-Nenova, above n 19, 1725.

[76] TVWF, Art 6(2) in conjunction with 6(1)(a) and (b). This definition is largely unchanged under the AVMS; see Art 1(n), points (i)–(iii).

[77] See Burri-Nenova, above n 51, 15–16.

and investment in the European industry.[78] However, this aspiration may remain unfulfilled, particularly as far as its contribution to cultural diversity in the European media is concerned. It appears that, despite good intentions, the AVMS lacks concrete solutions addressing cultural diversity. In the meantime, the concentration among the diverse players, both horizontally and vertically, has made designing an appropriate regulatory model even harder. To avoid a situation where cultural diversity becomes a mere political slogan, the EU may need to examine possible objective parameters for 'measuring' diversity to identify effective regulatory options and carve out more cultural measures compatible with the contemporary media ecology.

7.2.4 The ECJ and Cultural Diversity

The driving force behind the EC Treaty is to create a common market and eliminate trade barriers, instead of protecting culture. An entity defined by the EC Treaty as having a primarily economic mission,[79] the ECJ is empowered to uphold EC law and tends to emphasise economic concerns. Where cases before the ECJ place economic and cultural interests in conflict, the economic considerations usually prevail to the detriment of the cultural considerations.[80]

Prior to 1992, the ECJ lacked enshrined principles to guide its deliberations over matters possessing cultural dimensions. A survey of cases may reveal the Court's disregard for cultural concerns. In 1968, for example, the ECJ held that the free movement of goods admitted no legal difference between cultural goods and ordinary commercial products.[81] This case sets a precedent in line with the ECJ's devotion to facilitating the economic integration of Europe. Later, the vindication of the free movement of goods in *Procureur du Roi v Dassonville*[82] and *Rewe-Zentral AG v Bundesmonopolverwaltung für Branntwein* again showcased the ECJ's commitment to protecting the integrity of a common market. In *German Beer*, the ECJ determined that, despite the fact that the brewing and consumption of beer was a long-standing cornerstone of German culture, an interest in public health could not justify the marketing restrictions Germany had enacted.[83] In *Irish Souvenirs*, the ECJ struck down an Irish law as a quantitative restriction that violated the free movement of goods. The

[78] See European Commission, 'The Commission Proposal for a Modernization of the Television without Frontiers Directive', MEMO/05/475 (13 December 2005).

[79] Treaty of Amsterdam, Art 9; see also E Steyger, *National Traditions and European Community Law* (1997) 2.

[80] See Horst, above n 11, 183.

[81] See Case 7/68 *Commission v Italy* [1968] ECR 617.

[82] Case 8/74 *Procureur du Roi v Dassonville* [1974] ECR 837.

[83] Case 178/84 *Commission v Germany* [1987] ECR 1227.

ECJ was criticised as possibly depriving Ireland of the ability to control the commercial use of its cultural heritage.[84]

These pre-1992 cases demonstrate that the ECJ sought to vindicate the EC's fundamental economic interests and decided cases without due regard for cultural considerations. The addition of a Title on Culture in the Treaty of Maastricht in 1992 arguably should have led the ECJ to take heed of cultural issues in deciding cases.[85] After the Maastricht Treaty's entry into force, the ECJ dealt with a number of cases involving culture. Nevertheless, an examination of the ECJ's post-1992 cases tells a different story. It appears that the ECJ has not changed much in adjudicating cases involving culture since 1992. In these rulings, the Court did not refer to the new provisions of the Treaty, but continued to view cultural aspects in light of their relationship to the free movement of persons, services and capital.[86]

In *Federación de Distribuidores Cinemátograficos v Spain*, the ECJ did not even mention Article 151(4) of the EC Treaty.[87] This case concerned a Spanish royal legislative decree that restricted licences to distributors who undertook to distribute Spanish films. While the Spanish government argued that the decree had a cultural objective—protecting national film production[88]—the ECJ concluded that the link between the grant of licences and the distribution of national films had a purely economic objective.[89] The ECJ's remark that the decree applied irrespective of the content or quality of films demonstrates its doubts that the decree promotes genuine cultural diversity.

The tension between EC trade policy and the cultural values of Member States gained widespread attention when the ECJ determined that EC law precluded the application of long-standing national football association rules limiting the number of foreign players who could be fielded in competitive matches. In *Union Royale Belge des Societes de Football Association v Bosman*, the ECJ disregarded the Association's strong arguments that nationalism plays an important part in football and ruled that the players' rights to freedom of movement superseded any Member State's interest in watching their own footballers play in the national team.[90] This case indicates that such laws, regardless of any cultural

[84] Case 113/80 *Commission v Ireland* [1981] ECR 1625.

[85] See E Psychogiopoulou, 'EC Competition Law and Cultural Diversity: The Case of Cinema, Music and Book Publishing Industries' (2005) 30 *European Law Review* 838, 839.

[86] See V Mitsilegas, 'Culture in the Evolution of European Law: Panacea in the Quest for Identity?' in P Fitzpatrick and JH Bergeron (eds), *Europe's Other: European Law between Modernity and Postmodernity* (1998) 122.

[87] Case C-17/92 *Federación de Distribuidores Cinemátograficos v Spain* [1993] ECR I-2239, [1994] EMLR 153, 176 (1993).

[88] Ibid, 162 (1993).

[89] Ibid, 185.

[90] Case C-415/93 [1995] ECR I-5040, [1996] 1 CMLR 645 (1995).

impact, will not be sustained if they violate the EC Treaty's provisions on the Four Freedoms or competition rules.

There are other cases that reflect a similar standpoint on the part of the ECJ. In *Commission v Belgium*, Belgium tried to use Article 151 of the EC Treaty as a justification for its failure to comply with an EC directive that harmonises national laws on broadcasting activities. The ECJ held that a Member State could not control programmes from other Member States on the basis of Article 151. It further emphasised that the Community could still adopt measures to implement the fundamental Four Freedoms, even when cultural considerations had to be considered.[91] In *Daniele Annibaldi v Sindaco Del Comune di Guidonia e Presidente Regione Lazio*, the ECJ attempted to limit the Community's cultural competence by holding that a regional law establishing a park intended to protect and enhance environmental value and cultural heritage falls outside the scope of Community law.[92]

In *Greek Tour Guide*, Greece passed specific licensing requirements for non-resident tour guides in order to promote proper appreciation and understanding of its cultural treasures. The Commission asserted that the legislation violated Article 59 of the EC Treaty, which guarantees the freedom of EU nationals to provide services in other Member States on a temporary basis, and brought suit before the ECJ. The Court held that Greece went beyond what was necessary and that its action was disproportionate.[93] The Court used the same reasoning in another, near-identical Commission suit against France.[94]

These post-1992 cases highlight the economic bias that lies behind the proportionality standard applied by the ECJ and demonstrates the difficulties in incorporating Article 151 into other provisions of the EC Treaty. This indicates that Article 151 of the EC Treaty has not prompted the ECJ to adjust its analysis in cases involving culture. It is generally understood that, as 'an exceptional provision', Article 151 must 'be interpreted in a narrow sense' and 'cannot justify a shift in the institutional balance' of the EU.[95] This may partly explain why most of the ECJ's rulings have yielded little to engender confidence in the power of the culture clause. If the ECJ continues on this track and treats culture as it did prior to the implementation of the Maastricht Treaty, it may prevent Article 151 of the EC Treaty from performing its intended role.

It is worth noting that, in recent years, some of the ECJ's decisions have shown some regard for cultural concerns. For instance, in *Laserd-*

[91] Case C-11/95 [1996] ECR I-4153, [1997] 2 CMLR 289 (1996), 58–59.

[92] Case C-309/96 [1997] ECR I-7505, [1998] 2 CMLR 187 (1997), 24.

[93] Case C-198/89 *Commission v Hellenic Republic* [1991] ECR I-00727.

[94] Case C-154/89 *Commission v France* [1991] ECR I-00659.

[95] Case C-211/01 *Commission of the European Cmtys v Council of the European Union*, Opinion of Advocate General Alber [2003] ECR I-8913, 22.

isken APS v Kulturministeriet,[96] the ECJ's ruling arguably demonstrates that, as long as a legislative act of the Community declares its sensitivity to cultural issues, the Court will presume its compliance with Article 151, no matter how general the statements.[97] Though this pushed the culture clause closer to a procedural requirement rather than as a substantive limit on Community action, it shows that some attention has been paid to Article 151.

More progress is displayed in several other cases. In *Metronome Musik GmbH v Music Point Hokamp GmbH*, the ECJ recognised the relevance of Article 151(4) in the context of copyrighted works and invoked this clause to justify a Community action.[98] In *Centro di Musicologia Walter Stauffer v Finanzamt Munchen fur Korperschaften*,[99] the ECJ admitted that certain objects connected with the promotion of culture may constitute overriding reasons of general interest. In *IMPALA v Commission*, the ECJ noted that the merger of two major record labels would have some damaging consequences for culture by potentially limiting the originality and diversity of new artists and titles and found for applicants, not only faulting the Commission's market share analysis, but also criticising its decision for failing to take account of Article 151(4) and cultural diversity.[100]

These cases indicate that Article 151 of the EC Treaty gradually began to obtain some status in the ECJ's decisions. In the long term, the ECJ may realise the import of Article 151 and thereby take cultural issues into account in an attempt to limit the threat to cultural diversity imposed by its previous privileging of economic matters. In clarifying the actions required to stop threatening Member States' efforts at cultural preservation, the ECJ should apply Article 151 independently and include it as an explicit part of legal analysis when a party raises a reasonable cultural justification.[101]

That said, concrete suggestions have been put forward to guarantee that the ECJ decides cases in a manner respectful to culture. One approach to applying Article 151 has been its 'smooth' incorporation into the allegedly general principles of EC law, making a cultural concern one factor to be weighed within the balancing process. It is also advised that cultural concerns should be incorporated into a 'rule of reason' analysis or a 'rule of cultural integration'.[102] Another suggestion is a modified version of

[96] Case C-479/04 *Laserdisker ApS v Kulturministeriet* [2006] ECR I-8089.

[97] See Horst, above n 11, 193.

[98] Case C-200/96 *Metronome Musik GmbH v Music Point Hokamp GmbH* [1998] ECR I-1953, [1999] EMLR 93, 100 (1998).

[99] Case C-386/04 *Centro di Musicologia Walter Stauffer v Finanzamt Munchen fur Korperschaften* [2006] ECR I-8203.

[100] Case T-464/04 *IMPALA v Commission* [2006] ECR II-2289.

[101] European Council, Conclusions of the Ministers of Culture Meeting within the Council of 12 November 1992 on Guidelines for Community Cultural Action, [1992] OJ C336, 1, 2. See also Cunningham, above n 17, 139–40.

[102] See Kitz, above n 31, 388–98.

culturally informed proportionality review, which attempts to establish a new, objective standard of review for cultural issues and alter the ECJ's way of thinking.[103] Thus far, though none of these suggestions rests on a firm doctrinal basis or has gained wide recognition as a general principle in European law, they do indicate that the role of cultural issues in ECJ decisions is attracting more attention, and that there is more to be done in defending culture against judicial encroachment. The ECJ should take more notice of Article 151's potential, and the obligations that this article puts on all Community organs. Only then will Article 151 be in a position to develop its due force.

7.2.5 A Preliminary Remark on the Cultural Protection in the EC/EU

In its process of integration, the EC/EU seeks to unify or harmonise laws and regulations among its Member States, notwithstanding Europe's long-held concern about cultural homogeneity. As commonly noted, a purely economically oriented policy or regulation is inclined to wreak havoc on other values. To prevent this from happening in Europe, the EC/EU has made considerable efforts to enact and maintain an agenda on cultural diversity in recent years.[104] The creation of the European single market, which is the dominant goal of Community policies, allows the parallel existence of other objectives, including protection of culture. Culture enjoys an increasingly important role in EU affairs, particularly with the creation of the culture clause—Article 151 of the EC Treaty—and the European content quota contained in the EC directives TVWF and AVMS.

Notwithstanding these efforts, it is still not easy to strike the delicate balance between protecting national identities and promoting market integrity. In Europe, cultural protection has not become a legally permissible rationale for violating economically based treaty provisions. Therefore, the creation of a culture clause does not end the debate on cultural policy at the Community level. It is, however, a good start. At the same time, the EC/EU has to balance two competing but equally important objectives: the Community's interest in the effective operation of a common market and the Member States' right to cultural diversity.

The protection of cultural identities is an ingredient essential to the European model and a prerequisite for its wholehearted acceptance by

[103] While the ECJ permits limited derogations from the Four Freedoms, it judges them according to the strict standard of proportionality review. Very few culture-protective measures can survive. In order for the ECJ to participate constructively in the cultural evolution of Europe, it must reevaluate its priorities and strict standard of review. See Horst, above n 11, 194–209.

[104] See Burri-Nenova, above n 19, 1721.

its Member States. This should not be viewed as a constraint to pursuing economic integration or trade protection. There is no doubt that the EU will continue to develop policies that promote culture despite the inherent difficulties and outside pressure. However, since the globalisation of communication and the unification of Europe may render attempts to restrict the influx of foreign products ineffective, the EU needs to figure out more strategic ways to protect culture.

Looking forward, the EU faces a formidable task defined by the competing goals of harmonisation and enlargement. This adds more difficulties to devising a Community framework for culture, because European identity, if any, has changed and will continue to change dramatically with the presence of large immigrant populations and the multiculturalism brought by its enlargement.[105] Europe is a microcosm of the world community in the sense that it is a mosaic of overlapping, distinct ethnic groups with defined cultural differences.[106] Therefore, the European experience of effectively pursuing its economic and political interests while at the same time respecting cultural diversity may provide lessons as to how the world community can deal with similar problems.

7.3 NAFTA

Cultural industries risked being a major stumbling block during the negotiation of the 1988 Canada—United States Free Trade Agreement (CUSFTA).[107] Canada's concern rested in the US's role as a major exporter in cultural sector. Canada tried to exempt culture entirely from the Agreement; in contrast, the US wanted it included.[108] The topic became the subject of furious debate. In the end, a solution was reached and cultural industries were exempted under the notion of 'cultural exception'. This clause serves as a 'marker' or 'symbol' for cultural protection in regional settings.[109] The fact that the US agreed to the NAFTA cultural exception was later used as an important argument for the French and the EU to exempt culture in the GATS negotiation.[110]

[105] For the enlargement and European integration, see, eg I Ward, 'The Culture of Enlargement' (2005–06) 12 *Columbian Journal of European Law* 199.

[106] See Richardson, above n 7, 33.

[107] For more discussions on the NAFTA negotiation process, see, eg A. Baker Fox, *The Canada–United States Free Trade Agreement and the Cultural Industries* (1998).

[108] A comparative analysis of the Canadian and American approach to culture is given by Slotin. See I Slotin, 'Free Speech and the Visage Culture: Canadian and American Perspectives on Pop Culture Discrimination' (2002) 111 *Yale Law Journal* 2289.

[109] See C Carmody, 'Creating "Shelf Space": NAFTA's Experience with Cultural Protection and Its Relevance for the WTO' (2007) 2(2) *Asian Journal of WTO & International Health Law and Policy* 287, 287–88.

[110] See I Bernier, 'Cultural Goods and Services in International Trade Law' in D Browne (ed), *The Culture/Trade Quandary: Canada's Policy Options* (1998) 126.

7.3.1 Cultural Exception in NAFTA and Associated Problems

A formal cultural exception clause appeared in the CUSFTA[111] and was carried over, with little amendment, to the 1992 North America Free Trade Agreement (NAFTA).[112] NAFTA incorporates Article 2005 of CUSFTA[113] into its Article 2106[114] and Annex 2106.[115] The basic rule is that cultural industries are exempted from the general trade obligations between the US and Canada. The NAFTA cultural exception clause has aroused vociferous controversies since its initial inclusion. Several strands of criticism point to the exception in the context of free trade.

First, the clause is arguably contradictory to the goal of NAFTA.[116] Like the WTO framework, NAFTA is an agreement dedicated to free trade. The cultural exception clause enables Canada to maintain content quotas, government subsidies, tax incentives and other similar measures. It is emphatically asserted that adding exception, especially if the exception is abused, is antithetical to the spirit of NAFTA and may slowly erode the free trade commitment.[117] More importantly, the exception has not proved effective. The US's share of Canadian film revenues has not reduced since the inception of NAFTA. In addition, cultural exception might be held

[111] In 1988, Canadian negotiators introduced cultural exception doctrine into the Canada–United States Free Trade Agreement (CUSFTA). Under the doctrine, cultural industries, in principle, are exempted from the provisions of the Agreement, except as specifically provided in the Agreement. See CUSFTA, Art 2005 (Cultural Industries).

[112] NAFTA. *Cf* Arts 2005 and 2012 CUSFTA and Arts 2106 and 2017 and Annex 2106 NAFTA.

[113] Art 2005 of CUSFTA (Cultural Industries) reads as follows: '1. Cultural industries are exempt from the provisions of this Agreement, except as specifically provided in Article 401 (Tariff Elimination), paragraph 4 of Article 1607 (divestiture of an indirect acquisition) and Article 2006 and 2007 of this Chapter.

2. Notwithstanding any other provision of this Agreement, a Party may take measures of equivalent commercial effect in response to actions that would have been inconsistent with this Agreement but for paragraph 1.'

[114] Under NAFTA Art 2106 (Cultural Industries), Annex 2106 applies to the parties specified in that Annex with respect to cultural industries.

[115] Annex 2106: 'Cultural Industries: Notwithstanding any other provision of this Agreement, as between Canada and the United States, any measure adopted or maintained with respect to cultural industries, except as specifically provided in Article 302 (Market Access—Tariff Elimination), and any measure of equivalent commercial effect taken in response, shall be governed under this Agreement exclusively in accordance with the provisions of the Canada–United States Free Trade Agreement. The rights and obligations between Canada and any other Party with respect to such measures shall be identical to those applying between Canada and the United States.'

[116] The Preamble of the NAFTA states its goals as being to strengthen the bonds of friendship and cooperation, contribute to the harmonious development and expansion of world trade, reduce distortions to trade, foster creativity and innovation, and preserve flexibility to safeguard public welfare. See SR Konigsberg, 'Think Globally, Act Locally: North American Free Trade, Canadian Cultural Industry Exemption, and the Liberalization of the Broadcast Ownership Laws' (1994) 12 *Cardozo Arts & Entertainments Law Journal* 281, 320.

[117] See TA Larrea, 'Eliminate the Cultural Industries Exemption from NAFTA' (1997) 37 *Santa Clara Law Review* 1107, 1149.

unconstitutional as an impermissible content-based restriction of freedom of speech.[118]

Secondly, the final wording is a compromise that may lead to certain ambiguities. The question lingers whether culture is in the agreement or is left out.[119] *Black's Law Dictionary* defines 'exception' as 'something that is excluded from a rule's operation'; and there is no true exception where a right to retaliate exists. The problem here arises from the meaning of Article 2005(2). Taken literally, it introduces a serious limitation to 'cultural exception' and allows retaliation against cultural protection actions. For its part, the US maintains that, if Canada wants to protect culture, it has to pay for it.[120] In effect, the US brought a Section 301 suit against Canada pursuant to this provision after Canada passed a bill doubling the cost for Canadian advertisers to broadcast on the US stations that target the Canadian market. A Section 301 committee found the Canadian bill unreasonable and the US enacted mirror legislation authorised by Section 301.[121] There is also discord as to the scope of retaliation. Canada asserts that the right of retaliation is restricted to cultural industries, while the US regards it as universal, not specific to particular sectors.[122] There has been no case to address this issue yet.

Thirdly, the definition of 'cultural industries' provided in NAFTA Article 2107 is inadequate.[123] The definition seems to be broad enough to cover the various sectors making up cultural industries. However, new technology undermines the effectiveness of exception as well. In particular, the technological breakthrough in the telecommunication and audiovisual industries has led to many product classification problems. The definition seems ill suited to take this element into account and is likely to become obsolete

[118] See KN Holt, 'NAFTA's Cultural Industries Exemption: Its Constitutionality and the Australian Project Blue Sky Model for Free Trade of Content in North America' (2002–03) 9 *Southwestern Journal of Law and Trade in the Americas* 459, 464–76. Free speech rights may be implicated by the cultural exception clause. Films and other entertainment content in the US enjoy First Amendment protection. See Holt, ibid, 465–67.

[119] See G Carr, 'Trade Liberalization and the Political Economy of Culture: An International Perspective on FTA' (1991) 6 *Canadian–American Public Policy* 7–8.

[120] See Bernier, above n 111, 123.

[121] However, Section 301 failed to protect US interests in this case and the retaliatory action did cause Canada to repeal the bill. See Kessler, above n 14, 593.

[122] See K Acheson and C Maule, *Much Ado about Culture: North American Trade Disputes* (1999) 7–9.

[123] NAFTA, Art 2107: 'Definitions: For purposes of this chapter: Cultural industries means persons engaged in any of the following activities: (a) The publication, distribution, or sale of books, magazines, periodicals or newspapers in print or machine readable form but not including the sole activity of printing or typesetting any of the foregoing; (b) The production, distribution, sale or exhibition of film or video recordings; (c) The production, distribution, sale or exhibition of audio or video music recordings; (d) The publication, distribution or sale of music in print or machine readable form; or (e) Radio-communications in which the transmissions are intended for direct reception by the general public, and all radio, television and cable broadcasting undertakings and all satellite programming and broadcast network services.

in the digital age. Alternatively, whether the clause possesses sufficient terminological elasticity to cope with the rapid process of technology and convergence in cultural industries remains to be seen.

7.3.2 CMT Case: An Unwillingness to Resort to the NAFTA Cultural Exception?

When disputes involving cultural products arise, parties may resort to either administrative procedures or more powerful WTO dispute settlements instead of the NAFTA mechanism. The Country Music Television (CMT) dispute of 1995 provides an illustration of this situation. This case concerns the protection of Canadian-owned cable television services. In order to promote Canadian content, the Canadian Radio-television and Telecommunications Commission (CRTC) is empowered to determine the menu of domestic and foreign television signals from which Canadian viewers can choose. The outcome can influence the rates that viewers pay. Over time, however, the ability of CRTC's policy to promote Canadian content has declined as audiences can make choices from an increasing array of grey market signals over which the CRTC does not have influence.[124] In June 1994, the CRTC removed CMT from the list of authorised non-Canadian service providers, a status it had enjoyed for 10 years.[125] CMT argued that it was supportive of Canadian artists and the removal was requested on economic rather than cultural grounds.[126]

When CMT turned to the US government for assistance, the US did not choose to initiate a dispute resolution procedure under the NAFTA or the WTO. Instead, an agreement was eventually reached after lengthy negotiations between the private parties involved as a result of the USTR's intervention.[127] The CRTC had to change its delisting policy, and CMT ended up with 10% of Canadian service operating in Canada.[128] One benefit of such an informal process is the relatively lower costs. At the

[124] See Acheson and Maule, above n 123, 206–07.

[125] In 1994, the CRTC licensed a series of new Canadian speciality channels, among them the New Country Network (NCN). The licence was originally granted to a partnership between Maclean-Hunter and Rawlco Communications. Because of its policy that foreign services could not directly compete with Canadian services, the CRTC removed CMT from the list of eligible foreign services. NCN launched on 1 January 1995, and on that date, cable operators were no longer allowed to offer CMT.

[126] See Acheson and Maule, above n 123, 208–09.

[127] See Bernier, above n 111, 133–34.

[128] Under new policy, if a foreign channel is already available in Canada and a new Canadian equivalent is subsequently licensed, cable companies are no longer required to drop the foreign service. CMT would purchase a minority stake in the service. NCN relaunched as CMT Canada on 31 October 1996, with a format similar to the American service. See Acheson and Maule, above n 123, 219.

same time, however, doing so also reflects the US's unwillingness to test the NAFTA mechanism due to the cultural exception clause. Although NAFTA stipulates that it prevails in the case of any inconsistency with other agreements,[129] it allows the complaining party to choose its own forum for trade dispute settlement.[130]

Protection of Canadian-owned cable television services was the central issue in the dispute involving CMT. In the interests of Canadian culture, Canadian governments have enacted legislation that empowers the regulator, the CRTC, to determine the menu of domestic and foreign television signals from which Canadian viewers can choose, as well as influencing the rates they pay. As a condition of license, broadcasters must promote Canadian content. CMT tried and failed to seek Canadian administrative and judicial remedies. Next, it turned to the US government for assistance by filing a 301 petition on 23 December 1994, with the USTR complaining of its unfair treatment in Canada. As it had been barred from broadcast in Canada, CMT proposed to blacklist the distribution of Canadian music videos on its other services.[131]

In this case, neither NCN nor CMT used the dispute resolution procedures of NAFTA or of the WTO. They went head to head at the political level, using the Canadian courts, Section 301, the USTR, the CRTC, the FCC, private sanctions through video boycotts, threats of adverse consequences, lobbying, and diplomatic and private dispute settlement procedures. While the last led directly to the final outcome, the result was influenced by pressure from the two governments in the context of what had taken place in the other arenas and what issues were pending. A possible benefit of the informal process is the lower costs of reaching a settlement, especially if the process is disciplined by the knowledge that a formal process such as NAFTA or the WTO might be used.[132] Therefore, in the absence of a formal dispute resolution mechanism for cultural industries and an unwillingness to test the NAFTA cultural exemption, parties may invoke any leverage available to further their interests. If a private settlement is not reached, the dispute may be dealt with under NAFTA or the WTO.

[129] NAFTA, Art 103 (Relation to Other Agreements).
[130] NAFTA, Art 2005 (1).
[131] See Acheson and Maule, above n 123, 208–09.
[132] Ibid, 212, 219.

7.3.3 UPS Case: A Promising Sign to Use Cultural Exception?[133]

Though the CMT case displays an unwillingness to test the NAFTA cultural exception clause that leads to its underutilisation, another case shows a promising sign that the clause may be applied to fulfil the purpose of protecting cultural industries. The only case to date challenging the cultural exception appeared in a large action launched by United Parcel Services (UPS) primarily to address the allegation that Canada Post was cross subsidising its courier business with its monopoly over mail delivery.

In April 2000, UPS launched a claim before the International Centre for Settlement of Investment Disputes against the Canadian government under NAFTA Chapter 11, alleging that Canada gave its state-owned postal monopoly, Canada Post, favourable treatment over other companies. Specifically included in the case was the UPS challenge to the Publications Assistance Program (PAP) of the Department of Canadian Heritage (hereinafter the PAP claim), which subsidises the costs of Canada Post delivery of Canadian owned periodicals to Canadian subscribers to ensure equitable access to Canadian created content. The PAP is designed to promote the wider distribution of Canadian periodicals. To qualify for the subsidy, the publishers must deliver their products through Canada Post. The subsidy is paid from a government fund to a postal charge account in the name of the publishers.[134] UPS alleged that this is contrary to Canada's national treatment obligation.[135] UPS also argued that the

[133] See '*United Parcel Services of America Inc v Government of Canada*, Award on the Merits of the Arbitral Tribunal', 11 June 2007, available at http://www.international.gc.ca/trade-agreements-accords-commerciaux/disp-diff/parcel.aspx?lang=en (last accessed on 17 June 2012).

[134] The Publications Assistance Program is a government programme that pays subsidies for postal fees to publishers who distribute periodicals qualifying as 'cultural products' under this programme. The purpose of this programme is twofold: (i) to connect Canadians together through the preservation of accessible Canadian cultural products; and (ii) to sustain and develop the Canadian cultural publishing industry. See 'Publication Assistance Program (PAP)', available at http://www.pch.gc.ca/pgm/pap/index-eng.cfm (last accessed on 17 June 2012). Note that 2009 is the final year of operations for the PAP. A new programme, the Canada Periodical Fund (CPF), started in 2010 to replace both the PAP and the Canada Magazine Fund. See 'The Government of Canada Creates Canada Periodical Fund to Better Support Magazines and Community Newspapers', available at http://www.pch.gc.ca/pc-ch/infoCntr/cdm-mc/index-eng.cfm?action=doc&DocIDCd=CJM082334 (last accessed on 17 June 2012). For more information about CPF, see http://www.pch.gc.ca/pgm/fcp-cpf/index-eng.cfm (last accessed on 17 June 2012).

[135] The national treatment obligation arises from NAFTA Art 1102, which requires Canada to accord to US investors or investments in 'like circumstances' treatment 'no less favourable' than that accorded by Canada to its own investors and investments. In addressing this issue, the tribunal emphasised the distinction between the treatment of products imported and distributed by UPS Canada, and those imported and distributed by Canada Post. The tribunal concluded that there is a distinction between postal traffic and courier traffic. In light of this conclusion, the tribunal deemed UPS and Canada Post not to be in 'like circumstances', and as a result found that no violation of the national treatment obligation had occurred.

publishers qualifying under the PAP ought to have the freedom to choose their mail service provider. In defence of the PAP, Canada submitted that it falls within the scope of cultural exception under the NAFTA.[136] UPS admitted that the cultural exception clause applies to the measures giving assistance to publishers, but pointed out that Canada Post's role in the PAP is that of a mere 'delivery mechanism' and therefore is severable from any valid cultural purpose.

In its May 2007 decision on the case, a NAFTA tribunal ruled against UPS. The tribunal held that the PAP is a measure designed to assist Canadian cultural industries and fits into the NAFTA cultural exception clause. Furthermore, the tribunal contended that the delivery of the PAP materials through Canada Post was the best and most effective way to meet the Program's objectives; delivery is both integral and necessary to the attainment of the Program's statutory cultural objective. Therefore the requirement that publishers use Canada Post was found to be both rationally and intrinsically connected to assisting the Canadian publishing industry.[137]

The tribunal's decision includes a dissenting opinion from Dean Ronald A Cass, appointed by UPS. In considering the PAP claim, Cass noted that cultural exception excludes activities that are 'more mechanical activities that are less centrally related to the creative acts associated with cultural industries'. The PAP payments benefited Canada Post as a general package delivery entity rather than a firm engaged in a cultural industry. He then concluded that Canada Post's delivery service itself is not part of cultural industry and thus is not within the scope of cultural exception.[138] At the same time, in considering whether the activity in question was 'reasonably connected' to the exception, Cass maintained that less deference should be afforded to a host nation's domestic decision-making policies when relying on an exception. He then concluded that Canada Post's role in the PAP had no reasonable connection to cultural exception. Thus, the PAP programme treated UPS less favourably.[139]

The *UPS* case furnishes an apt example of the NAFTA cultural exception clause's application in a dispute. In this case, the tribunal appears to have afforded broad deference to Canada's domestic cultural policies by reading the exception broadly to include the nature, scope, objective and operation of an exempted measure connected to the cultural industry. The dissenting opinion, on the other hand, interpreted the cultural exception clause strictly, within a narrow scope. The tribunal's finding that the

[136] Canada submitted that the PAP supports the Canadian publishing industry by providing 'distribution assistance' to publishers and is therefore a 'measure with respect to cultural industries'. *United Parcel Services of America Inc v Government of Canada*, above n 134, ¶156.

[137] Ibid, ¶¶147–68.

[138] Ibid, ¶138.

[139] Ibid, ¶147.

delivery aspect is integral to the PAP and therefore protected under the cultural exception clause suggests that, where certain commercial aspects of a service that fall under the exception are considered integral to delivery of the service, they can be protected by the exception as well. Critics argue that it appears incongruous that the delivery aspect of a subsidy to publishers is considered to be an 'integral' part of the exception; they suggest that this finding is a privileges culture under a broad interpretation of the NAFTA cultural exception clause. In this sense, it may have some bearing on future cases involving cultural industries.

Neither the majority nor the dissenting opinion in this case ever questioned the motive or rationale for the PAP. Instead, the majority narrowed the issue and questioned whether UPS could have carried out the objectives of the PAP. The tribunal found that the PAP fitted within the cultural exception clause partly based on technical grounds.[140] This seems to illustrate the tribunal's reluctance to question Canada's policy objectives. The dissent examined whether the particular domestic policy was designed or implemented in a fair manner, but did not question the validity of the domestic policy itself. This may indicate that cultural exception is a highly sensitive issue, and the determination of whether a particular aspect of a programme falls under the NAFTA cultural exception clause remains largely based on fact. In every sense, however, the UPS case suggests a promising scenario in which the culture clause can be applied to protect domestic cultural industries. The broad interpretation of the cultural exception in the UPS case should be welcomed.

7.4 THE INTERFACE BETWEEN REGIONAL AND GLOBAL TRADE AGREEMENTS: THE ISSUE OF FORUM SHOPPING, AMONG OTHERS

The EU, NAFTA and the WTO each struggles with identical problems and challenges with respect to culture and trade. Some striking similarities can be discerned in the legal responses to the cases concerning cultural products that arise in each of these fora. Chief among them is the issue of culture as a possible spoiler to the unhindered flow of products. Thus, it came as no surprise that the Europeans touted the NAFTA cultural exception during the Uruguay Round as a precedent requiring the US to grant the EU an exemption.

The overall structure of these trade arrangements varies greatly due to a variety of determinants of economic integration. As a result, the normative

[140] See R Hauk, 'NAFTA's Chapter 11: Lessons Learned from the UPS Case' (2008) 8 *Asper Review of International Business & Trade Law* 125, 140–43.

approach to cultural industries displayed by each differs greatly as well.[141] Both the EC Treaty culture clause and the NAFTA cultural exception signal that cultural values are being considered alongside the promotion of trade and economic development. Notwithstanding a positive trend in the practice of the EU and NAFTA, there is a great deal of room for improvement with regard to the treatment of culture in the WTO framework. There is no special status granted to cultural products under the WTO, except for GATT Article IV, which has not been tested thus far in practice. In its two cases involving cultural products, *Canada—Periodicals* and *China—Publication and Audiovisual Services*, the WTO tribunals did not give full consideration to the specificity of cultural products.

The institutional inconsistencies between NAFTA and the WTO are readily apparent in *Canada—Periodicals*. The primary, clearly defined purpose of NAFTA's cultural exception clause is to protect Canada from losing its cultural identity in the face of a massive influx of American products. In this case, it is likely that the Canadian measures could be justified under the NAFTA cultural exception clause. However, the US initiated dispute settlement before the WTO. This choice apparently weakened the effect of the NAFTA cultural exception clause.[142] NAFTA was not mentioned in the dispute, probably because of the uncertainty as to whether a NAFTA clause could be considered under the WTO context. This case exemplifies how the NAFTA cultural exception clause encounters a de facto rejection if a case is brought to the WTO, which recognises no equivalent to such an exception.

Because of the institutional inconsistency between NAFTA and other trade regimes (especially the WTO), what remains of the NAFTA cultural exception seems to be a matter of uncertainty. From a practical perspective, the US's choice of forum was a strategic decision undertaken to circumvent NAFTA's cultural exception clause that in fact rendered the clause virtually meaningless. These cases demonstrate the need for an objective appraisal of the NAFTA cultural exception clause. The related question is whether such an exception is the best way to protect culture in the era of economic globalisation. In particular, as a result of the proliferation of regional trade agreements, the forum shopping engaged in by the US in *Canada—Periodicals* could become a routine practice in dispute resolution involving cultural products.[143]

[141] See RJ Neuwirth, 'The "Cultural Industries": A Clash of Basic Values?—A Comparative Study of the EU and the NAFTA in Light of the WTO' in F Palermo and GN Toggenburg (eds), *European Constitutional Values and Cultural Diversity* (2003) 104–05.

[142] See Bernier, above n 111, 124.

[143] It is suggested that the GATT should be modified. For example, a provision could be added stating that if a country agrees to a provision in a regional trade agreement that is GATT-consistent but is not specifically provided for in the GATT then the GATT cannot be used to resolve the dispute. Instead, the dispute must be resolved under the regional trade agreements. A provision like this would substantially cut down on the potential to utilise

In the wake of *Canada—Periodicals*, Canada realised that, in order not to restrict its ability to pursue cultural policy, it should move in the direction of developing a multilateral instrument with like-minded countries designed specifically to promote and preserve cultural diversity.[144] Canada's experience with the formal cultural exception in NAFTA proved to be helpful in Canada's championing of the negotiation and conclusion of the UNESCO Convention on Cultural Diversity.

In another WTO case, *Mexico—Soft Drinks*, the relationship between the WTO and regional trade agreements arose acutely again. This case began when the US filed a complaint protesting against a discriminatory tax scheme imposed by Mexico. Mexico defended its measures by requesting that the WTO dispute settlement system decline to exercise jurisdiction over the matter in favour of an arbitral panel under Chapter 20 of NAFTA.[145] Mexico's jurisdictional deference to the NAFTA tribunal contravenes that of the WTO and creates a tough political situation for the WTO. In considering Mexico's request, the Appellate Body noted that Mexico could not identify a legal basis that would allow it to raise the market access claims it was pursuing under NAFTA in a WTO dispute settlement proceeding.[146] The Appellate Body finally rejected Mexico's claim by upholding the general kompetenz-kompetenz of WTO panels—that is, the overall right of an international judicial body to determine the scope of its own authority.[147] The decision implies that the WTO dispute settlement system could be used to determine rights and obligations outside the covered agreements.

7.5 FURTHER OBSERVATIONS

The growing number of bilateral agreements on trade or investment concluded in recent years is also of relevance in discussing the treatment of culture. For example, in addition to the cultural protection clauses it

one trade agreement to avoid the obligations of another. Countries would be more confident that the obligations they negotiate in an agreement could not be circumvented through the use of the WTO. See A Scow, 'The *Sports Illustrated Canada* Controversy: Canada "Strikes Out" In Its Bid to Protect Its Periodical Industry from US Split-Run Periodicals' (1998) 7 *Minnesota Journal of Global Trade* 245, 284. However, this author holds that such suggestions seem unrealistic for the time being due to the complicated relationship between the WTO and RTAs.

144 See Recommendation 21 on Culture in Government of Canada, Government Response to the Report of the Standing Committee on Foreign Affairs and International Trade: Building an Effective New Round of WTO Negotiations: Key Issues for Canada, 3 October 2002, available at http://www.international.gc.ca (last accessed on 17 June 2012).

145 WTO, *Mexico—Tax Measures on Soft Drinks and Other Beverages*, Report of the Panel, WT/DS308/R, 7 October 2005, ¶7.1.

146 See WTO, *Mexico—Tax Measures on Soft Drinks and Other Beverages*, Report of Appellate Body, WT/DS308/AB/R, 6 March 2006, 18.

147 Ibid, 23.

has enacted in multilateral agreements, Canada has concluded bilateral free trade and foreign investment protection agreements. Those concluded in recent years all contain a provision that excludes cultural industries from the scope of the agreement.[148] For instance, in its bilateral trade agreements with Chile and Israel, Canada insisted on and obtained an absolute cultural exception clause that does not allow for retaliatory measures of equivalent commercial effect.[149]

It is also worth noting that the recent FTAs concluded by the US, including US–Chile, US–Singapore, CAFTA (the US with Central American Countries) and US–Australia,[150] mark a new development in the way that the US envisages the treatment of cultural products in trade agreements. Interestingly, the abilities of the negotiating parties to withstand American demands for trade liberalisation in cultural products accurately reflect the negotiating capacity of the states involved, capacities which map well onto per capita GDP.[151] In general, the analysis shows that these FTAs are closely related in their design. They have a significant impact in cultural sectors and demonstrate a new US strategy towards cultural products in the digital era. This strategy clearly rests on the view that measures that do not conform to free trade rules can be tolerated as they presently exist in the traditional sectors because they are bound to disappear with time. However, no such tolerance can be accepted for the digitally delivered content that is at the heart of the new communication economy. As such, new sectors should remain free from cultural protectionism.[152] Clearly, the new strategy avoids a 'cultural exception' approach and has a political objective to counter attempts by other countries to exclude cultural sectors in totality or in part from bilateral or regional FTAs. This strategy undoubtedly provides improved access to American cultural products among contracting parties.

[148] Canada's bilateral free trade agreements with Chile, Costa Rica and Israel all contain cultural protection clauses, as do many of Canada's bilateral foreign investment protection agreements. A list of such agreements is available at http://www.international.gc.ca/tna-nac/fipa_list-en.asp (last accessed on 17 June 2012).

[149] See, eg Free Trade Agreement between Canada and Chile (entered into force on 5 July 1997), Art O-06 and Annex O-06; Free Trade Agreement between Canada and Israel (entered into force on 1 January 1997), Art 10.5. The cultural exemption clause of the Canada–Chile Free Trade Agreement reads as follows: 'Nothing in this Agreement shall be construed to apply to measures adopted or maintained by either Party with respect to cultural industries except as specifically provided in Art C-02 (Market Access-Tariff Elimination)'. The wording of the Canada–Israel Agreement is essentially the same.

[150] The FTA signed between the US and Australia contains a cultural exception, which is considered very weak by the Australian audiovisual industry. See Gómez, above n 117, 33. A series of FTAs concluded by the US can be found at http://www.ustr.gov/trade-agreements/free-trade-agreements (last accessed on 17 June 2012).

[151] See CM Bruner, 'Culture, Sovereignty, and Hollywood: UNESCO and the Future of Trade in Cultural Products' (2008) 40 *International Law and Politics* 351, 366–67.

[152] See I Bernier, 'The Recent Free Trade Agreements of the United States As Illustration of their New Strategy Regarding the Audiovisual Sector', available at http://www.diversite-culturelle.qc.ca/index.php?id=133&L=1 (last accessed on 17 June 2012).

A challenge for the WTO in the context of the culture and trade quandary comes from the universalism versus regionalism, or centralism versus decentralisation, debate, and, more precisely, in successive questions about the compatibility, utility and significance of various regional economic integration projects with multilateral WTO rules.[153] RTAs, like the EU and NAFTA, are often recognised as having achieved a higher degree of integration. Therefore, even if cultural products enjoy special treatment on a regional level, it might still be difficult to protect them in a global context. The cultural exception clause in NAFTA and the cultural clause in Article 151 of the EU Treaty have no equivalent arrangement in the WTO framework. However, if there is a constant interaction between the actual legal framework in place and the ideas about its improvement over time, these clauses may have an argumentative weight in dealing with the trade and culture quandary on a global level. As more and more regional instruments contain cultural protection clauses, they may become viewed as embodying custom and thereby affect the attitude of the WTO on this issue.

[153] See RJ Neuwirth, 'The Cultural Industries and the Legacy of Art IV GATT: Rethinking the Relation of Culture and Trade in Light of the New WTO Round', paper presented at the Conference 'Cultural Traffic: Policy, Culture, and the New Technologies in the European Union and Canada', Carleton University, 22–23 November 2002, 7.

8

Reform Proposals for the Culture and Trade Quandary

> In general, the protective system of our day is conservative, while the free trade system is destructive . . . In a word, the free trade system hastens the social revolution. It is in this revolutionary sense alone, that I vote in favor of free trade.
>
> Karl Marx[1]

8.1 INTRODUCTION

THE ISSUE OF 'free trade v protectionism' has remained periodically relevant as long as markets and capitalism have existed. In a speech delivered in early 1848 in response to the repeal of the English Corn Law, Karl Marx articulated an interesting relationship between protectionism and free trade. He basically maintained that the protectionist system is nothing but a means of establishing large-scale industry in a given country, that is to say, of making it dependent on the world market, and from the moment that dependence on the world market is established, there is already more or less a dependence on free trade. Besides this, he holds, a protective system helps to develop free trade competition within a country.[2] This insight perhaps has some actual bearing on how we tackle the issue of free trade and cultural protectionism.

As discussed thus far, one debate over global governance is framed as a conflict between trade and culture—between unhindered free trade and homogenising forces of globalisation on the one hand and the protection of domestic cultures for the sake of diversity on the other.[3] Accordingly,

[1] K Marx, 'Speech to the Democratic Association of Brussels at its Public Meeting of January 9, 1848—On the Question of Free Trade', available at http://www.marxists.org/archive/marx/works/1848/01/09ft.htm#marx (last accessed on 18 June 2012). The address was a response to the repeal of England's Corn Laws by the English bourgeoisie in 1846 and ensuing discussions over free trade issues. The repeal of the Corn Laws was widely viewed as England's transition from protective trade to a free trade system.

[2] Ibid.

[3] Franck framed this opposition international legal discourse as one between 'legal-culture' on the one hand—whose staple is equal application of legal rules to all regardless

the regulation of the relationship between trade and culture has come into the international spotlight. The WTO and UNESCO, in charge of trade liberalisation and the protection and promotion of cultural diversity respectively, have to face the challenge of whether and how the aspects of culture and its sensibilities, as an important non-trade social concern, may be considered within a trade framework. In fact, within the WTO, culture-related issues have long stalled trade negotiations and are garnering momentum with domestic policymakers and trade experts as the WTO limps towards the conclusion of its current negotiation. Outside of the WTO, the trade and culture nexus appears in the recent development of a series of cultural instruments by the UNESCO featuring the Convention on Cultural Diversity.

The need for a solution that allows for synergy between the traditionally separate fields of culture and trade becomes increasingly clear, though it is never easy to put cultural issues into a trade framework. Grounded on the research presented in the previous chapters, this chapter aims to develop a layered and multifaceted framework at both the national and international levels, advising how different legal systems with inherently divergent missions might function together to cement a harmonious regime on trade and culture.

This chapter begins with a recap of the interaction between trade and culture with a view to providing rationales for the reform proposals. Subsequently, given the fact that any initiative to trade liberalisation through multilateral negotiations cannot be successful without the necessary support of domestic mechanisms, the chapter analyses how to formulate WTO-compatible cultural policy and measures, suggesting that a proper reconciliation of the clash between trade and culture tends to enhance the acceptability and desirability of the WTO trade system. Next, the chapter explores how the WTO system could be more culture conducive by amending or revising WTO agreements, clarifying cultural exception in general exception clauses and revisiting 'like product' determinants, among other actions.

The most pressing task is to explore the reconciliation and cooperation between the WTO rules and the UNESCO Convention. This chapter suggests several possible routes to bring the two systems together—including norm integrity and authority integrity, treaty interpretation and dispute settlement—in order to create synergy between trade norms and cultural concerns. Lastly, the chapter touches upon the application of the margin of appreciation doctrine and its potential extrapolation to the trade and culture field.

of difference—and 'culture-culture' on the other—whose main concern is the protection of diversity in the face of the homogenising forces of an egalitarian application of international law. See T Franck, 'The Legal-Culture and the Culture-Culture' (1999) 93 *American Society for International Law Proceedings* 271, 278.

8.2 A RECAP OF THE INTERACTION BETWEEN TRADE AND CULTURE

A big challenge presented by globalisation for nations committed to cultural diversity is the protection and promotion of their unique cultures, through both domestic policy measures and international legal systems. Prior to exploring how to tackle this challenge, a fundamental inquiry concerns how trade and culture interact with each other, and whether these two values truly conflict with opposing interests. This section recaps the interaction between trade and culture, plainly positing that, in the context of globalisation, trade norms and cultural values are both essential to human development and social progress, and neither can be forsaken. This constitutes the foundation for the reform proposals advanced later in this chapter.

8.2.1 On the Specificity of Cultural Products

As discussed in the previous chapters, cultural values express not only a cultural, but also an anthropological, human identity. Different cultures have different intellectual or institutional means of expressing and operationalising identity, although human dignity, the experience of freedom and the ideal of cooperation are common across all cultures. Cultural production is rooted in local culture, and cultural consumption is not only a leisure activity but also a consequential social practice. Despite the claim that trade may provide consumers with the cultural products that they desire, on closer examination, the application of unrestricted trade principles to cultural products may thwart consumer preference in some cases.[4]

The paradigms of comparative advantage and competition that underlie trade liberalisation only acknowledge a product's immediate physical qualities rather than its value as a product of cultural expression. Accordingly, free trade principles, which play an integral role in global economic system, cannot adequately account for the specificity of cultural products. This generates the conflict between the respect for cultural diversity and the trading system. Given the tremendous influence of trade in cultural products on the systematic indoctrination of individuals with ideological

[4] For more seasoned analysis in this regard, see CE Baker, 'An Economic Critique of Free Trade in Media Products' (2000) 78 *North Carolina Law Review* 1357, 1435; see also P Francois and T van Ypersele, 'On the Protection of Cultural Goods' (2002) 56 *Journal of International Economics* 359 (discussing economic models that trade restrictions may enhance welfare which involves the US and France).

values and lifestyles, trying to convince all countries that free trade is not a menace to local culture does not seem to be a wise strategy.[5]

In an era of increasing homogeneity and growing convergence, it is particularly necessary to protect the natural occurrence of culture for the collective good. One path towards this goal is through the non-economic value of cultural products, which can be employed to ascertain how much weight should be vested in pertinent concerns in assessing cultural derogation from trade rules. In fact, sophisticated economists who appreciate free trade theory understand that 'non-economic objectives' constitute an important element of the theory.[6] They recognise the virtues of free trade, but also note that non-economic values such as culture should be accommodated.

8.2.2 On the Dynamics and Openness of Culture

The interaction between trade and culture cannot be fully addressed without understanding culture's dynamics and its inherent openness. Almost all cultures are multiculturally constituted.[7] Cultures have historically evolved through generations in a never-ending process of exchange with each other. It remains the case today that all cultures are in a state of constant flux, driven by internal and external forces. Cultures are influenced by and in turn influence other cultures. In other words, no culture is a hermetically sealed entity, and a culture might be gradually extinguished in the absence of interaction with others. Any culture can benefit by drawing on other cultures; culture is not the achievement of relevant communities alone, but also of others.[8] One case in point: some lament Hollywood's global reach, but the success of Hollywood can be partly attributed to its ceaseless incorporation of exotic elements from across the world.

Another concern relates to whether the influx of foreign cultural products will destroy the propagation of significantly different local cultures and inevitably lead to cultural homogenisation.[9] As widely noted,

[5] See BI Moran, 'Curb Center Special Feature: United States' Trade Policy and the Exportation of United States' Culture' (2004) 7 *Vanderbilt Journal of Entertainment Law & Practice* 41, 54–55.

[6] See J Bhagwati, *The Wind of the Hundred Days: How Washington Mismanaged Globalization* (2000) 210.

[7] See B Parekh, *Rethinking Multiculturalism: Cultural Diversity and Political Theory* (2002) 163.

[8] See UNESCO, 'Our Creative Diversity': Report of the World Commission on Culture and Development (finalised by J Pérez de Cuéllar, 1995), Executive Summary, 54.

[9] Considering that the trade protectionism cloaked in cultural diversity often contains a subjective, affective element—ie the fear of homogeneity—this question addresses this concern. For an account of homogenisation theory see OR Goodenough, 'Defending the

economic development tends to create homogeneity and heterogeneity at the same time, and there are difficulties in reconciling what may be the final outcome.[10] In the trade and culture discourse, most protectionists assert an affirmative connection between free trade and cultural homogenisation.[11] A common statement is that cultural diversity is impoverished or even extinguished as the globalised flow of modern entertainment coming from Hollywood dominates and homogenises world cultures.[12] However, in accordance with the theory of culture transmission and the resilient nature of cultures, culture itself is not a passive inheritance but an active process of creating meaning; it is not given, but is constantly redefined and reconstituted.[13] Cultural transmission is not one-way traffic in the sense that people are not solely depositories of culture; rather, they are active participants in the process, uniquely selecting, modifying and incorporating cultural stimuli to fit their visions. Therefore, the strongest and richest culture is the one that develops naturally, when people have opportunities to gain knowledge and to access creative inputs from any source.[14]

This means that foreign influences may produce a healthy culture if the uncritical and wholesale assimilation of foreign culture can be avoided. A reasonable choice is to undertake the momentous task of creatively reinterpreting one's own culture and judiciously incorporating those elements of foreign culture that can be approved and assimilated.[15] Cowen counters the anxiety that globalisation may make all regions culturally uniform by noting that individuals will have more choices, since trade heightens the pace of change and raises the level of diversity per unit of time.[16] Thus far there has been no convincing link between exposure to foreign products and a change in domestic values to hold that homogenisation is an inevitable outcome of free trade.[17]

Imaginary to the Death? Free Trade, National Identity, and Canada's Cultural Preoccupation' (1998) 15 *Arizona Journal of International and Comparative Law* 203, 241.

[10] See EL Jones, *Cultures Merging: A Historical and Economic Critique of Culture* (2006) 249.

[11] See R Collins, 'The Screening of Jacques Tati: Broadcasting and Cultural Identity in The European Community' (1993) 11 *Cardozo Arts & Entertainments Law Journal* 361; see also MA Harper, 'Comment, International Protection of IP Rights in the 1990's: Will Trade Barriers and Pirating Practices in the Audiovisual Industry Continue?' (1994) 25 *California Western International Law Journal* 153, 157.

[12] See M Burri-Nenova, 'Cultural Diversity and the EC Audiovisual Media Services Directive: Beyond the Handsome Rhetoric', NCCR Trade Regulation Working Paper No 2009/09 (2 April 2009) 24–25.

[13] See Parekh, above n 39, 152–53.

[14] See RL Van Harpen, 'Mamas, Don't Let Your Babies Grow Up to Be Cowboys: Reconciling Trade and Cultural Independence' (1995) 4 *Minnesota Journal of Global Trade* 165, 189–90.

[15] See Parekh, above n 39, 164–66.

[16] See T Cowen, *Creative Destruction: How Globalization is Changing the World's Cultures* (2002) 137–45.

[17] See Goodenough, above n 9, 241.

In sum, culture and cultural identity are not static or fixed, but are a dynamic reality. The observed increases in cultural homogeneity and heterogeneity show that they are not opposing processes, but two sides of the same coin. By the same token, cultural homogenisation and heterogenisation are not alternatives or substitutes; rather, they tend to occur together.[18] These features reflect the dynamics of culture, which highlight the importance of constant cultural exchange as a prerequisite to maintaining a culture's viability.

8.2.3 On Cultural Diversity and Trade Liberalisation

Viewed broadly, both trade and culture are expressions of human activity under sociological and anthropological theories. Many critics of globalisation focus on cultural specifics, rather than on a comprehensive notion of culture. Tyler Cowen's book *In Praise of Commercial Culture* offers an outstanding contribution to the debate on the issue of trade and culture. Cowen demonstrates the fertility of market culture and points out that, compared with the competitive American cultural market, government-sponsored art tends to be lifeless. He advocates that capitalism and competition are good for the arts, and suggests that markets relax the constraints on internal creativity.[19] Despite the criticisms one may levy against Cowen's arguments, it should be recognised that Cowen understands that, in modern times, trade serves as an essential tool for enhancing cultural flows and exchanges, and leads to close ties between and greater interaction among cultures.

While the social costs of free trade are often considerable, free trade increases consumers' choices and overall welfare. Economic theory further articulates that trade and competition often strengthen domestic industries, while protection weakens them. This partly accounts for trade lawyers' routine suspicion and scepticism towards cultural issues and their frequent attitude towards culture as an excuse for derogation from trade rules.[20] A recurrent argument for cultural protectionism is the economic weakness of domestic cultural industries exposed to the onslaught of American cultural products. Cairncross even comments that if France or Italy were to once again become global centres of artistic excellence, the pressures for trade protection would probably fade away.[21] Therefore, when various pressures mount to establish legal mechanisms of cultural protection that

[18] See Cowen, above n 16, 16.

[19] See generally, T Cowen, *In Praise of Commercial Culture* (1998).

[20] See H Loeb, 'The Management and Resolution of Cross Border Disputes As Canada/US Enter the 21st Century: Telecommunication and Culture: Transborder Freedom of Information or Cultural Identity?' (2000) 26 *Canada–US Law Journal* 303, 304.

[21] See F Cairncross, *The Death of Distance: How the Communications Revolution will Change our Life* (1997) 251.

entail trade restrictions, one has to ask whether curtailing trade might indeed prevent cultural exchange.[22]

In short, the conventional wisdom suggested by cultural economics and the openness and dynamics of culture itself maintain that trade may serve as a catalyst for cultural evolution and an inspiration for cultural diversity in the context of globalisation. Under this premise, the national interest paradigm espoused by cultural protectionists might be ill-suited to the particularities of cultural products.[23] Further, an unalloyed protection is not necessarily the best way to maintain cultural identity and improve cultural diversity.

In sum, free trade and cultural diversity are not, and should not become, enemies. In the rapidly changing global environment, trade norms and culture policies, and the values upon which they are respectively based, frequently collide and diverge. However, cultural preservation motivated by nationalism does not yield positive results for culture.[24] By and large, promotion seems to be the better solution for culture. By the same token, principle in this area calls for a better trade framework that does not necessarily contradict cultural goals.[25] Thus the key issue with regard to maintaining culture in framing a trade regime is not 'whether', but 'how', such a reconciliation can be realised.

8.3 DESIGNING WTO-COMPATIBLE DOMESTIC POLICY MEASURES

The conception of national culture in an international framework helps to mould international policy, which in turn shapes domestic cultural policy and measures. Among other things, domestic measures aimed at protecting local culture or cultural industries may lead to the violation of trade obligations and, if challenged, could result in trade disputes. Thus, the design of WTO-compatible domestic cultural policy measures plays a consequential role in the effort to resolve the quandary of trade and culture. In one way or another, this may be regarded as a solution *ex ante*. It is more cost efficient than the complicated, *ex post* dispute settlement triggered by cases involving cultural products.

[22] See T Broude, 'Taking "Trade and Culture" Seriously: Geographical Indications and Cultural Protection in WTO Law' (2005) 26 *University of Pennsylvania Journal of International Economic Law* 623, 692.

[23] See J Devlin, 'Canada and International Trade in Culture: Beyond National Interests' (2004) 14 *Minnesota Journal of Global Trade* 177, 178–79.

[24] Ibid, 197.

[25] See DP Steger, 'The Boundaries of the WTO: Afterword: The "Trade and . . ." Conundrum—A Commentary'(2002) 96 *American Journal of International Law* 135.

8.3.1 The Challenges in Designing Domestic Cultural Policy Measures

Chapter 3 examined the tension between trade liberalisation and the pursuit of cultural policies by national governments. In brief, the duality of cultural products, together with the nature of public goods inherent in these products and the externalities that they generate, theoretically justify policy intervention in order to increase the consumption of domestic products. In practice, domestic pressures to fortify cultural diversity and a certain degree of self-interest have often compelled governments to maintain various policy instruments to combat the complete liberalisation of cultural sectors and deviate from their trade obligations. An array of measures is incorporated into many states' domestic cultural regulation, including foreign investment restrictions in cultural industries, tariffs and content quotas, subsidies and grants, tax incentives, and a range of miscellaneous enactments.

The acceptability of these measures, however, has been gradually called into question as progressive trade liberalisation has included more measures within its scope and subjected them to increasing regulatory scrutiny. In fact, the ability of a nation to protect itself from the invasive effects of foreign cultural influence has been growing increasingly suspect. In Chapter 3, I submit that trade rules have placed undeniable constraints on the pursuit of national cultural policies and measures by limiting the role government can play in the provision of cultural products both at home and abroad. Here, it is sufficient to emphasise particular challenges in designing cultural polices and measures.

First, almost every political and economic action carries certain cultural consequences. The reverse holds true: most cultural policies have political or economic dimensions.[26] Lack of political will or commitment is not a prominent challenge to formulating domestic policy measures. Rather, it is a misconstrual or partial recognition of the cultural policy objective itself: culture. In an era of globalisation, when culture is understood as one of the bases for social development, any policy for development should be profoundly sensitive to and inspired by culture.[27] Thus, the notion of cultural policy has to be considerably broadened to reflect the importance of the cultural dimension of development. When culture has become a key component of a society's soft power, the design of cultural policy should be placed within a broader social context and considered from a comprehensive perspective.

Secondly, while technological innovations may hold promise for greater efficiency and innovation, these developments challenge the ability of cultural industries to maintain a strong national presence in an expanding

[26] See N Horst, 'Creating an Ever Closer Union: The European Court of Justice and the Threat to Cultural Diversity' (2008) 47 *Columbian Journal of Transnational Law* 165, 200.

[27] See UNESCO, 'Our Creative Diversity', above n 8, 232.

global marketplace.[28] Trade barriers imposed upon cultural products are becoming less advantageous and increasingly difficult to implement in light of a changing technology environment. For instance, advances in broadcasting and digital technology have greatly muted the impact of content requirements and other trade policy instruments.[29] Exposure to cultural products has become a matter of individual choice, less and less subject to the influence of government intervention. The technological changes that are now taking place are much more profound than those faced in the past.[30] At whatever level the issues of communication are envisaged, there arises the shared challenge of organising our considerable capacities in ways that support cultural diversity.[31] These new technologic modalities and the broader transformed technology environment need to be cautiously examined to craft an appropriate and efficient regulation toolbox.

Thirdly, the convergence of cultural industries and the shift in power from public to private sectors also pose new challenges to formulating sustainable cultural policies. The convergence raises a number of questions regarding the scope and tradability of cultural products.[32] The activities of private sectors are in some ways replacing the cultural strategies typified by broadcast quotas and film subsidies, which make the behaviour of corporate actors an important element in devising cultural policies. These developments coincide with a more general transformation of public policy from direct to indirect intervention.[33]

In sum, there are ever-evolving challenges facing cultural policy measures today. Many conventional policy measures are the remnants of an ill-conceived perception of globalisation and its effects on culture;[34] they do not sufficiently accommodate the changed regulatory environment, nor do they have the potency to appropriately address the new challenges. Notwithstanding the tensions that governments face between trade rules reflecting commercial interests and the desire to maintain cultural representation of their identities, this reality does not spell the end of cultural

[28] See S Scott, 'The Impact of Technological Change on Canada's Cultural Industries' in D Browne (ed), *The Culture/Trade Quandary: Canada's Policy Options* (1998) 54.

[29] See HB Feigenbaum, *Globalization and Cultural Diplomacy* (2001) 32.

[30] A single communications medium, the internet, has so cheapened communication that its effect on information is much like the effect of free trade on commerce. See generally L Lessig, 'The Zones of Cyberspace' (1996) 48 *Stanford Law Review* 1403 (discussing issues of legal extraterritoriality connected with the rise of the internet).

[31] See UNESCO, 'Our Creative Diversity', above n 8, 107.

[32] See J Middleton, 'The Effectiveness of Audiovisual Regulation Inside the European Union: The Television without Frontiers Directives and Cultural Protectionism' (2003) 31 *Denver Journal of International Law & Policy* 607, 625–26.

[33] See HB Feigenbaum, 'Public Policy and the Private Sector in Audiovisual Industries' (2002), 49 *UCLA Law Review* 1767, 1768.

[34] See M Burri-Nenova, 'Trade versus Culture in the Digital Environment: An Old Conflict in Need of a New Definition' (2009) 12(1) *Journal of International Economic Law* 17, 40–41.

autonomy and government regulation. Rather, policymakers need to reconsider traditional approaches to protecting and promoting cultural diversity in the light of the evolving regulatory environment. Policymakers have to refocus on the goal of cultural policies and determine the best vehicles by which to achieve that goal.

8.3.2 A Guiding Principle: Distinguishing Cultural Protection from Cultural Protectionism

Like many other 'trade-linkage' problems, the essential challenge of the trade and culture nexus lies in designing workable legal mechanisms to distinguish genuine cultural protection measures from those measures whose intention is merely the protection of domestic industries and, therefore, the distortion of trade flows. This reflects precisely the juxtaposition between free trade and cultural policies. A state's regulatory autonomy generally encompasses two aspects: its autonomy with respect to the policy objectives it chooses to pursue and its autonomy with regard to the means by which it chooses to pursue those objectives.[35] In applying this theory to the relationship between cultural policy and trade obligations, the first issue that arises is whether the promotion or preservation of culture through the protection of cultural industries or products is a legitimate regulatory objective in the context of the WTO. Next comes the issue of whether WTO Members are entitled to fully pursue that objective, including the right to resort to discriminatory measures.

The difficulties in answering these issues are clear. Given the potential negative effects from cultural imports,[36] protection becomes part and parcel of the cultural policies of a significant group of countries. Importing states attempt to assert cultural claims as a strategy for resisting trade disciplines.[37] Again, because of the duality of cultural products and industries which often represent huge economic interests, it is often the case that, when a state asserts claims of cultural autonomy to protect itself from cultural imports, its claims are dismissed as a pretext for economic protectionism or a restraint on the free flow of cultural products and the information they contain. This generates a source of tensions among WTO Members. Cultural claims may be accepted only to the extent that they do not impose unnecessary barriers to trade liberalisation, which rarely happens in practice.

[35] See G Verhoosel, *National Treatment and WTO Dispute Settlement: Adjudicating the Boundaries of Regulatory Autonomy* (2002) 51.

[36] See JR Paul, 'Cultural Resistance to Global Governance' (2000) 22 *Michigan Journal of International Law* 1, 7, 38 (cultural products shape the expectations and values of citizens. and cultural imports, to some extent, may displace domestic cultural industries and then influence the nation's values and behaviours).

[37] See Feigenbaum, above n 33, 1774.

Voon examined these issues and discussed how cultural policy measures could be evaluated or scrutinised within the WTO framework.[38] Her claim, which I second here, is that the core task in easing this tension is to distinguish between trade interventions intended to promote the economic success of cultural undertakings and those intended to protect cultural heritage or promote the cultural development of a community. Conceivably, in a context where industrial interests are often dressed in cultural concerns, a twin-track approach is needed to recognise that, on the one hand, cultural products come under the ordinary rules of trade agreements, while on the other hand, state intervention should be made possible in order to ensure a viable domestic cultural production and consumption that favours the diversity of cultural expressions.[39] It is not a simple choice between free trade and cultural resistance. Rather, policymakers want to promote free trade alongside some form of cultural protection. To achieve this goal, an approach that would distinguish between industrial interests and the cultural objectives of government intervention is preferred. This approach may hopefully help determine which policy or measure is compatible with WTO rules and serves as a better vehicle to promote cultural diversity. This argument suggests a number of principles that national policymakers should follow in devising cultural policy measures.

First, in drawing the boundaries between cultural protection and trade protectionism, culture itself should be taken seriously as a non-trade social norm. The range of manifestations that governments choose to see as relevant to their cultural policies has broadened in recent years, as the production of and the demand for artistic goods for mass consumption have expanded alongside the awareness that cultural identity is shaped by many different forms of cultural expressions.[40] As far as culture sectors are concerned, however, few governments have a clearly formulated policy that contains a general vision of culture.[41]

The flag of culture is easily unfurled in the name of cultural protection. When policymakers intend to afford various advantages to national producers, they should first consider whether locally produced items substantively express national culture. Government measures, by and large, should essentially protect those products that substantively express their cultures. To this end, were we to accept the wider anthropological approach to culture, cultural diversity would need to be recognised in many matters; there would be no universal recipe for good practice. In any case, governments should make special efforts to support activities

[38] See T Voon, *Cultural Products and the World Trade Organization* (2007) 38–39.

[39] See I Bernier, Cultural Goods and Services in International Trade Law, in Browne above n 28, 147.

[40] See UNESCO, 'Our Creative Diversity', above n 8, 233.

[41] Ibid.

in several areas, such as the study of national history, helping its citizens understand their past and their shared conditions today.[42] This consumer-oriented effort would lend itself to increasing intellectual consumption of domestic cultural content.[43] Furthermore, if culture is to be taken seriously as a justification for trade-restrictive policies, it must also be proven that these policies contribute to the protection of local culture and to the safeguarding of cultural diversity.[44] This is a key test for any cultural policy: only then may it be allowed to establish digressions from general trade rules. This may seem to be a 'trade first' approach, but it is no less a 'culture first' attitude; it would not tolerate those policy measures that may look good on paper but have no real effect on culture in practice.

Secondly, trade obligations cannot be ignored in the guise of defending culture. Whatever their effectiveness in achieving their charged cultural aims, domestic cultural policies can affect international trade by artificially sustaining the competitiveness of domestic producers and limiting competition from foreign sources.[45] Generally, imported products compete with domestic products and may threaten local producers. If consumers prefer imported products, domestic producers have to either compete harder or suffer losses. This alone does not offer a strong rationale for treating imports differently. Rather, it is the duality of cultural products that justifies appropriate government intervention. As discussed earlier, even though cultural imports are not the same as other imports, protectionist policies still often make little economic and cultural sense.[46] In brief, an excessively protectionist policy does not aid, and may even hinder, the goal of cultural preservation and jeopardises diversity in the marketplace by discouraging cultural imports. Such a policy is also inconsistent with human rights agreements that protect the free transmission of information and ideas.[47]

To strike a proper balance, government interference in the market should be in a position to protect local culture without any unnecessary effects of trade distortion. At its most basic, this means that the respect for cultural diversity is essential, but it must go hand-in-hand with the promotion of

[42] For instance, the Canadian government launched some initiatives in this regard and succeeded in its aims. See B Schwartz, 'Canadian Cultural Policy in a World Context' (2002) 2 *Asper Review of International Business & Trade Law* 1, 17.

[43] See Broude, above n 22, 691–92.

[44] See F Pinto, 'Book Review—Blockbusters and Trade Wars: Popular Culture in a Globalized World' (2004) 7 *Journal of International Economic Law* 922, 925–26.

[45] See S Andreano and PL Iapadre, 'Audiovisual Policies and International Trade: The Case of Italy' in Guerrieri, P et al (eds), *Cultural Diversity and International Economic Integration: The Global Governance of the Audio-Visual Secto* (2005) 109.

[46] See K Acheson and C Maule, *Much Ado about Culture: North American Trade Disputes* 332 (1999). See also WM Shao, 'Is There No Business Like Show Business? Free Trade and Cultural Protectionism' (1995) 20 *Yale Journal of International Law* 105, 140–41; see also Voon, above n 38, 53–54.

[47] See Harpen, above n 14, 194.

cultural exchange and dialogue through trade and other channels. Indeed, contrary to restricting trade in cultural products, some governments have at times viewed trade as a necessary condition of cultural development and developed policies based on the view that cultural exchange through trade is beneficial to promoting domestic cultures.[48]

Ideally, in assessing whether a given measure is a genuine cultural policy measure rather than the product of protectionist inclinations, an objective trade-restrictiveness test should be imposed instead of a test that evaluates the subjective motives behind the measure. The WTO could sanction those measures that are no more trade-restrictive than necessary to achieve their declared cultural goals. A WTO framework for minimising the trade-restrictiveness of cultural policy measures could take two forms. First, the Members could agree on a broad rule that a number of measures are allowed provided that they are no more trade-restrictive than necessary to meet the relevant cultural goals. This wording constitutes the chapeau in the general exceptions clauses in the GATT and GATS. If challenged, individual cultural policy measures would be evaluated by the DSB. Secondly, WTO Members could establish more concrete and comprehensive rules, reflecting a multilateral decision *ex ante* about the types of measures that will allow Members to pursue their cultural goals in the least trade-restrictive manner.[49] This approach may increase certainty while reducing the flexibility to adapt to different circumstances.

8.3.3 Designing WTO-Compatible Domestic Cultural Policy Measures

A close interdependence exists between trade rules and domestic regulations. For trade rules to be effective, domestic regulations should not restrain trade and competition too much. Viewed this way, trade disciplines play a crucial role in shaping domestic regulatory systems. WTO agreements, including the GATT, GATS and TRIPS, have an important impact on the design of cultural policy measures. Some of the cultural policies or measures currently in place are unsustainable under WTO rules. For example, some measures intended to enhance diversity, such as local content rules and preferential co-production agreements for films and audiovisual productions, are hard to reconcile with the principles of national treatment and MFN treatment. These two principles stand at the cornerstone of non-discrimination policy in the trade system. In addition, those measures opposing liberalisation, such as denying market access to foreign cultural industries, would have to be countered with

[48] Ibid, 187.

[49] See Voon, above n 38, 66–68.

restricted access to foreign markets. This outcome may be costly, since foreign market access is of great economic interest to domestic exporters.

Countries undertaking trade obligations in cultural sectors have to accept certain constraints to their domestic regulations and ensure that they do not constitute unnecessary barriers to international trade. This requires an overhaul of domestic cultural policies as well as the criteria informing their application. It should be noted that, if the measures at issue only concern cultural services, they may not be in violation of the GATS; the GATS's current structure includes exemptions to the MFN rules, and both market access and national treatment are only required when specific commitments are made by the WTO Members. Many cultural policy measures potentially fall within the meaning of market access or national treatment as defined in the GATS.[50] The current Doha Round of WTO negotiation on service has been considering establishing the disciplines of service subsidies and emergency safeguard measures. Until the relevant rules are put into place, subsidies for audiovisual services or safeguard measures will not be subject to the scrutiny of the GATS.

On the other hand, the GATS is committed to progressive liberalisation. WTO Members have agreed that exemption from the MFN obligation should not, in principle, exceed 10 years. If most WTO Members cannot reach consensus on a treaty that de facto requires the permanent continuation of MFN exemptions related to cultural products, some domestic measures concerning cultural services may risk violating the GATS in the future, if they do not already.

In formulating cultural policy measures, policymakers need to look critically for means by which a nation can protect its culture through domestic policy measures. It is essential that, whatever measures are favoured and ultimately adopted, the costs of domestic industry protection be minimised.[51] Among the various options, a targeted, non-export subsidy to chosen domestic producers is more likely to result in more products that promote domestic culture. Such subsidies are overall less distortive of trade flow than quotas, and therefore less costly to the economic system. Furthermore, carefully designed subsidies are compatible with the current WTO rules, which state that trade regulations shall not prevent 'payment

[50] For instance, in the area of market access, these measures include prohibitions on dubbing of foreign films and dubbing licensing restrictions; in the area of national treatment, they include domestic content requirements, especially measures regulating radio and television broadcasting content, as well as discriminatory regulatory/licensing restrictions, and discriminatory subsidies. For more analysis in this regard see, eg A Beviglia-Zampetti, 'WTO Rules in the Audiovisual Sector' in P Guerrieri et al (eds), *Cultural Diversity and International Economic Integration: The Global Governance of the Audio-Visual Sector* (2005) 263–64.

[51] See CN Smith, 'International Trade in Television Programming and GATT: An Analysis of Why the European Community's Local Program Requirement Violates the General Agreement on Tariffs and Trade' (1993) 10 *International Tax & Business Law* 97, 134–35.

of subsidies exclusively to domestic producers'.[52] The Appellate Body has held that the form of subsidies is not limited to actual grants of monetary aid, but may include indirect aid, such as the exemption of domestic products from internal taxes and the application of special transportation and postal rates.[53]

On a practical level, such a government subsidy can be easily linked to the quality, local cultural content and commercial viability of domestic products in order to promote local culture.[54] In addition to a subsidy, a thorough review of the way in which safeguard measures may be applied to cultural products is also recommended. There are some striking examples of measures that are not currently caught by the WTO rules, such as anti-competitive behaviours in cultural industries. In recent years, some more constructive and active approaches to promoting domestic cultural industries, such as exportation promotion, have gained much support and should be greatly encouraged.[55]

In sum, the very nature of the tension between cultural protection and the integrity of trade systems begs for a compromise. Guided by this basic understanding, WTO Members should balance their market access openings with the need to preserve domestic culture by developing more specific disciplines. It would be wise to use the WTO rules as a reference point for undertaking the domestic reforms necessary to design more sustainable cultural policy measures.

8.4 SEARCHING FOR SOLUTIONS WITHIN THE TRADE SYSTEM

The WTO trade system has been an extraordinary success. It provides an increasingly integrated world economy with a foundation of predictability and liberalism, protecting global economy from the arbitrary interventions of national governments. Despite its success, however, the system has

[52] General Agreement on Tariffs and Trade, 30 October 1947, 61 Stat A-11, 55 UNTS 194, Art III 8(b). In a fully market-driven trade scheme, government subsidies may also count as trade barriers; such subsidies could be made consistent with WTO law under the Agreement on Subsidies and Countervailing Measures. See JD Donaldson, 'Television without Frontiers: The Continuing Tension between Liberal Free Trade and European Cultural Integrity' (1996) 20 *Fordham International Law Journal* 90, 180.

[53] WTO, *Canada—Certain Measures Concerning Periodicals* (hereinafter WTO, *Canada—Periodicals*), Report of the Appellate Body, WT/DS31/AB/R, 30 June 1996, 34.

[54] Korea may offer a good example in this respect. See CH-K Kim, 'Building the Korean Film Industry's Competitiveness: Abolish the Screen Quota and Subsidize the Film Industry' (2000) 9 *Pacific Rim Law & Policy* 353, 353–78.

[55] For example, Canada has been actively seeking to promote culture exports. Under the 'Tomorrow Stars Today' programme, $32 million will be allotted over three years to help Canadian businesses export cultural products. Ironically, the government fact sheet on the programme stresses the impact these exports have on the Canadian economy; the US and EU as the largest export markets. See Schwartz, above n 42, 2.

long been fiercely criticised as an intrusion into the domestic affairs of sovereign states. One common line of attack is based on the premise that social norms are inextricably linked to trade systems. The claim is that to regard the WTO rules as solely a code of economic conduct ignores a great deal about the wider social environment in which they operate.[56]

As discussed above, social, economic and legal arguments provide a rationale for government support of domestic cultural expression. Multilateral consensus has recognised the value of culture and the appropriateness of governmental measures protecting and promoting domestic culture. It is thus unwise for the WTO to ignore the resonance of cultural issues, not only because cultural concerns relate to each WTO Member, but also because integrating social norms into trade policy would ensure more open, efficient and fair markets.[57]

In fact, the framers of the GATT and other trade proponents have realised that certain public welfare goals must be considered alongside the economic benefits associated with free trade. The current WTO framework also provides certain flexibility for Members to pursue cultural objectives in connection with cultural products.[58] In brief, in addition to the leeway for screen quotas contained in GATT Article IV, several other provisions scattered within the WTO agreements relate to culture to a certain extent. Nonetheless, as examined in Chapter 5, these provisions are not in a position to break the current impasse between trade and culture. This section aims to articulate possible reform strategies that would establish a coherent relationship between trade and culture within the WTO system. The profound challenge in this regard is using a concept as indeterminate as 'culture' to provide a principled basis for distinction in the WTO rules. With this in mind, the following explores several options through which the WTO framework can become more culture conducive.

8.4.1 Exempting Cultural Products from General Trade Rules

The first option is to exempt cultural products from general trade disciplines. The confluence of trade policy and cultural identity can be viewed through an assessment of the genesis, evolution and current vitality of

[56] See M Wolf, 'What the World Needs From the Multilateral Trading System' in GP Sampson (ed), *The Role of the World Trade Organization in Global Governance* (2001) 196.

[57] See GP Sampson, 'Is There a Need for Restructuring the Collaboration among the WTO and UN Agencies so as to Harness their Complementarities?' in E-U Petersmann (ed), *Reforming the World Trading System: Legitimacy, Efficiency, and Democratic Governance* (2005) 528.

[58] See WTO Council for Trade in Services, 'Communication from the United States—Audiovisual and Related Services', S/CSS/W/21 (18 December 2000), ¶¶7–8; see also B Richardson, 'Hollywood's Vision of a Clear, Predictable Trade Framework Consistent with Cultural Diversity' in CB Graber et al (eds), *Free Trade versus Cultural Diversity: WTO Negotiations in the Field of Audiovisual Services* (2004) 111, 121–22.

cultural exception doctrine.[59] The term 'cultural exception' reflects the premise that, given the duality of cultural products, the trade system should grant such products a special brand of protection by exempting them from general trade rules.[60]

Although the doctrine seems to be an effective slogan, it has resulted in a long-running international public relations battle, alternatively couched in the rhetoric of 'anti-Americanisation'. The doctrine fails not only because the term 'exception' conveys a negative connotation that carries with it the suspicion of protectionist intent, but also because the bite of cultural exceptions occurs at the level of popular culture, not the high culture that seems more related to 'national culture'.[61] Operationally, the precise meaning of 'cultural exception' is not clear-cut; it is extremely hard to identify which products and measures should be covered by the exception and which should not. When a state invokes a culture exception to its trade obligations, the international community questions its legitimacy and generally rejects the claim as a pretext for trade protectionism. After the Uruguay Round trade negotiation, it was boldly proclaimed that 'the cultural exception is dead' as the result of the exigencies of the new global economy and technology, coupled with globalisation's hallmark consolidation, integration and harmonisation.[62]

The rejection of a blanket 'cultural exception' does not mean that cultural products should be treated exactly like conventional products. Their unique cultural qualities call for appropriate distinction in treatment. Here, I suggest a revised understanding of 'cultural exception', different from that which France and Canada proposed during the Uruguay Round. My re-articulation of the doctrine does not require a blanket exemption of cultural products from the general trade system, but rather a targeted allowance for specific cultural products. I suggest that efforts should be made to permit derogatory interventions by Members or to allow them

[59] See Loeb, above n 20, 311–12.

[60] See generally M Hahn, 'A Clash of Cultures? The UNESCO Diversity Convention and International Trade Law' (2006) 9 *Journal of International Economic Law* 515 (discussing the value of culture in the face of present WTO trading obligations and proposing a general cultural exception to the national treatment obligations of the GATT and GATS).

[61] It is advised that the term 'cultural recognition' would provide a more positive orientation in describing efforts to deal with this matter in negotiations between countries. See D Throsby, *Economics and Culture* 133 (2001).

[62] See FS Galt, 'The Life, Death, and Rebirth of the "Cultural Exception" in the Multilateral Trading System: An Evolutionary Analysis of Cultural Protection and Intervention in the Face of American Pop Culture's Hegemony' (2004) 3 *Washington University Global Studies Law Review* 909, 909. Subsequent to the demise of cultural exception doctrine, advocates of cultural protection recognised that a new concept was needed to defend the legitimacy of cultural values. Then, in the 1990s, the concept of cultural diversity first entered the scene of international law and was chosen to serve as a new policy goal to respond to the trade system's negative impact on culture. European Commission, 'Communication to the Council and the European Parliament, The EU Approach to the WTO Millennium Round', COM(1999) 331 final (8 July 1999).

to enact necessary policies to protect cultural products in specific circumstances.

The question is how this revised 'cultural exception' would proceed in practice. One suggestion is that the WTO avail itself of the general exception clauses contained in GATT Article XX and GATS Article IVX to introduce a 'cultural exception'. It is noted that, as currently interpreted and applied, the general exception clauses lack explicit exceptions for the protection of cultural values. Although the clauses enumerate exceptions to the principles underlying the trade regime for measures 'necessary to protect public morals' and for measures 'imposed for the protection of national treasures of artistic, historic or archaeological value', the exact wording of these exceptions does not suggest a direct applicability to cultural products; they are not intended to protect domestic cultural industries from the onslaught of cultural products from Hollywood.

The promotion and preservation of culture through cultural products should not be regarded as an illegitimate regulatory objective for WTO Members merely because of its exclusion from general exception clauses.[63] Culture, as an integral part of a common heritage of mankind that contributes to a rich world, is itself a cultural treasure, rooted in the national culture and an inalienable part of the world's artistic value. One could imagine that national treasures of artistic value in modern time include popular culture. A new 'cultural exception' may be introduced into the general exception clauses, similar to those existing measures that accommodate other non-trade social concerns. The standard conditions for other exceptions can also be extended to the proposed cultural exception clause.

The proposed exception itself must be limited in scope, and only claimed and defended if there are no suspicions of economic intention.[64] Arguably, an exception could be made for the preservation of cultural and linguistic diversity, including national culture.[65] It is also possible to distil the aspects of 'cultural products' in a manner that would best facilitate a 'cultural exception' analysis, namely, that cultural products that have historic value and embrace traits fundamentally linked to a nation and its people.[66] Determining the concrete rules and their application is a complex issue; experience drawn from regional trade agreements may shed some light on this question. The exemption of cultural industries contained in NAFTA might be used as a reference in designing a cultural exception applicable to cultural goods.

[63] See Voon, above n 38, 9–11, 41–42.

[64] See Shao, above n 46, 149–50.

[65] See Bernier, above n 39, 147.

[66] See D Beppu, 'When Cultural Value Justifies Protection: Interpreting the Language of the GATT to Find a Limited Cultural Exception to the National Treatment Principle' (2008) 29 *Cardozo Law Review* 1765, 1767–68.

A cultural exception doctrine is backed by sensible policy justifications that point to the overall importance and value of culture in modern times. A properly defined and limited cultural exception would be designed to avoid usurping the fundamental justification of trade disciplines, and to respect the sovereignty of states by allowing them to define culture on their own terms as well.[67] While there may not be sufficient political support among WTO Members for the inclusion of specific cultural exceptions in general clauses, this may change in the light of new challenges to national cultures.[68] It should be emphasised that this form of 'cultural exception' would be an ambitious process, which requires not only Members' consensus but also a practical, precise definition of qualifying cultural products. Also note that in dispute settlement practice the Appellate Body is often reluctant to read general exception clauses broadly; the chapeau of exception clauses articulate further limits on measures intended to protect cultural products.

As a practical concern, a revised cultural exception included only in the GATT and GATS general exception clauses might be incomplete; cultural industries touch upon many aspects of trade. As such, the aspects scattered across different WTO agreements—including GATT, GATS, TRIPS, TRIMs and subsidies—must be combined. To this end, it is advised that a specific instrument be adopted to deal with the special treatment of cultural products or related cultural industries.[69] This mild option does not seek to exempt cultural products from trade rules, but instead attempts to provide some special rules for trade in cultural products. I make this recommendation with a view to enhancing the WTO's fairness and efficiency through greater coherence and a more holistic spirit.

8.4.2 Requesting Waiver for Cultural Policy Measures

Two relatively recent decisions adopted by the WTO General Council, 'TRIPS Waiver'[70] and 'Kimberly Waiver',[71] have brought the waiver

[67] See Hahn, above n 60, 528–30; see also Beppu, ibid, 1794.

[68] See P Van Den Bossche, 'Free Trade and Culture: A Study of Relevant WTO Rules and Constraints on National Cultural Policy Measures', Maastricht Faculty of Law Working Paper No 2007-4 (2007) 138–39.

[69] See ME Footer and CB Graber, Trade Liberalization and Cultural Policy' (2000) 3 *Journal of International Economic Law* 115, 136–37.

[70] This is the 2003 decision of the General Council on the implementation of para 6 of the Doha Declaration on the TRIPS Agreement and Public Health. See WTO General Council, Implementation of Paragraph 6 of the Doha Declaration on the TRIPS Agreement and Public Health, Decision of 30 August 2003, WT/L/540, 2 September 2003.

[71] See WTO General Council, Waiver Concerning Kimberley Process Certification Scheme for Rough Diamonds, Decision of 15 May 2003, WT/L/518, 27 May 2003. The waiver was extended in 2006 by the WTO General Council Decision of 15 December 2006, WT/L/676, 19 December 2006.

process to the attention of those seeking to find ways to overcome the allegedly narrow focus of the WTO on economic matters.[72] The legal basis for requesting a waiver is contained in Article IX(3) of the WTO Agreement, which authorises the Ministerial Conference to waive a Member's or Members' obligation imposed by the WTO Agreement or any of the multilateral trade agreements.[73] Waiver decisions share common features whether they take the form of an exception or a rule-making instrument. The only substantive requirement for waivers set out in this putative provision is the existence of 'exceptional circumstances'; this has never been specified in the past and does not prove to be a substantive limitation to the waiver power.[74]

Waiver competence has been used pragmatically and creatively throughout the history of the GATT/WTO. Here, the question is whether a WTO Member can apply for a waiver based on cultural protection. The rationale for the waiver proposal lies partly in the nearly paralysed state of political organs in the WTO that has resulted from its practice of consensus decision-making. Feichtner elaborates on the desirability of political debates and explores the potential for the waiver procedure to create a space for political lawmaking within the WTO. As she convincingly argues, the waiver competence of the WTO bears a specific potential to open the WTO for political debates on the coordination and reconciliation of competing norms and interests.[75] Waiver decisions, as binding legal instruments, are the outcome of a political process. According to her analysis, it seems that requesting a waiver for cultural policy measures is both possible and feasible. The political debates on granting waivers may result in two different legal instruments. In the context of the current WTO framework, which does not address cultural concerns, cultural protection in particular demands the political will of Members. On the one hand, the waiver power allows for a general modification of WTO norms to take better account of non-economic interests, including cultural values. On the other hand, it can affect trade by restricting the WTO's jurisdiction with respect to specific measures mandated by another international legal regime.[76] This may present some opportunities to coordinate WTO rules and cultural measures enacted under the UNESCO Convention.

[72] See I Feichtner, 'The Waiver Power of the WTO: Opening the WTO for Political Debate on the Reconciliation of Competing Interests' (2009) 20 *European Journal of International Law* 615, 618–19.

[73] See WTO General Council, Decision-Making Procedures Under Art IX and XII of the WTO Agreement, Decision of 15 November 1995, WT/L/93, 24 November 1995.

[74] See D Marinberg, 'GATT/WTO Waivers: "Exceptional Circumstances" as Applied to the Lomé Waiver' (2001) 19 *Boston University International Law Journal* 129 (criticising the waiver practice under the WTO).

[75] See Feichtner, above n 72, 618.

[76] Ibid, 629–44.

Waivers are not only granted to individual Members; collective waiver decisions can be adopted to suspend obligations for all, or groups of, Members. Two types of collective waiver decisions can be distinguished. First, collective waivers can be granted for concretely defined measures or situations, such as the coordination of WTO law with other international legal regimes.[77] This may furnish a rationale to legalise measures mandated by the UNESCO Convention on Cultural Diversity and thus avoid norm conflict. Secondly, waiver decisions have been adopted to legalise abstractly defined measures for all, or groups of, Members.[78] If cultural concern can be equated with public health, it is conceivable for WTO Members to adopt a cultural waiver similar to the TRIPS waiver.

This brief survey of waiver practice shows that the waivers may serve the function of a safety valve when an individual Member is unable to perform its obligations. Moreover, the waiver option can be used more broadly, allowing, for example, regional economic integration and the justification of non-reciprocal trade preferences for the products from developing countries.[79] Carmody proposes reconciling cultural concerns with trade obligations by way of a carefully defined waiver for cultural industries.[80]

The right of WTO Members to request a cultural waiver may provide an opportunity to place their cultural concerns on the WTO agenda and have them debated. This can generate some bearing on potential norm change that would favour cultural protection and diversity within the WTO system. However, it is never easy to materialise a waiver competence to legalise non-compliant cultural measures. To successfully request a cultural waiver the cultural sectors concerned should first be clearly identified; secondly, the support of three-quarters of the WTO Members is required. This is a conceivable barrier, given that the US's strong opposition would make it extremely hard to obtain the required quorum for adopting a cultural waiver.

[77] The Kimberley waiver is an example of a waiver decision falling into this category. For an analysis of this waiver, see Feichtner, ibid, 622–25. In this case, had the WTO waiver not been granted, the fragmentation of political authority between the UN and the WTO would have been acute because an ostensible clash between UN and WTO authorities would have occurred. See T Broude, 'Principles of Normative Integration and the Allocation of International Authority: The WTO, The Vienna Convention on the Law of Treaties, and the Rio Declaration' (2008) 6 *Loyola University of Chicago International Law Review* 173, 178.

[78] The TRIPS waiver is a classic example of this type. For more discussion, see Feichtner, above n 72, 625–29.

[79] See WTO, *Analytical Index I, Marrakesh Agreement* (2003) ¶183; WTO, *Analytical Index, Guide to GATT Law and Practice* (1995) ii, ¶¶892–906.

[80] For more analysis of a waiver proposal, see C Carmody, 'When "Cultural Identity Was Not At Issue": Thinking about Canada—Certain Measures Concerning Periodicals' (1999) 30 *Law & Policy International Business* 231.

8.4.3 Other Options

The proposals for cultural protection within the WTO system discussed above—cultural exception or cultural waiver—aside from the obvious difficulties in formulating them in a non-arbitrary and enforceable manner and obtaining the necessary WTO Members' consent, are 'regressive' in the sense that they decrease the already achieved level of trade liberalisation.[81] This is especially true where the GATT is concerned. There might be other positive options to be considered.

First, in view of the changing environment, one avenue for improving the WTO framework regarding the treatment of culture is to reform the existing service classification to clarify the status of audiovisual services. Technological convergence, economic concentration,[82] and classification and scheduling issues in the services sector have long been acknowledged as problematic. The problems of the classification system used for services[83] with reference to the United Nations Central Product Classification[84] include its inconsistency with the purpose of scheduling, overlapping categories and the Members' non-compliance in their commitments.[85] Chapter 5 also mentions that, in the current WTO system, it is hard to distinguish between goods and services in audiovisual sectors and, accordingly, to decide whether the GATT or GATS rules should apply to the transactions at issue. In practice, the need for a careful classification and scheduling has been stressed in several cases, such as *US—Gambling* and *China—Publications and Audiovisual Services*.[86] Meanwhile, in the specific context of the digital environment, more attention should be paid to cultural products supplied by electronic means. This can be reduced to the question of whether matter traded digitally should be categorised

[81] See T Voon, 'A New Approach to Audiovisual Products in the WTO: Rebalancing GATT and GATS' (2007) 14 *UCLA Entertainment Law Review* 1, 27.

[82] See P Guerrieri et al (eds), *Cultural Diversity and International Economic Integration: The Global Governance of the Audio-Visual Sector* (2005) 2.

[83] See WTO, 'Services Sectoral Classification List', WTO Doc MTN.GNS/W/120 (10 July 1991).

[84] UN Provisional Central Product Classification (CPC), UN Statistics Papers, Series M, No 77, Version 1.1, E. 91.XVII.7, 1991. The CPC has in fact been revised twice since the end of the Uruguay Round. See respectively, CPC, Version 1.0, UN Statistics Papers, Series M, No 77, 1998, E.98.XVII.5; CPC, Version 1.1, UN Statistics Papers, Series M, No.77, 2002, ESA/STAT/SERM/77/Ver.1. The CPC Version 1.2 is in draft and pending adoption. However, these updates have not been integrated into the current negotiations.

[85] See Burri-Nenova, above n 34, 51.

[86] WTO, United States—Measures Affecting the Cross-Border Supply of Gambling and Betting Services, Panel Report, WT/DS285/R, adopted 10 November 2004, Appellate Body Report, WT/DS285/AB/R, adopted 7 April 2005. WTO, China—Measures Affecting Trading Rights and Distribution Services for Certain Publications and Audiovisual Entertainment Products, Panel Report, WT/DS363/R, adopted 12 August 2009, Appellate Body Report, WT/DS363/AB/R, adopted 21 December 2009. See also S Wunsch-Vincent, 'The Internet, Cross-Border Trade in Services, and the GATS: Lessons from *US—Gambling*' (2006) 5 *World Trade Review* 319, 324.

as goods or services. Due to the starkly different positions held by the US and the EU, one can predict that there will be a lengthy battle before any clear-cut solution is reached. In this regard, the uncertain boundary between telecommunications and radio and television transmission adds another layer of complexity to the issue. A clearer, better structured and more up-to-date system of classification, especially with regard to sectors pertinent to culture and the rapidly changing audiovisual and telecommunication sector, could allow more finely tuned scheduling and facilitate deeper market access commitments in the service sectors. This should rank high on the list of possible reforms.

Secondly, a 'reference paper' document, similar to that applying to basic telecommunication services in the current WTO system, is suggested for cultural sectors.[87] A reference paper for audiovisual services would provide a safeguard for cultural policy measures in the form of a universal service clause. Such a document would advance national treatment and market access commitments while, at the same time, achieving a balance between the drive for liberalisation and cultural objectives. In a narrower sense, a reference paper on audiovisual subsidies is proposed to allow subsidies for cultural purposes while banning subsidies for industrial ends.[88]

Thirdly, inspired by the special arrangements crafted for agricultural, textile, steel and other sectors, it does not seem impossible to design an agreement that deals with cultural products and their associated industries.[89] This option aims to develop a set of more integrated rules for protecting cultural values, either by introducing necessary changes to different WTO rules or disciplines, or by inserting new provisions into existing documents. The core task is to make the overall WTO framework more culture conducive and grant Members room to pursue their cultural policy measures.

8.4.4 Towards a Jurisprudence of 'Jus Gentium of International Trade'?

In reconciling the clash between trade and culture, notwithstanding the differences in trade rules resulting from the different levels of integration, it is notable that the trade rules of all of these regimes are often too abstract to preclude multiple interpretations. This abstractness tends to develop evolutionary trade jurisprudence that reflects changing circumstances. During this process, the role of judicial organs is critical because their interpretations and hermeneutics retain controlling power in defining

[87] See Burri-Nenova, above n 34, 49.

[88] See Emmanuel Cocq and P Messerlin, 'French Audio-Visual Policy: Impact and Compatibility with Trade Negotiations' in P Guerrieri et al (eds), *Cultural Diversity and International Economic Integration: The Global Governance of the Audio-Visual Sector* (2005) 48–49.

[89] See Acheson and Maule, above n 46, 338–39.

the actual obligations governing the behaviours of treaty members. At the same time, the practical difficulties in amending or revising treaty provisions also highlight the role judicial organs may play.[90] The fluid nature of trade rules and the essential role of judicial organs together facilitate jurisprudential evolution, which creates a fertile ground for the hermeneutic convergence of different trade regimes.

Another factor driving this convergence in domestic dimension lies in the 'constitutional' nature of the interface between free markets and state regulation. Jackson has conceptualised this issue as a 'trade constitution', which represents a 'very delicate mix of economic and governmental policies, political constraints, and above all an intricate set of constraints imposed by a variety of rules or legal norms in a particular institutional setting'.[91]

In recent years, there has been a discernible convergence of WTO, EU and NAFTA trade jurisprudence concerning how to address the dual crisis of trade and regulatory failure and the corresponding clash between free markets and state regulation.[92] First, in the past, the interpretative focus of trade tribunals tended to emphasise questions such as whether certain exceptions were 'necessary' or sufficiently 'relating' as to take precedence over free trade principles. In contrast, trade tribunals are now inclined to focus scrutiny on whether a state has attempted to comply with and implement its trade obligations in good faith. Secondly, trade tribunals in the past tended to condemn a piece of domestic regulation legislation when they found it to be unnecessary to attain a certain regulatory objective and therefore not qualified for an exception. In contrast, they now tend to leave such legislation intact, choosing instead to concentrate on narrowing the scope of its application.

Cho aptly describe the gist of this converging and evolving jurisprudence as a shift in the focus of judicial scrutiny from considerations of

[90] See S Cho, *Free Markets and Social Regulation: A Reform Agenda of the Global Trading System* (2003) 89.

[91] See JH Jackson, *The World Trading System: Law and Policy of International Economic Relations*, 2nd edn (1997) 339; JH Jackson, 'Reflections on International Economic Law' (1996) 17 *University of Pennsylvania Journal of International Economic Law* 17, 25–28.

[92] See J Weiler, 'Epilogue: Towards a Common Law of International Trade' in J Weiler (ed), *The EU, the WTO and the NAFTA: Towards a Common Law of International Trade* (2000) 201 (discussing the convergence phenomenon of the WTO and the EU jurisprudence); see also R Howse, 'Managing the Interface between International Trade Law and the Regulatory State: What Lessons Should (or Should Not) Be Drawn from the Jurisprudence of the United States Dormant Commerce Clause' in T Cottier and PC Mavroidis (eds), *Regulatory Barriers and the Principle of Non-discrimination in World Trade Law* (2000) 159 (observing that 'the jurisprudence of the dormant commerce clause can provide a useful reference point for critical reflection on the way the WTO panels have managed the interface between free trade rules and the regulatory state). Similarly, Professor Sykes identifies the striking 'regularity' among the WTO, the NAFTA, the EU and the US's trade system in prohibiting 'regulatory protectionism'. See AO Sykes, 'Regulatory Protectionism and the Law of International Trade' (1999) 66 *University of Chicago Law Review* 1.

'substance' or 'content' to considerations of 'process' or 'manner'.[93] Based on the phenomenon of convergence, Cho further advocates that a unified set of norms, or 'legal reference', be employed to reconcile the clash between free markets and state regulation without regard to which trade system is involved.[94] This common legal precept, which falls under the rubric of a 'jus gentium of international trade', can be defined as 'a system of general legal discipline, applicable to all trade systems in addressing the interface of trade and regulation'. In this sense, it can be translated into a 'law of trading nations'. Here the 'jus gentium of international trade' consists of a 'jus cogens of international trade' and 'customary international trade law'.[95]

The 'jus gentium of international trade' generates legitimacy in the highly integrative global marketplace in the sense that it transcends narrow and overly contextualised legal doctrines, which have addressed the clash only in specific institutional settings.[96] As a reference for managing the clash between free trade and social values, the proposed 'jus gentium of international trade' attempts to crystallise, on the one hand, general principles of trade laws, while reflecting, on the other hand, the integrative *telos* legitimising the communitarian duty to cooperate on social concerns.[97] This legal precept may serve to enhance the predictability of trading systems as a whole.

Given that cultural protection falls into the sphere of state regulation, and the conflict between free trade and cultural values is not significantly different in nature from the conflicts between free trade and other societal values, it is safe to assume that the converging jurisprudence concerning trade and regulation has important bearings on dealing with the culture and trade issue. A similar approach to reconciliation may be envisaged to reconcile the conflict between cultural concern and trade liberalisation. Here, the basic idea is to respect the most fundamental trade principles, such as non-discriminatory policy, while allowing a state to invoke internationally recognised legal norms to protect cultural values. More needs to done in developing a systematic theory in this regard.

In sum, there are a number of ways that the WTO framework may be rendered more culture conducive. Apart from cultural exception and waiver options, those suggestions which are not themselves culturally motivated but rather seek to improve the overall WTO structure of rules and make it more flexible, comprehensive and transparent deserve more attention. For example, 'neutral' pathsm like an improved classification system, new rules on subsidies for services or a reference paper

[93] See Cho, above n 90, 90.
[94] Ibid, 180.
[95] Ibid 175–94.
[96] Ibid, 9.
[97] Ibid, 193.

for audiovisual services within the WTO framework, may help to readily achieve cultural objectives. These suggestions, albeit positive, also need the strong support and political will of WTO Members.

8.5 THE RELATIONSHIP BETWEEN THE UNESCO CONVENTION AND WTO AGREEMENTS

The 2005 UNESCO Convention on Cultural Diversity, championed by France and Canada, is one prominent outcome of the international effort to protect cultural diversity. Nevertheless, a problem arises immediately from the problematic fragmentation of international law, so it should be determined which rules shall prevail in the case of conflict between the Convention and other international rules. WTO jurisprudence has not yet been clarified with respect to the relationship between WTO rules and the UNESCO Convention. Since the WTO's system of mandatory dispute settlement is a relatively strong enforcement mechanism, WTO law is likely to prevail in the case of conflict.[98] After examining the sustainability of reform strategies within the WTO framework, this section attempts to discuss the trade and culture linkage from the perspectives of treaty interpretation, norm conflict and authority integration.

8.5.1 A Background Note: Norm Integration in International Law

As widely noted, a pressing contemporary problem in international law is less the availability of legal instruments than their coherent and efficient application in practice. In the face of growing concerns over the fragmentation of international law,[99] two approaches are suggested to overcome the dangers of fragmentation. First, legal doctrine and other relevant tools which general international law provides can be utilised to address the potential norm conflict. To this end, conflict norms are employed, as are the rules of interpretation, and evidence is frequently needed to determine the hierarchisation of international legal norms.[100] Secondly, the cooperation and coordination between different actors during the process of norm creation is paid increasing attention in order to help prospectively

[98] This is referred to as the 'factual hierarchy of regimes'. See H Hestermeyer, *Human Rights and the WTO, the Case of Patents and Access to Medicines* (2007) 193.

[99] The International Law Commission (ILC) has started to address the issue. See ILC, 'Fragmentation of International Law-Difficulties Arising from the Diversification and Expansion of International Law, Report of the Study Group of the International Law Commission' (finalised by Martti Koskenniemi) A/CN.4/L.682 (13 April 2006); see also G Rafner, 'Pros and Cons Ensuing from Fragmentation of International Law' (2004) 25 *Michigan Journal of International Law* 849.

[100] These works focus by and large on the doctrinal tools to address norm conflict and are presented in ILC, above n 99.

avoid conflict. Accordingly, institutional solutions to conflicts are proposed that aim not to doctrinally reconcile norms but, rather, to explore the potential of various institutional arrangements to mitigate the effects of the conflict.[101]

These methods coincide with an increasingly cogent advocacy for the principles of normative integration of international legal rules. Note that normative integration maintains a distinct correlative and functional relationship with authority integration. The success of norm integration may threaten the particular authorities of decision-making bodies in international law, and, further, can be associated with the unpopular idea of centralised global 'government'.[102] This is often the difficulty in accepting authority integration that sustains the controversy over normative integration. Arguably, a model of normative integration that creates fewer pressures towards authority integration has a better chance of attaining its normative goals.

That said, legal principles of normative integration are not merely technical, lawyerly methods for producing consistent legal outcomes. Rather, they have broad-reaching political significance for the international system's structure of authority and governance. Consequently, the outcome ought not only to be normative consistency, coherence and regularity, but also a trend towards greater centralisation and rationalisation of governance and/or harmonisation of authority.[103] In the meantime, since the conflicts arising from the fragmentation of international law are due not only to a lack of information and coordination, but also frequently to an expression of underlying interests and value conflicts, it is essential for political processes to be involved in solving such conflicts.[104]

8.5.2 Norm Integration versus Authority Integration: The Case of the WTO and UNESCO

The WTO practice is an exercise in elaborating and/or applying international trade norms. Since trade has significant social implications, trade governance requires a set of institutions that are coherent, mutually consistent and supportive, and operate in an effective, accountable and

[101] See, eg Y Shany, *The Competing Jurisdictions of International Courts and Tribunals* (2003).

[102] See Broude, above n 77, 174.

[103] Ibid, 175–76.

[104] See, eg A Fischer-Lescano and G Teubner, 'Regime-Collisions: The Vain Search for Legal Unity in the Fragmentation of Global Law' (2004) 25 *Michigan Journal of International Law* 999, 1004 (discussing the reason for fragmentation lies in contradiction between society-wide institutionalised rationalities); see also I Scobbie, 'Wicked Heresies or Legitimate Perspectives? Theory and International Law' in MD Evans (ed), *International Law*, 2nd edn (2006) 83, 86 (arguing that social conflict needs to be solved by political means).

legitimate manner. Trade norms cannot be created and operated in isolation from other areas of public policy.[105] The challenge depends largely on the conditions governing the organisation of an international legal order as a whole, particularly concerning the role played by various actors and their horizontal as well as vertical interaction. This explains why the search for solutions to the trade and culture conundrum cannot be limited to the WTO system. Rather, the WTO must cooperate with UNESCO to secure a satisfactory outcome. I argue that, like other areas of norm integration, the problem arising from authority integration between the UNESCO and WTO might be an obstacle to the integration of cultural norms into the trade system.

The work of the GATT/WTO impacts matters routinely dealt with by some UN Agencies, such as human rights, the environment and sustainable development, and culture. An effective structure of trade governance should harness the complementarities and cooperation between the WTO and the UN or its specialised agencies.[106] Such a collaboration, whose objective is to provide an illustration of the WTO and the UN agencies pursuing common goals, has indeed been formally recognised by the WTO.[107] The 1948 UNESCO Beirut Agreement[108] may serve as an early positive example of this inter-institutional cooperation.[109] A more recent, striking example concerns human rights and trade. In the realm of human rights, the UN High Commissioner for Human Rights has proposed a 'human rights approach' to trade and the WTO, whereby the norms and standards of human rights are used as a legal framework for the social dimensions of trade liberalisation.[110] A human rights approach to trade in

[105] See C Martin, 'The Relationship between Trade and Environment Regimes: What Needs to Change?' in GP Sampson, *The Role of the World Trade Organization in Global Governance* (2001) 151.

[106] Some areas dealt with by UN bodies have been proposed as candidates for collaboration with the WTO, such as core labour standards. This collaboration is required to increase the complementarities of the WTO and the UN or its specialised agencies. See Sampson, above n 57, 532.

[107] The WTO Agreement obliges the General Council to 'make appropriate arrangements for effective cooperation with other intergovernmental organisations that have responsibilities related to those of the WTO' and similar arrangements for 'consultation and cooperation with non-governmental organisations (NGOs) concerned with matters related to those of the WTO'. WTO Agreement, Art V (Relations with Other Organizations).

[108] UNESCO, Agreement for Facilitating the International Circulation of Visual and Auditory Materials of an Educational, Scientific and Cultural Character with Protocol of Signature and model form of certificate provided for in Art IV of the above-mentioned Agreement 1948, adopted in Beirut on 10 December 1948, entered into force 12 August 1954.

[109] The first draft prepared by the UNESCO Secretariat was submitted to a meeting of the Contracting Parties to the GATT, where it was revised. See UNESCO, *A Guide to the Operation of the Agreement on the Importation of Educational, Scientific and Cultural Materials*, 4th edn (Paris, UNESCO, 1969) 5.

[110] See UN Commission on Human Rights, 'Globalization and Its Impact on the Full Enjoyment of Human Rights: Report of the High Commissioner for Human Rights Submitted in Accordance with Commission on Human Rights Resolution 2001/32', E/CN.4/2002/54

cultural products is premised on cultural rights and freedom of expression. Instead of serving as a cloak for protectionism,[111] according to a further proposal by Voon, [112] human rights may assist in minimising trade restrictions arising from non-trade concerns such as cultural protection. It is also suggested that human rights instruments be used to interpret general exceptions clauses.[113] This approach may lay foundations for invoking the clauses for the purpose of cultural protection and diversity.

Another interesting case study concerns the relationship between the WTO and the trade provisions in the UN Multilateral Environment Agreements.[114] The WTO also established the Committee on Trade and Environment, which has a broad mandate that covers environmental issues and trade in goods, services and trade-related intellectual property rights.[115] This is a big step towards forming a multilateral forum to discuss trade and environment issues.

Furthermore, several WTO cases, such as *US—Shrimp*[116] and *EU—Asbestos*,[117] indicate that the complementarities between the WTO rules and UN instruments are important in addressing the interplay between trade and non-trade social norms. Notwithstanding these collaborations between the WTO and UN agencies to deal with trade and environment and trade and human rights, such partnerships have not been formalised; it is also hard to envisage the creation of a Committee on Trade and

(15 January 2002) ¶10; see also UN Commission on Human Rights, Sub-Commission on the Promotion and Protection of Human Rights, 'Globalization and Its Impact on the Full Enjoyment of Human Rights: Final Report Submitted by J Oloka-Onyango and Deepika Udagama, in Accordance with Sub-Commission Decision 2000/105', E/CN.4/Sub.2/2003/14 (25 June 2003) ¶26; UN, Office of the United Nations High Commissioner for Human Rights, 'Human Rights and Trade', Statement to the Fifth Ministerial Conference of the WTO, 10–14 September, 2004, ¶4.

111 See, eg JH Jackson, 'Reflections on the Possible Research Agenda for Exploring the Relationship between Human Rights Norms and International Trade Rules' in F Abbott et al (eds), *International Trade and Human Rights: Foundations and Conceptual Issues* (2006) 19, 26.

112 See Voon, above n 38, 149–55.

113 See, eg R Howse, 'Human Rights in the WTO: Whose Rights, What Humanity? Comment on Petersmann' (2002) 13(3) *European Journal of International Law* 651, 657; E-U Petersmann, 'Time for a United Nations "Global Compact" for Integrating Human Rights into the Law of Worldwide Organizations: Lessons from European Integration' (2002) 13(3) *European Journal of International Law* 619, 621–22; J Pauwelyn, 'Human Rights in WTO Dispute Settlement' in T Cottier et al (eds), *Human Rights and International Trade* (2005) 205, 208.

114 See Sampson, above n 57, 530–31.

115 See JMF Olsen et al, 'Trade and Environment at the World Trade Organization: The Need for a Constructive Dialogue' in GP Sampson (ed), *The Role of the World Trade Organization in Global Governance* (2001) 160.

116 See WTO, *United States—Import Prohibition of Certain Shrimp and Shrimp Products* (hereinafter WTO, *US—Shrimps*), Report of the Appellate Body, WT/DS58/AB/R, 12 October, 1998, ¶128.

117 See WTO, *European Communities—Measures Affecting Asbestos and Asbestos-Containing Products* (hereinafter WTO, *EC—Asbestos*), Report of the Appellate Body, WT/DS135, 5 April, 2001.

Culture within the WTO in the near future.[118] During the negotiation debates of the UNESCO Convention, the US expressed its concern that the trade system would be encroached upon by the Convention. Because the WTO is not a system of world government, incorporating many standards that do not have much to do with trade into this framework might be a perilous undertaking; it may destroy the fundamental attributes of the trading system.[119] This gives rise to the question of how far any such arrangement could stretch in reality.

8.5.3 The Relationship between the UNESCO Convention and the WTO Rules

The UNESCO Convention has added impetus to the ongoing debates on the issue of trade and culture. The Convention's intention to create a safe haven for cultural policies and protect them from the WTO disciplines manifests itself substantively, in particular by empowering states to support their domestic industries and restrict the influx of foreign cultural products. The question becomes whether such policy measures are permissible under the WTO rules. This section examines the relationship between the UNESCO Convention and WTO rules.

8.5.3.1 An Overview of the Relationship Prescribed in the UNESCO Convention

Part V of the Convention contains two articles dealing with its relationship to other legal instruments: Articles 20 and 21. Given the proximate grouping of these two articles, they should be seen as interrelated and complementary. The articles, however, pursue different objectives. Article 20 is an interpretative provision that aims to clarify the link between the Convention and other treaties. Article 21, on the other hand, presents non-binding encouragement to the parties to promote the objectives and principles of the Convention in other international forums and to consult each other for this purpose.[120] Under Article 21, no *inter se* modification of pre-existing WTO obligations exists, which constitutes the basis and

[118] See Sampson, above n 57, 531.
[119] See Wolf, above n 56, 201–02.
[120] See I Bernier, 'The Relationship between the UNESCO Convention on the Protection and Promotion of the Diversity of Cultural Expressions and Other International Instruments: The Emergence of a New Balance in the Interface between Commerce and Culture', available at http://www.cdc-ccd.org/Les-relations-entre-la-Convention?lang=en (last accessed on 18 June 2012), 21.

condition *sine qua non* for its overwhelming support in the final vote. It also conforms to the general rules of international law.[121]

The central operative provision for bringing about the desired shielding effect for domestic policies is contained in Article 20. Indeed, this article, entitled 'Mutual Supportiveness, Complementarity and Non-subordination', is intended as an antidote for the perceived or real grievances resulting from the application of WTO rules to cultural products. A review of its content may shed some light on whether the Convention can live up to the charged mission of safeguarding domestic cultural industries against foreign competition.

Article 20 incorporates the critical 'conflict of laws' rules and was at the centre of intense discussions throughout the negotiations. It first reaffirms a basic tenet of international law on the relationship between treaties, that they must be executed in good faith and that, unless there are special provisions establishing a relationship of superiority or inferiority between the treaties, they hold the same legal status. Furthermore, Article 20 not only reaffirms the principle of equal status, but also provides positive methods for the parties to encourage mutual support and take relevant provisions into account when interpreting and applying other agreements or acceding to other international commitments. In this sense, Article 20 may be considered a progressive provision, the true significance of which will be revealed through the practice of the parties.[122] At the same time, Article 20 leaves much room for interpretation and clarification, and makes it impossible for the Convention to effectively shield cultural sectors from free trade.

8.5.3.2 'Mutual Supportiveness' in Article 20(1)

Article 20 contains two paragraphs. The first sentence of Article 20(1) (a) repeats a universally recognised principle of international law, under which every treaty in force is binding upon the parties to it and must be performed by them in good faith.[123] Next the article orders its signatories to foster 'mutual supportiveness' between the Convention and the other treaties to which they are parties. 'Mutual supportiveness', a key term in addressing tensions between competing regimes, is a principle according to which international legal rules are to be understood and applied as

[121] Treaty law prohibits parties to a multilateral treaty from concluding an agreement to modify the treaty unless such modification is permitted by the treaty itself. See United Nations: Vienna Convention on the Law of Treaties, done at Vienna on 23 May 1969 and entered into force on 27 January 1980 (hereinafter VCLT), Art 41.

[122] See Bernier, above n 120, 21–22.

[123] VCLT, Art 26 (stating that every treaty in force is binding upon the parties to it and must be performed by them in good faith).

reinforcing each other with a view to fostering harmonisation and complementarity, as opposed to conflict.[124]

The baptism of 'mutual supportiveness' in the international arena can be traced to Agenda 21, an important programmatic document adopted by the 1992 UN Conference on Environment and Development.[125] Coined to deal with the tensions between environment and trade, the principle of 'mutual supportiveness' has the potential to spill over and apply to other contexts or situations characterised by a plurality of equally applicable competing legal frameworks.[126] In fact, the principle, while it leaves room for interpretation, has been successfully introduced into a number of new international instruments.[127] The emergence of 'mutual supportiveness' between competing regimes serves as an important conceptual tool with significant consequence to the creation and interpretation of international law norms. The multiple references to the principle should not be simply dismissed as mere political statements devoid of any normative significance.

As the core element of Article 20, the principle of 'mutual supportiveness' demands complementarity and synergy in interpreting and implementing the Convention and other treaties. It translates itself into a specific obligation of conduct incumbent upon states, ie a duty to pursue good faith negotiations aimed at achieving formal modifications in the law, which are necessary to restore the integrity of the international legal order.[128] This is especially important for the progressive clarification of the normative value of the principle. As such, it may be seen as a corollary of the general principle of good faith performance of treaty obligation.

Though 'mutual supportiveness' is a soft and flexible obligation, its normative content is supplied by the article's second paragraph, which goes a step further by proposing a concrete means of enhancing complementarity between the Convention and other treaties.[129] Article 20(1)(b) requires that 'when entering into other international obligations, Parties shall take into account the relevant provisions of this Convention'. This provision distinguishes between two situations. The first scenario occurs when parties to the Convention interpret and apply other instruments of

[124] See M Lück, 'Harmonization, Systematic Integration, and Mutual Supportiveness as Conflict-Solution Techniques: Different Modes of Interpretation as a Challenge to Negative Effects of Fragmentation?' (2006) 17 *Finnish Yearbook of International Law* 39 (discussing the notions of harmonisation, presumption against conflicts, and systematic integration).

[125] Agenda 21, ¶2.3(b), available at http://www.un.org/esa/dsd/agenda21/res_agenda21_00.shtml (last accessed on 18 June 2012).

[126] See R Pavoni, 'Mutual Supportiveness as a Principle of Interpretation and Law-Making: A Watershed for the "WTO-and-Competing-Regimes" Debate?' (2010) 21 *European Journal of International Law* 649, 650–51.

[127] International Treaty on Plant Genetic Resources for Food and Agriculture, FAO Resolution 3/2001. The Treaty came into force on 29 June 2004.

[128] See Pavoni, above n 126, 650.

[129] Ibid, 659.

international law. This becomes relevant if WTO panels are confronted with a trade dispute involving a Member's cultural policy measures, and will be elaborated in the next section.

The second arises when parties to the Convention enter into other international treaties. This refers to the parties' conducting negotiations regarding either the conclusion of new treaties or the amendment of existing treaties. Parties are obliged to take account of the Convention's provisions in such negotiations. This obligation is further complemented by Article 21, which imposes on parties the undertaking to promote the objectives and principles of the Convention in other international fora and to consult each other for this purpose. In reality, when a less affluent country negotiating bilateral treaties with the US is exposed to the pressure to liberalise its trade in cultural products, the UNESCO Convention may present a legal, or at least diplomatic, hurdle to the attainment of the US trade agenda.[130] In short, Article 20(1) clearly states that the undertaking to achieve 'mutual supportiveness' is, in principle, not intended to subordinate the Convention to any other treaty per se, nor affect the integrity of other treaty obligations. This indicates that every effort should be made to reconcile the conflicting obligations imposed by the constantly emerging treaties.

8.5.3.3 When the Issue Gets Tough: Article 20(2)

Article 20(1) attempts to follow a desirable trend in international governance that gives equal weight to cultural and trade concerns. However, one way or another, 'mutual supportiveness' between the UNESCO Convention and WTO law is a demanding task, based on the general rules of treaty interpretation set out in the Vienna Convention on Law on Treaties (VCLT), the hierarchy of international law and WTO jurisprudence.[131] In this sense, the principle of 'mutual supportiveness' is more political than legal. The Convention's ability to perform its mission as an antidote to the grievances resulting from trade in cultural products remains uncertain.

Beyond this, Article 20(2) makes the issue even tougher when it comes to the question of whether the parties of the UNESCO Convention could apply the Convention rules *inter se* if they conflict with WTO laws. The answer seems to be negative for several reasons. According to Article 20(2), nothing in the Convention shall be interpreted as modifying the rights and obligations of the parties under any other treaties to which they are parties. This provision prescribes no *inter se* modification of WTO obligations among the Convention's signatories. In fact, treaty law, as enshrined in VCLT, prohibits two or more parties to a multilateral

[130] See CM Bruner, 'Culture, Sovereignty, and Hollywood: UNESCO and the Future of Trade in Cultural Products' (2008) 40 *International Law and Politics* 351, 377–78.

[131] See Hahn, above n 60, 543–46.

treaty from concluding another agreement to modify the treaty obligations among themselves unless the modification in question is allowed by the treaty.[132] Viewed this way, the general claim to non-subordination in Article 20(1) is modified in Article 20(2). It should be noted here that, given the lack of substantive consensus in negotiations, in particular US consent, Article 20(2) had to become part of the package and was even the condition *sine qua non* for the overwhelming support for the Convention in the final vote.

In short, Article 20 of the UNESCO Convention faithfully reflects the desire shared by the vast majority of contracting parties to exclude any form of subordination between the Convention and other treaties,[133] but it contains a certain amount of ambiguity and may not have the real effect of shielding cultural sectors from WTO rules and obligations. The 'mutual supportiveness' between the Convention and WTO agreements is more difficult to achieve than would be desirable, both for the integrity of the trading system and the promotion of cultural diversity.[134] The future of this article is tied more closely to its application and the way it is interpreted by dispute settlement bodies in the context of the Convention or other treaties, such as the WTO.

8.6 CONNECTING WTO RULES WITH THE UNESCO CONVENTION: THE PERSPECTIVE OF DISPUTE SETTLEMENT

A domestic cultural measure justified under the UNESCO Convention is likely to be in violation of WTO laws. Given the difficulties in dealing with the twin regimes of trade and environment, labour, human rights, etc, it is doubtful whether the WTO tribunals would exercise a degree of deference to the UNESCO Convention when applying WTO trade rules under the current framework. As a consequence, in addressing how to reconcile this conflict, the overarching issue remains the possible channels of connection between the UNESCO Convention and the WTO rules. One solution to the difficulties in the treatment of cultural products within the current WTO framework is to leave the treaty provisions as they stand, while allowing the tribunals to resolve uncertainties and develop pragmatic compromises in practice.[135] Indeed, this is the way that WTO Members have tackled many problems and ambiguities in the context of the WTO since it was founded in 1995.

[132] VCLT, Art 41.
[133] See Bernier, above n 120, 1.
[134] See Hahn, above n 60, 543–46.
[135] See Voon, above n 38, 123.

Drawing on the insights set out in the relevant literature, this section assesses how the WTO's predominant reliance on its dispute settlement mechanism can be a sustainable proposition to deal with the growing incidence of disputes arising from the policy interface between culture and trade. In particular, it tries to analyse the possible linkages between the WTO rules and the UNESCO Convention from the perspective of treaty interpretation. Treaty interpretation in WTO law continues to represent a topic of high theoretical and practical importance. This section is devoted to the discussions of how a tribunal should respond to the argument that an allegedly WTO-inconsistent trade measure is justified under the UNESCO Convention.

8.6.1 Identifying the Legal Basis for Linking WTO Rules with the UNESCO Convention

In general, WTO panels and the Appellate Body have to make findings based on the interpretation of the 'covered agreements' within the WTO framework. They are not allowed to decide whether a challenged measure would conform to an outside international legal agreement. Hence, when a trade dispute involving cultural products arises, it is necessary to justify a WTO tribunal's linking of the WTO provisions with the UNESCO Convention.

International law affects the interpretation of WTO provisions in dispute settlement through DSU Article 3.2. In connection with the use of international law in WTO disputes, Article 3.2 imposes two key requirements. First, public international law clearly plays a part, at least to the extent that it provides customary rules regarding the interpretation of WTO agreements. Secondly, public international law cannot be used to replace or supplement the WTO agreements if this would amount to increasing or diminishing the rights and obligations provided under those agreements.[136] It is often contended that the second requirement limits the application of non-WTO international law within WTO dispute settlement.[137] In Howse's view, however, which I second, these two principles fit together neatly: 'when the Appellate Body is interpreting existing provisions in

[136] WTO, Dispute Settlement Understanding (DSU). Art 3.2 reads: 'The dispute settlement system of the WTO is a central element in providing security and predictability to the multilateral trading system. The Members recognize that it serves to preserve the rights and obligations of Members under the covered agreements, and to clarify the existing provisions of those agreements in accordance with customary rules of interpretation of public international law. Recommendations and rulings of the DSB cannot add to or diminish the rights and obligations provided in the covered agreements.'

[137] See, eg Voon, above n 38, 125–26.

accordance with the customary rules, it is not, impermissibly, adding to or diminishing . . . existing obligations'.[138]

It is well settled in WTO case law that the principles codified in the VCLT, particularly Article 31 and Article 32, are customary rules of interpretation within the meaning of DSU Article 3.2.[139] As pointed out, it does not matter that the US and some other WTO Members are not party to the VCLT as these rules form part of customary international law.[140] As a principle, the VCLT calls for treaty interpretation in good faith and in light of the treaty's objective and purpose.[141] The different interpretive approaches provided include the investigations of the 'ordinary meaning' of the words, the historical context or intentions of the parties, and the teleological reasons or aims for the adoption of the text.[142] The VCLT also stipulates that a special meaning shall be given to a term if it is established that the parties so intended.[143] If the application of this rule leaves the meaning ambiguous or obscure, or leads to absurd results, recourse may be had to supplementary means of interpretation, including the preparatory work of the treaty and the circumstances of its conclusion.[144]

8.6.2 Connecting WTO Rules with the UNESCO Convention under VCLT Article 31(1)

Article 31 is of paramount significance in the context of WTO dispute settlement. The Appellate Body has used international law to interpret WTO provisions primarily based on Article 31(1),[145] which contains the basis for considering other international instruments in interpreting the 'ordinary meaning' of terms used in the WTO agreements. According to this provision, the Appellate Body must utilise the so-called textual

[138] See R Howse, 'The Most Dangerous Branch? WTO Appellate Body Jurisprudence on the Nature and Limits of the Judicial Power' in T Cottier and P Mavroidis, *The Role of the Judge in International Trade Regulation: Experience and Lessons from WTO* (2003) 11, 15.

[139] Art 3.2 of the DSU refers implicitly to Arts 31 and 32 of the VCLT. In several cases, WTO tribunals have explicitly recognised that Arts 31 and 32 of the VCLT are authoritative modifications of the customary rules of interpretation of public international law. See, eg WTO, *US—Carbon Steel*, Appellate Body Report, ¶61; WTO, *US—Standards for Reformulated and Conventional Gasoline* (hereinafter WTO, *US—Gasoline*), WT/DS2/R, Report of the Panel, 29 January 1996.

[140] See M Lennard, 'Navigating by the Stars: Interpreting the WTO Agreements' (2002) 5(1) *Journal of International Economic Law* 17, 18–19.

[141] VCLT, Art 31.

[142] See, eg GG Fitzmaurice, 'The Law and Procedure of the International Court of Justice: Treaty Interpretation and Certain other Treaty Points' (1951) 28 *British Yearbook of International Law* 1.

[143] VCLT, Art 31(4).

[144] VCLT, Art 32.

[145] VCLT, Art 31(1), which reads: 'A treaty shall be interpreted in good faith in accordance with the ordinary meaning to be given to the terms of the treaty in their context and in the light of its object and purpose'.

approach. There is no doubt that the textual approach to treaty interpretation has contributed to the consistency and coherence of Appellate Body reports as well as to lending the multilateral trading system desirable security and predictability.[146] In this sense, ignoring the contextual and teleological dimensions of treaty interpretation may undermine the legitimacy of DSB reports and the dispute settlement mechanism as a whole.[147]

However, the problem associated with the textual approach is that a WTO Member would be less able to justify its cultural policy measures if the interpretation is merely grounded on the text without regard to the implications of international law and the legitimacy of cultural objectives. Embracing a holistic approach to treaty interpretation and recognising the hermeneutic value of each individual dimension of the general rule encapsulated in Article 31(1) would allow the flexibility necessary for the DSB to accommodate the broader policy considerations underlying any interpretative exercise. In fact, the increased relevance of the WTO regime within the system of global governance demands such flexibility, particularly in light of the growing interface between WTO norms and other societal values, including cultural diversity.[148] It is interesting to note that the Appellate Body has been shifting away from strict textualism in recent years.[149] Several Appellate Body decisions indicate its willingness to consider international law in determining the 'ordinary meaning' of particular words under Article 31(1).[150]

A guiding principle evident in a number of landmark cases implies that WTO law is not supposed to be read in 'clinical isolation' from other fields of international law.[151] For instance, in *US—Gasoline*, the first case it decided, the Appellate Body applied the general rules of treaty interpretation provided in the VCLT and stated this principle.[152] This interpretative approach is also visible in *US—Shrimp*.[153] In this landmark

[146] See C-D Ehlermann, 'Six Years on the Bench of the "World Trade Court"' in F Ortino and E-U Petersmann (eds), *The WTO Dispute Settlement System 1995–2003* (2004), 509–10.

[147] See F Ortino, 'Treaty Interpretation and the WTO Appellate Body Report in *US—Gambling*: A Critique' (2006) 9 *Journal of International Economic Law* 117, 146.

[148] See Ortino, ibid, 148; Broude, above n 22, 625–26.

[149] See Voon, above n 38, 127–28.

[150] See WTO, *US—Shrimp*, Report of Appellate Body, ¶¶110–32; WTO, *US—Gasoline*, Report of Appellate Body, 17; WTO, *India–Patent Protection for Pharmaceutical and Agricultural Chemical Products*, WT/DS50/AB/R, ¶46; WTO, *Japan—Taxes on Alcoholic Beverages* (Alcoholic Beverages II), WT/DS8/AB/R, WT/DS10/AB/R, WT/DS11/AB/R, ¶10.2; WTO, *United States—Anti-dumping Duty on Dynamic Random Access Memory Semiconductors (DRAMs) of One Megabit or Above from Korea*, WT/DS99/R, ¶6.13.

[151] See Martin, above n 105, 151–52; G Marceau, 'A Call for Coherence in International Law—Praise for the Prohibition against "Clinical Isolation" in WTO Dispute Settlement' (1999) 33(5) *Journal of World Trade* 87.

[152] WTO, *US—Gasoline*, Report of the Appellate Body, 17.

[153] WTO, *US—Shrimp*, Report of the Appellate Body, ¶130. In this case, India, Malaysia, Pakistan and Thailand challenged a US ban on certain shrimp imports, purportedly imposed to protect sea turtles from accidental capture during shrimp harvesting. In its decision, the

case, when the Appellate Body was faced with defining 'an exhaustible natural resource', it clearly stated that to some extent standards, such as environmental standards, could be taken into account in the interpretation of WTO clauses. It then made reference to a list of environmental conventions, considered as 'a living reality', to assist in interpreting the term, despite the fact that not all parties to the dispute were signatories to those agreements.[154] Making extensive use of these documents, the Appellate Body found that the term includes 'living biological resources', such as sea turtles. This finding is important in arriving at the conclusion that the US laws at issue fell within the terms of the general exception clause in GATT Article XX(d). *US—Shrimp* indicates that the WTO could open up to general principles set out in other international treaties. On the use of Article 31(1) as an avenue for invoking international law to interpret WTO law, the ILC Study Group comments that 'taking other treaties' into account as evidence of 'ordinary meaning' appears to be a rather contrived way of preventing the 'clinical isolation' of WTO law from the rest of public international law.[155]

There is a concern that rulings like this might cause criteria and concepts to be imported from other international organisations into WTO law without the consent of Members.[156] As Paulwelyn explains, however, the Appellate Body was perhaps relying on non-WTO international instruments, not so much to establish the 'ordinary meaning' of particular words in WTO provisions, but more as a 'factual reference' in examining whether there has been discrimination in the sense of the chapeau of GATT Article XX.[157] Viewed this way, these concepts are not imported into WTO law. Voon holds the same position, pointing out that the Appellate Body is hesitant to rely on outside conventions to which only some WTO Members are party but is willing to use such a convention as a factual rather than a legal reference.[158]

On the other hand, while the WTO tribunals have avoided the absolute normative insularity of the WTO regime, in practice they eschew the application of non-WTO substantive norms in their jurisprudence.[159] For

Appellate Body drew support from other international instruments, including United Nations on the Law of the Sea and the Convention on International Trade in Endangered Species of Wild Fauna and Flora to interpret the meaning of 'exhaustible natural source'.

[154] WTO, *US—Shrimp*, Report of Appellate Body, ¶129.

[155] ILC, above n 99, ¶450.

[156] For example, India expressed this concern when the DSB adopted the AB Report for *EC—Tariff Preference*. See WTO, 'Minutes of Meeting Held in the Center William Rappard on 20 April 2004', WT/DSB/M/167, (27 May 2004) ¶49.

[157] See J Pauwelyn, *Conflict of Norms in Public International Law—How WTO Law Relates to Other Rules of International Law* (2003) 269.

[158] See Voon, above n 38, 134, 142.

[159] See Ortino, above n 147, 117 (arguing that, although the Appellate Body appears to emancipate itself from a rigorous textual approach, it has not yet embraced a holistic approach to treaty interpretation, one in which the treaty interpreter looks thoroughly at

example, in *EC—Biotech*,[160] the panel backed away from applying an outside protocol (the Cartagena Protocol on Biosafety, [161] CPB) as an interpretative aid on the basis that not all the disputants had ratified it.[162] Two observations can be made in this regard. First, the statement in *EC—Biotech* was made by the panel, not the Appellate Body; the latter is superior in the WTO's interpretative hierarchy. In any event, the panel in this case did not purport to overrule the opinion made by the Appellate Body in *US—Shrimp*. Secondly, it is possible to reconcile these two cases by reasoning that the WTO dispute settlement system has been gradually developing a more nuanced approach to the interpretative use of non-WTO norms. The difference in treatment exhibited in these cases may be regarded as consistent if one compares the Convention on International Trade in Endangered Species (CITES), where there is no record of non-ratification, with the CPB, where there is. In another example, the panel in *EU—GMOs* observed that the mere fact that one or more disputing parties are not parties to a convention does not necessarily mean that a convention cannot shed light on the meaning and scope of a treaty term that needs to be interpreted.[163]

When it comes to whether the WTO tribunals may extend their consideration to the UNESCO Convention, the answer should be very case dependent. Thus far there have been no clear-cut rules to guide the WTO tribunals in using non-WTO international instruments to interpret WTO agreements; uncertainties do exist in this regard. However, it is safe to claim that Article 31(1) of the VCLT provides a possible avenue to improving the chances of the UNESCO Convention's influencing the interpretation of WTO rules.

8.6.3 The Relevance of the UNESCO Convention under VCLT Article 31(3)(c): An Observation on Customary International Law

In interpreting WTO agreements, the Appellate Body also refers to non-WTO norms in reliance on VCLT Article 31(3)(c). This provision articulates that, as part of the general rule of treaty interpretation, any 'relevant rules of international law' applicable in the relations between the

all the relevant elements of the general rule on treaty interpretation pursuant to VCLT Art 31(1)); A Lindroos and M Mehling, Dispelling the Chimera of "Self-Contained" Regimes in International Law and the WTO' (2006) 16 *European Journal of International Law* 857.

[160] WTO, *European Communities—Measures Affecting the Approval and Marketing of Biotech Products* (hereinafter WTO, *EC—Biotech*), WT/DS291, complaint by the US, the Panel Report (WT/DS291/R) was adopted on 29 September 2006.

[161] Cartagena Protocol on Biosafety to the Convention on Biological Diversity, 29 January 2000, 39 ILM 1027 (2000).

[162] See above n 160. Report of the Panel, ¶7.94.

[163] Ibid, ¶7.53.

parties shall be taken into account in addition to context.[164] Article 31(3)(c) is aimed at incorporating and conciliating international rules for treaty interpretation that may apply between the parties. In order to achieve this goal, it mandates the consideration of non-WTO international legal rules in the course of interpreting WTO provisions, through which values or interests other than trade liberalisation may be prioritised. This represents a juridical reasoning instrument of normative integration.[165] The ILC study group report heralds this method of normative integration as a principle of 'systemic integration' and strongly advocates its adoption.[166]

WTO tribunals have thus far not followed a very consistent method in applying Article 31(3)(c) in dispute settlement. For instance, the panel in *EC—Biotech* was burdened with the delicate task of interpreting the WTO Agreement on the Application of SPS Agreement.[167] There were claims that the panel should account for non-WTO treaty norms, especially the Convention on Biodiversity[168] and the CPB, in its interpretation of SPS Agreement. Against some resistance, the panel chose to restrict the application of Article 31(3)(c), reducing it to apparent insignificance. The panel interpreted Article 31(3)(c) as engaging only non-WTO treaties to which all WTO Members have subscribed, instead of a more inclusive approach that would have taken into account all mutual obligations that apply between the parties to a particular dispute.[169] However, in *US—Shrimp*, in stark contrast to its rejection of the strict integrationist confines of Article 31(3)(c), the DSB decision closely follows the loose imperatives of the 1992 Rio Declaration on Environment and Development adopted by the UN. It is argued that the panel tends to reject the application of Article 31(3)(c) as an effective norm-integrating tool if it finds that the outcome would generate indirect yet intrusive authority-integrating implications.[170] This is interesting because it reinforces the relationship between norm integration and authority integration, that is, the path of normative integration seems easier to follow when it is chosen by decision-makers and, as such, does not threaten integration of authority.

According to Article 38(1) of the Statute of the International Court of Justice (ICJ),[171] 'relevant rules of international law' include international

[164] VCLT, Art 31(3)(c).

[165] See R Howse, 'Adjudicative Legitimacy and Treaty Interpretation in International Trade Law: The Early Years of WTO Jurisprudence' in J Weiler (ed), *The EU, the WTO and the NAFTA: Towards a Common Law of International Trade* (2000) 35, 55.

[166] See ILC, above n 99, ¶¶209–13; Broude, above n 77, 196.

[167] WTO, Agreement on the Application of Sanity and Phytosanitary Measures, 15 April 1994, Marrakesh Agreement Establishing the World Trade Organization, Annex 1A, Legal Instruments—Results of the Uruguay Round, 33 ILM 1125 (1994).

[168] Convention on Biological Diversity, 5 June 1992, 1760 UNTS 79, 31 ILM 818 (1992).

[169] WTO, *EC—Biotech*, Report of the Panel, ¶¶7.67–71.

[170] See Broude, above n 77, 198–200.

[171] Statute of International Court of Justice, Art 38(1), which reads: 'The Court, whose function is to decide in accordance with international law such disputes as are submitted

conventions, international customs and the general principles of law. Note that this reference to customary international law raises important questions about the substantive relevance of other sources of international law. This is of particular relevance with the question of whether the UNESCO Convention may serve as customary international law in this context. International law enunciates two classic requirements for customs: (i) consistent state practice and (ii) *opinio juris*. These requirements have, however, traditionally been problematic. In the case of state practice, it is hard to determine the real practice of states as a whole; in the case of *opinio juris*, it is even harder to determine whether states have acted out of a sense of legal obligation.[172] It thus comes as no surprise that the question of whether a source constitutes customary international law often leads to hot debate.

A recent phenomenon worth noting is that, alongside the growing importance of international organisations like UNESCO, scholars have begun to observe the creation of so-called 'new' or 'modern' customs in international law.[173] The traditional distinction between hard treaty and soft law obligations is no longer as clear-cut as it previously was. Sometimes it is hard to tell whether certain institutional products impose obligations only for those who have notified particular treaties, and are therefore a species of contractual obligation, or are general obligations on all, and therefore a new phenomenon: a species of international legislation.[174] This new kind of custom, increasingly composed of 'intertwined forms of treaty and custom', is said to be the product of a deliberative and deliberate process in international organisations.[175]

The work of UNESCO is arguably providing a shortcut to finding custom. The UNESCO Convention on Cultural Diversity is the latest in a series of efforts by UNESCO to ward off the spread of cultural homogeneity through the excessive exportation of cultural products by economically dominant countries into cultures at a relative economic disadvantage. The Convention is a breakthrough in that it brings an obscure soft-law notion of cultural diversity into international law. With

to it, shall apply: a. international conventions, whether general or particular, establishing rules expressly recognized by the contesting states; b. *international custom, as evidence of a general practice accepted as law*; c. the general principles of law recognized by civilized nations; d. subject to the provisions of Article 59, judicial decisions and the teachings of the most highly qualified publicists of the various nations, as subsidiary means for the determination of rules of law' (emphasis added).

[172] For more discussions, see JL Goldsman and E Posner, 'A Theory of Customary International Law' (1999) 66 *University of Chicago Law Review* 1113; A Guzman, 'Saving Customary International Law', UC Berkeley Public Law Research Paper No 708721 (April 2005).

[173] See A Roberts, 'Traditional and Modern Approaches to Customary International Law: A Reconciliation'(2006) 95 *American Journal of International Law* 757.

[174] See J Alvarez, *International Organizations as Lawmakers* (2006).

[175] Ibid, 589.

its far-reaching consequences, it may function as a frame of reference for cultural protection and promotion and lay the groundwork for achieving greater cultural diversity. In this sense, the Convention may be regarded as an illustration of the 'new' customs in action and interpreted as a conventional and customary source of international law in the field of cultural protection. Furthermore, the determination of customs in international law frequently turns on purpose or value.[176] An instrument like the UNESCO Convention that emphasises a culturally sensitive order of analysis helps identify and reinforce the purpose or value behind any particular measure that is challenged under trade rules. The Convention's puissance and legitimacy in dispute resolution is strengthened by the rapid process with which it was concluded and entered into force. Although the Convention is ambiguous in some clauses, it contains a number of process mechanisms that may permit that ambiguity to be creatively sharpened over time.

The Convention can be considered alongside the development of customary international law in the area as an important attempt to secure international cultural 'shelf space'.[177] Although it faces the criticism that the strategy of systematically creating WTO-contradicting multilateral agreements in non-WTO fora is legally misguided and politically unwise,[178] the UNESCO Convention certainly reflects the contemporary cultural concern of international community. The WTO system would be ill-advised not to accommodate the Convention's leitmotif of cultural diversity protection and promotion. The US's opposition, however, presents a clear barrier to this route, especially with regard to interpreting the UNESCO Convention as relevant customary international law. It remains doubtful that one could argue that the Convention constitutes custom applicable to the US given its consistent opposition to the Convention.

In sum, the use of international law by the Appellate Body in the previous cases has precedential value via either VCLT Article 31(1) or Article 31(3)(c).[179] One can therefore expect the Appellate Body to approach non-WTO international law in future disputes in a manner that

[176] See C Carmody, 'Creating "Shelf Space": NAFTA's Experience with Cultural Protection and Its Relevance for the WTO' (2007) 2(2) *Asian Journal of WTO & International Health Law and Policy* 287, 306.

[177] The term 'shelf space' gained popularity in Canada in the late 1980s after Canada sought a measure of protection for Canadian culture in its 1988 free trade agreement with the US. See Carmody, ibid, 288.

[178] See Hahn, above n 60, 546–47.

[179] The DSU imposes no formal principle of stare decisis on panels or the Appellate Body. See generally, R Bhala, 'The Myth about Stare Decisis and International Trade Law' (1999) 14 *American University International Law Review* 845. In practice, however, WTO Panels and the Appellate Body routinely take previous decisions made by the panels and the Appellate Body into account, and panel and the Appellate Body reports are therefore typically consistent with previous Appellate Body reports, even when not with previous panel reports. See generally, R Bhala, The Precedent Setters: De Facto Stare Decisis in WTO Adjudication' (1999) 9 *Journal of International Law & Policy* 1; R Bhala, 'The Power of

is broadly in line with its previous decisions.[180] Following this logic, if the UNESCO Convention is used in the same way that the Rio Declaration or CITES was employed in *US—Shrimp*, it may bolster a culturally sensitive form of WTO interpretation. Nevertheless, one may need to consider the strong US opposition to reach any objective judgment as to whether to invoke the UNESCO Convention to interpret WTO norms.

8.6.4 A Procedural Link to Connect the WTO Rules and the UNESCO Convention?

Simply referring to the UNESCO Convention to interpret WTO provisions through treaty interpretation may not solve the present stalemate between culture and trade. It would be beneficial for WTO Members to set up a mechanism under which both WTO law and the UNESCO Convention could be considered by the WTO tribunals when a culture-related trade dispute emerges. To this end, WTO Members may develop some rules or, *de minimis*, a set of guidelines, in the form of a statement or an interpretation, to guide the tribunals' practice in the event that they need to deal with culture-related trade disputes.[181] In order to complement the treaty interpretation method discussed above, this section discusses how to establish a procedural interface between the UNESCO Convention and WTO rules.

The first challenge lies in finding a proper place in the WTO architecture to insert such a link. One option is to create such an interface by amending the Preamble of the WTO Agreement. In *US—Shrimp*, the Appellate Body emphasised the importance of the Preamble of the WTO Agreement, stating that it adds colour, texture and shading to the interpretation of trade agreements. The proposed addition can be realised in one of two ways: by including the goal of cultural diversity next to that of sustainable development, or by obliging Members to recognise cultural diversity as a key principle in a globalised society.[182] However, given the difficulties in amending the Preamble, a more feasible suggestion would be to insert a link to the UNESCO Convention into the body of WTO agreements in the form of a Ministerial Decision. Such a link would oblige Members to take the UNESCO Convention into account when interpreting and applying WTO rules to cultural products.

the Past: Towards De Jure Decisis in WTO Adjudication' (2001) 33 *George Washington International Law Review* 873.

[180] See Voon, above n 38, 129.

[181] See J-B Harelimana, 'Eye on Recent Trade versus Culture Decision Case, USA–China: Clash or Beautiful Friendship between the UNESCO Diversity Convention and International Economic Law?' available at http://www.multipol.org (last accessed on 18 June 2012).

[182] See CB Graber, 'The New UNESCO Convention on Cultural Diversity: A Counterbalance to the WTO?' (2006) 9 *Journal of International Economic Law* 553, 571–72.

Another solution, following financial services models and developments in WTO dispute settlement,[183] is to add a procedural rule to the DSU mandating that the WTO tribunals include one cultural expert in trade disputes involving cultural products. Such an approach would not, admittedly, constitute a direct channel for accommodating cultural concerns, but it would ensure that necessary expertise is brought to bear on analysis of the complex conflicts between trade and culture. This option may also increase the legitimacy of tribunals' decisions in such disputes.[184] In this regard, Canada goes even further, suggesting a specific Cultural Dispute Resolution Body.[185]

There is also an opportunity for the UNESCO Convention to serve as a point of reference in defining boundaries between trade and culture in future WTO negotiations or dispute settlement procedures. The boldest proposal thus far suggests delegating cultural protection in the sphere of trade to UNESCO—probably through a panel established in the WTO—which in turn could use all its resources to further its principal goals. Alternatively, UNESCO could rely on the WTO's economic expertise for a more efficient and successful implementation of its own activities.[186] I am of the view that the prospect for putting these ambitious proposals into practice in the foreseeable future is slim indeed, considering the huge gap that exists between these two institutions and their inherently conflicting missions. Nevertheless, it may be helpful to examine the role that the Intergovernmental Committee, as provided by Article 23 of the UNESCO Convention, might play in writing opinions or authoritative interpretations. If a WTO tribunal decides to seek clarification in a dispute settlement, the Committee could substantially contribute to strengthening the normative impact of the Convention.

The establishment of this link would mirror the principle of 'mutual supportiveness' between the UNESCO Convention and WTO rules. Moreover, such a proposal does not waive any existing WTO obligations; such a modest approach is relatively pragmatic. In assessing the desirability of these various options, one has to evaluate the practical difficulties that potentially attend each option, especially when a proposal requires an amendment to the existing WTO legal framework. It is very hard to secure an agreement from the required three-quarters of WTO

[183] See Graber, ibid, 571.

[184] In *Mexico—Measures Affecting Telecommunication Services*, an expert in the field of telecoms was appointed as a member of the panel. From a legal sociology perspective, enhanced isomorph between the legal system and the areas of society it seeks to regulate furthers the acceptance of such regulation. See G Teubner, 'How the Law Thinks: Towards a Constructive Epistemology of Law' (1989) 23(5) *Law & Society Review* 727, 747–49.

[185] See The Cultural Industries Sectoral Advisory Group on International Trade (SAGIT), 'An International Agreement for Cultural Diversity: A Model for Discussion, Article X (Cultural Disputes Resolution Body)' (September 2002), available at www.international.gc.ca/trade-agreements-accords../assets/../sagit_eg.pdf (last accessed on 18 June 2012).

[186] See Graber, above n 182, 574.

membership to approve a general exemption from current WTO obligations; the proposal requiring such an amendment risks failure. Opposition from the US adds more uncertainty to the possible success of such an amendment.

The consideration of a link between the WTO rules and the UNESCO Convention attempts to determine whether WTO tribunals may consider the Convention in making decisions in a culture-related trade dispute. Moreover, if a challenged measure serves legitimate cultural aims, it does not have to give way to stringent trade principles. Central to all these inquiries, I argue, is the question of whether WTO tribunals are willing to balance the interests at stake when they interpret contested trade measures. There have, thus far, been only two disputes involving cultural products decided by the WTO tribunals, so there is considerable room for speculation about the practical value of these theoretical musings. However, the analysis in this section may lead to more discussion of how cooperation and coordination between the WTO and UNESCO might reconcile the twin pursuits of market openness and cultural diversity.

8.7 THE MARGIN OF APPRECIATION DOCTRINE: RIPE FOR EXTRAPOLATION?

As discussed in Chapter 2, the margin of appreciation is one of the legal methods deliberately aimed at the reconciliation of formally disparate elements of international law. Recent years have witnessed an increased readiness on the part of international courts to embrace a margin of appreciation methodology in their decisions. This section touches upon the possibility of extrapolating this doctrine to the field of trade and the likelihood that WTO tribunals might use the doctrine to grant room for domestic cultural policy measures.

8.7.1 The Application of Margin of Appreciation Doctrine

The margin of appreciation doctrine has long been applied in different cases by courts other than the ICJ, most famously by the European Court of Human Rights (ECtHR).[187] The ECtHR has developed loosely principled standards in applying the doctrine which are critical to the enforcement of the European Human Rights Convention.[188] The European

[187] See, eg *Engel v Netherlands* (1976) 1 EHRR 647; *De Wilde v Belgium* (1971) 1 EHRR 373; *Goodwin v UK* (1996) 22 EHRR 123; *Pretty v UK* (2002) 35 EHRR 1; *Lehideux v France* (2000)30 EHRR 665.

[188] See TA O'Donnel, 'The Margin of Appreciation Doctrine: Standards in the Jurisprudence of the European Court of Human Rights' (1982) 4(4) *Human Rights Quarterly* 474, 477.

Court of Justice (ECJ) has adopted a similar approach, particularly in cases related to exception clauses.[189]

Aside from the application of the doctrine by the courts, a number of arbitral tribunals have recently adopted margin-of-appreciation-type methodology in certain cases. For example, the tribunal in *Heathrow Charges* held that the UK is entitled to a margin of appreciation in setting airport charges.[190] Similarly, in *SD Myers, Inc*, a NAFTA Chapter 11 tribunal held that a breach of NAFTA Article 1105 occurs only when it can be shown that an investor has been treated in such an unjust or arbitrary manner that the treatment can be deemed unacceptable from an international perspective. That determination must be made in light of the high measure of deference that international law generally extends to the right of domestic authorities to regulate matters within their own borders.[191] In contrast, several decisions made by the ICJ, such as *Oil Platforms*, and *Wall in the Occupied Palestinian Territory*, reflect the ICJ approach to the application of the doctrine, ie no room for discretion.[192] This seems to be out of sync with the emerging consensus on the topic.

The support for the doctrine stemming from the jurisprudence of international courts and tribunals serves as a strong indicator of the growing acknowledgement of the doctrine's utility. This readiness is partly premised on the fact that different international legal norms are endowed with different levels of inherent certainty. Some law-application exercises—ie the interactions between facts and law—are by their nature less certain than others and hinge upon intrinsically indeterminate circumstances.[193] In the cases where the application of law is inherently or inevitably uncertain, there are strong policy reasons that support recourse to the margin of appreciation doctrine.

The question of whether international courts should embrace non-intrusive standards of review under a margin-of-appreciation-type decision-making methodology is also linked to contemporary discussions on the subsidiary nature of international law, ie whether international law should embrace a centralised or decentralised organisational model.

[189] See Shany, above n 101, 927–28.

[190] Award on the first question. US/UK Arbitration concerning Heathrow Airport User Charges, 30 November 1992, ch 5, p 84, ¶2.2.6, cited in D Witten, 'The US–UK Arbitration Award Concerning Heathrow Airport User Charges' (1995) 89 *American Journal of International Law* 174, 187 note 56.

[191] *SD Myers, Inc v Canada (Partial Award)*, 40 ILM 1408, 1438 (2001). For a discussion on the suitability of the margin of appreciation doctrine to NAFTA obligations, see EM Freeman, 'Regulatory Expropriation under NAFTA Chapter 11: Some Lessons from the European Court of Human Rights' (2003) 42 *Columbia Journal of Transnational Law* 177, 211–12.

[192] The decision in *Oil Platforms and Wall in the Occupied Palestinian Territory* rejected the doctrine, explicitly or implicitly, whereas in *Avena*, the Court adopted a more hospitable attitude towards its application. See Shany, above n 101, 908.

[193] See Shany, ibid, 913.

In this regard, although the ECtHR has repeatedly stated that the margin of appreciation doctrine goes hand-in-hand with European supervision, the principle of subsidiarity links the ECtHR and the state organs of the contracting states.[194] This reflects the area of friction between international supervision and national sovereignty.

Three factors are identified as particularly pertinent to the scope of margin afforded to national authorities: the comparative advantage of local authorities, the indeterminacy of the applicable standard and the nature of the contested interests.[195] First, the courts commonly take the subject matter of protected rights as a factor in deciding the width of the margin.[196] The more fundamental the right considered, the narrower the margin is allowed. Secondly, the legitimate aims pursued by the restriction to ensure the rights in question is identified as a key factor affecting how the courts apply the doctrine.[197] In weighing community interest, the margin is generally wider when the rights of others are at stake.[198] Thirdly, the existence of similar patterns of practice or regulation in different states legitimises a wider margin of appreciation for the state that stays within that framework, and, indeed, delegitimises attempts to part ways with the framework.[199] Notwithstanding the identification of these factors in granting margin, discussion on the rationale and scope of application of the doctrine is unsatisfactory in practice. The fact remains that different courts often hold inconsistent positions towards the acceptability of the doctrine.

8.7.2 Extrapolating the Margin of Appreciation Doctrine to the Area of Trade

The application of margin of appreciation brings the status of the doctrine to the forefront of contemporary debates on the legitimacy and effectiveness of international adjudication in general, and its ability to introduce rule of law restrictions on state actions in particular. It is advocated that the doctrine is ready to be extrapolated to the global level, whether to

[194] See J Schokkenbroek, 'The Basis, Nature and Application of the Margin of Appreciation Doctrine in the Case-Law of the European Court Rights—General Report (1998) 19 *Human Rights Law Journal* 30, 35.

[195] See E Brems, 'The Margin of Appreciation Doctrine in the Case-Law of the European Court of Human Rights' (1996) 56 *Heidelberg Journal of International Law* 240, 256.

[196] See *Handyside v The United Kingdom*, Judgment of 7 December 1976, Series A No 24, (1979-80) 1 EHRR 523; see also *Sunday Times Case*, Judgment of 26 April 1979, Series A No 30, (1979-80) 2 EHRR 245.

[197] See I De La Rasilla Del Moral, 'The Increasingly Marginal Appreciation of the Margin of Appreciation Doctrine' (2006) 7(6) *German Law Journal* 612, 616.

[198] See Schokkenbroek, above n 194, 35–36.

[199] See De La Rasilla, above n 197, 617.

the human rights field[200] or, more generally, to other areas of international law.[201] With regard to human rights, the doctrine is purported to be a means of introducing flexibility in universal human rights standards in response to non-Western human rights discourse. In the same vein, the extrapolation of the doctrine to other fields of international law has been put forward on the basis of a variety of worldwide case law and a disparate array of policy arguments.[202]

The trade and culture issue presents a fundamental relationship between the need for meaningful normative guidance for free trade on the one hand and the attainment of the substantive goals of specific cultural norms on the other. The need to respect the 'margin of appreciation' of each country raises the question of whether the WTO tribunals might take into account the doctrine in culture-related trade disputes and offer its Members certain 'margin' to maintain their cultural measures. Several factors suggest an affirmative answer.

First, a variety of widely recognised policy arguments relating to the quality and legitimacy of the WTO's operation support, by and large, a flexible reading of WTO law per se. WTO agreements also offer the possibility of developing a margin of appreciation doctrine in relation to certain categories of non-trade norms governing the state conduct of its Members.[203]

Secondly, the doctrine is essentially only suitable for certain types of international norms that are intrinsically uncertain or that consciously sacrifice legal certainty for pluralism. Given the indefiniteness of the concept of 'culture', culture and cultural diversity fit into this category of uncertain norms. As a key component of human rights, cultural rights are inherently compatible with the margin of appreciation. More and more national and international cultural norms have come into being in recent years. This provides a rationale for applying the doctrine to the settlement of culture-related disputes.

Thirdly, the WTO tribunals' deferential decision-making methodology is generally compatible with the margin of appreciation doctrine in the sense that they both denote judicial restraint and acknowledge the need to address normative ambiguity in particular fields. It is not impossible that, where appropriate, WTO tribunals would be willing to offer certain margin to a specific cultural norm.

An explicit standard of review is provided in the WTO Antidumping Agreement, which requires panels to exercise deference to both legal

[200] See H Yourow, *The Margin of Appreciation Doctrine in The Dynamics of European Human Rights Jurisprudence* (1996).

[201] See Shany, above n 101, 907.

[202] See De La Rasilla, above n 197, 622.

[203] See, eg GATS, Art VI (Domestic Regulation).

and factual national determinations.[204] In a series of cases, GATT/WTO tribunals have adopted a non-intrusive standard of review towards discretionary determinations made by the national authorities of Member States.[205] For example, in *EC—Asbestos*, the Appellate Body held that WTO Members have the indisputable right to determine the level of health protection that they consider appropriate in a given situation.[206] This approach is generally consistent with the 1994 decision taken by a GATT panel in *US—Tuna*.[207] In the recent *China—Publications and Audiovisual Services*, the panel and Appellate Body both recognise that China is fully entitled to decide the level of protection of public morals within its territory, though the means used to achieve that goal must conform to China's trade obligations.

The margin of appreciation doctrine might serve as a basis for the WTO to grant certain regulatory room for domestic cultural policy measures. The acceptance of the doctrine would improve the quality and perceived legitimacy of WTO legal pronouncements, promote the accountability of the WTO tribunals' decisions by producing a more realistic match between trade law application and cultural protection practice, and encourage the application of inter-institutional comity. There are, however, a number of caveats in extrapolating the margin of appreciation doctrine to culture-related trade disputes. In Shany's opinion, national authorities enjoy comparative institutional advantages over international courts with regard to fact-finding and fact-assessing exercises, but not in relation to norm-interpretation projects. Consequently, a general margin of appreciation doctrine should mainly govern fact-intensive law-application decisions and not norm-intensive law-interpretation processes,[208]

[204] WTO, Anti-dumping Agreement, Art 17.6. For more discussion, see C-D Ehlermann amd N Lockhart, 'Standard of Review in WTO Law' (2004) 7 *Journal of International Economic Law* 491, 500.

[205] See, eg WTO, *EC—Measures Concerning Meat and Meat Products*, WT/26/AB/R (1998), ¶115 ('The standard of review . . . must reflect the balance established in that [SPS] Agreement between the jurisdictional competences conceded by the Members to the WTO and the jurisdictional competences retained by the Members for themselves'); WTO, *US—Restrictions on Imports of Cotton and Man-Made Fiber Underwear*, WT/DS24/R (1996); WTO, *Argentina—Safeguard Measure on Imports of Footwear*, WT/DS121/AB/R (2000). For more analysis, see Ehlermann and Lockhart, ibid, 493. One may link the debate over the status of the margin of appreciation doctrine to the constitutionalisation of international law: see S Zleptnig, 'The Standard of Review in WTO Law: An Analysis of Law, Legitimacy and the Distribution of Legal and Political Authority' (2002) 6 *European Integration online Papers* No 17, available at http://eiop.or.at/eiop/pdf/2002–017.pdf (last accessed on 18 June 2012), 9–10.

[206] WTO, *EC—Asbestos*, Report of Appellate Body, ¶168.

[207] GATT, *US—Restrictions on Imports of Tuna*, 33 ILM 839 (1994), ¶3.73. However, earlier GATT case law on the applicable standards of review matter is inconsistent; see, eg SP Croley and JH Jackson, 'WTO Procedures, Standard of Review, and Deference to National Governments' (1996) 90 *American Journal of International Law* 193, 196–97 (discussing the *Hatter Fur*, *Transformer Imports* and *Polyacetal Resins* cases).

[208] See Ehlermann and Lockhart, above n 204, 497.

whose ultimate elaboration should remain the exclusive province of the international judiciary.[209] This may give rise to difficulties in applying the doctrine to cultural measures because cultural norms, in most cases, do not concern fact-finding or fact-assessing exercises, but rather relate to norm interpretation, which seems to fall within the realm of WTO tribunals.

Meanwhile, it is always hard to determine the degree of judicial deference to be granted. Judicial deference varies in the light of such considerations as the importance of the interests implicated by the relevant norms, the degree of normative uncertainty, and the comparative decision-making facilities and domestic institutions. It is not hard to conceive of potential difficulties in applying the doctrine to cultural measures; this is particularly true given the conceptual uncertainties of culture and cultural diversity, and the lack of clear-cut rules. The scope of margin should also be flexible and sensitive to emerging cultural norms. Therefore, if a WTO tribunal considers granting margin to a domestic cultural policy measure, many practical difficulties would arise, which may also generate a high risk of legal uncertainty in WTO dispute settlement.

8.8 CONCLUSION

In pulling the strings discussed in this chapter together and attempting to outline an appropriate modus operandi for safeguarding cultural diversity in the era of globalisation, this chapter sets out a number of options for dealing with the confrontation between trade and culture. This chapter focuses on how to minimise the undesirable incongruence between trade rules and cultural protection. It explores, on the one hand, how domestic cultural policy and measures should be devised in compatibility with trade obligations, and, on the other hand, how the WTO could integrate cultural diversity into its agenda of progressive liberalisation. I suggest that, in designing domestic policy measures, WTO Members should take cultural concerns seriously and distinguish genuine cultural protection from disguised trade protection. At the same time, the new digital media landscape requires a readjustment of regulatory priorities and new tools to achieve cultural diversity.

As set out in Chapter 5, the WTO framework embodies this new *telos*, bringing implications that go beyond the parameters of trade. The WTO should follow this track and take further innovative steps to transform trade in cultural products into a 'positive-sum' exercise for all Members. In an effort to search for the free synergies between culture and trade at an international level, this chapter proposes two reform paths. The first is bottom-up, and relates to the clarification and improvement of the existing

[209] See Croley and Jackson, above n 207, 202.

WTO rules, including completing the GATS regulatory architecture, increasing the clarity and consistency of scheduling and commitments, and inserting rules that establish a procedural link to the UNESCO Convention. The second is top-down, and contemplates the need for a concerted global process to appropriately distribute tasks between the WTO rules and the UNESCO Convention.

This chapter proposes a number of ways through which the WTO rules might be connected with the Convention so that both trade and culture issues are considered when the WTO tribunals hear a culture-related trade dispute. Besides suggesting an evolutionary treaty interpretation method that would invoke the UNESCO Convention where appropriate, this chapter proposes a procedural link to guide the DSB's practice, such as engaging a cultural expert in resolving disputes. Furthermore, given the developments in applying the margin of appreciation doctrine, this chapter questions whether it is possible to extrapolate the doctrine to the field of trade and culture.

It is hard to predict which option will prove superior. One trend, however, seems clear: the more neutral a path is, the more likely it is to succeed. The political intensity of any measure to do with culture—and, by extension, national sovereignty—requires a neutral method to deal with the matters of trade and culture. This chapter does not purport to exhaust all potential reform proposals; I do hope, though, that the suggestions made herein can articulate a jurisprudence that meshes free trade with cultural diversity in a manner that makes it an advisable resource for authoritative decision makers encountering this perplexing issue in international law.

9

Concluding Remarks

> The flame knows no rest, for it lives in perpetual conflict between two opposite tendencies. On the one hand, it cleaves to its wick, drinking thirstily of the oil that fuels its existence. At the same time, it surges upward, seeking to tear free of its material tether.
>
> Yanki Tauber[1]

No commitment to globalisation comes free of cost. This book opens with the observation that, in the era of globalisation, 'trade linkage' problems present good examples of the fragmentation of international law. Among a wide array of concepts deemed incompatible with trade liberalisation, culture is one of the most dynamic and comprehensive, and hence the most difficult to outline. Few other areas have generated so much debate on the political, economic and institutional limits and legitimacy of regional and global integration processes.

The fragmentation of international law is caused largely by the severe interest-and-value conflicts among states. The different interests and values are often pursued under separate international legal regimes; what is justified and protected under one regime may be neglected or challenged under another. These conflicts play out in full complexity and dynamism in the trade and culture linkage. On one hand, international law recognises culture as part of universal human rights and an essential feature of human relations,[2] and cultural diversity among nation-states as a fundamental human value.[3] On the other hand, international law greatly bolsters trade liberalisation through the powerful WTO regime. Critics argue that the WTO frustrates the realisation of internationally acknowledged cultural interests and values.

Two issues lie at the heart of this debate, one a practical reality and the other a value position: the reality is the overwhelming presence of American cultural products in most countries; the value position is whether culture products should be subject to free trade principles that govern other products. The dilemma is further characterised by indivisible

[1] Y Tauber, *Beyond the Letter of the Law: A Chassidic Companion to the Ethics of the Fathers* (1995) 220.

[2] See AS Akermark, *Justifications of Minority Protection in International Law* (1997) 78–83.

[3] See I Bernier, 'Cultural Goods and Services in International Trade Law' in D Browne (ed), *The Culture/Trade Quandary: Canada's Policy Options* (1998) 146–47.

conflicts between two incommensurable public goals: the economic benefits of deeper international integration versus the social value of non-economic principles, including cultural protection and diversity.

The culture-and-trade conflict has posed considerable difficulties for a long time. These difficulties persist on present global and regional trade agendas. It is hard to decide where to sympathise in this intricate debate. The problem further manifests itself in the potential conflict between the WTO trade rules and the UNESCO instruments on cultural diversity.

International law is an instrument for universalisation and a reflection of ambivalent particularities, as well as a means of domination and a space for cooperation and emancipation.[4] Simply put, international law is part of the problem and part of the solution. Today, international law aims not only at the delimitation of sovereign spheres, but also at the reconciliation of opposed interests.[5] As such, it has begun pursuing and protecting societal interests and engaging in the regulation of social life, a mission hitherto the exclusive domain of domestic regulation.[6]

There is a pressing need for a better understanding and management of free trade and cultural diversity. Over the years, international lawyers have been struggling to address the inherent contradictions and have made a variety of proposals for the doctrinal and practical construction of a unified international legal order to mitigate the conflict. Several observations flow from this research in the challenge of relating cultural objectives with trade objectives.

First, when culture is put on the table, it prompts complex discussions on the relationship between the economic and non-economic value of products—that is, the value attributed to those products that does not have an assigned price. The disagreements over cultural diversity and free trade centre around the understanding of how cultural products can fit into either global or regional trade regimes. International trade agendas and regional economic agreements present major challenges to the survival of cultural diversity. The key to addressing this issue is to acknowledge that cultural products have cultural as well as commercial value.[7] I subscribe to the view that culture is not just about the creation of a commodity or a service to be traded, promoted or invested in, but rather must include concern for the sustainable diversity of cultural expression. Cultural products construct and convey cultural values, produce and

[4] See E Jouannet, 'Universalism and Imperialism: The True–False Paradox of International Law?' (2007) 18 *European Journal of International Law* 379, 406.

[5] See I Feichtner, 'The Waiver Power of the WTO: Opening the WTO for Political Debate on the Reconciliation of Competing Interests' (2009) 20 *European Journal of International Law* 615, 615.

[6] See J Weiler and L Motoc, 'Taking Democracy Seriously: The Normative Challenge to the International System' in Griller, S (ed), *International Economic Governance and Non-Economic Concerns: New Challenges for the International Legal Order* (2003), 47, 63.

[7] See T Voon, *Cultural Products and the World Trade Organization* (2007) XXXI.

represent cultural identity, and contribute to social cohesion; at the same time, they constitute a key sector in national economies and generate enormous export interests.

Secondly, while there is a concern that preserving the legal primacy of free trade may eliminate a good measure of cultural diversity,[8] the same logic exists that the desire to protect local culture may undermine the wisdom of trade liberalisation.[9] It is worth mentioning that free trade and cultural protection are, in this context, shorthand for the two sides of a debate in which arguments are advanced with an unusual degree of high-handed self-righteousness. The free traders are not necessarily interested in creating more choice for consumers, but rather tend to promote economic liberalisation. The culture sector, on the contrary, has a strong profit motivation of its own for creating red tape for foreign competitors. This partly explains why the international community generally does not support practices that implicate trade with cultural concerns. By contrast, gender norms and roles are recognised to be intrinsic to national culture and are accorded great deference.[10] As a result, retaining a formal sovereign right to develop cultural policies is no longer adequate if programme and structural measures put in place by a country are constantly assessed (or challenged) against the standards set for trade in goods or services.[11]

Thirdly, despite the importance of preserving national cultures through appropriate measures, cultures are encouraged to grow and flourish through exchange and interaction with other cultures.[12] A strong and viable domestic cultural base is the primary goal, and the domestic market remains the primary audience for products supported through domestic cultural policies. It is equally important that free trade not be cast as the villain in the process of cultural exchange. Economic growth spurred by trade liberalisation tends to favour social conditions in a domestic setting, while a domestic regulatory reform may boost trade by eliminating unnecessary barriers. Trade conducted according to multilateral rules has been a major contributor not only to the enormous expansion of the world economy but also to the diminution of international conflict. Thus, reform of the current trading system should be done with care in order to preserve the system's strengths while responding to legitimate cultural concerns. Meanwhile, trade challenges are not the only way to examine the rationale for cultural policies and national cultural objectives.

[8] See J Chen, 'Globalization and Its Losers' (2000) 9 *Minnesota Journal of Global Trade* 157, 214.

[9] See Voon, above n 7, 11.

[10] See JR Paul, 'Cultural Resistance to Global Governance' (2000) 22 *Michigan Journal of International Law* 1, 2–3.

[11] See V Rabinovitch, 'The Social and Economic Rationales for Domestic Cultural Policies' in D Browne (ed), *The Culture/Trade Quandary: Canada's Policy Options* (1998) 44.

[12] See Voon, above n 7, 11–12.

Carefully guiding the process of globalisation-with-a-human-face always remains a challenging task. Having acknowledged the collision of cultural concerns and trade values, this book seeks to contribute to the reconciliation of culture and trade by utilising a systematic approach to examine the culture and trade quandary from both exogenous and endogenous perspectives, including the duality of cultural products, the evolution of the new media environment and the dual track of international legislations. It continues with a trend analysis of trade in cultural products from the theoretical, legislative and judicial perspectives, trying to offer an understanding of the past dichotomy, current quandary and need for future synergy between culture and trade.

Free trade and cultural diversity do not stand in complete opposition. Neither the 'pro-trade' nor the 'pro-culture' option reflects a genuine appreciation of culture and trade issues, or prescribes a solution to this quandary. Consequently, it is wrong to assume that either free trade or cultural exception will finally 'win'. Both the global flow of cultural products and a variety of cultural protection should continue. With this in mind, I have proposed a jurisprudence for breaking the culture and trade impasse, featuring a balanced framework that could guarantee market access for cultural products on the one hand, and the cultural rights of a nation and its citizens and diversity of consumer choice on the other. The solution is based on the premise that genuine cultural expressions should be protected from unbridled trade disciplines on the one hand, while cultures can reap benefits from trade on the other.

The issue of culture and trade has now acquired prime strategic significance. To adapt a well-known declaration, development will be cultural in the twenty-first century, or it will not be at all.[13] To echo those who advocate the universal history of cultures as a rich source that enhances our understanding of trade,[14] I suggest that there should be a synergy between culture and trade. Further, the potentially synergistic aspect of the interface of trade and culture calls for a coherent response in the spirit of mutual complementarity.

The solution to the problems arising from trade in cultural products can only be successful if the underlying relationship between the different countries is less polarised than the dynamics reflected in the current rhetorical exchanges.[15] A pragmatic approach featuring a compromise and an operational middle route holds the key to devising the mechanism under which the values of both trade and culture are respected and

[13] See UNESCO, 'Our Creative Diversity: Report of the World Commission on Culture and Development' (finalised by J Pérez de Cuéllar, 1995), Executive Summary, 232.

[14] See, eg J Weiler (ed), *The EU, the WTO and the NAFTA: Towards a Common Law of International Trade* (2000) 24.

[15] See K Acheson and C Maule, *Much Ado about Culture: North American Trade Disputes* (1999) 4.

maintained through coordination and cooperation. I hold that, in order to ensure a sustainable multilateral trading system in the long term, we must develop a moderate protection for cultural diversity, rather than a blanket exemption of cultural products from trade disciplines.

To conclude, the basic melody of this book calls for transforming the interaction of culture and trade from a tenor of dichotomy to one of quandary, and then, eventually, to one of synergy. The possible synergy between culture and trade would play a consequential role in the life of both individual and nation; it should, therefore, be incorporated into contemporary international legal considerations. I am, however, fully aware of the complexity of the negotiation process, and hold no fantasy that there will be a sudden substantial advancement in any of the discussed aspects. More focused research is needed to clarify all of the options, weigh their associated costs and benefits, and prioritise their negotiation in order to awaken the interest of the policy makers and advance concrete and feasible solutions. The key challenge, I should emphasise here, is to move from principle to practice. Notwithstanding the difficulties in putting cultural objectives into a trade framework, this book ends on a note of vacillating optimism that a reformed policy and corresponding legal framework could end the battle between trade and culture.

Bibliography

Acheson, K and Maule, C, *Much Ado about Culture: North American Trade Disputes* (Ann Arbor, University of Michigan Press, 1999).

Acheson, K and Maule, C, 'Convention on Cultural Diversity' (2004) 28 *Journal of Cultural Economics* 243.

Acheson, K and Maule, C, 'Canada's Audio-visual Policies: Impact on Trade' in P Guerrieri et al (eds), *Cultural Diversity and International Economic Integration: The Global Governance of the Audio-Visual Sector* (Cheltenham, Edward Elgar Publishing, 2005).

Ackerman, BA, 'The Storrs Lectures: Discovering the Constitution'(1984) 93 *Yale Law Journal* 1013.

Addis, A, 'Who's Afraid of Foreigners? The Restrictions on Alien Ownership of Electronic Media' (2000) 32 *Columbian Human Rights Law Review* 133.

Adlung, R, 'Services Negotiations in the Doha Round: Lost in Flexibility?' (2006) 9 *Journal of International Economic Law* 865.

Adorno, TW and Bernstein, JM, *The Culture Industry: Selected Essays on Mass Culture*, 2nd edn (London, Routledge, 2001).

Adorno, TW and Horkheimer, M. 'The Culture Industry: Enlightenment as Mass Deception' in TW Adorno and M Horkheimer (eds), *Dialectic of Enlightenment* (1997) 120–67.

Agdomar, M, 'Removing the Greek from Feta and Adding Korel to Champagne: The Paradox of Geographical Indications in International Law' (2008) 18 *Fordham Intellectual Property, Media & Entertainment Law Journal* 541.

Akande, D and Williams, S, 'International Adjudication on National Security Issues: What Role for the WTO?' (2003) 43 *Virginia Journal of International Law* 365.

Akermark, AS, *Justifications of Minority Protection in International Law* (Leiden, Martinus Nijhoff, 1997).

Alston, P, 'Resisting the Merger and Acquisition of Human Rights by Trade Law: A Reply to Petersmann' (2002)13(4) *European Journal of International Law* 815.

Alvarez, J, *International Organizations as Lawmakers* (New York, Oxford University Press, 2005).

Alvarez-Jiménez, A, 'The WTO Appellate Body's Exercise of Judicial Economy' (2009) 12 *Journal of International Economic Law* 393.

Andreano, S and Iapadre, PL, 'Audiovisual Policies and International Trade: The Case of Italy' in P Guerrieri et al (eds), *Cultural Diversity and International Economic Integration: The Global Governance of the Audio-Visual Sector* (Cheltenham, Edward Elgar Publishing, 2005).

Annan, K, 'Laying the Foundations of a Fair and Free World Trade System' in GP Sampson (ed), *The Role of the World Trade Organization in Global Governance* (Tokyo, United Nations University Press, 2001).

Aolain, FN, 'The Emergency of Diversity: Differences in Human Rights Jurisprudence' (1995) 19 *Fordham International Law Journal* 101.

Arnold, M, *Culture and Anarchy* (London, Routledge, 1869/1994).

Asmal, K, 'What the Convention Means to Me' in N Obuljen and J Smiers (eds), *UNESCO's Convention on the Protection and Promotion of the Diversity of Cultural Expressions: Making It Work* (Zagreb, Institute for International Relations, 2006).

Baker, CE, 'Turner Broadcasting: Content-Based Regulation of Persons and Presses' in DJ Hutchinson et al (eds), *The Supreme Court Review* (Chicago, University of Chicago Press, 1994).

Baker, CE, 'An Economic Critique of Free Trade in Media Products' (2000) 78 *North Carolina Law Review* 1357.

Baker Fox, A, *The Canada–United States Free Trade Agreement and the Cultural Industries* (distributed by the Institute for the Study of Diplomacy, Pew Case Study Center, Georgetown University, 1988).

Barfield, T (ed), *The Dictionary Anthropology* 98 (Boston, MA, Wiley, 1997).

Baudin, L, *Free Trade and Peace* (Geneva, International Institute of Intellectual Co-operation, League of Nations, 1939).

Baumol, WJ, 'Applied Welfare Economics' in R Towse, (ed), *A Handbook of Cultural Economics* (Cheltenham, Edward Elgar Publishing, 2003).

Beale, A, 'Communication Policy, Media Industries, and Globalization: Identifying a Policy Hierarchy' in D Crane et al (eds), *Global Culture: Media, Arts Policy, and Globalization* (London, Routledge, 2002).

Benvenisti, E, 'Margin of Appreciation, Consensus, and Universal Standards' (1999) 31 *New York University Journal of International Law & Policy* 843.

Beppu, D, 'When Cultural Value Justifies Protection: Interpreting the Language of the GATT to Find a Limited Cultural Exception to the National Treatment Principle' (2008) 29 *Cardozo Law Review* 1765.

Berg, GC, 'An Economic Interpretation of "like Products"' (1996) 30 *Journal of World Trade* 195.

Bernhart, R et al (eds), *Encyclopedia of Public International Law* (Amsterdam, North-Holland, 1992).

Bernier, I, 'Cultural Goods and Services in International Trade Law' in D Browne (ed), *The Culture/Trade Quandary: Canada's Policy Options* (Ottawa, Center for Trade Policy and Law, 1998).

Bernier, I and Fabri, HR, 'Implementing the Convention' in N Obuljen and J Smiers (eds), *UNESCO's Convention on the Protection and Promotion of the Diversity of Cultural Expressions: Making It Work* (Zagreb, Institute for International Relations, 2006).

Beviglia-Zampetti, A, 'WTO Rules in the Audiovisual Sector' in P Guerrieri et al (eds), *Cultural Diversity and International Economic Integration: The Global Governance of the Audio-Visual Sector* (Cheltenham, Edward Elgar Publishing, 2005).

Bhagwati, CJ, *In Defense of Globalization* (Oxford, Oxford University Press, 2004).

Bhagwati, CJ, *The Wind of the Hundred Days: How Washington Mismanaged Globalization* (Cambridge, MA, The MIT Press, 2000).

Bhala, R, 'The Myth about Stare Decisis and International Trade Law' (1999) 14 *American University International Law Review* 845.

Bhala, R, 'The Precedent Setters: De Facto Stare Decisis in WTO Adjudication' (1999) 9 *Journal of International Law & Policy* 1.

Bhala, R, *International Trade Law: Theory and Practice*, 2nd edn (New York, Lexis Pub, 2001).

Bhala, R, 'The Power of the Past: Towards De Jure Decisis in WTO Adjudication' (2001) 33 *George Washington International Law Review* 873.

Bierman, L et al, 'The General Agreement on Tariffs and Trade from a Market Perspective' (1996) 17 *University of Pennsylvania Journal of International Economic Law* 821.

Binder, G, 'Cultural Relativism and Cultural Imperialism in Human Rights Law' (1999) 5 *Buffalo Human Rights Law Review* 211.

Blackhurst, R and Henderson, D, 'Regional Integration Agreements, World Integration and the GATT' in K Anderson and R Blackhurst (eds), *Regional Integration and the Global Trading System* (Hemel Hempstead, Harvester Wheatsheaf, 1993).

Bogart, L, *Commercial Culture: The Media System and the Public Interest* (Oxford University Press, 1995).

Bogdandy, A von, 'The European Union as Situation, Executive, and Promoter of the International Law of Cultural Diversity—Elements of a Beautiful Friendship' (2008) 19 *European Journal of International Law* 241.

Borofsky, R, 'Cultural Possibilities' in UNESCO, *World Culture Report* (1998) 64 .

Boryskavich, K and Bowler, A, 'Trade and Culture: Hollywood North: Tax Incentives and the Film Industry in Canada' (2002) 2 *Asper Review of International Business & Trade Law* 25.

Bosland, J, 'The Culture of Trade Marks: An Alternative Cultural Theory Perspective' (2005) 10(2) *Media & Arts Law Review* 99.

Bozeman, A, *Strategic Intelligence and Statecraft* (Brassey's, 1992).

Braun, M and Parker, L, 'Trade in Culture: Consumable Product or Cherished Articulation of a Nation's Soul?' (1993) 22 *Denver Journal of International Law and Policy* 155.

Brems, E, 'The Margin of Appreciation Doctrine in the Case-Law of the European Court of Human Rights' (1996) 56 *Heidelberg Journal of International Law* 240.

Brewer, TL and Young, S, 'The Multilateral Agenda for Foreign Direct Investment: Problems, Principles, and Priorities for Negotiations at the OECD and WTO', *World Competition*, June 1995.

Brilmayer, L, *American Hegemony—Political Morality in a One-Superpower World* (New Haven, CT, Yale University Press, 1994).

Brooks, E, 'Cultural Imperialism vs Cultural Protectionism: Hollywood's Response to UNESCO Efforts to Promote Cultural Diversity' (2006) 5 *Journal of International Business & Law* 112.

Broude, T, 'Taking "Trade and Culture" Seriously: Geographical Indications and Cultural Protection in WTO Law' (2005) 26 *University of Pennsylvania Journal of International Economic Law* 623.

Broude, T, 'Principles of Normative Integration and the Allocation of International Authority: The WTO, The Vienna Convention on the Law of Treaties, and the Rio Declaration' (2008) 6 *Loyola University of Chicago International Law Review* 173.

Brown, C, *Sovereignty, Rights and Justice: International Political Theory Today* (Australia, Polity Press, 2002).

Browne, D (ed), *The Culture/Trade Quandary: Canada's Policy Options* (Ottawa, Center for Trade Policy and Law, 1998).

Bruner, CM, 'Culture, Sovereignty, and Hollywood: UNESCO and the Future of Trade in Cultural Products' (2008) 40 *International Law and Politics* 351.

Burri-Nenova, M, 'The Law of the World Trade Organization and the Communications Law of the European Community: On a Path of Harmony or Discord?' 41 *Journal of World Trade* 833 (2007).

Burri-Nenova, M, 'The New Audiovisual Media Services Directive: Television without Frontiers, Television without Cultural Diversity' (2007) 44 *Common Market Law Review* 1689.

Burri-Nenova, M, 'Trade versus Culture in the Digital Environment: An Old Conflict in Need of a New Definition' (2009) 12(1) *Journal of International Economic Law* 7.

Burt, EM, 'Developing Countries and the Framework for Negotiations of Foreign Direct Investment in the World Trade Organization' (1997) 12 *American University Journal of International Law & Policy* 1015.

Cahn, S and Schimmel, D, 'The Cultural Exception: Does it Exist in GATT and GATS Frameworks? How Does it Affect or is it Affected by the Agreement on TRIPS?' (1997) 15 *Cardozo Arts & Entertainments Law Journal* 281.

Cairncross, F, *The Death of Distance: How the Communications Revolution will Change our Life* (Cambridge, MA, Harvard Business School Press, 1997).

Calaguas, MJ, 'A Rose by Any Other Name: Protecting Geographical Indications for Wines and Spirits in China' (2006) 3 *Loyola University of Chicago International Review* 257.

Canclini NG, 'Cultural Policy Options in the Context of Globalization' in UNESCO, *World Culture Report* (Paris, 1998).

Carmody, C, 'When "Cultural Identity Was Not At Issue": Thinking about Canada—Certain Measures Concerning Periodicals' (1999) 30 *Law & Policy International Business* 231.

Carmody, C, 'Creating "Shelf Space": NAFTA's Experience with Cultural Protection and Its Relevance for the WTO' (2007) 2(2) *Asian Journal of WTO & International Health Law and Policy* 287.

Carozza, PG, 'Subsidiarity as a Structural Principle of International Human Rights Law' (2003) 97 *American Journal of International Law* 38.

Carrington, PD, 'Diversity!' [1992] *Utah Law Review* 1105.

Chan-Tibergien, J, 'Cultural Diversity as Resistance to Neoliberal Globalization: The Emergence of a Global Movement and Convention' (2006) *Journal of Cultural Economics* 52.

Chao, TW, 'GATT's Cultural Exemption of Audiovisual Trade: The United States May Have Lost the Battle but not the War' (1996) 17 *University of Pennsylvania Journal of International Economic Law* 1127.

Chen, J, 'Globalization and Its Losers' (2000) 9 *Minnesota Journal of Global Trade* 157.

Cho, S, *Free Markets and Social Regulation: A Reform Agenda of the Global Trading System* (London, Kluwer Law International, 2003).

Choi, W-M, *'Like Products' in International Trade Law: Towards a Consistent GATT/WTO Jurisprudence* (Oxford, Oxford University Press, 2003).

Civic, MA, 'A Comparative Analysis of International and Chinese Human Rights Law—Universality Versus Cultural Relativism' (1995–96) 2 *Buffalo Journal of International Law* 285.

Emmanuel Cocq and P Messerlin, 'French Audio-Visual Policy: Impact and Compatibility with Trade Negotiations' in P Guerrieri et al (eds), *Cultural Diversity and International Economic Integration: The Global Governance of the Audio-Visual Sector* (Cheltenham, Edward Elgar Publishing, 2005).

Collins, R, 'The Screening of Jacques Tati: Broadcasting and Cultural Identity in The European Community' (1993) 11 *Cardozo Arts & Entertainments Law Journal* 361.

Cowen, T, *In Praise of Commercial Culture* (Cambridge, MA, Harvard University Press, 1998).

Cowen, T, *Creative Destruction: How Globalization is Changing the World's Cultures* (Princeton, NJ, Princeton University Press, 2002).

Crawford, J (ed), *The Rights of Peoples* (Oxford, Clarendon Press, 1992).

Croley, SP and Jackson, JH, 'WTO Procedures, Standard of Review, and Deference to National Governments' (1996) 90 *American Journal of International Law* 193.

Cunningham, CB, 'In Defense of Member State Culture: The Unrealized Potential of Article 151(4) of the EC Treaty and the Consequences for EC Cultural Policy' (2001) 34 *Cornell International Law Journal* 119.

Curtis, J, 'Culture and the Digital Copyright Cinema: Assessing the International Regulatory System of the Music Industry in Relation to Cultural Diversity' (2006) 13(1) *International Journal of Cultural Property* 59.

De La Rasilla, I, 'The Increasingly Marginal Appreciation of the Margin of Appreciation Doctrine' (2006) 7(6) *German Law Journal* 612.

Demaret, P, 'The Metamorphoses of the GATT: From the Havana Charter to the World Trade Organization' (1995) 34 *Columbia Journal of Transnational Law* 123.

Devlin, J, 'Canada and International Trade in Culture: Beyond National Interests' (2004) 14 *Minnesota Journal of Global Trade* 177.

Diebold, NF, 'The Morals and Order Exception in WTO Law: Balancing the Toothless Tiger and the Undermining Mole' (2008) 11 *Journal of International Economic Law* 43.

Diebold, NF, *Non-discrimination in International Trade in Services: Likeness in WTO/GATS* (Cambridge, Cambridge University Press, 2010).

Donald, S, Keane, M and Hong, Y (eds), *Media in China: Consumption, Content, and Crisis* (RoutledgeCurzon, 2002).

Donaldson, JD, 'Television without Frontiers: The Continuing Tension between Liberal Free Trade and European Cultural Integrity' (1996) 20 *Fordham International Law Journal* 90.

Donnelly, J, 'Cultural Relativism and Universal Human Rights' (1984) 6(4) *Human Rights Quarterly* 400.

Dowler, K, 'The Cultural Industries Policy Apparatus' in M Dorland (ed), *The Cultural Industries in Canada: Problems, Policies and Prospects* (Toronto, James Lorimer & Co, 1996).

Doyle, G and Hibberd, M, 'The Case of the UK Audiovisual System' in P Guerrieri et al (eds), *Cultural Diversity and International Economic Integration: The Global Governance of the Audio-Visual Sector* (Cheltenham, Edward Elgar Publishing, 2005).

Drake, M and Nicolaidis, K, 'Global Electronic Commerce and GATS: The Millennium Round and Beyond' in P Sauvé and R Stern (eds), *GATS 2000: New Directions in Services Trade Liberalization* (Washington, DC, The Brookings Institution Press, 2000).

Drijber, BJ, 'The Revised Television without Frontiers Directive: Is it Fit for the Next Century?' (1999) 36 *Common Market Law Review* 87.

Drimmer, J, 'Hate Property: A Substantive Limitation for America's Cultural Property Laws' (1998) 65 *Tennessee Law Review* 691.

DSB, 'Minutes of the Meeting Held on 19 November 2007', WT/DSB/M/242 (11 February 2008).

Eberschlag, R, 'Culture Clash: Canadian Periodical Policies and the World Trade Organization' (1998) 26 *Manchester Law Journal* 65.

Eckert, A, 'The Global and Local: Reconciling Universal Human Rights and Cultural Diversity' (2002) 2(2) *Human Rights & Human Welfare* 2.

Ehlermann, C-D, 'Six Years on the Bench of the "World Trade Court"' in F Ortino and E-U Petersmann (eds), *The WTO Dispute Settlement System 1995–2003* (London, Kluwer Law International, 2004).

Ehlermann, C-D and Lockhart, N, 'Standard of Review in WTO Law' (2004) 7 *Journal of International Economic Law* 491.

Eide, A, 'Cultural Rights as Individual Rights' in Eide, A, et al (eds), *Economic Social and Cultural Rights*, 2nd edn (London, Kluwer Law International, 2001).

Endelman, HM, 'Regulating Culture: Controversy in the GATT Accord' (1995) 18 *Boston College International & Competition Law Review* 443.

European Commission, 'Interim Report Realities and Tendencies in European Television: Perspectives and Opinions', COM(1983) 229 final (25 May 1983).

European Commission, 'Television without Frontiers: Green Paper on the Establishment of the Common Market for Broadcasting, Especially by Satellite and Cable', COM(84) 300 (May 1984).

European Commission, 'Green Paper on the Development of A Common Market for Telecommunication Services and Equipment', COM(1987) 290 final (30 June 1987).

European Commission, 'Communication to the Council and the European Parliament, The EU Approach to the WTO Millennium Round', COM(1999) 331 final (8 July 1999).

European Commission, 'Fourth Report on the Application of Directive 89/552/EEC Television without Frontiers', COM(2002) 778 final (6 January 6 2003).

European Commission, 'The Commission Proposal for a Modernization of the Television without Frontiers Directive', MEMO/05/475 (13 December 2005).

European Commission, 'Commission Communication on a European Agenda for Culture in a Globalizing World', COM(2007) 242 final (10 May 2007).

European Commission, 'Inventory of Community Actions in the Field of Culture, Accompanying Document to the Communication on a European Agenda for Culture in A Globalizing World', SEC(2007) 570 (10 May 2007).

Ezetah, C, 'Patterns of an Emergent World Trade Organization Legalism: What Implications for NAFTA Cultural Exemption?' (1998) 21(5) *World Competition* 93.

Fabri, HR, 'Reflections on Possible Future Legal Implications of the Convention' in N Obuljen and J Smiers (eds), *UNESCO's Convention on the Protection and Promotion of the Diversity of Cultural Expressions: Making It Work* (Zagreb, Institute for International Relations, 2006).

Falkenberg, KF. 'The Audio-Visual Sector' in JHJ Bourgeois et al (eds), *The Uruguay Round Results: A European Lawyer's Perspective* (Oxford, Peter Lang, 1999).

Fazeskas, A de, 'Free Trade and Culture: An Alternative Approach' (1993) 2 *Dalhousie Journal of Legal Studies* 141.

Feddersen, C, 'Focusing on Substantive Law in International Economic Relations: The Public Morals of GATT's Article XX(a) and "Conventional" Rules of Interpretation' (1998) 7 *Minnesota Journal of Global Trade* 75.

Feichtner, I, 'The Waiver Power of the WTO: Opening the WTO for Political Debate on the Reconciliation of Competing Interests' (2009) 20 *European Journal of International Law* 615.

Feigenbaum, HB, *Globalization and Cultural Diplomacy* (Center for Arts and Culture Issue Paper, 2001).

Feigenbaum, HB, 'Public Policy and the Private Sector in Audiovisual Industries' (2002), 49 *UCLA Law Review* 1767.

Feingold, CS, 'The Doctrine of Margin of Appreciation and the European Convention of Human Rights' (1977) 53 *Notre Dame Law Review* 90.

Filipek, J, 'Culture Quotas, The Trade Controversy over the European Community's Broadcasting Directive' (1992) 28 *Stanford Journal of International Law* 323.

Fischer-Lescano, A and Teubner, G, 'Regime-Collisions: The Vain Search for Legal Unity in the Fragmentation of Global Law' (2004) 25 *Michigan Journal of International Law* 999.

Fitzmaurice, GG, 'The Law and Procedure of the International Court of Justice: Treaty Interpretation and Certain other Treaty Points' (1951) 28 *British Yearbook of International Law* 1.

Fitzmaurice, GG, 'The Law and Procedure of the International Court of Justice 1951–4: Treaty Interpretation and Other Treaty Points' (1957) 33 *British Yearbook of International Law* 203.

Footer, ME and Graber, CB, 'Trade Liberalization and Cultural Policy' (2000) 3 *Journal of International Economic Law* 115.

Forrest, A, 'Can Community Support Measures Have A Decisive Impact on European Film and Television Production?' (1996) 8 *European Business Journal* 36.

Franck, TM, *The Power of Legitimacy among Nations* (New York, Oxford University Press, 1990).

Franck, T, 'The Legal-Culture and the Culture-Culture' (1999) 93 *American Society for International Law Proceedings* 271.

Francioni, F, 'Beyond State Sovereignty: The Protection of Cultural Heritage As A Shared Interest of Humanity' (2004), 25 *Michigan Journal of International Law* 1209.

Francois, P and van Ypersele, T, 'On the Protection of Cultural Goods' (2002) 56 *Journal of International Economics* 359.

Freeman, EM, 'Regulatory Expropriation under NAFTA Chapter 11: Some Lessons from the European Court of Human Rights' (2003) 42 *Columbia Journal of Transnational Law* 177.

Friedman, J, *Cultural Identity and Global Process* (London, Sage Publications, 1994).

Friedman, TL, *The Lexus and the O Tree: Understanding Globalization* (New York, Harper Collins Publishers, 1999).

Galperin, H, 'Cultural Industries in the Age of Free Trade Agreements' (1999) 24 *Canadian Journal of Communications* 49.

Galt, FS, 'The Life, Death, and Rebirth of the "Cultural Exception" in the Multilateral Trading System: An Evolutionary Analysis of Cultural Protection and Intervention in the Face of American Pop Culture's Hegemony' (2004) 3 *Washington University Global Studies Law Review* 909.

Gao, H, 'The Mighty Pen, the Almighty Dollar, and the Holy Hammer and Sickle: An Examination of the Conflict between Trade Liberalization and Domestic Cultural Policy with Special Regard to the Recent Dispute between the United States and China on Restrictions on Certain Cultural Products' (2007) 2 *Asian Journal of WTO & International Health Law & Policy* 313.

Garnham, N, *Capitalism and Communication* (London, Sage Publications, 1990).

Garrett, LL, 'Commerce versus Culture: The Battle between the United States and the European Union Over Audiovisual Trade Policies' (1994) 19 *North Carolina Journal of International Law and Commercial Regulation* 553.

Germann, C, 'Towards a Global Cultural Contract to Counter Trade Related Cultural Determination' in N Obuljen and J Smiers (eds), *UNESCO's Convention on the Protection and Promotion of the Diversity of Cultural Expressions: Making It Work* (Zagreb, Institute for International Relations, 2006).

Ghoneim, AF, 'The Audiovisual Sector in Egypt' in P Guerrieri et al (eds), *Cultural Diversity and International Economic Integration: The Global Governance of the Audio-Visual Sector* (Cheltenham, Edward Elgar Publishing, 2005).

Gibbons, T, 'The Impact of Regulatory Competition on Measures to Promote Pluralism and Cultural Diversity in the Audiovisual Sector' (2006–07) 9 *Cambridge Yearbook of European Legal Studies* 239.

Gibson, J, *Community Resources: Intellectual Property, International Trade and Protection of Traditional Knowledge* (London, Ashgate, 2005).

Globerman, S, *Culture, Governments, and Markets: Public Policy and the Cultural Industries* (Vancouver BC, The Fraser Institute, 1987).

Goldberg, D et al, *EC Media Law and Policy* (Oxford, Oxford University Press, 1998).

Goldsman, JL and Posner, E, 'A Theory of Customary International Law' (1999) 66 *University of Chicago Law Review* 1113.

Goodenough, OR, 'Defending the Imaginary to the Death? Free Trade, National Identity, and Canada's Cultural Preoccupation' (1998) 15 *Arizona Journal of International and Comparative Law* 203.

Gordon, R, 'Symposium: Critical Race Theory and International Law: Convergence and Divergence Foreword' (2000) 45 *Williamette Law Review* 827.

Goulet, D, 'The Evolving Nature of Development in the Light of Globalization' (2004) 6 *Journal of Law & Social Challenges* 1.

Graber, CB et al (eds), *Free Trade versus Cultural Diversity: WTO Negotiations in the Field of Audiovisual Services* (Zürich, Schulthess, 2004).

Graber, CB, 'The New UNESCO Convention on Cultural Diversity: A Counterbalance to the WTO?' (2006) 9 *Journal of International Economic Law* 553.

Granastein, JL, *Yankees Go Home: Canadians and Anti-Americanism* (Toronto, Harper Collins Publisher, 1996).

Grant, JM, '"Jurassic" Trade Disputes: The Exclusion of the Audiovisual Sector from the GATT' (1995) 70 *Indiana Law Journal* 1333.

Grant, PS and Wood, C, *Blockbusters and Trade Wars: Popular Culture in a Globalized World* (Vancouver, Douglas & McIntyre, 2004).

Gray, J, *False Dawn: The Delusions of Global Capitalism* (London, Granta Books, 1998).

Griffiths, F, *Strong and Free: Canada and the New Sovereignty* (Toronto, Stoddart, 1996).

Grossberg, L, 'Identity and Cultural Studies: Is That All There Is?' in ST Huall and P Du Gay (eds), *Questions of Cultural Identity* (London, Sage Publications, 1996) 87–107.

Guerrieri, P et al (eds), *Cultural Diversity and International Economic Integration: The Global Governance of the Audio-Visual Sector* (Cheltenham, Edward Elgar Publishing, 2005).

Hadjioannou, M, 'The International Human Right to Culture: Reclamation of the Cultural Identities of Indigenous Peoples under International Law' (2005) 8 *Chapman Law Review* 201.

Hafner, G, 'Risk Ensuring from Fragmentation of International Law', ILC Report on the Work of its 52nd session, General Assembly Official Records, 56th session, supplement No 10 (A/55/10), 321–29.

Hahn, M, 'A Clash of Cultures? The UNESCO Diversity Convention and International Trade Law' (2006) 9 *Journal of International Economic Law* 515.

Hansen, P, 'The Cultural Short Cut: A Road to Exclusion? Notes on Identity Politics in the European Union' in J Gundara and Sidney Jacobs (eds), *Intercultural Europe—Diversity and Social Policy* (London, Ashgate, 2000).

Harpen, RL Van, 'Mamas, Don't Let Your Babies Grow Up to Be Cowboys: Reconciling Trade and Cultural Independence' (1995) 4 *Minnesota Journal of Global Trade* 165.

Harper, MA, 'Comment, International Protection of IP Rights in the 1990's: Will Trade Barriers and Pirating Practices in the Audiovisual Industry Continue?' (1994) 25 *California Western International Law Journal* 153.

Harrison, LE and Huntington, SP (eds), *Culture Matters: How Values Shape Human Progress* (New York, Basic Books, 2000).

Hauk, R, 'NAFTA's Chapter 11: Lessons Learned from the UPS Case' (2008) 8 *Asper Review of International Business & Trade Law* 125.

Heiberg, CE, 'American Films in China: An Analysis of China's Intellectual Property Record and Reconsideration of Cultural Trade Exceptions Amidst Rampant Piracy' (2006) 15 *Minnesota Journal of International Law* 219.

Held, D and A McGrew (eds), *Global Transformations: Politics, Economics and Culture* (Palo Alto, CA, Stanford University Press, 1999).

Henkin, L, 'That "S" Word: Sovereignty, and Globalization, and Human Rights, et cetera' (1999) 68 *Fordham Law Review* 1.

Herman, ES and Chomsky, N, *Manufacturing Consent: The Political Economy of the Mass Media* (New York, Pantheon Books, 1988).

Herold, A, 'Between Art and Commerce: Constitutional Contradictions within the Framework of the EU Film Policy' in F Palermo and GN Toggenburg (eds), *European Constitutional Values and Cultural Diversity* (Berlin, EURAC Research, Europäische Akademie, 2003).

Hestermeyer, H, *Human Rights and the WTO, the Case of Patents and Access to Medicines* (Oxford, Oxford University Press, 2007).

Higgins, TE, 'Anti-Essentialism, Relativism, and Human Rights' (1996) 19 *Harvard Women's Law Journal* 89.

Holt, KN, 'NAFTA's Cultural Industries Exemption: Its Constitutionality and the Australian Project Blue Sky Model for Free Trade of Content in North America' (2002–03) 9 *Southwestern Journal of Law and Trade in the Americas* 459.

Horst, N, 'Creating an Ever Closer Union: The European Court of Justice and the Threat to Cultural Diversity' (2008) 47 *Columbian Journal of Transnational Law* 165.

Hoskins, C et al, 'Television and Film in a Freer International Trade Environment: US Dominance and Canadian Responses' in EG McAnany and KT Williams (eds), *Mass Media and Free Trade: NAFTA and Cultural Industries* (Austin, University of Texas Press, 1996).

Howse, R, 'Adjudicative Legitimacy and Treaty Interpretation in International Trade Law: The Early Years of WTO Jurisprudence' in JHH Weiler (ed), *The EU, the WTO and the NAFTA: Towards a Common Law of International Trade* (New York, Oxford University Press USA, 2000).

Howse, R, 'Managing the Interface between International Trade Law and the Regulatory State: What Lessons Should (or Should Not) Be Drawn from the Jurisprudence of the United States Dormant Commerce Clause' in T Cottier and PC Mavroidis (eds), *Regulatory Barriers and the Principle of Non-discrimination in World Trade Law* (Ann Arbor, University of Michigan Press, 2000).

Howse, R, 'From Politics to Technocracy–and Back Again: The Fate of the Multilateral Trading Regime' (2002) 96 *American Journal of International Law* 94.

Howse, R, 'Human Rights in the WTO: Whose Rights, What Humanity? Comment on Petersmann' (2002) 13(3) *European Journal of International Law* 651.

Howse, R, 'The Most Dangerous Branch? WTO Appellate Body Jurisprudence on the Nature and Limits of the Judicial Power' in T Cottier and P Mavroidis, *The Role of the Judge in International Trade Regulation: Experience and Lessons from WTO* (Ann Arbor, University of Michigan Press, 2003).

Hudec, R, 'GATT/WTO Constraints on National Regulation: Requiem for an "Aim and Effects" Test' (1998) 32 *International Lawyer* 619.

Hudec, RE, '"Like Products": The Differences in Meaning in GATT Article I and III' in T Cottier and P Mavroidis (eds), *Regulatory Barriers and the Principle of Non-discrimination in World Trade Law* (Ann Arbor, University of Michigan Press, 2000.

Hughes, J, 'Champagne, Feta, and Bourbon: The Spirited Debate about Geographical Indications' (2006) 58 *Hastings Law Journal* 299.

Hunter, JD, 'The Enduring Culture War' in JD Hunter and A Wolfe (eds), *Is There a Culture War?—A Dialogue on Values and American Public Life* (Washington, DC, The Brookings Institution Press, 2006).

Huntington, SP, *The Clash of Civilizations and the Remaking of World Order* (New York, Simon & Schuster, 1996).

Huntington, SP, *Who Are We? The Challenges to America's National Identity* (New York, Simon & Schuster, 2004).

Huntington, SP et al, 'Samuel P Huntington's 'The Clash of Civilizations?' The Debate, [1993/1996] *Foreign Affairs* 29.

Idleman, SC, 'Multiculturalism and the Future of Tribal Sovereignty' (2004) 35 *Columbia Human Rights Law Review* 589.

ILC, 'Fragmentation of International Law-Difficulties Arising from the Diversification and Expansion of International Law, Report of the Study Group of the International Law Commission' (finalised by Martti Koskenniemi), A/CN.4/L.682 (13 April 2006).

Jackson, JH, *World Trade and the Law of GATT* (Indianapolis, IN, The Bobbs Merril Company, 1969).

Jackson, JH, *The World Trading System: Law and Policy of International Economic Relations* (Cambridge, MA, The MIT Press, 1989).

Jackson, JH, 'National Treatment Obligations and Non-Tariff Barriers' (1989) 10 *Michigan Journal of International Law* 207.

Jackson, JH, 'Reflections on International Economic Law' (1996) 17 *University of Pennsylvania Journal of International Economic Law* 17.

Jackson, JH, *The Jurisprudence of GATT and the WTO: Insights on Treaty Law and Economic Relations* (New York, Cambridge University Press, 2000).

Jackson, JH, 'Reflections on the Possible Research Agenda for Exploring the Relationship between Human Rights Norms and International Trade Rules' in F Abbott et al (eds), *International Trade and Human Rights: Foundations and Conceptual Issues* (Ann Arbor, University of Michigan Press, 2006).

Jäckel, A, 'The Inter/Nationalism of French Film Policy' (2007) 15(1) *Modern & Contemporary France* 21.

James, CP, 'Trade, Culture and Technology: A Test of Canada's Cultural Mettle' (1997) 8(7) *Entertainment Law Review* 253.

Jameson, F, 'Globalization and Strategy', *New Left Review*, July/August 2000, 49.

Jennings, R and Watts, A (eds), *Oppenheim's International Law*, 9th edn (Oxford, Oxford University Press, 1992).

Jones, EL, *Cultures Merging: A Historical and Economic Critique of Culture* (Princeton, NJ, Princeton University Press, 2006).

Jones, P, 'Human Rights and Diverse Cultures: Continuity or Discontinuity?' in ST Caney and P Jones (eds), *Human Rights and Global Diversity* (London, Frank Cass Publishers, 2001) 27–50.

Jones, S, 'Mass Communication, Intellectual Property Rights, International Trade, and the Popular Music Industry' in EG McAnany and KT Williams (eds), *Mass Media and Free Trade: NAFTA and Cultural Industries* (Austin, University of Texas Press, 1996).

Jouannet, E, 'Universalism and Imperialism: The True–False Paradox of International Law?' (2007) 18 *European Journal of International Law* 379.

Kahn, J, 'Culture: Demise or Resurrection?' (1987) 9(2) *Critique of Anthropology* 17.

Kant, I, 'Perpetual Peace: A Philosophical Sketch (1795)' in H Reiss (ed), *Kant's Political Writings* (Cambridge, Cambridge University Press, 1991).

Kapcznski, A, 'Walter B after the 20th Century: The Future of a Past: Historicism, Progress, and the Redemptive Constitution' (2005) 26 *Cardozo Law Review* 1041.

Kaplan, LGC, 'The European Community's "Television Without Frontiers" Directive: Stimulating Europe to Regulate Culture' (1994) 8 *Emory International Law Review* 255.

Karpe, CR, 'European Cultural Protectionism and the Socioeconomic Forces that will Defeat it' (1995) 5 *Indiana International & Comparative Law Review* 425.

Kaul, I and Stern, M (eds), *Global Public Goods: International Cooperation in the 21st Century* (Oxford, Oxford University Press, 1999).

Keane, M, 'Exporting Chinese Culture: Industry Financing Models in Film and Television' (2006) 3(1) *Westminster Papers in Communication and Culture* 11.

Kennedy, D, 'New Approaches to Comparative Law: Comparativism and International Governance' [1997] *Utah Law Review* 545.

Kennedy, KC, 'A WTO Agreement on Investment: A Solution in Search of Problem?' (2003) 24 *University of Pennsylvania Journal of International Economic Law* 77.

Kessler, KL, 'Protecting Free Trade in Audiovisual Entertainment: A Proposal for Counteracting the European Union's Trade Barriers to the US Entertainment Industry's Exports' (1995) 26 *Law & Policy International Business* 563.

Khachaturian, A, 'The New Cultural Diversity Convention and Its Implications on the WTO International Trade Regime: A Critical Comparative Analysis' (2006) 42 *Texas International Law Journal* 191.

Kim, CH-K, 'Building the Korean Film Industry's Competitiveness: Abolish the Screen Quota and Subsidize the Film Industry' (2000) 9 *Pacific Rim Law & Policy* 353.

Kim, SJ, 'Comment, Viewer Discretion Is Advised: A Structural Approach to the Issue of Television Violence' (1994) 142 *University of Pennsylvania Law Review* 1383.

Kitz, V, 'The Difference between Books and Chocolate Bars—How EC Treaty Art 151(4) Affects Community Actions' (2004) 32 *AIPLA Quarterly Journal* 361.

Knight, T, 'The Dual Nature of Cultural Products: An Analysis of the World Trade Organization's Decisions Regarding Canadian Periodicals' (1999) 57 *University of Toronto Faculty of Law Review* 165.

Konigsberg, SR, 'Think Globally, Act Locally: North American Free Trade, Canadian Cultural Industry Exemption, and the Liberalization of the Broadcast Ownership Laws' (1994) 12 *Cardozo Arts & Entertainments Law Journal* 281.

Kroeber, AL, *The Nature of Culture* (1952).

Krugman, P, 'Competitiveness: A Dangerous Obsession' (1994) 73 *Foreign Affairs* 2.

Kulovesi, K, *The WTO Dispute Settlement System-Challenges of the Environment, Legitimacy and Fragmentation* (London, Kluwer Law International, 2011).

Kuper, A, *Culture—The Anthrologists' Account* (Cambridge, MA, Harvard University Press, 1999).

Kymlicka, W, *Multicultural Citizenship: A Liberal Theory of Minority Rights* (New York, Oxford University Press USA, 1996).

Kymlicka, W, *The Rights of Minority Cultures* (New York, Oxford University Press USA, 1995).

Landers, D, *The Wealth and Poverty of Nations* (New York, Norton, 1998).

Landers, D, 'Culture Makes Almost All the Difference', in LE Harrison and SP Huntington (eds), *Culture Matters: How Values Shape Human Progress* (New York, Basic Books, 2000) 2.

Landsman, ML, 'Restricting Foreign Television Programming in Europe: The European Community's Television Quota Reappraised' (1999) 8 *Media Law & Policy* 29.

Larrea, TA, 'Eliminate the Cultural Industries Exemption from NAFTA' (1997) 37 *Santa Clara Law Review* 1107.

Leal-Arcas, R, 'The Resumption of the Doha Round and the Future of Services Trade' (2007) 29 *Loyola of Los Angeles International and Comparative Law Journal* 339.

Ledet, C, 'Causation of Injury in Safeguards Cases: Why the US Can't Win' (2003) 34 *Law & Policy International Business* 713.

Lee, B and Bae, H-S, 'The Effect of Screen Quotas on the Self-Sufficiency Ratio in Recent Domestic Film Markets' (2004) 17(3) *Journal of Media Economics* 163.

Lee, K, 'The Little State Department: Hollywood and the MPAA's Influence on US Trade Relations' (2008) 28 *Northwestern Journal of International Law & Business* 371.

Lee, S, 'Heritage Conventions Intertwine with the Concept of Cultural Diversity: Asian and European Perspectives' in N Obuljen and J Smiers (eds), *UNESCO's Convention on the Protection and Promotion of the Diversity of Cultural Expressions: Making It Work* (Zagreb, Institute for International Relations, 2006).

Leebron, D, 'Linkages' (2002) 96 *American Journal of International Law* 5.

Lennard, M, 'Navigating by the Stars: Interpreting the WTO Agreements' (2002) 5(1) *Journal of International Economic Law* 17.

Lessig, L, 'The Zones of Cyberspace' (1996) 48 *Stanford Law Review* 1403.

Levy, DAL, *Europe's Digital Revolution: Broadcasting and Regulation: The EU and the Nation States* (London, Routledge, 1999).

Lewin, A, 'Convergences and Divergences: The United States and France in Multilateral Diplomacy' (2006) 58 *Maine Law Review* 395.

Lickova, M, 'European Exceptionalism in International Law' (2008) 19 *European Journal of International Law* 463.

Liebman, BH and Tomlin, KM, 'Safeguards and Retaliatory Threats' (2008) 51 *Journal of Law & Economics* 351.

Lindroos, A and Mehling, M, 'Dispelling the Chimera of "Self-Contained" Regimes in International Law and the WTO' (2006) 16 *European Journal of International Law* 857.

Liss, J, 'The Impact of Globalization and Technological Change on Culture and National Identity: A Call for Visionary Pragmatism' in D Browne (ed), *The Culture/Trade Quandary: Canada's Policy Options* (Ottawa, Center for Trade Policy and Law, 1998).

Liss J, 'The Impact of Technology Change on Canada's Affirmative Policy Model in the Cultural Industry and New Media Sectors' (1999) 25 *Canada—US Law Journal* 379.

Little, V, 'Audiovisual Media Services Directive: Europe's Modernization of Broadcast Services Regulations' [2008] *University of Illinois Journal of Law, Technology & Policy* 223.

Loeb, H, 'The Management and Resolution of Cross Border Disputes As Canada/US Enter the 21st Century: Telecommunication and Culture: Transborder Freedom of Information or Cultural Identity?' (2000) 26 *Canada—US Law Journal* 303.

Lodge, AJ, 'Globalization: Panacea for the World or Conquistador of International Law and Statehood?' (2005) 7 *Oregon Review of International Law* 224.

Logan, W, *UNESCO, Cultural Diversity, Cultural Heritage and Human Rights* (London, Routledge, 2009).

Loisen, J, 'Can the Existing WTO Legal Framework Take into Account the Cultural Specificity of the Audiovisual Sector' in N Obuljen and J Smiers (eds), *UNESCO's Convention on the Protection and Promotion of the Diversity of Cultural Expressions: Making It Work* (Zagreb, Institute for International Relations, 2006).

Lück, M, 'Harmonization, Systematic Integration, and Mutual Supportiveness as Conflict-Solution Techniques: Different Modes of Interpretation as a Challenge to Negative Effects of Fragmentation?' (2006) 17 *Finnish Yearbook of International Law* 39.

Macklem, P, 'Distributing Sovereignty: Indian Nations and Equality of Peoples' (1993) 45 *Stanford Law Review* 1311.

Magder, T, 'Franchising the Candy Store: Split Run Magazines and the New International Regime for Trade and Culture' [1998] *Canadian–American Public Policy* 1.

Mahoney, P, 'Marvelous Richness of Diversity or Invidious Cultural Relativism?' (1998) 19 *Human Rights Law Journal* 4.

Mandelbaum, M, *History, Man and Reason* (Washington, DC, The Johns Hopkins University Press, 1974).

Mandle, J, 'Globalization and Justice' (2000) 570 *Annals* 126.

Marceau, G, 'A Call for Coherence in International Law—Praise for the Prohibition against "Clinical Isolation" in WTO Dispute Settlement' (1999) 33(5) *Journal of World Trade* 87.

Marinberg, D, 'GATT/WTO Waivers: "Exceptional Circumstances" as Applied to the Lomé Waiver' (2001) 19 *Boston University International Law Journal* 129.

Martin, C, 'The Relationship between Trade and Environment Regimes: What Needs to Change?' in GP Sampson, *The Role of the World Trade Organization in Global Governance* (Tokyo, United Nations University Press, 2001).

Martin, L, 'The Political Economy of International Cooperation' in I Kaul and M Stern (eds), *Global Public Goods: International Cooperation in the 21st Century* (Oxford, Oxford University Press, 1999).

Martinez, GA, 'Latinos, Assimilation and the Law: A Philosophical Perspective' (1999) 20 *Chicano-Latino Law Review* 1.

Matheny, RL, 'In the Wake of the Flood: "Like Products" and Cultural Products After the World Trade Organization's Decision in Canada Certain Measures Concerning Periodicals' (1998) 147 *University of Pennsylvania Law Review* 245.

Matsushita, M, et al, *The World Trade Organization, Law, Practice, and Policy* (New York, Oxford University Press USA, 2006).

Matsushita, M, 'Export Control of Natural Resources: WTO Panel Ruling on the Chinese Export Restrictions of Natural Resources' (2011) 3 *Trade, Law and Development* 286.

Mattoo, A, 'China's Accession to the WTO: The Services Dimension' (2003) 6 *Journal of International Economic Law* 299.

Mavroidis, P, *The General Agreement on Tariffs and Trade: A Commentary* (Oxford, Oxford University Press, 2005).

McAnany, EG and Williams, KT (eds), *Mass Media and Free Trade: NAFTA and Cultural Industries* (Austin, University of Texas Press, 1996).

McCulloch, JR, *The Works of David Ricardo* (London, John Murray, 2002).

McGonagle, T, 'The Promotion of Cultural Diversity via New Media Technologies: An Introduction to the Challenges of Operationalization' (2008) 2008(6) *IRIS-Plus* 1.

McRae, DM, 'GATT Article XX and the Appellate Body' in M Bronckers and R Quick (eds), *New Directions in International Economic Law: Essays in Honor of John H Jackson* (London, Kluwer Law International, 2000).

Mead, M, *Keep Your Powder Dry: An Anthropologist Looks at America* (Oxford, Berghahn Books, 1943).

Mensch, E, 'The History of Mainstream Legal Thought' in D Kayris (ed), *The Politics of Law: A Progressive Critique*, 2nd edn (New York, Basic Books, 1998).

Merrilis, JG, *The Development on International Law by the European Court of Human Rights* (Manchester, Manchester University Press, 1993).

Meyerhoff, H, 'Introduction' in H Meyerhoff (ed), *The Philosophy of History in our Time: An Anthology Selected, and with an Introduction and Commentary* (New York, Doubleday, 1959).

Middleton, J, 'The Effectiveness of Audiovisual Regulation Inside the European Union: The Television without Frontiers Directives and Cultural Protectionism' (2003) 31 *Denver Journal of International Law & Policy* 607.

Mises, L von, *Theory and History* (New Haven, CT, Yale University Press, 1957).

Mitchell, AD, *Legal Principles in WTO Disputes* (Cambridge, Cambridge University Press, 2008).

Mitsilegas, V, 'Culture in the Evolution of European Law: Panacea in the Quest for Identity?' in P Fitzpatrick and JH Bergeron (eds), *Europe's Other: European Law between Modernity and Postmodernity* (Sudbury, MA, Dartmouth Publishing Inc, 1998).

Moran, B, 'Curb Center Special Feature: United States' Trade Policy and the Exportation of United States' Culture' (2004) 7 *Vanderbilt Journal of Entertainment Law & Practice* 41.

Morgan-Foster, J, 'A New Perspective on the Universality Debate: Reverse Moderate Relativism in the Islamic Context' (2003) 10 *ILSA Journal of International & Comparative Law* 35.

Morgenthau, HJ, *Politics among Nations: The Struggle for Power and Peace*, 3rd edn (New York, McGraw-Hill, 1962).

Murden, S, 'Culture in World Affairs' in J Bayliss and S Smith (eds), *The Globalization of World Politics: An Introduction to International Relations* (New York, Oxford University Press USA, 1997).

Murray, TM, 'The US–French Dispute over GATT Treatment of Audiovisual Products and the Limits of Public Choice Theory: How an Efficiency Market Solution was "Rent-Seeking"' (1997) 21 *Maryland Journal of International Law & Trade* 203.

Neuwirth, RJ, 'The "Cultural Industries": A Clash of Basic Values?—A Comparative Study of the EU and the NAFTA in Light of the WTO' in F Palermo and GN Toggenburg (eds), *European Constitutional Values and Cultural Diversity* (Berlin, EURAC Research, Europäische Akademie, 2003).

Neuwirth, RJ, 'The Fragmentation of the Global Market: The Case of Digital Versatile Discs (DVDs)' (2009) 27 *Cardozo Arts & Entertainments Law Journal* 409.

Newman, F and Weissbrodt, D, *International Human Rights: Law, Policy, and Process* (New York, LexisNexis, 1996).

Niec, H, 'Casting the Foundation for the Implementation of Cultural Rights' in H Niec (ed), *Cultural Rights and Wrongs: A Collection of Essays in Commemoration of the 50th Anniversary of the Universal Declaration of Human Rights* (Builth Wells, UNESCO Institute of Art and Law, 1998).

Ninkovich, FA, *The Diplomacy of Ideas: US Foreign Policy and Cultural Relations* (Cambridge, Cambridge University Press, 1981).

Niu, Z, 'The Door Is Wedged Open: China's Regulation on Foreign Access to Audiovisual Markets' (2007) 18(8) *Entertainment Law Review* 265.

Nozick, R, *Anarchy, State and Utopia* (1974).

Obuljen, N and Smiers, J (eds), *UNESCO's Convention on the Protection and Promotion of the Diversity of Cultural Expressions: Making It Work* (Zagreb, Institute for International Relations, 2006).

O'Donnel, TA, 'The Margin of Appreciation Doctrine: Standards in the Jurisprudence of the European Court of Human Rights' (1982) 4(4) *Human Rights Quarterly* 474.

Oesch, M, 'Commentary on *EC—Asbestos*' (2003) 6 *International Trade Law Reports* 441.

Oh, J, 'International Trade in Film and the Self-Sufficiency Ratio' (2001) 14(1) *Journal of Media Economics* 31.

Olsen, JMF et al, 'Trade and Environment at the World Trade Organization: The Need for a Constructive Dialogue' in GP Sampson (ed), *The Role of the World Trade Organization in Global Governance* (Tokyo, United Nations University Press, 2001).

Ortino, F, 'Treaty Interpretation and the WTO Appellate Body Report in *US—Gambling*: A Critique' (2006) 9 *Journal of International Economic Law* 117.

Ostry, B, 'Culture and Trade: One Policy/No Options' in D Browne (ed), *The Culture/Trade Quandary: Canada's Policy Options* (Ottawa, Center for Trade Policy and Law, 1998).

Otto, D, 'Rethinking the "Universality" of Human Rights Law'(1997) 29 *Columbia Human Rights Law Review* 1.

Palermo, F and Toggenburg, GN (eds), *European Constitutional Values and Cultural Diversity* (Berlin, EURAC Research, Europäische Akademie, 2003).

Palka, StE, 'Canada's Cultural Industries, the United States, and Trade Law: Tension, Conflict, and Possibilities' (2000) 10 *Windsor Review of Legal and Social Issues* 105.

Parekh, B, *Rethinking Multiculturalism: Cultural Diversity and Political Theory* (New York, Palgrave Macmillan, 2006).

Paul, JR, 'Cultural Resistance to Global Governance' (2000) 22 *Michigan Journal of International Law* 1.

Pauwelyn, J, 'The Role of Public International Law in the WTO: How Far Can We Go?' (2001) 95 *American Journal of International Law* 535.

Pauwelyn, J, *Conflict of Norms in Public International Law—How WTO Law Relates to Other Rules of International Law* (Cambridge, Cambridge University Press, 2003).

Pauwelyn, J, 'Human Rights in WTO Dispute Settlement' in T Cottier et al (eds), *Human Rights and International Trade* (Oxford, Oxford University Press, 2005) 205.

Pavoni, R, 'Mutual Supportiveness as a Principle of Interpretation and Law-Making: A Watershed for the "WTO-and-Competing-Regimes" Debate?' (2010) 21 *European Journal of International Law* 649.

Perino, G and Schulze, GG, 'Competition, Cultural Autonomy and Global Governance: The Audio-Visual Sector in Germany' in P Guerrieri et al (eds), *Cultural Diversity and International Economic Integration: The Global Governance of the Audio-Visual Sector* (Cheltenham, Edward Elgar Publishing, 2005).

Petersmann, E-U, *The GATT/WTO Dispute Settlement System—International Law, International Organizations and Dispute Settlement* (New York, Kluwer Law International, 1997).

Petersmann, E-U, 'The Transformation of the World Trading System through the 1994 Agreement Establishing the World Trade Organization' (1995) 6 *European Journal of International Law* 161.

Petersmann, E-U, 'Time for a United Nations "Global Compact" for Integrating Human Rights into the Law of Worldwide Organizations: Lessons from European Integration' (2002) 13(3) *European Journal of International Law* 619.

Petersmann, E-U (ed), *Reforming the World Trading System: Legitimacy, Efficiency, and Democratic Governance* (Oxford, Oxford University Press, 2005).

Petito, DS, 'Sovereignty and Globalization: Fallacies, Truth, and Perception' (2001) 17 *New York Law School Journal of Human Rights* 1139.

Petzold, H, 'The Convention and the Principle of Subsidiarity' in R Macdonald et al (eds), *The European System for the Protection of Human Rights* (London, Springer, 1993) 41.

Piciocchi, C, 'Europe Faces Cultural Diversity: Towards a European Multicultural Model?' in F Palermo and GN Toggenburg (eds), *European Constitutional Values and Cultural Diversity* (Berlin, EURAC Research, Europäische Akademie, 2003).

Piérola, F, 'The Availability of a GATT Article XX Defence with Respect to a Non-GATT Claim: Changing the Rules of the Game?' (2010) 5 *Global Trade and Customs Journal* 172.

Pieterse, JN, *Globalization and Culture—Global Mélange* (New York, Rowman & Littlefield Publishers, Inc, 2004).

Pinto, F, 'Book Review—Blockbusters and Trade Wars: Popular Culture in a Globalized World' (2004) 7 *Journal of International Economic Law* 922.

Porter, ME, 'Attitudes, Values, Beliefs, and the Microeconomics of Prosperity' in Harrison, LE and Huntington, SP (eds), *Culture Matters: How Values Shape Human Progress* (New York, Basic Books, 2000).

Prestowitz, C et al, 'The Fight over Competitiveness: A Zero-Sum Debate?' (1994) 73 *Foreign Affairs* 4.

Prodi, R, 'Globalization and Cultural Diversity: The Contribution of European Institutions'in Ricciardelli, M, et al (eds), *Globalization and Multicultural Societies—Some Views from Europe* (Notre Dame, IN, University of Notre Dame Press, 2003) 137.

Prowda, JB, 'US Dominance in the "Marketplace of Culture" and the French "Cultural Exception"' (1997) 29 *New York University Journal of International Law & Policy* 193.

Psychogiopoulou, E, 'EC Competition Law and Cultural Diversity: The Case of Cinema, Music and Book Publishing Industries' (2005) 30 *European Law Review* 838.

Puche, JS, 'Regionalism and the WTO' in The WTO Secretariat (ed), *From GATT to the WTO: The Multilateral Trading System in the New Millenium* (Dordrecht, Kluwer Law International, 2000).

Qin, JY, 'The Challenge of Interpreting "WTO-Plus" Provisions' (2010) 44(1) *Journal of World Trade* 127.

Qin, JY, 'The Predicament of China's "WTO-Plus" Obligation to Eliminate Export Duties: A Commentary on the *China–Raw Materials* Case' (2012) 11 *Chinese Journal of International Law* 239.

Rabinovitch, V, 'The Social and Economic Rationales for Domestic Cultural Policies' in D Browne (ed), *The Culture/Trade Quandary: Canada's Policy Options* (Ottawa, Center for Trade Policy and Law, 1998).

Rafner, G, 'Pros and Cons Ensuing from Fragmentation of International Law' (2004) 25 *Michigan Journal of International Law* 849.

Ramirez, SA, 'A General Theory of Cultural Diversity' (2001) 7 *Michigan Journal of Race & Law* 33.

Reeves, J, *Culture and International Relations: Narratives, Natives and Tourists* (London, Routledge, 2004).

Reichert, E, 'Human Rights: An Examination of Universalism and Cultural Relativism' (2006) 22(1) *Journal of Comparative Social Welfare* 23.

Reisman, WM, 'Autonomy, Interdependence, and Responsibility' (1993) 103 *Yale Law Journal* 401.
Reisman, WM, 'Law, International Public Policy (So-called) and Arbitral Choice in International Commercial Arbitration' in AJ Van Den Burg (ed), *International Arbitration 2006: Back to Basics?* (New York, Kluwer Law International, 2008).
Reisman, WM and Schreiber, AM, *Jurisprudence: Understanding and Shaping Law: Cases, Readings, Commentary* (New Haven, CT, New Haven Press, 1987).
Reitz, C, 'Enforcement of the General Agreement of Tariffs and Trade' (1996) 17 *University of Pennsylvania Journal of International Economic Law* 555.
Richardson, B, 'Hollywood's Vision of a Clear, Predictable Trade Framework Consistent with Cultural Diversity' in CB Graber et al (eds), *Free Trade versus Cultural Diversity: WTO Negotiations in the Field of Audiovisual Services* (Zürich, Schulthess, 2004).
Richardson, J, 'The European Union in the World—A Community of Values' (2002) 26 *Fordham International Journal* 12.
Risse, T, 'A European Identity? Europeanization and the Evolution of Nation-State Identities' in MG Cowles et al (eds), *Transforming Europe: Europeanization and Domestic Change* (Ithaca, NY, Cornell University Press, 2001).
Roberts, A, 'Traditional and Modern Approaches to Customary International Law: A Reconciliation'(2006) 95 *American Journal of International Law* 757.
Rojas, H, 'Stop Cultural Exclusions (in Chile)!: Reflections on the Principle of Multiculturalism' (2003) 55 *Florida Law Review* 121.
Rosas, A, 'Non-Commercial Values and the World Trade System: Building on Article XX' in K Van Der Borght et al (eds), *Essays on the Future of the WTO: Finding a New Balance* (London, Cameron, 2004).
Rose, IM, 'Note, Barring Foreigners from Our Airways: An Anachronistic Pothole on the Global Information Highway'(1995) 95 *Columbia Law Review* 1188.
Roy, M, 'Audiovisual Services in the Doha Round: Dialogue de Sourds, The Sequel?' (2005) 6(6) *Journal of World Investment and Trade* 923.
Ryn, CG, 'Defining Historicism' (1998) 11(2) *Humanitas*.
Sampson, GP, 'Greater Coherence in Global Economic Policymaking: A WTO Perspective' in AO Krueger (ed), *The WTO as an International Organization* (Chicago, University of Chicago Press, 1998).
Sampson, GP, *The Role of the World Trade Organization in Global Governance* (Tokyo, United Nations University Press, 2001).
Sampson, GP, 'Is There a Need for Restructuring the Collaboration among the WTO and UN Agencies so as to Harness their Complementarities?' in E-U Petersmann (ed), *Reforming the World Trading System: Legitimacy, Efficiency, and Democratic Governance* (Oxford, Oxford University Press, 2005).
Samuelson, P, 'Implications of the Agreement on Trade Related Aspects of Intellectual Property Rights for the Cultural Dimension of National Copyright Laws'(1999) 23 *Journal of Cultural Economics* 95.
Sauvé, P and Steinfatt, K, 'Towards Multilateral Rules on Trade and Culture: Protective Regulation or Efficient Protection?' in *Achieving Better Regulation of Services,* Conference Proceedings, AusInfo, Canberra (Productivity Commission and Australian National University, November 2000).

Schlesinger, AM, *Disuniting of America: Reflections on a Multicultural Society* (New York, WW Norton & Co, 1991).

Schloemann, HL and Ohlhodd, S, 'Constitutionalization and Dispute Settlement in the WTO: National Security as an Issue of Competence' (1999) 93 *American Journal of International Law* 424.

Schokkenbroek, J, 'The Basis, Nature and Application of the Margin of Appreciation Doctrine in the Case-Law of the European Court Rights—General Report (1998) 19 *Human Rights Law Journal* 30.

Schooley, KY, 'Cultural Sovereignty, Islam, and Human Rights—Toward A Communitarian Revision' (1995) 25 *Cumberland Law Review* 651.

Schulze, GG, 'International Trade in Art' (1999) 23 *Journal of Cultural Economics* 109.

Schwartz, B, 'Canadian Cultural Policy in a World Context' (2002) 2 *Asper Review of International Business & Trade Law* 1.

Scobbie, I, 'Wicked Heresies or Legitimate Perspectives? Theory and International Law' in MD Evans (ed), *International Law*, 2nd edn (Oxford, Oxford University Press, 2006).

Scott, S, 'The Impact of Technological Change on Canada's Cultural Industries' in D Browne (ed), *The Culture/Trade Quandary: Canada's Policy Options* (Ottawa, Center for Trade Policy and Law, 1998).

Scow, A, 'The *Sports Illustrated Canada* Controversy: Canada "Strikes Out" In Its Bid to Protect Its Periodical Industry from US Split-Run Periodicals' (1998) 7 *Minnesota Journal of Global Trade* 245.

Segrave, K, *American Television Abroad: Hollywood's Attempt to Dominate World Television* (Jefferson, NC, McFarland, 1998).

Serageldin, I, 'Cultural Heritage As Public Good: Economic Analysis Applied to Historic Cities' in I Kaul and M Stern (eds), *Global Public Goods: International Cooperation in the 21st Century* (Oxford, Oxford University Press, 1999).

Shaffer, GC and Meléndez-Ortiz, R (eds), *Dispute Settlement at the WTO—The Developing Country Experience* (Cambridge, Cambridge University Press, 2010).

Shany, Y, *The Competing Jurisdictions of International Courts and Tribunals* (New York, Oxford University Press USA, 2003).

Shany, Y, 'Towards a General Margin of Appreciation Doctrine in International Law?' (2006) 16 *European Journal of International Law* 907.

Shao, WM, 'Is There No Business Like Show Business? Free Trade and Cultural Protectionism' (1995) 20 *Yale Journal of International Law* 105.

Shi, J and Chen, W, 'The Specificity of Cultural Products versus the Generality of Trade Obligations-Reflecting on "China—Publications and Audiovisual Services"' (2011) 45(1) *Journal of World Trade* 159.

Sinclair, I, *The Vienna Convention of the Law of Treaties*, 2nd edn (Manchester, Manchester University Press, 1984).

Sinclair, J, 'Culture and Trade: Theoretical and Practical Considerations' in EG McAnany and KT Williams (eds), *Mass Media and Free Trade: NAFTA and Cultural Industries* (Austin, University of Texas Press, 1996).

Skinner, M, 'Locating Indigenous Power: Cultural Relativism, Universalism and State Sovereignty Preface' (2001) 7 *New England International & Comparative Law Annual* 69.

Slotin, I, 'Free Speech and the Visage Culture: Canadian and American Perspectives on Pop Culture Discrimination' (2002) 111 *Yale Law Journal* 2289.

Smith, B, 'Art Objects and Historical Usage' in I McBryde (ed), *Who Owns the Past?* (Oxford, Oxford University Press, 1985).

Smith, CN, 'International Trade in Television Programming and GATT: An Analysis of Why the European Community's Local Program Requirement Violates the General Agreement on Tariffs and Trade' (1993) 10 *International Tax & Business Law* 97.

Smith, F and Woods, L, 'A Distinction without Difference: Exploring the Boundary between Goods and Services in the World Trade Organization and the European Union' (2005) 12(1) *Columbia Journal of European Law* 1.

Smith, RC, 'The UNESCO Convention on the Protection and Promotion of Cultural Expressions: Building a New World Information and Communication Order?' (2007) 1 *International Journal of Communication* 24.

Snape, WJ III and Lefkowitz, NB, 'Searching for GATT's Environmental Miranda: Are "Process Standards" Getting "Due Process"?' (1994) 27 *Cornell International Law Journal* 777.

Snelson, JH, 'Can GATT Artcle III Recover From Its Head-On Collision With United States Taxes on Automobiles?' (1996) 5 *Minnesota Journal of Global Trade* 467.

Steger, DP, 'The Boundaries of the WTO: Afterword: The "Trade and . . ." Conundrum—A Commentary'(2002) 96 *American Journal of International Law* 135.

Stenou, K (ed), *UNESCO and the Question of Cultural Diversity 1946–2007—Review and Strategies: A Study Based on A Selection of Official Documents* (Paris, UNESCO, 2007).

Stewart, RB. 'International Trade and Environment: Lessons from the Federal Experience' (1992) 49 *Washington & Lee Law Review* 1329, 1330..

Steyger, E, *National Traditions and European Community Law* (Sudbury, MA, Dartmouth Publishing Inc, 1997).

Stocking, GW, *Race, Culture, and Evolution: Essays in the History of Anthropology* (Chicago, University of Chicago Press, 1968/82).

Strong, SI, 'Banning the Cultural Exclusion: Free Trade and Copyrighted Goods' (1993) 4 *Duke Journal of Comparative & International Law* 93.

Sullivan, P, 'Antidumping Law and the Dumping of Services' (1992) 24 *New York University Journal of International & Policy* 1677.

Sutherland, P, et al, 'Challenges Facing the WTO and Policies to Address Global Governance' in GP Sampson (ed), *The Role of the World Trade Organization in Global Governance* (Tokyo, United Nations University Press, 2001) 92.

Sweeney, JA, 'Margins of Appreciation: Cultural Relativity and the European Court of Human Rights in the Post-Cold War Era' (2005) 54 *International & Comparative Law Quarterly* 461.

Sykes, AO, 'Regulatory Protectionism and the Law of International Trade' (1999) 66 *University of Chicago Law Review* 1.

Sykes, A, 'Comparative Advantage and the Normative Economics of International Trade Policy' (1998) 1(1) *Journal of International Economic Law* 49.

Sykes, AO, 'The Persistent Puzzles of Safeguards: Lessons from the Steel Dispute' (2004) 7 *Journal of International Economic Law* 523.

Tauber, Y, *Beyond the Letter of the Law: A Chassidic Companion to the Ethics of the Fathers* (Brooklyn, NY, Vaad Hanochos Hatmimim, 1995).

Tesón, FR, 'The Kantian Theory of International Law' (1992) 92 *Columbia Law Review* 53.

Teubner, G, 'How the Law Thinks: Towards a Constructive Epistemology of Law' (1989) 23(5) *Law & Society Review* 727.

Thompson, JH, 'Canada's Quest for Cultural Sovereignty: Protection, Promotion, and Popular Culture' in SJ Randell et al (eds), *North America without Borders?* (Calgary, Alberta, University of Calgary Press, 1992).

Thompson, JH, 'Canada's Quest for Cultural Sovereignty: Protection, Promotion, and Popular Culture' in SJ Randall and HW Konrad (eds), *NAFTA in Transition* (Calgary, Alberta, University of Calgary Press, 1995).

Throsby, D, *Economics and Culture* (Cambridge, Cambridge University Press, 2001).

Toggenberg, GN, 'Cultural Diversity at the Background of the European Debate on Values—An Introduction' in F Palermo and GN Toggenburg (eds), *European Constitutional Values and Cultural Diversity* (Berlin, EURAC Research, Europäische Akademie, 2003).

Tomlinson, J, *Globalization and Culture* (Chicago, Chicago University Press, 1999).

Trachtman, JP, 'Unilateralism, Bilateralism, Regionalism, Multilateralism, and Functionalism: A Comparison with Reference to Securities Regulation' (1994) 4 *Transnational Law and Contemporary Problems* 69.

Trachtman, JP, 'Trade and . . . Problems, Cost–Benefit Analysis and Subsidiarity' (1998) 9 *European Journal of International Law* 32.

Tunstall, J, *Media are American* (New York, Columbia University Press, 1977).

Tyagi, M, 'Flesh on a Legal Fiction: Early Practice in the WTO on Accession Protocols' (2012) 15 *Journal of International Economic Law* 398.

Ul Haq, M, *Reflections on Human Development* (Oxford, Oxford University Press, 1995).

UN Commission on Human Rights, Sub-Commission on the Promotion and Protection of Human Rights, 'The Impact of the Agreement on Trade-Related Aspects of Intellectual Property Rights on Human Rights: Report of the High Commissioner', E/CN.4/Sub.2/2001/13 (27 June 2001).

UN Commission on Human Rights, 'Globalization and Its Impact on the Full Enjoyment of Human Rights: Report of the High Commissioner for Human Rights Submitted in Accordance with Commission on Human Rights Resolution 2001/32', E/CN.4/2002/54 (15 January 2002).

UN Commission on Human Rights, Sub-Commission on the Promotion and Protection of Human Rights, 'Liberalization of Trade in Services and Human Rights: Report of High Commissioner', E/CN.4Sub.2/2002/9 (25 June 2002).

UN Commission on Human Rights, Sub-Commission on the Promotion and Protection of Human Rights, 'Globalization and Its Impact on the Full Enjoyment of Human Rights: Final Report Submitted by J Oloka-Onyango and Deepika Udagama, in Accordance with Sub-Commission Decision 2000/105', E/CN.4/Sub.2/2003/14 (25 June 2003).

UN Commission on Human Rights, Human Rights, Trade and Investment, 'Report of the High Commissioner for Human Rights', E/CN.4/Sub.2/2003/9, ¶3 (2 July 2003).

UNCTAD and World Bank, *Liberalizing International Transactions in Services: A Handbook* (1994).

UNESCO, *A Guide to the Operation of the Agreement on the Importation of Educational, Scientific and Cultural Materials*, 4th edn (Paris, UNESCO, 1969).

UNESCO, *Cultural Industries: A Challenge for the Future of Culture* (Paris, UNESCO, 1982).

UNESCO, 'Our Creative Diversity: Report of the World Commission on Culture and Development' (finalised by J Pérez de Cuéllar, Paris, UNESCO, 1995).

UNESCO, *World Culture Report 2000* (Paris, UNESCO, 2000).

United Nations, Office of the United Nations High Commissioner for Human Rights, Human Rights and World Trade Agreements, 'Using General Exception Clauses to Protect Human Rights', HR/PUB/05/5.

Verhoosel, G, *National Treatment and WTO Dispute Settlement: Adjudicating the Boundaries of Regulatory Autonomy* (Oxford, Hart Publishing, 2002).

Voon, T, 'UNESCO and the WTO: A Clash of Cultures?' (2006) 55 *International & Comparative Law Quarterly* 635.

Voon, T, 'A New Approach to Audiovisual Products in the WTO: Rebalancing GATT and GATS' (2007) 14 *UCLA Entertainment Law Review* 1.

Voon, T, *Cultural Products and the World Trade Organization* (Cambridge, Cambridge University Press, 2007).

Vyver, JD van der, 'Book Review: Culture and Equality: An Egalitarian Critique of Multiculturalism by Brian Barry' (2002) 17 *Connecticut Journal of International Law* 323Veeser, HA, *The New Historicism* (London, Routledge, 1989).

Walker, RBJ (ed), *Culture, Ideology and World Order* (Boulder, CO, Westview Press, 1984).

Ward, I, 'The Culture of Enlargement' (2005–06) 12 *Columbian Journal of European Law* 199.

Warnock, JW, *Free Trade and the New Right Agenda* (Vancouver, BC, New Star Books, 1988).

Warouw, A, 'Realistic and Prospects of the Current Services Negotiations: Indonesia Perspectives' (2006) 1 *Asian Journal of WTO & International Health Law & Policy* 141.

Weiler, HN, 'Withdrawing from UNESCO: A Decision in Search of Argument' (1986) 30(1) *Comparative Education Review* 132.

Weiler J (ed), *The EU, the WTO and the NAFTA: Towards a Common Law of International Trade* (New York, Oxford University Press USA, 2000).

Weiler, J and Motoc, L, 'Taking Democracy Seriously: The Normative Challenge to the International System' in Griller, S (ed), *International Economic Governance and Non-Economic Concerns: New Challenges for the International Legal Order* (New York, Springer, 2003).

Weston, BH, 'Human Rights and Nation-Building in Cross-Cultural Settings' (2008) 60 *Maine Law Review* 317.

Wheeler, M, 'Supranational Regulation: Television and the European Union' (2004) 19(3) *European Journal of Communication* 349.

Wiedemann, HN, 'Empowering Audiovisual Services for the Future' in N Obuljen and J Smiers (eds), *UNESCO's Convention on the Protection and Promotion of the Diversity of Cultural Expressions: Making It Work* (Zagreb, Institute for International Relations, 2006).

Wildman, SS and Siwek, SE, *International Trade in Films and Television Programs* (Toronto, Harper Collins Publishers, 1988).

Williams, JC, 'Culture and Certainty: Legal History and the Reconstructive Project' (1990) 76 *Virginia Law Review* 713.

Williams, R, *Keywords: A Vocabulary of Culture and Society* (New York, Oxford University Press USA, 1985).

Witten, D, 'The US–UK Arbitration Award Concerning Heathrow Airport User Charges' (1995) 89 *American Journal of International Law* 174.

Wolf, M, 'Why Trade Liberalization Is a Good Idea' in JM Finger and A Olechowski (eds), *The Uruguay Round: A Handbook on the Multilateral Trade Negotiations* (Washington, DC, World Bank, 1987).

Wolf, M, 'What the World Needs From the Multilateral Trading System' in GP Sampson (ed), *The Role of the World Trade Organization in Global Governance* (Tokyo, United Nations University Press, 2001) 183–86.

Wright, S, 'The Politicization of Culture'(1998) 14(1) *Anthropology Today* 7.

WTO, 'GATS Services Sectoral Classification List, Note by the Secretariat', MTN.GNS/W/120 (10 July 1991).

WTO, *GATT Analytical Index: Guide to GATT Law and Practice* (1994).}

WTO 'Arrangement for Effective Cooperation with other Intergovernmental Organizations between the WTO and the UN: Communication from the Director-General', WTO Doc WT/GC/W/10 (3 November 1995).

WTO, 'Audiovisual Services, Background Note by the Secretariat of the Council of Trade in Services', S/C/W/40 (15 June 1998).

WTO, 'Work Program on Electronic Commerce Adopted by the General Council on 25 September 1998', WT/L/274 (30 September 1998).

WTO, 'WTO Programme on Electronic Commerce: Background Note by the Secretariat', G/C/W/128 (5 November 1998).

WTO, 'Minutes of Meeting Held in the Center William Rappard on 6 November 1998', WT/DSB/M/50 (14 December 1998).

WTO, 'Argentina—Safeguard Measure on Imports of Footwear, Report of Appellate Body', WT/DS121/AB/R (2000).

WTO, 'EC—Measures Affecting Asbestos and Asbestos-Containing Products, Report of Appellate Body', WTO Doc WT/DS135/AB/R (2001).

WTO, 'Working Party on the Accession of China—Report of the Working Party on the Accession of China', WT/ACC/CHN/49 (1 October 2001).

WTO, 'Protocol on the Accession of the People's Republic of China', WT/L/432 (23 November 2001).

WTO, 'Minutes of Meeting Held in the Center William Rappard on 20 April 2004', WT/DSB/M/167, (27 May 2004).

WTO, 'Minutes of Meeting Held in the Center William Rappard on 24 March 2006', WT/DSB/M/208 (28 April 2007).

WTO, 'China–Measures Affecting Trading Rights and Distribution Services for Certain Publications and Audiovisual Entertainment Products, the Report of Panel', WT/DS363/R (12 August 2009).

WTO, 'China—Measures Affecting Trading Rights and Distribution Services for Certain Publications and Audiovisual Entertainment Products, the Report of Appellate Body', WT/DS363/AB/R (21 December 2009).

WTO Council for Trade in Services, 'Audiovisual Services: Background Note by the Secretariat', S/C/W/40 (15 June 1998).

WTO Council for Trade in Services, 'Communication from the United States—Audiovisual Services', S/C/W/78 (8 December 1998).

WTO Council for Trade in Services, 'Communication from the European Communities and their Member States: Electronic Commerce Work Programme', S/C/W/183 (30 November 2000).

WTO Council for Trade in Services, 'Report of the Meeting Held on 19–22 March 2002: Note by the Secretariat', TN/S/M/1 (5 June 2002).

WTO Council for Trade in Services Special Session, 'Communication from the United States—Audiovisual and Related Services', S/CSS/W/21 (18 December 2000).

WTO Council for Trade in Services Special Session, 'Communication from Switzerland—GATS 2000: Audio-visual Services', S/CSS/W/74 (4 May 2001).

WTO Council for Trade in Services Special Session, 'Communication from Brazil—Audiovisual Services', S/CSS/W/99 (9 July 2001).

WTO Council for Trade in Services Special Session, 'Communication from Hong Kong China, Japan, Mexico, The Separate Customs Territory of Taiwan, Penghu, Kinmen and Matsu, and United States—Joint Statement on the Negotiation on Audiovisual Services', TN/S/W/49 (30 June 2005).

WTO Secretariat, 'Fifth Dedicated Discussion on Electronic Commerce under the Auspices of the General Council on 16 May and 11 July 2003: Summary by the Secretariat of the Issues Raised', WT/GC/W/509 (31 July 2003).

WTO Working Party on GATS Rules, 'Communication from Argentina and Hong Kong, China: Development of Multilateral Disciplines Governing Trade Distortive Subsidies in Services', S/WPGR/W/31 (16 March 2000).

WTO Working Party on GATS Rules, 'Subsidies and Trade in Services: Note by the Secretariat', S/WRGR/W/9 (6 March 1996).

Wunsch-Vincent, S, 'The Internet, Cross-Border Trade in Services, and the GATS: Lessons from *US—Gambling*' (2006) 5 *World Trade Review* 319.

Wunsch-Vincent, S, *The WTO, the Internet and Trade in Digital Products: EC–US Perspectives* (Oxford, Hart Publishing, 2006).

Yourow, HC, *The Margin of Appreciation Doctrine in The Dynamics of European Human Rights Jurisprudence* (Leiden, Martinus Nijhoff Publishers, 1996).

Yu, PK, 'Three Questions That Will Make You Rethink the US–China Intellectual Property Debate' (2008) 7 *John Marshall Review of Intellectual Property Law* 412.

Yúdice, G, *The Expediency of Culture: Uses of Culture in the Global Era* (Durham, NC, Duke University Press, 2003).

Zampetti, AB, 'WTO Rules in Audio-Visual Sector', HWWA-Report (Hamburg, Hamburg Institution of International Economics, 2003).

Zechenter, EM, 'In the Name of Culture: Cultural Relativism and the Abuse of the Individual' (1997) 53 *Journal of Anthropological Research* 319.

Zedalis, RJ, 'The Theory of GATT "like" Product Common Language Cases' (1994) 27 *Vanderbilt Journal of Transnational Law* 33.

Zeiler, TW, *Free Trade, Free World* (Chapel Hill, The University of North Carolina Press, 1999).

Zleptnig, S, 'The Standard of Review in WTO Law: An Analysis of Law, Legitimacy and the Distribution of Legal and Political Authority' (2002) 6 *European Integration online Papers* No 17.

Index